THE VIKING PORTABLE LIBRARY

ROMAN READER

Each volume in The Viking Portable Library either presents a representative selection from the works of a single outstanding writer or offers a comprehensive anthology on a special subject. Averaging 700 pages in length and designed for compactness and readability, these books fill a need not met by other compilations. All are edited by distinguished authorities, who have written introductory essays and included much other helpful material.

The Portable

Roman Reader

Edited and with an introduction by
BASIL DAVENPORT

PENGUIN BOOKS

PENGUIN BOOKS
Published by the Penguin Group
Penguin Group (USA) Inc., 375 Hudson Street, New York, New York 10014, U.S.A.
Penguin Books Ltd, 80 Strand, London WC2R 0RL, England
Penguin Books Australia Ltd, 250 Camberwell Road, Camberwell, Victoria 3124, Australia
Penguin Books Canada Ltd, 10 Alcorn Avenue, Toronto, Ontario, Canada M4V 3B2
Penguin Books India (P) Ltd, 11 Community Centre, Panchsheel Park, New Delhi – 110 017, India
Penguin Group (NZ), cnr Airborne and Rosedale Roads, Albany, Auckland 1310, New Zealand
Penguin Books (South Africa) (Pty) Ltd, 24 Sturdee Avenue,
Rosebank, Johannesburg 2196, South Africa

Penguin Books Ltd, Registered Offices: 80 Strand, London WC2R 0RL, England

First published in the United States of America
by Viking Penguin Inc. 1951
Paperbound edition published 1959
Reprinted 1961, 1962, 1963, 1964, 1966 (twice),
1967, 1969, 1970 , 1972, 1974, 1975
Published in Penguin Books 1977

20

Copyright 1951 by Viking Penguin Inc.
Copyright © renewed Viking Penguin Inc., 1979
All rights reserved

LIBRARY OF CONGRESS CATALOGING IN PUBLICATION DATA
Davenport, Basil, 1905–1966, ed.
The Portable Roman reader.
1. Latin literature—Translations into English.
2. English literature—Translations from Latin.
I. Title.
[PA6163.D38 1977]   870'.8   76-48083
ISBN 0 14 015.056 0

Printed in the United States of America
Set in Linotype Caledonia

Page v constitutes an extension of this copyright page.

*

Acknowledgments

The editor wishes to thank the following for permission to use excerpts from English translations of Latin texts:

George Allen & Unwin, Ltd., London: Poems VIII and LVIII, Catullus, *Translations from Latin Poetry*, translated by R. C. Trevelyan.

Cambridge University Press, London: Poems IX and LXXXV, Catullus, translated by Hugh Macnaghten; and F. L. Lucas and the Cambridge University Press: *Pervigilium Veneris*, translated by F. L. Lucas.

Dodd, Mead & Company, New York: extracts from *Trimalchio's Dinner* (Petronius) by Harry Thurston Peck, copyright 1898 by Dodd, Mead & Company (copyright renewed).

E. P. Dutton & Co., Inc., New York, and J. M. Dent & Sons, Ltd., London: excerpt from *On the Nature of Things*, Lucretius, translated by William Ellery Leonard; and E. P. Dutton & Co., Inc.: Poem XLVI, *The Poems of Catullus* by William Appleton Aiken, copyright 1950 by William A. Aiken.

Harvard University Press, Cambridge: excerpts from volumes in the Loeb Classical Library: *Gallic War*, Caesar, translated by H. J. Edwards; *De Senectute*, Cicero, translated by William A. Falconer; *In Catilinan*, Cicero, translated by Louis E. Lord; *Roman History*, Livy, translated by B. O. Foster; *Germania*, Tacitus, translated by William Peterson; *Annals*, Tacitus, translated by John Jackson.

Henry Holt and Company, Inc., New York, and The Society of Authors, London, as the Literary Representative of the Trustees of the Estate of the late A. E. Housman: Ode IV:7, Horace, *The Collected Poems of A. E. Housman*, copyright 1936 by Barclays Bank, Ltd., 1940 by Henry Holt and Company, Inc.

Longmans Green & Co., Limited, and the Representatives of the late Andrew Lang, London: Poems XXXI and CI, Catullus, *The Poetical Works of Andrew Lang*.

Routledge and Kegan Paul, Ltd., London: epigrams, Martial, *The Twelve Books of Epigrams* by J. A. Pott and F. A. Wright.

Russell & Volkening, Inc., New York: Ode I:7, Horace, translated by Lord Dunsany.

The University of Chicago Press, Chicago: "Medea," *Tragedies of Seneca* by Frank Justus Miller.

Contents

vii

CONTENTS ix

CONTENTS

THE PORTABLE

ROMAN READER

*

Introduction

NOT long ago I was talking to a young friend of mine, a college graduate, intelligent, well read, and very fond of books. He happened to speak of *The Ides of March,* Thornton Wilder's novel of Cæsar and Cleopatra, and referred to it as illustrating conditions "toward the end of the Roman Empire." I was more than startled. The idea that anybody at all could suppose that Julius Cæsar flourished toward the end of the Roman Empire filled me with the same sort of horror and pity that filled the elder Mrs. Day at the thought that in a Christian country anybody could miss being baptized. These emotions remained with me, and led me to reflect both on the probable number of men of my friend's age who knew no more of Rome than he did, and on why it seemed to me such a loss for them.

A generation ago the answer to the latter question would have been prompt. One must know the history of Rome because one learned valuable lessons from it. Upon further inquiry as to what one learned, it appeared to be that from the rise of Rome one learned how to build a great state, and from the fall of Rome how to keep it from falling. Moreover, if the answer was given by an Englishman or an American, it was with a comfortable sense that the first of these lessons had been well learned, and there would be no need for the second just yet. We were still as confident as Gibbon, when, in finishing his *Decline and Fall of the Roman Empire,* he congratulated himself that there were no powerful barbarians ready to overrun civilization; if he had dared,

1

he might have added that the Christianity he saw around him did not seem sufficiently enthusiastic to be a menace to the state. Now, with the barbarians at the gate, when we inquire what did cause the fall of Rome, we are given a bewildering choice of answers. Rome fell because of persecuting the Christians, and of being converted by them; because of the invasions of the Goths, and of the Anopheles mosquito; because of bread and circuses, and of the natural aging of an organism. All of us who have old-fashioned church-going upbringings can remember earnest preachers maintaining (like Thomas Wolfe's schoolma'am, who declared that the wages of Falstaff's sin was death at a ripe old age) that the crimes of Nero led to the fall of Rome some four centuries later; and perhaps some of us have found Gibbon more brilliant, but no more convincing. What we can be sure of is, first, that Rome established what, considering the conditions of communication, can be called a world state, a society of many peoples and languages united in a common citizenship, and that for some hundreds of years she gave them peace and on the whole good government; and, second, that the Empire was established at the cost of a period of civil wars, political assassinations, secret denunciations, and party purges, and was later maintained by a bureaucracy so efficient that it kept the Empire alive when it is quite arguable that it would have been better dead. Compared with our grandfathers, we are nearer the world state as an ideal, and nearer the blood baths in reality.

The Rome that did this is one of the great formative facts of our world. Not to know Rome is not to know the character of one of one's own immediate ancestors— an ancestor who has of late been less thought of than Athens and Jerusalem, and deservedly so, but an ancestor all the same, whose traits keep turning up in his descendants. And not to know Roman history is not to know one of the great historic dramas. The story of Rome is not indeed a tragedy in Aristotle's sense. Greece of the Golden Age, and the Southern Confederacy, are examples among the nations of the Aristotelian tragic hero—the great man who by a certain flaw in his nature is brought to a downfall greater than he deserved. And, like classic heroes, both the Golden Age and the Confederacy fell with a crash. Rome is like George Eliot's Tito Melema, the brilliant young man whose flaw grows and grows until his downfall is deserved; Rome is like Ethan Frome, the cripple who goes on living too long. It is a tragedy, perhaps, even more to the modern taste. And both the history and the mind of Rome are reflected, more, probably, than those of any other people, in its literature. Sherlock Holmes' ideal reasoner, who from a single drop of water could deduce an Atlantic or a Niagara, could undoubtedly deduce the rise, greatness, and decline of Rome from reading, in order, Plautus, Virgil, and Juvenal; and without being an ideal reasoner one can still feel, in every work of Latin literature, the quality of Romanness. *Ex pede Herculem*—from the foot alone you may infer Hercules.

In the beginning, and for a long time thereafter, the Romans were a nation of soldiers. Throughout her history Rome was almost continuously at war somewhere along her lengthening or shrinking frontiers, and during the Republic every Roman was a soldier—potentially at least, and most often actually. That may be the reason for a certain hard-bitten realism and practicality in the Roman attitude toward life. Their plastic arts are for the most part imitated from the Greeks, and coarsened in the imitating; their great contributions are the arch, the aqueduct, the Roman road—and the portrait bust, which shows not an ideal athlete but an actual general

or emperor, warts and all. One of the earliest pieces of
Roman literature is a treatise on practical farming by
the elder statesman Cato; one of the masterpieces of
the Golden Age is the *Georgics* of Virgil, a solitary in-
stance of a treatise on practical farming which is also
fine poetry. The *Works and Days* of the Greek Hesiod is
much less complete and more mythological; it opens
with a myth of the Origin of Evil—which, as in Genesis,
is why farming is necessary. In passing, it is significant
that Hesiod is writing as a man who farms his own acres,
Virgil as a gentleman farmer whose land is tilled by
slaves; the Roman, at least the Roman who read and
wrote, was far richer than the corresponding Greek. In
this connection it is also significant that the practical
Cato lays it down as a maxim that a slave should be
either working or sleeping, and also recommends selling
off old slaves for what they will fetch, to save their keep.
Roman philosophy, in contrast to the metaphysical and
æsthetic speculations of the Greeks, is almost entirely
concerned with ethics. The exception, the great Roman
philosopher Lucretius, is entirely concerned with two
points: the Nature of Things—not the Nature of Reality
but the way things actually are, as a matter of observa-
tion and deduction; and the eminently practical goal of
Peace of Mind. And in both comedy and tragedy, the
Romans delighted in *sententiæ*, short, pithy observa-
tions on the proper conduct of life.

The proper conduct of life was a matter of *gravitas,
pietas,* and *virtus*—three words that look as if they
meant "gravity," "piety," and "virtue," which they do
not. *Gravitas* means much the same as "dignity," though
the quality was more important to the Romans than to
us. *Pietas* was close to "duty"; it meant performing one's
duties in every relationship: as father, son, soldier, citi-
zen, friend, slave-owner, worshiper. Toward the gods

it required neither beliefs nor morals, but the proper performance of the proper ceremonies. But toward mankind it meant giving every man his due, one of the greatest legacies that Rome has left to us. It was Rome who first formed the concept of the Law of Nations, the idea that beyond the statutes of any particular locality there was an abstract standard of right and wrong which all men recognized and were bound by. Greece had conceived the equality of citizens before the law, but it was Rome that constantly extended the rights of citizen-ship. A Greek had no rights outside his own city; under the Roman Empire, Paul, a Jew of Tarsus, could make a provincial governor revoke his sentence of a flogging by merely saying, "I am a Roman citizen"; he could say, "I appeal to Cæsar," and receive the only possible answer, "Thou hast appealed unto Cæsar; unto Cæsar shalt thou go." The Romans first conquered their neigh-bors in their own peninsula, and then led those con-quered neighbors to fight as loyal Romans against the strangers beyond the seas and mountains—strangers who would in their turn be made vassals, then subject allies, then Roman citizens.

Virtus was the quality that distinguished the man, *vir,* from the mere human creature, *homo.* There is no exact word for it; but if we wish to know what a nation ad-mires we can go to its nursery tales, the old stories of Washington and the Cherry Tree, Alfred and the Cakes, Bruce and the Spider. For the Roman, such stories were those Livy tells of the beginnings of the Republic; they are concerned not with truthfulness or democracy or perseverance, but with valor and complete devotion to country. Every Roman schoolboy knew the stories of Horatius at the Bridge, of Quintus Curtius leaping his horse into the gulf, of Lucius Junius Brutus, who com-manded and witnessed the execution of his own sons for conspiracy against the city. There was the story of the other Horatius, who supplied the subject of a play by Corneille; in the service of the city, he killed the man his sister loved, and killed his sister because she mourned for him; he was sentenced for the killing of his sister to a purely nominal punishment, that justice might be preserved. There was Gaius Mucius, who slipped into the camp of the besieging Lars Porsena with intent to kill him, but killed one of his followers by mistake and was taken prisoner. He declared to Lars Porsena that though he had failed, there were three hundred men in Rome who had sworn to attempt Porsena's life, one after the other. When Porsena threatened him with torture unless he revealed their names, he smiled and held his own right hand in the brazier until it was burned off. Lars Porsena thought it wiser to come to terms with the Romans, and Mucius was given the name of Scævola, or Left-handed, which was borne by his descendants down to imperial times.

The story is important as showing what the Romans admired, even though I think it is probable that it was invented later to explain a nickname "Lefty" bestowed in the ordinary way. There was a similar story about the name Brutus, which means "Stupid" or "Brutish"—Hamlet's pun to Polonius was better than he knew. The story is that Lucius Junius Brutus, like Hamlet, feigned idiocy to escape the suspicion of his uncle, the last of the kings. Possibly; but the original Lefty and Stupid may have been called so for no such complimentary reason. The Romans had a schoolboyish aptitude for names based on personal peculiarities. Cicero means "Warty"; Cæsar probably "Hairy." It is part of the quality in them which led, on the one hand, to the only two art forms they invented, the portrait bust and the satire; and on the other, to the abuse and smut of some of the epigrams.

For, as Aristotle says, every virtue is a mean between two vices, one consisting of its defect, the other of its excess, and, it may be added, the virtue and the excess are sometimes present in the same person. It is not hard to see the excess in the stories of Horatius's murder of his sister, and even of Brutus's execution of his sons. To us, the phrase "a Roman father" implies a somewhat doubtful virtue. As the Romans might have said if they could have thought of it, in their anxiety not to be unmanly they became inhuman. Even in their carefully maintained indifference to death and pain there came to be something almost theatrical, an attitude that reaches its full expression in the epic poets of the Silver Age, and in the tragedies of Seneca, whose characters are the ancestors of all the declamatory seventeenth-century heroes, Corneille's and Dryden's. And from disregarding their own pain they came to disregard that of others, or to enjoy it. Their *virtus* was always liable to be stained by the vice to which the soldier is tempted, ruthlessness and cruelty. Julius Cæsar was in general a humane commander, but once he cut off the hands of his prisoners, to teach them not to revolt. The cruelty of the arena, at first occasional, became habitual, so that it could be said of one of the late emperors, "he never dined without human blood."

The soldier's vices are two, cruelty and loot; and of the two the loot was probably the more serious for Rome. The King of Brobdingnag, looking at Rome with the superiority that comes of being sixty feet high, might have said that, from the Punic Wars on, her internal history is that of a successful gang of cutthroats quarreling over the division of the swag. Already, before the end of the Republic, the raped wealth had begun to pour into Italy. The rich got richer and the poor got poorer; the struggle between the Haves and Have-Nots led to the civil wars which brought an end to the Republic. Under the Empire, the appetite for wealth grew by what it fed on; men already rich spent their lives fawning on others for more riches. Tacitus, Suetonius, and Juvenal have left us a picture of the final corruption of Roman society. No doubt it is somewhat exaggerated, but it is a fact that with those three names Roman literature comes to a virtual end. The Roman Empire of the West lasted some three hundred years more, but the spirit had gone out of it. Scattered here and there are the beginnings of something new, writing that should be called Romanesque rather than Roman; but the old Roman world is like the men whose souls Dante met in Hell though their bodies were still walking about on earth.

A NOTE ON SELECTIONS AND TRANSLATIONS

In choosing the material for this volume, my aim has been twofold: to give so far as possible a comprehensive picture of Roman literature; and to produce a readable book. If these seemed to conflict, I have perhaps weighted the scales a little in favor of the latter, feeling that, as Horace says that silver buried in the ground is of no color, so a book which is not read has no real existence. At best too many of us feel about Roman authors generally as the lieutenant in *Tom Jones* did about Homer, even though we might not express it so vigorously: "Don't talk to me of Homer! I have the marks of him in my a— yet" (I follow Fielding's spelling). I have tried to overcome this prejudice by finding passages which are readable both in themselves and in their English rendering. In some cases the difficulty or impossibility of this has led to what may seem, or may be, faults of proportion. The *Odes* of Horace, for instance, by their absolute importance in literature, deserve more space; but Horace is the most translated and most untranslatable of poets; it seemed better to leave him underpresented than misrepresented. For the other shortcomings in this, the apology has been made once for all by Æschylus: τέχνη δ'ἀνάγκης ἀσθενεστέρα μακρῷ—"Art is far weaker than Necessity."

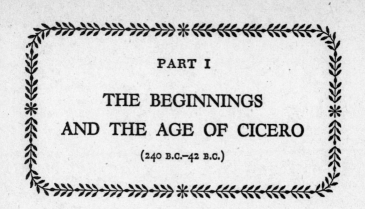

PART I

THE BEGINNINGS
AND THE AGE OF CICERO

(240 B.C.–42 B.C.)

IT IS not often that the beginning of a literature can be precisely dated; but it can be said that the first work of Latin literature—except for a handful of charms, the first piece of Latin writing—appeared in 240 B.C., the year after the end of the First Punic War, and was the work of a Greek freedman bearing a Roman name. Both facts are almost too obviously significant. All through history the conquered Greeks were to be Rome's teachers and models; and Rome had no time to spare for literature until she had defeated her immediate neighbors. The Roman conquest of Italy was completed by the Pyrrhic War, which ended in 272 B.C. with the capture of Tarentum; besides bringing the whole of the Italian peninsula under Roman domination, this war brought the Romans into contact with the Greeks of southern Italy. A certain Andronicus, a Greek of Tarentum, was taken to Rome as a captive and became the slave of a Roman named Livius; Andronicus acted as tutor to his children, was rewarded for his services with the gift of his freedom, and, as was customary, added to his own name that of his late master, by which he is known. (The Greeks customarily bore one name apiece, the Romans three.) Livius Andronicus continued to act as a teacher of Greek and Latin, and also as an actor and stage manager. For his theater he translated Greek plays, and the first of these were produced in 240 B.C., a comedy and a tragedy, which someone spoke of with surprise as "plays with plots!" Livius also translated the *Odyssey* into the rough Roman Saturnian meter. Native Roman verse was based not, like Greek, upon quantity or longs and shorts, but, like ours, upon

stress accent; one of their favorite meters was the Sa-
turnian, which is approximately that of the feminine
lines in "Sing a song of sixpence"—"The queen was in
her parlor, eating bread and honey."

Five years after the first production of a play by
Livius there appeared a native Roman writer called
Nævius. He also did translations or adaptations of Greek
plays; besides this, he wrote a long poem on the subject
of the Punic War, also in the Saturnian meter. In his
first two books he goes back to the founding of Rome,
and (according to a surviving account) anticipates
Virgil in making Venus appeal to Jupiter on behalf of
Æneas, and Jupiter give a promise of the greatness of
Rome. Already the Romans had begun to think of their
state as a City of Destiny. But most of his work, so far
as we can judge from what is left of it, was a jog-trot
chronicle.

Both these authors survive only in scraps of a dozen
lines or so, but enough to show that in what is lost we
are not missing much. The same may be said of Ennius,
"the Father of Latin Poetry." He produced Greek adap-
tations in many forms, but his chief claims to the pater-
nity of Latin poetry are the somewhat contradictory
ones that he domesticated the Greek hexameter and
that he originated the only distinctive Roman form, the
literary satire. The word comes from *satura,* a hodge-
podge, and was originally applied to a sort of informal
entertainment at the harvest festival, consisting of songs
and personal banter, much of it coarse and even obscene.
These *saturæ* were driven off the stage by Livius's as-
tonishing innovation, a play with a plot; Ennius adopted
the fugitive and adapted it to a written form, writing in
a go-as-you-please fashion and making fun of his neigh-
bors. This was the beginning of the form which was to
serve the elegant persiflage of Horace and the savage in-

dignation of Juvenal. Ennius's most important work is
the *Annals*, a history of Rome from the arrival of Æneas
down to 172 B.C., only three years before his own death
—toward the end he must have been racing to keep up
with events, like Upton Sinclair's Lanny Budd saga. For
this he used the quantitative hexameter employed by
the Greeks, and his success, or else the prestige of the
Greek originals, was so great that the native accentual
verse was driven underground and did not reappear
until the tottering Empire was giving way to the earliest
Middle Ages. It is really an astonishing phenomenon. It
is as though certain Elizabethan experimenters had suc-
ceeded in their attempt to write English verse on the
French model, basing it on number of syllables instead
of stress, and as if the whole body of subsequent Eng-
lish poetry had managed to ignore the fact that English
is a stress-accented language. But the spirit of the Latin
language makes itself heard, in the preponderance of
long syllables, which make its hexameters move much
more heavily than the Greek. It is the Roman *gravitas*.

As with Livius and Nævius, only small fragments of
Ennius are left, and, as with them, one cannot honestly
say that one is hungry for more. The first Roman writer
who is survived by completed works is Plautus, Ennius's
slightly older contemporary, and the second is Terence,
a generation later than Plautus. Both these men are
writers of comedies modeled on the late Greek form
known as the New Comedy, to distinguish it from the
comedy of Aristophanes, which was more like musical
comedy with a satiric plot. The New Comedy is a school
of farce, made up of situation comedies and stock char-
acters. The young man, with the advice of his clever
slave, gets the better of the heavy father, or of the girl's
heavy father; twins are mistaken for each other; it turns
out that the slave girl is the long-lost daughter of one's

neighbor, so one may safely marry her. Among the
characters we meet the Boastful Soldier, the Sponge,
the Hen-pecked Husband, and so on. It is noteworthy
that without exception the plays have settings which
are nominally somewhere in Greece, and, indeed, the
world they depict—the world of young lovers, confiden-
tial slaves, witty courtesans, and cowardly soldier-brag-
garts—is Alexandrine Greece rather than Rome. Never-
theless, like the wood in A *Midsummer Night's Dream*,
which is nearer to England than to Athens, the setting
of these plays is actually nearer to Rome than to Greece.
Magistrates appear with Roman titles, ædiles and *tres-
viri*; characters speak of walking in the Forum and
visit the Capitol; they worship the Roman household
gods and speak contemptuously of the Greeks. If it is a
Greek world, it is inhabited by Roman characters. The
characters are Roman because that is what the audience
knew and cared for; the world is Greek because in that
way Roman dignity could be maintained. It is all very
well to show an Athenian heavy father hoodwinked by
a clever slave, or a Theban husband cuckolded by Jupi-
ter; it would never do to show a Roman in such situa-
tions.

Roman literature seems now to be well launched.
The Romans have learned to write from the Greeks, but
they have learned well; they have developed their own
themes, characters, even their own form; everything
is going swimmingly. Then, suddenly, there is a gap of
half a century when nothing of importance appears.
Roman literature began when the frontiers, where the
wars were always going on, were pushed out far enough
so that the fighting was not on Rome's doorstep. Roman
literature paused when fighting broke out in Italy again,
the civil wars which did not really stop until the over-
throw of the Republic, although the Age of Cicero

marks a period of apparent peace, when the war, as
has been said of diplomacy, was carried on by other
means. The expansion of Rome meant, of course, that
the Republic must sooner or later come to an end. Just
as an amœba is bound to split in two when its area needs
more food than its perimeter can supply, the Republic
was bound to break down when it tried to administer a
state the size of Italy by the methods of the town meet-
ing. Even if they had thought of representative govern-
ment, that would hardly have helped unless they had
also been able to invent some form of rapid transport.
But the end of the Republic was quicker and more bitter
because of the strife between the Haves and Have-Nots.
The spoils of Empire were changing Rome from a landed
to a money economy. The great proprietors, enriched
by the wars, were working their vast estates like fac-
tories, with slave labor; to do this they turned off their
free tenants and bought up their poor neighbors by fair
means or foul. The city of Rome, the only place where it
was possible to cast a vote, became full of landless men;
men with legitimate grievances to place before the legis-
lators, but men who were peculiarly liable to be misled
by the promises of any man whose platform was cheap
bread, and let the Italians pay the taxes.

The old general Marius, who had covered himself
with glory in the wars against the kingdom of Numidia,
became involved in the intrigues of two demagogues,
turned against them, and went into retirement for a
while, until he thought he saw a chance to regain his
lost prestige by getting the command of the war in the
East against Mithridates, the command that had been
given to the younger general Sulla. He succeeded in
getting the popular assembly to vote him in. Sulla, how-
ever, was the actual commander of the army. He
marched it on Rome; Marius fled; and with Sulla and

his army at the doorstep the popular assembly reversed its decree and confirmed Sulla in his command. Sulla went off to fight his war. As soon as he was at a safe distance Marius returned, at the head of his anti-Senatorial or popular party, and murdered the leading men of the Senate and the governing class, a blood bath from which the Senatorial order never recovered. By the time Sulla returned victorious, Marius was dead, but Sulla had his revenge upon everybody else. He had already shown for the first time that the man who commanded the army could put himself in command of Rome. Now he taught another lesson to those who came after him; he had himself appointed dictator without conditions.

The office of dictator was fundamental in the Roman constitution. That constitution, like the American, originated in opposition to kingship and was a system of checks and balances; but the checks were so effective that sometimes it was impossible to get anything done at all. At the head of the Republic, for instance, were two consuls, each with a right to veto the other. Considering this and other veto powers, the Romans found that in time of emergency it was necessary to vest extraordinary powers in one man. He was appointed dictator, or virtual autocrat, but was still subject to certain limitations; he could not touch the treasury, he was accountable at the end of his term, and none of the early dictators kept his office for more than six months. Sulla had the title granted to himself without restrictions, a precedent for the legal fictions by which the Republic was transformed into an empire.

This was the background of the Rome of Julius Cæsar and Cicero—Cicero, a conservative by inclination and connections, and Cæsar, the ambitious young politician, nephew by marriage of Marius. Sulla was dead, after putting through some conservative reforms, but the struggle went on and broke out into violence in such affairs as the conspiracy of Catiline. Catiline was a ruined noble, ruined, like so many nobles before and since, partly by his own dissipation, partly by the change from a land economy and from a rural to an urban culture. In the early days of the Republic, land-owners had been content to live on their holdings; when they wished to live in the city, they borrowed on their lands, and the interest on the mortgages soon outran the income from the estates. Catiline and a group of others first tried to push through a law containing the simple and revolutionary measure of an arbitrary reduc-tion of all debts; and when he failed in this, gathered a private army and plotted to murder the leading mem-bers of the government, and increase the confusion by firing their houses. Cicero got wind of the conspiracy, denounced it, and secured passage of the emergency decrees: "Let the Consuls see to it that the Republic take no harm"—the last legitimate use of the old, limited dictatorship; and after the arrest of the con-spirators Cicero himself was guilty of an unconstitutional act in having them strangled without giving them the right to appeal against the death penalty to the assembly of the people.

The conspiracy of Catiline was followed by others, by riots and the use of private armies of gangsters on one side and the other. The situation had become desperate through the failure of the executive, and the only hope seemed to be to invest one man with full power to make the laws and see that they were obeyed—then, perhaps, they could go back to constitutional government. For this position there were two obvious candidates, the two successful generals Pompey and Julius Cæsar. Pompey was backed by the Senate and the old land-owning class; Cæsar by the opposition. When their rivalry led to a civil war in which Pompey was defeated, Cæsar was the only man in Rome. He consolidated his position by following the example of Sulla: he was Dictator, Pontifex Maximus or Supreme Head of the Church, Commander-in-Chief of the Army, and, like Pooh-Bah, several minor officials as well. Of all these, the most important was commander-in-chief; witness the fact that the Latin word for it, *imperator,* gave us the title "emperor." Cæsar was killed by a group of conspirators who hoped to restore the Republic; but it was too late for that.

The great prose writers of this time were two of the great actors in it, Cæsar and Cicero. There were also two poets, who, like most great poets, are not of an age but for all time, Lucretius and Catullus. Lucretius' work is that unique epic of thought, *On the Nature of Things.* It is very different from the brilliant speculations and myths of the Greeks. Zeno of Elea, for instance, maintained that if Achilles, the swiftest of mortals, tried to overtake a tortoise, he could never catch it, since before he could go the whole distance he must go half, and there would always be half of some distance remaining; this and a series of other paradoxes had a serious purpose, to show that the very natures of time, space, and motion were self-contradictory. Plato explains love by saying that we are all made double and split apart, and one wonders how far to believe him. The Roman Lucretius looks straight at the world and tries to see how it is made. In his own way he is no less astonishing than Plato. The atomic theory, organic evolution and the Mendelian principle, the origin of kingship with a foreshadowing of Rousseau, a theory of dreams—they are all here. And here is the triumphant, rapturous denial of immortality, stated with such eloquence that while one reads, at least, it really seems what it seemed to Lucretius, good news.

Catullus was the most brilliant of a circle of brilliant young men who cultivated Greek literature and wrote imitations of it. Through the body of his verse it is possible to know him as one knows few men in history. He shares with us the rapture of first love, the anguish of disillusionment, the pang of bereavement, even his friendships and his quarrels. Catullus, Lucretius, and the philosophic writings of Cicero remind us of what is so hard to remember in reading history—that even in periods of the greatest crisis men still ponder abstract themes, they still fall in love.

※≫※≪≪

PLAUTUS

(Titus Maccius Plautus, 254? B.C.–184 B.C.)

※

Amphitryon

Translated by Sir Robert Allison

CHARACTERS

MERCURY, *disguised as Sosia*
SOSIA, *slave of Amphitryon*
JUPITER, *disguised as Amphitryon*
ALCMENA, *wife of Amphitryon*
AMPHITRYON, *leader of the Theban army*
BLEPHARO, *a pilot*
BROMIA, *maid-servant of Alcmena*
THESSALA (persona muta), *a maid-servant*

SCENE: *A street in Thebes in front of the house of Amphitryon.*

PROLOGUE

MERCURY (*disguised as Sosia*): As you in all your mer-
   chandisings wish,
Whether you buy or sell, that I should help
And render aid in everything you do,
And see that all your businesses and plans
Should turn out well, whether they be at home
Or else abroad, and bless you with a rich
And full reward in all you are engaged,
Or will engage in, still to you and yours

22

Bring tidings of success, and still report
Of all that may be for your common good;
For you already know the gods have given
And granted me a preference as to news
And trade; and, as you wish, I still should try
To bless, and bring to you perpetual gain;
Listen in silence to this comedy,
As fair, impartial arbiters should do.
Now I will tell at whose command I come,
And wherefore, and will give my name as well.
Jove is my master; Mercury my name;
He sent me here as his ambassador;
Although he knew his word would be for you
As good as a command, and that you fear
And reverence his name, as well you should;
But still he bid me now to come to you,
Entreatingly, with kind and gentle words.
For sure this Jove as much as any one
Of you, dreads ill mischance; born as he is
Like you of mortal mother, mortal sire,
'Tis nothing strange, if he fears for himself.
And I too, I who am the son of Jove
Infected am with this same dread of ill.
Therefore with kindly feeling 'tis I come
And bring the same to you; from you I ask
But what is just and feasible; as one
Who justice does, justice he asks from you.
To ask unfairness from the fair were wrong;
And to ask fair play from the unfair were but
To lose one's time; they know not what is right
Nor try to do it. Now attend to me.
You ought to wish the same as we; for we,
I and my father, have deserved well
Of you and of your State. Why needs recall
How I in plays have seen the other gods,

Neptune and Virtue, Victory and Mars,
Aye, and Bellona, tell the good that they
Have done to you, while of that very good
My sire, who reigns in Heaven, was architect.
But sure, it never was my father's way
To throw the good he's done in people's teeth;
He thinks you're grateful for his services;
And ne'er regrets what he has done for you.
Now first I'll tell you what I come to say;
And then explain the plot, which underlies
This tragedy; but why contract your brows,
When I say tragedy? For I'm a god
And soon can change it; if you like I'll make
These selfsame verses be a comedy.
Shall I or not? But sure I am a fool,
Being a god, and yet not knowing what you wish.
Ah, yes! I know your mind; and I will make it
A tragicomedy; for it is not right
To make a play where kings and gods do speak
All comedy. But since a slave takes part
I'll make it for you tragicomedy.
Now Jupiter desires I ask of you
That the detectives look the seats all through,
And if they find there men who are suborned
To clap the actors, that they take their cloaks
To be security to meet the charge.
And so those actors who have sought to arrange,
Whether by letter written, or themselves,
Or intermediaries, to have the palm,
Or that the magistrates should act unfairly,
Then Jove has granted that the law apply
The same as if they had conspired to get
An office for themselves, or some one else.
You victors, he has said, must fairly win,
And not by canvassing and treachery.

Why should not that be law to actors too
As is to greatest men? By merit we
Should seek to win, and not by hired applause.
Virtue's its own reward to well-doers,
If those who are in power act fairly by them.
And he has further given a command,
That there shall be detectives, who shall see
If any actor has arranged for men
To applaud himself, or to prevent some other
Receiving his applause, that they shall flay
His dress and hide in pieces with a scourge.
I would not ye should wonder that Jove cares
For the actor's welfare; he'll be one himself.
Why be amazed, as though 'twere something new
For Jove to turn an actor? Even last year
When the actors did invoke him on the stage
He came and helped them out; in tragedy
He certainly appears. And so today
He'll act in this and I will do the same.
And now attend: I will relate the plot.
This city's Thebes; and in that house there dwells
Amphitryon, of Argive blood, and born
At Argos; he is wedded to a wife,
Alcmena, daughter of Electryon.
He was the leader of the army when
The Thebans and the Teloboans fought.
But ere he joined the army in the field,
He left Alcmena pregnant; now you know,
I think, by this time that my father is
In these same matters somewhat free, and when
The fancy takes him, loves with all his strength;
Thus he began to love Alcmena, and
Borrowed her, as it were, all unbeknown,
And left her pregnant too. So, as you see,
Alcmena has a double progeny.

My father now is in the house with her;
And for that reason this night has been made
Longer than usual, that he may take
His pleasure with her as he will. And then
He has disguised himself, so that he's like
Amphitryon. And do not wonder at
This dress of mine, and that I've come today
In likeness of a slave; believe me 'tis
A novel rendering of an ancient theme;
And therefore I come dressed in novel garb.
My father is within, in likeness of
Amphitryon; all the servants think 'tis he;
So clever is he to transform himself,
Just as he chooses. I have taken the form
Of Sosia, who went with him to the war.
In this way I can serve my father; and
The servants do not ask me who I am,
When thus they see me passing to and fro.
For when they think I am their fellow-slave
No one will ask my name, or why I came.
My father now within enjoys himself
Just as he will, with her he loveth most;
He tells her what has happened at the war;
She thinks it is her husband. So he tells
What forces of the foe he's put to rout,
What costly gifts he has received from them.
The things thus given to Amphitryon
We carried off; an easy task for him
Who can do as he likes. But now today
Amphitryon will return, and he whose form
I've taken as a slave; and that you may
Distinguish 'tween us I will wear a plume
Upon my hat; while with the same intent
My father wears a tassel under his;
Amphitryon will not have one, but these marks

No one will see, but only you alone.
But see, here's Sosia, Amphitryon's slave,
Fresh from the port, his lantern in his hand.
I'll keep him from the house—and see, he's there.
'Twill be worth while, I think, to the spectators here
As actors to see Jove and Mercury appear.

ACT I, SCENE I

(Enter Sosia from the harbour, holding a lantern.)

SOSIA *(to himself)*: Is there a bolder or more valiant man
Than I, who know the habits of our youth,
Yet walk abroad by night and all alone?
And what if the night-watchmen in their rounds
Put me in jail, and from the prison's cell
Tomorrow I was handed over to
The whipping-post, no one to take my part,
And no help from my master; none to think
Me worthy; eight strong fellows then would flay
My back as 'twere an anvil; such would be
The public welcome that I should receive,
On thus returning from a foreign shore.
My master's haste has this to answer for,
Who for no purpose forces me by night
To leave the harbour; was it not as well
To let me go by day? Hard, hard, it is
To serve a wealthy man; and this is why
A rich man's slave more miserable is;
By night and day enough and more to do,
And something still which must be said or done
To rob you of your rest; your lord himself
Rolling in wealth, and all unused to toil,
Thinks everything that comes into his head
Can easily be done; he thinks it fair,
And never reckons what the cost may be,

Nor thinks if what he wants be just or no.
We then have much to suffer, we poor slaves;
The burden must be borne what'er the toil.
MERCURY (*aside*): I have more reason to complain
　　today;
For I was free, his father was a slave;
And yet this fellow, who was born a slave,
Thinks he may grumble. I a slave in name
Have just as much to suffer.
SOSIA:　　　　　　　　　Now it comes
Into my head to pay my grateful thanks
On landing to the gods for what they've done;
For, if they treated me as I deserve,
They'd send some fellow who would smash my face,
Because for all the good that they have done
I ne'er have thanked them.
MERCURY (*aside*):　　　　Well, this fellow does
What is not common; his deserts he knows.
SOSIA: What I, nor any ever thought would happen,
That we should reach our homes all safe and sound,
Has come to pass; we are the conquerors,
The enemy have lost; our legions come;
The war's all over; what a war it was,
With hosts of slain; the town, which bitter trouble
Has wrought the Theban people, is destroyed
Under Amphitryon's happy leadership.
With booty rich, and land, and great renown,
He has repaid his soldiers; and secured
The crown to Creon. From the harbour he
Sent me straight home to tell his wife the news,
How under him as guide the State has fared.
And I must think how best to tell it her.
If I tell lies, I'm doing as I'm wont;
For when they fought the most, I furthest fled;
Yet still I must pretend that I was there,

And tell what I have heard; yet in what words,
And how I am to tell it, I must think.
I'll begin thus: when first we did arrive,
First touched the land, Amphitryon did choose
His leaders out, and sent them to the foe,
To announce his terms; if they, without being forced,
Their booty and its captors would restore,
If they returned what they had carried off,
He would withdraw his army home again,
The Argives would have the land, and peace be theirs.
But if they're otherwise disposed, nor grant
What he demands, then he with all his force
Will straight besiege their town. And when they heard
From those whom thus Amphitryon had sent
What were his terms, these proud and mighty men,
Strong in their valour, and their sense of power,
Fiercely attack our envoys; say that they
Can well defend themselves and theirs in war;
And that the army must at once withdraw.
And when our envoys told Amphitryon
What had been said, he leads his army out;
The Teloboans in their turn come forth,
And range their legions, clad in armour bright.
Then was there marshalling on either side;
Leaders and regiments each set in their place,
We in our wonted fashion, they in theirs.
Then comes a leader out on either side;
They hold a parley there, and then agree
Whichever loses in the fight, should give
His land and city, hearths and altars up;
That done, the trumpets sound on either side;
The earth responsive rings, the armies shout,
The leaders, both on this side and on that,
Make prayer to Jove, and call upon their troops;
Each soldier to his utmost strength and power

Strikes with his sword; the lances splinter then,
And heaven rings with mingled shouts of men.
The breath of men, the panting of the steeds,
Rises in clouds; the while on every side
Stricken with wounds they fall; at length our troops
Prove themselves better; we have conquered them;
On every side they fall; our men rush on;
Yet no one turns to flight, and no one leaves
The place appointed to him; rather they
Would lose their lives than stir from where they stand.
So each lies where he stood, and keeps his rank.
This when Amphitryon, my master, saw,
He straightway bids his cavalry to charge
On the right wing; immediately they go,
And fall with shouts and clamour on the foe,
Still urging onwards, while beneath their feet
They tread and trample on the impious men.
MERCURY (*aside*): So far at least this man's said nothing
      wrong;
For I was there, when this great fight was fought,
I and my father too.
SOSIA: At last they take
To flight; this gives fresh courage to our men,
And as they fly their backs are filled with darts.
With his own hand Amphitryon slew their king.
And so the fight went on from morn till eve.
I know it was so, for I went undined.
Night stayed the battle by its coming on.
On the day after, to our camp there came
Their princes all in tears, with clasped hands,
Beseeching us to pardon their offense,
And promising to give themselves, their children,
Their city, all things human and divine,
Into the keeping of the Theban people.
And then was given to Amphitryon,

In token of his valour, the gold cup
Which Pterela had used. This will I tell
My mistress. Now, as bidden by my master,
I will go home, and do as he has said.

MERCURY (*aside*): Ah, he is coming! But I'll go before
    him;
Nor shall this man approach this house today.
Since I am masquerading in his form
'Tis certain I can cheat him; and, besides,
If I have ta'en his form I also take
His manner and his actions; I must be
A rascal, sly, astute; with his own arms
Of roguery I'll keep him from the house.
But what is that? He's gazing at the sky;
I will observe him.

SOSIA: If there's anything
One may believe or know, I am quite sure
The God of night has drunk too much tonight;
For neither Charles's Wain moves in the sky,
Nor does the Moon, who is just where she rose;
Nor do Orion, Venus, or the Pleiads set;
The constellations keep their stated posts;
And night no longer gives place to the day.

MERCURY (*aside*): Proceed, Night, as you have begun;
    obey
My sire's command; great favour you have done,
And great will be the reward you shall receive.

SOSIA: I never saw a longer night than this,
Save that when I was scourged and hung by the heels;
And this I think is longer ev'n than that.
The Sun 'twould seem is sleeping, and has drunk
Too much; 'tis strange, if he's not been too free
At dinner-time.

MERCURY (*aside*): And say you so, you wretch?
D'ye think the gods are somewhat like yourself?

I'll hold you to account for what you say;
Come here, you rascal; you'll not find it pleasant.
SOSIA: Where's that vile herd that cannot sleep alone?
This night will bring some gain to those they hire.
MERCURY (*aside*): Then if this fellow's right my father
    has
Been wise to stay within Alcmena's bed,
Following his own sweet will.
SOSIA: And now I'll go
And tell Alcmena as my master bade. (*He sees Mercury*)
But who's this man I see before the house?
I do not like it.
MERCURY (*aside*): There is not, I'm sure,
A greater coward than he.
SOSIA: It seems to me
This man intends perhaps to steal my cloak.
MERCURY (*aside*): He's in a fright; I'll cheat him.
SOSIA: I'm undone.
My teeth all chatter; this man surely will
Receive me in a most pugnacious way.
Yet he has pity; and because my master
Has made me stay up all the night out here,
His fist will lull me into sleep again.
I am quite ruined; see how strong is he!
MERCURY (*aside*): I'll speak out clearly; he'll hear what
    I say;
And so will be the more afraid. (*Aloud*) Now, fists,
Bestir yourselves; for long you've had no food;
'Tis ages since you sent four men to rest
And stole their clothes.
SOSIA (*aside*):   I'm terribly afraid
He'll change my name, and make of me the fifth,
And Quintus in the future I'll be called.
Four men already he has sent to rest,
I fear that I shall to their number add.

MERCURY: Ha! there! I'm ready for him.

SOSIA (*aside*):   He's prepared.
He's making haste.

MERCURY: He shan't escape a beating.

SOSIA (*aside*): Who shan't?

MERCURY: Whoever comes here eats my fists.

SOSIA (*aside*): I do not eat at night; and I have dined;
Pray give your supper unto those who starve.

MERCURY: This is a weighty fist.

SOSIA (*aside*):   I am undone.
He weighs his fist.

MERCURY: What if I stroke him gently
That he may sleep.

SOSIA (*aside*):   You've hit upon the thing;
For three long nights I have been watching now.

MERCURY: But this won't do! My fist, you must not learn
To strike him feebly. Whom you even graze,
Must have himself all changed, and take again
Another form.

SOSIA (*aside*): That man will touch me up
And make my face quite different.

MERCURY: If you hit
Him fair and square, I'm sorry for his bones.

SOSIA (*aside*): Strange if he does not bone me like an eel.
Away with one who bones his fellow-men!
I'm done for, if he sees me.

MERCURY: There's a smell,
I think, of man—which bodes no good to him.

SOSIA (*aside*): What have I done?

MERCURY: He cannot be far off;
Though he was far enough just now.

SOSIA (*aside*):   This man
Is sure a wizard and a sorcerer.

MERCURY: And now my fists are itching to begin.

SOSIA (*aside*): If you are going to use them upon me,

Try the wall first.

MERCURY: A voice has reached my ear,
Flying on wings.

SOSIA (*aside*):   Unhappy that I am,
Not to have clipped the wings; I seem to have
A birdlike voice.

MERCURY: He evidently wants
A thrashing for his beast.

SOSIA (*aside*):   I have no beast.

MERCURY: He must be loaded with my fists.

SOSIA (*aside*):   Nay, sir,
I am weary of my voyage on the sea,
And still am sick; even without a load,
I scarce can walk; and with one I believe
I should not walk at all.

MERCURY: Some one, I think,
Is talking here.

SOSIA (*aside*): So I am safe at last;
He sees me not; some one, he says, is talking;
But I am Sosia.

MERCURY: Somewhere on the right
This voice would seem to strike my ear.

SOSIA (*aside*):   I fear
'Tis not my voice that strikes his ear that will
Be struck, but I myself.

MERCURY: He is advancing.

SOSIA: I'm stiff with fright; if any ask, I know
Not where I am; nor can I move from fear;
Now all is over; and my master's mission
And Sosia himself go down together.
Howe'er, I'll try to speak as bold as may be,
And then perhaps he'll keep his hands off me.

MERCURY: And whither, carrying Vulcan in your lamp
Of horn?

SOSIA: And who made you inquisitor,

Who say you knock men's teeth out with your fists?

MERCURY: Are you a slave or free?

SOSIA: Both if I choose.

MERCURY: Aye, say you so?

SOSIA: Why, yes, I do indeed.

MERCURY: You lie; I'll make you learn to speak the truth.

SOSIA: What need of that?

MERCURY: Now I must know at once

Whither you go, as well as whose you are

And why you came.

SOSIA: Well, then, I'm coming here;

I am my master's slave. Is that enough?

MERCURY: I'll stop that wretched tongue of yours today.

SOSIA: You cannot; 'tis as good and clean as yours.

MERCURY: And do you quibble? What have you to do

Here at this house?

SOSIA: Why, what is that to you?

MERCURY: King Creon stations separate sentinels

To watch by night.

SOSIA: So doing he does well;

While we're abroad our house is safe and sound.

But go and say the servants have arrived.

MERCURY: Well, I know nought of that; unless you go

At once, I will arrange that your reception

Is not the sort that family servants get.

SOSIA: But I live here, and am these people's slave.

MERCURY: Dost thou know how? I'll have you carried
    out

Upon a litter, in your pride of state.

SOSIA: How, pray?

MERCURY: You will not need to walk, but will

Be carried off if once I take my stick.

SOSIA: But I assert, I am this family's slave.

MERCURY: Look to't—you'll soon be ready for a beating,

Unless you go at once.

SOSIA: Do you pretend
To stop me coming home who've been abroad?
MERCURY: Is this your home?
SOSIA: Why, yes, it is indeed.
MERCURY: And who's your master?
SOSIA: 'Tis Amphitryon,
The general of the Theban army, he
Who's married to Alcmena.
MERCURY: What's your name?
SOSIA: They call me Sosia, the son of Davus.
MERCURY: Then you have come today with made-up
     tales
And patched-up lies, thou height of impudence!
SOSIA: Nay, if you like, with patched-up clothes, not lies.
MERCURY: And now you lie again; upon your feet
You came, not on your clothes.
SOSIA: Yes, very true!
MERCURY: Then take that for your lies. (*Striking him*)
SOSIA: That will I not.
MERCURY: Whether you will or no; for this is sure;
It is no matter of opinion.
SOSIA: Be civil, please.
MERCURY: And dare you say that you
Are Sosia, when I myself am he. (*Still striking him*)
SOSIA: I'm killed entirely.
MERCURY: That is but a small
Instalment of what will be. Whose are you now?
SOSIA: Why yours; your fists have marked me for your
     own—
Your help, ye citizens of Thebes!
MERCURY: Do you
Call out, you rascal? Say for what you came.
SOSIA: To be a target for your fists, good sir.
MERCURY: Whose are you then?
SOSIA: Amphitryon's slave.

MERCURY: Therefore, the more you shall be beaten for
Your idle talk; 'tis I am Sosia.

SOSIA: I wish you were, and I was beating you.

MERCURY: And are you murmuring?

SOSIA: I will be quiet.

MERCURY: Who is your master?

SOSIA: Any one you like.

MERCURY: What then? How are you called?

SOSIA: As you may bid.

MERCURY: You said you were Amphitryon's slave,
And Sosia called.

SOSIA: 'Twas a mistake I made.
I meant Amphitryon's associate.

MERCURY: I knew that none but I was Sosia.
You made a slip.

SOSIA: Would that your fists had, too.

MERCURY: I am that Sosia that you said you were.

SOSIA: I pray you let us have a truce between us
And no more blows.

MERCURY: An armistice be it,
If you have aught to say.

SOSIA: I will not speak
Unless there be a peace; for you are stronger.

MERCURY: Then call it what you like; I will not hurt
you.

SOSIA: But can I trust you?

MERCURY: Me?

SOSIA: What if you fail?

MERCURY: Then Mercury will revenge himself on Sosia.

SOSIA: Now, sir, observe, since I may freely speak,
I'm really Sosia, Amphitryon's slave.

MERCURY: Do you repeat that?

SOSIA: Yes, I made a truce,
The peace is signed, I speak the very truth.

MERCURY: Take that then. (*Striking him again*)

SOSIA: Do just as you please to me,
Your fists are stronger; but whate'er you do
On this I'll not be silent.
MERCURY: While you live
You will not make me any one today
But Sosia.
SOSIA: And you will never make
Me other than myself. Nor is there here
A slave save Sosia, who went from hence
To join the army with Amphitryon.
MERCURY: The man is mad.
SOSIA: Nay, that disease is yours.
What the plague, am I not Sosia the slave,
Amphitryon my master; did not the ship
Which came to port tonight bring me with it?
Did not my master send me? Did I stand
Before the house, a lantern in my hand?
Do I not speak? Not watch? Did not this man
Attack me with his fists? He did indeed;
And even now my cheeks smart with his blows.
How can I doubt all this? And why not go
Into our house?
MERCURY: Your house?
SOSIA: 'Tis so, indeed.
MERCURY: In what you said just now, you lied, you know.
I am Amphitryon's Sosia; our ship
This night returned home from foreign lands;
And where King Pterela reigned, we took the town,
Destroyed by force the Teloboan troops:
Amphitryon himself in savage flight
Cut off King Pterela's head.
SOSIA (*aside*):   I scarce believe
Myself when thus I hear this fellow talk.
He knows by heart the deeds that were done there.
(*Aloud*) But say; what was the Teloboans' gift

To King Amphitryon?

MERCURY: The golden cup
King Pterela used.

SOSIA (*aside*):   He's right. (*Aloud*) Where is the
    cup?

MERCURY: It's in a chest, stamped with Amphitryon's
    seal.

SOSIA: What's on the seal?

MERCURY: The sun arising, with
Four horses in his car. Why do you try
To trip me up?

SOSIA (*aside*): He wins in argument;
And I must seek another name myself;
How has he seen these things? Now I will catch
Him nicely; what I did was within my tent,
Alone, when no one else was there to see,
That, anyhow, he cannot say. (*Aloud*) If you
Are Sosia, tell me what took place the while
The battle was going on, within my tent.
If you can say, you win.

MERCURY: There was a cask
Of wine from whence I filled myself a jug—

SOSIA (*aside*): On the right road!

MERCURY: And that I drained it
    pure,
As it came from the grape.

SOSIA (*aside*):   A wondrous tale,
Unless himself was hid within the cask;
'Tis true I drank it pure, without a drop
Of water in it.

MERCURY: Now is't true that you
Are not our Sosia?

SOSIA: You deny I am?

MERCURY: What else to do when I am he myself?

SOSIA: I swear by Jove I'm he, and that's no lie.

MERCURY: And I by Mercury declare that Jove
Does not believe you. He would rather trust
To me unsworn, than you upon your oath.
SOSIA: Then if not Sosia, who the deuce am I?
MERCURY: When I'm not Sosia, you, of course, are he;
Now when I am, unless you go, you wretch,
You will be beaten.
SOSIA (*aside*):   When I see this man
And contemplate my own appearance too
(I've often done it in a glass), I see
How like he is to me. He has on him
A hat and coat like mine; as like to me
He is indeed as I am to myself.
His calf, his foot, his stature, beard and eyes,
His nose, his cheeks, the way he wears his hair,
His neck, the whole—what need of further words?
If but his back is scarred, then nothing can
Be more alike than he; yet when I think
I really am just what I always was.
I know my master; know our house; can think
And feel; I won't mind what he says; I'll knock
Upon the door.
MERCURY: Where are you off to now?
SOSIA: To home.
MERCURY: Ev'n if you take Jove's car itself
And fly from hence, you shan't escape from ill.
SOSIA: May I not tell my mistress what my master
Bids me to say?
MERCURY: Your own tell what you like,
But not to mine; if you provoke me further,
You'll take a broken back from hence today.
SOSIA: I'll off. (*Aside*) Ye gods immortal, give me help!
Where did I lose myself? Where was I changed?
Where did I lose my shape? Did I forget
Myself when going to the war abroad

And leave myself at home? For sure this man
Has all the appearance that I did possess.
I'll to the port, and tell my master all.
Ev'n he, perhaps, won't know me; grant he mayn't,
That I today with head all shorn and bare
The glorious cap of liberty may wear.

(Sosia departs to the harbour.)

ACT I, SCENE II

MERCURY: (to himself): With all good luck this day has
   passed for me;
This piece of work's proceeded splendidly;
I have removed the greatest obstacle
That could prevent my sire's illicit joys.
For when this fellow comes before his master,
He'll tell how Sosia drove him from the door;
His master straightway will believe he lies,
And that he never went as he was bid.
I'll fill them both with error and mistake
And all Amphitryon's family beside,
Until my sire has tasted to the full
The joys he wishes; after, all will know
What's taken place; and Jove himself will bring
Alcmena into favour with her lord.
For sure Amphitryon will have a row
With her, accusing her of doing wrong;
And then my sire will end the strife between them
And bring back peace. (To audience) Now, as I left
   unsaid
A while ago, Alcmena will bring forth
Today two sons, the one a ten months' child,
The other seven: one Amphitryon's,
The other Jove's; the greater father to
The younger boy, the lesser to the other,
You understand. My sire has taken care

That for Alcmena's sake both should be born
Together, so to hide the secret wrong.
Yet, as I said, in the end Amphitryon
Will know the truth. What then? Does any think
The worse of poor Alcmena? The god will not
Allow his sin and fault to fall upon
A mortal's head. And now I'll end my speech,
The door has creaked; the false Amphitryon
Comes out, and with him comes his borrowed spouse.

Act I, Scene III

(*Enter Jupiter and Alcmena from the house*)

JUPITER: Good-bye, Alcmena, look well to the house,
As you are wont, and of yourself take care;
I must go hence; do you bring up the child.

ALCMENA: What is't, my husband, that you haste away
So soon?

JUPITER: 'Tis not because you weary me.
But when the general is not with the force,
What should not be, comes quicker than what should.

MERCURY (*aside*): He is a clever rogue, and 'tis no won-
    der,
Since he's my father; watch how he will coax
The woman.

ALCMENA: Now I clearly see how much
You value me.

JUPITER: Is't not enough there is
No other lady that I love so much?

MERCURY (*aside*): But if your wife should hear of these
    proceedings,
You'd rather be Amphitryon than Jove.

ALCMENA: I'd rather taste your love than hear of it.
You've hardly come; you came at mid of night,
And now you go; pray, is it kindly done?

MERCURY (*aside*): I'll go and talk to her and back him
    up.
(*To Alcmena*) I do not think that any man e'er loved
His wife to such distraction as he does.
JUPITER: Do I not know you, wretch? Out of my sight!
What care of yours to interfere with me,
Or even mutter? With this staff of mine—
MERCURY: Oh, don't!
JUPITER: One word and—
MERCURY (*aside*):   So my first ap-
    pearance
As flatterer has turned out rather poorly.
JUPITER: As to your words, dear wife, you must not be
Angry with me; I left upon the sly;
I stole these moments for you, so that you
Might learn the progress of affairs; I've told
You all; unless I loved you very much
I could not do it.
MERCURY (*aside*): Just as I did say:
He soothes her fears and pets her.
JUPITER: Lest the troops
Perceive my absence I must now return.
Let them not say that I preferred my wife
To state affairs.
ALCMENA: Your going leaves your wife
In tears.
JUPITER: Nay, nay, don't spoil your eyes, my dear,
I'll come again, and soon.
ALCMENA: That soon is long.
JUPITER: I do not leave you gladly.
ALCMENA: So it seems,
For the same night sees you both come and go.
JUPITER: Why keep me thus? I wish to leave the city
Before the dawn. And now this cup which they
Have given me for my valour, which the king

Did use himself, the king my hand has slain,
I give it to you.

ALCMENA: You do as you're wont.
In truth a noble gift, like him who gave it.

MERCURY: Indeed a noble gift, worthy of her
To whom 'tis given.

JUPITER: Will you not depart,
You wretch? And can I not escape you yet?

ALCMENA: And don't, my dear Amphitryon, be vexed
With Sosia for my sake.

JUPITER: That as you like.

MERCURY (*aside*): Though he's in love, he can be pretty
cross.

JUPITER: Hast aught you wish?

ALCMENA: Yes, that you love me
well,
Ev'n when I am away.

MERCURY: Amphitryon,
'Tis time to go. The day begins to dawn.

JUPITER: Sosia, go first; and I will follow thee.

(*Mercury departs*)

Want you aught more?

ALCMENA: Yes, that you soon return.

JUPITER: I'll come before you've time to think of it.
Be of good cheer. (*As Alcmena goes into her house*)
Now, Night, who stayed your course
To speed my plans, depart; give place to day,
That men may have its bright and shining light;
And by how much this night was longer than
The last, by so much shall the day that dawns
Be shorter; so there'll be equality,
And night succeed to day even as it's wont.
Now I will go and follow Mercury.

(*Jupiter departs*)

Act II, Scene I

(Enter Amphitryon and Sosia from the harbour; attendants follow with luggage)

AMPHITRYON: Go you behind.

SOSIA: I follow close to you.

AMPHITRYON: You are the greatest rascal I have known.

SOSIA: And why?

AMPHITRYON: Because what you tell me is not,
Nor was, nor will be.

SOSIA: Sure, a pretty state!
You won't believe your servants when they speak.

AMPHITRYON: What is't? I will cut off that wretched
     tongue
Of yours!

SOSIA: I am your slave, and I suppose
That you will do exactly as you choose.
Yet you shall not deter me; I will tell
Things as they are.

AMPHITRYON: You rascal, do you dare
To say you are at home, who'rt here with me.

SOSIA: I speak the truth.

AMPHITRYON: The gods will punish you
For this: and I will do the same today.

SOSIA: That's in your hand; for me, I am your slave.

AMPHITRYON: And do you dare to mock your master
     thus?
You dare to say what no man ever saw,
Nor yet can be, that at the selfsame time
A man may in two places be at once?

SOSIA: It was as I have said.

AMPHITRYON: The gods destroy you!

SOSIA: What harm through me has happened your af-
     fairs?

AMPHITRYON: D'ye ask that even when you're mocking
    me?

SOSIA: Blame, if you like, if matters are not so;
I do not lie; I speak things as they are.

AMPHITRYON: The man is drunk.

SOSIA: I only wish I were.

AMPHITRYON: You need not wish; you are.

SOSIA: What, I?

AMPHITRYON: Yes, you.
Where did you get it?

SOSIA: I've had none at all.

AMPHITRYON: What can I do with him?

SOSIA: A dozen times
I've said I am at home; d'ye hear me now?
And also I am here, the selfsame man.
Now is that clear, and have I spoken plain?

AMPHITRYON: Off with you!

SOSIA: What's the matter?

AMPHITRYON: You've the plague.

SOSIA: Why say you that? I am alive and well.

AMPHITRYON: But I, today, will give you your deserts;
Make you less well, more full of misery,
If I return home safe. Now follow me,
Who mock your master with such idle tales.
You have neglected my express commands,
And now have come to laugh at me besides.
Things which could never be, and which no one
Has ever heard of, these you now put forward.
You wretch, your back shall pay for these your lies.

SOSIA: Amphitryon, the greatest trouble that befalls
An honest servant when he speaks the truth
Is, sure, to find that truth rammed down his throat
And disbelieved.

AMPHITRYON: How can it be, you wretch,

That you're both here and yet at home as well?
Argue it out, I want you to explain it.

SOSIA: I am both here and there. It may seem strange
And 'tis as strange to me as any one.

AMPHITRYON: But how?

SOSIA: 'Tis not a jot more wonderful
To you than to myself; nor by the gods
Did I, this Sosia, believe the tale
Until that other Sosia made me do so.
In proper order all that happened when
We met the enemy he did disclose;
And took my very shape, my name as well.
Milk's not more like to milk than he to me.
For when before the dawn you sent me home—

AMPHITRYON: What then?

SOSIA: Why long before I ever came,
I stood before the house.

AMPHITRYON: What silly nonsense!
Say, are you sane?

SOSIA: Just as you see me here.

AMPHITRYON: Some wizard has bewitched this wretched
    man
After he left me.

SOSIA: That is true enough;
I'm bruised all over.

AMPHITRYON: Who has beaten you?

SOSIA: Why, I myself, the one that's now at home.

AMPHITRYON: Just answer what I ask. And first of all
Who is this Sosia?

SOSIA: He is your slave.

AMPHITRYON: It seems I have more Sosias than I need;
Yet since my birth I never had but you.

SOSIA: And yet, Amphitryon, I warrant you
Will find another Sosia waiting there

When you arrive; born of the selfsame father,
Same form and age as I. Need I say more?
There is a double Sosia born to you.

AMPHITRYON: These things are strange. But did you see
my wife?

SOSIA: I was not even allowed to come within.

AMPHITRYON: Who stopped you?

SOSIA: Why, this other Sosia,
Who used his fists upon me.

AMPHITRYON: Who is he?

SOSIA: 'Tis I, I say. How often have I told you!

AMPHITRYON: How can it be? Pray did you go to sleep?

SOSIA: No, never in the world.

AMPHITRYON: I thought perhaps
That you had seen this Sosia in your dreams.

SOSIA: I never sleep when following your behests;
I was quite wide awake as I am now
And as I speak to you; and wide awake
I was when he attacked me with his fists.

AMPHITRYON: Who did?

SOSIA: This other Sosia, can't you hear?

AMPHITRYON: How can one when you prate such silly
tales?

SOSIA: Well, soon you'll know.

AMPHITRYON: Know whom, d'ye mean?

SOSIA: That other Sosia.

AMPHITRYON: Then follow me, for first
I must enquire. Let all be disembarked.

SOSIA: I will take care that all you wish is done.
I have not swallowed your commands
As they were wine.

AMPHITRYON: May the gods grant to me
That nought of what you say has come to pass.

Act II, Scene II

(Enter Alcmena from the house, not seeing them)

ALCMENA *(to herself)*: How little pleasure there remains in life
When placed beside the sorrows we endure;
Such is the lot of man, the will of gods
That pain should still accompany pleasure here,
And that the more we have of good, the more
Of ill will follow. I find this at home,
And in my own experience, to whom
But little pleasure's come; a single night
Was all my husband could remain with me.
And suddenly before the dawn he went.
Now I am here alone; and he is gone
Whom most I love; more sorrow do I find
Now he has gone than pleasure when he came.
But this is well that he has won the fight
And comes back full of honour to his home.
'Tis that consoles me, that with glory won
He now returns; with courage and in faith
I'll bear his absence to the very end;
If only this reward be given to me
That he is hailed the conqueror in war,
That is enough; it is the best reward;
And valour comes before all other things.
Our liberty, our health, our life and wealth,
Our country and our friends are safe and sound
When there is valour; it possesseth all things.
And he who valour has, has all things else.

AMPHITRYON *(to Sosia)*: Yes, I believe my wife is longing for
My quick return; she loves me well, I know,
And I love her. And now that all's gone well

And far beyond our expectation, we
Have routed all our foes; in the first encounter,
Under my leadership, we won the day.
And so I'm sure she will be glad to see me.

SOSIA: And don't you think my spouse will be as much
  so?

ALCMENA (*aside*): It is my husband.

AMPHITRYON: Now keep close to me.

ALCMENA (*aside*): But why does he return who said just
  now
He must depart? Was't but a trial of me?
If that was it, to see if I deplored
His absence, I rejoice at his return.

SOSIA: We'd best return to the ship, Amphitryon.

AMPHITRYON: And why?

SOSIA: Because there's nothing here to eat.

AMPHITRYON: And how comes that into your mind, I
  pray?

SOSIA: Because we come so late.

AMPHITRYON: And how is that?

SOSIA: I see Alcmena has already dined.

AMPHITRYON: She was with child when last I went
  away.

SOSIA: Oh! What a nuisance!

AMPHITRYON: What is it to you?

SOSIA: I've just come home in time to carry water
For the child's bath according to your reckoning.

AMPHITRYON: Be of good cheer!

SOSIA: D'ye know how brave I am?
If once I take the bucket, ne'er believe
Aught that I say in any sacred matter,
If I don't draw the well to the very bottom.

AMPHITRYON: Now follow me: I'll find another slave
To do that work. Don't fear.

ALCMENA (*aside*):   I think that I

Will better do my duty if I go
To meet him now.

AMPHITRYON (*to Alcmena*):   Amphitryon salutes
His darling wife, the best, her husband says,
That ever was in Thebes, and whom as well
The citizens of Thebes most highly think of.
How are you? Are you glad to see me back?

SOSIA (*aside*): Not much of that, I think; she would
   receive
A dog as well.

AMPHITRYON: I'm glad to see you thus
With such a goodly bulk spread out as this.

ALCMENA: I pray you don't salute and speak me thus,
In way of mockery, as if you had
Not lately seen me; and for the first time
After the war were now returning home,
And talk as if it was a long time past
Since you had seen me.

AMPHITRYON: Till this moment I
Have never seen you anywhere today.

ALCMENA: But why deny it?

AMPHITRYON: 'Tis the truth I say.
I've learned to speak the truth.

ALCMENA: He does not well
Who what he's learned unlearns. D'ye wish to know
What mind I'm of? But why so soon returned?
Was it some omen that delayed your start,
Or does the weather stay you, and prevent
Your going to the army, as you said
You must just now?

AMPHITRYON: Just now? And how was that?

ALCMENA: Art trying me? Why, just a moment since—

AMPHITRYON: I ask you how it's possible?

ALCMENA: D'ye think that I
In turn should try to fool you, who declare

That you've just come, when you've just gone away?

AMPHITRYON: She's talking nonsense.

SOSIA: Wait a little while,
Until she sleeps her sleep out.

AMPHITRYON: Aye, she dreams,
While waking.

ALCMENA: I am wide awake, and tell
All that has taken place; how long ago
Before the dawn I saw both him and you.

AMPHITRYON: And in what place?

ALCMENA: Of course the house you live in.

AMPHITRYON: Never; it never was.

SOSIA: What if the ship
Brought us to shore asleep?

AMPHITRYON: Do you assist her?

SOSIA: What can one do? For don't you know that if
You wish to cross a raving maenad you
Will make her worse; and sometimes they will strike;
But if you humour them you will escape
With a single blow.

AMPHITRYON: But I'm determined now
To rate her well, because she did omit
To welcome me again on my return.

SOSIA: You'll raise a nest of hornets.

AMPHITRYON: Do be quiet!
Alcmena, I would ask one question of you.

ALCMENA: Ask what you will.

AMPHITRYON: Is't folly or is't pride
That overmasters you?

ALCMENA: Why ask the question?

AMPHITRYON: Because at coming you were wont to
    greet me,
To speak to me as modest wives are wont;
But now I came upon you, nor did find

The usual welcome.

ALCMENA: Yesterday, my lord,
I certainly did greet you when you came,
Inquired most carefully how you had been,
And took you by the hand and gave a kiss.

AMPHITRYON: You greeted me?

ALCMENA: I did, and Sosia too.

SOSIA: Amphitryon, I thought that she would have
A boy; I was mistaken.

AMPHITRYON: What then is't?

SOSIA: 'Tis folly she produces.

ALCMENA: I'm quite sane,
And pray the gods that I may have a boy.
But you will have a thrashing if he does
What is his duty; from your prophecy
You'll get, my prophet, what you well deserve.

SOSIA: A pregnant woman in her day should have
An apple given to gnaw, if she feel sick.

AMPHITRYON: You saw me yesterday?

ALCMENA: I did indeed;
I can repeat it ten times if you like.

AMPHITRYON: Perhaps in dreams?

ALCMENA: No, I was wide awake.

AMPHITRYON: Alas!

SOSIA: Why, what's the matter?

AMPHITRYON: She is mad.

SOSIA: 'Tis bile she has; naught makes men mad so soon.

AMPHITRYON: When first were you affected by it, wife?

ALCMENA: I am quite well and sound.

AMPHITRYON: Then why d'ye say
You saw me yesterday, who only came
This night to port; and there I dined and slept
The whole night in the ship, nor ever put
My foot into the house since first I went

Against the Teloboans and subdued them.

ALCMENA: You supped with me, and slept with me as
    well.

AMPHITRYON: How's that?

ALCMENA: 'Tis true.

AMPHITRYON: Not certainly, in this;
The rest I know not.

ALCMENA: At first blush of dawn
You left me for the army.

AMPHITRYON: How was that?

SOSIA: She says what she remembers; she relates
Her dreams. But surely, ma'am, when you awaked,
You should have given a salted cake or incense
To Jove, who wards off omens such as these.

ALCMENA: May you be hanged!

SOSIA: 'Tis for your interest
To see it done.

ALCMENA: This man, for the second time,
Is rude, and yet receives no punishment.

AMPHITRYON (to Sosia): Be still! (To Alcmena) You say
    I went from here at dawn?

ALCMENA: Who but yourself has told me that there was
A battle?

AMPHITRYON: You know that?

ALCMENA: And how you'd stormed
A mighty town and slain King Pterela.

AMPHITRYON: I told you this?

ALCMENA: With Sosia standing by.

AMPHITRYON (to Sosia): Did you hear this?

SOSIA: Where was I when I heard?

AMPHITRYON: Ask her.

SOSIA: No such event took place when I
Was present.

ALCMENA: 'Tis a wonder if he does
Not contradict his master.

AMPHITRYON: Sosia,
Look here!

SOSIA: I do.

AMPHITRYON: And please to speak the truth,
Not merely to agree with me; did you
Hear me say these things which she says I did?

SOSIA: And are you mad as well to ask me this?
I who now see her here for the first time.

AMPHITRYON: Now hear him, wife.

ALCMENA: I do, and hear him lie.

AMPHITRYON: You don't believe your husband, nor yet
    him?

ALCMENA: Because I do believe and know these things
Were as I say.

AMPHITRYON: I came here yesterday?

ALCMENA: Do you deny you went from here today?

AMPHITRYON: Most certainly; this is my first visit.

ALCMENA: And will you say you have not given me
A golden cup today, which you declared
Was given you there?

AMPHITRYON: I neither gave't nor said so;
But still I did intend, and do so still,
To give it you. But who was it who said so?

ALCMENA: 'Twas your own lips, and from your hand I
    took it.

AMPHITRYON: Stay, stay, I do beseech you! Yet I won-
    der,
Sosia, who told her that I had received
The golden cup, unless yourself did so?

SOSIA: I told her not, nor have I seen her save
With you.

AMPHITRYON: What sort of man is this?

ALCMENA: Would you
That I produce the cup?

AMPHITRYON: I wish it so.

ALCMENA: It shall be done. (*Calling inside*) Now, Thessala, bring the cup
My husband gave today.

AMPHITRYON: Sosia, come here,
For this will be the strangest thing on earth
If she should have this cup.

SOSIA: Can you believe it?
I have it in this box, sealed with your seal.

AMPHITRYON: And is the seal untouched?

SOSIA: Why, look at it.

AMPHITRYON: 'Tis right; just as I made the seal myself.

SOSIA: Why not command that she be purified
As being a lunatic?

AMPHITRYON: It must be done.
Her head is full of fancies; she's bewitched.

(*Enter Thessala with cup*)

ALCMENA: What need of further words? See, there's
your cup.

AMPHITRYON: Pray hand it here.

ALCMENA: Yes, look at it, yóu who
Deny what's taken place; I will convince
You openly 'tis so. Is that the cup?

AMPHITRYON: What do I see, great Jupiter? It is
The cup. Ah, Sosia, I am quite undone!

SOSIA: Either this woman is the greatest witch
Or else the cup's in here.

AMPHITRYON: Open the box.

SOSIA: Why open it? The box is firmly sealed
And all is going well. You have brought forth
Amphitryon the second, I in turn
A second Sosia, and if the cup
Has done the like, we all are doubled now.

AMPHITRYON: It must be opened and inspected then.

SOSIA: Look at the seal lest you should blame me after.

AMPHITRYON: Just open it; this woman by her words

Does make one mad.

ALCMENA: Whence comes this cup, I pray,
Unless by you 'twas given?

AMPHITRYON: I must enquire.

SOSIA: By Jupiter!

AMPHITRYON: What is't?

SOSIA: There is no cup.

AMPHITRYON: What do I hear?

SOSIA: You hear what's true enough.

AMPHITRYON: If 'tis not found you will be crucified.

ALCMENA: 'Tis found and here.

AMPHITRYON: Who gave it to you, then?

ALCMENA: The man who asks.

SOSIA (to Amphitryon):   You're trying to catch me;
You ran before me from the ship by stealth
Some other way, you took the cup from hence,
Then gave it to her and replaced the seal.

AMPHITRYON: Alas, her madness you encourage too.
(To Alcmena) D'ye say we came here yesterday?

ALCMENA: I do.
And coming you saluted me, I you,
And kissed you.

SOSIA: That kiss does not quite please.

AMPHITRYON: I will pursue my enquiries.

ALCMENA: Then you bathed.

AMPHITRYON: What then?

ALCMENA: You came to supper.

SOSIA: Excellent!
Enquire about that.

AMPHITRYON: Don't interrupt. (To Alcmena) Go on.

ALCMENA: Dinner was served; we sat together there.

AMPHITRYON: On the same couch?

ALCMENA: The same.

SOSIA: He does not like
The dinner.

AMPHITRYON: Let her state her arguments.
What after we had dined?
ALCMENA: You said that you
Were sleepy; so the table was removed.
We went to bed.
AMPHITRYON: Where did you sleep, I pray?
ALCMENA: In the same bed with you.
AMPHITRYON: O God!
SOSIA: How now?
AMPHITRYON: She's good as killed me.
ALCMENA: Why, what is it, dear?
AMPHITRYON: Don't speak to me!
SOSIA: What is it?
AMPHITRYON: I'm undone!
To all the troubles of my absence this
Is added that the honour of my wife
Is lost.
ALCMENA: And why, my lord, do I hear you say so?
AMPHITRYON: What! I your lord! Nay, do not use that
    name!
SOSIA: The matter is at a deadlock indeed
If she has changed him now from lord to lady.
ALCMENA: What have I done you should address me so?
AMPHITRYON: You tell the tale, yet ask how you have
    sinned?
ALCMENA: I was with you I married, where's the sin?
AMPHITRYON: You were with me? A more audacious lie
Was never told; and even if you have
No modesty, you might assume a little.
ALCMENA: Such conduct as you hint does not become
My race; and if you try to prove a charge
Against me of immodesty you'll fail.
AMPHITRYON: Now, Sosia, by the gods, at least you
    know me!
SOSIA: Why, rather!

AMPHITRYON: Yesterday I dined on board?
SOSIA: We've many witnesses to speak to that.
I know not what to say unless there be
Amphitryon the second who looks after
Your business in your absence, and can fill
Your place; to have another Sosia
Was strange; but it was stranger still to find
A new Amphitryon standing in your shoes.
AMPHITRYON: Some witch, I think, this lady does befool.
ALCMENA: By the high heaven, by Juno too, herself,
Whom most of all I reverence and regard,
I swear that no one else has ever come
Near me to wreck my modesty.
AMPHITRYON: I wish
Indeed 'twere so.
ALCMENA: I speak the truth, but you
Will not believe.
AMPHITRYON: You are a woman still,
And swear audaciously.
ALCMENA: Who has not sinned
Must needs be bold, and speak with confidence,
Aye, ev'n and forwardness, in her defence.
AMPHITRYON: Boldly enough, I grant.
ALCMENA: As one who is
Quite innocent.
AMPHITRYON: Yes, you are so in word.
ALCMENA: A dowry, sir, is not what people deem;
But love and modesty, and all desires
Controlled in fitting bounds, the fear of Heaven,
Respect of parents, good will to my friends,
Conforming in my likings to your own,
Bounteous in kindly service for your good,
These things I had, and these my dowry were.
SOSIA: If she speaks true she's innocence itself.
AMPHITRYON: I am bewitched; I know not who I am.

SOSIA: You are Amphitryon surely; see that you
Don't let another man your name usurp
And take it to himself (men change so much),
Now that we have at last arrived at home.
AMPHITRYON: I'll probe this matter to the very bottom.
ALCMENA: That as you choose.
AMPHITRYON: What say you? Answer me.
What if I bring your kinsman Naucrates,
Who sailed on board with me, and he denies
That what you say is true, what would be fair?
Can you say aught why I should not divorce you?
ALCMENA: Naught if I so have sinned.
AMPHITRYON: 'Tis settled then.
You, Sosia, bring these in; and I will fetch
This Naucrates from off the ship with me.
         (*Amphitryon departs towards the harbour*)
SOSIA: We are alone; now tell me seriously,
Is there another Sosia still inside?
ALCMENA: Leave me, thou slave, who such a master fits.
SOSIA: I go if so you will. (*Goes into the house*)
ALCMENA (*to herself*): It is too strange
That to my husband it should now occur
To charge me falsely with this grievous sin;
But still my kinsman Naucrates will tell us all.
              (*Alcmena goes inside.*)

ACT III, SCENE I

(*Enter Jupiter*)

JUPITER (*to the audience*): Friends, I am still Amphi-
    tryon whose slave
Is Sosia now, but when occasion serves
Is Mercury again; I live above
In the top attic; when it pleases me
I Jupiter become. At other times

When I come here I am Amphitryon,
And change my dress. Now for your sake I come,
Lest I should leave the comedy unfinished;
I also come to give Alcmena help
Who by her husband is accused of sin,
Being innocent herself; for 'tis my blame
If all the trouble I have caused should fall
On innocent Alcmena's head. And now
I will pretend to be Amphitryon
And in this family will introduce
The greatest mischief; then at length again
I'll make all clear, and to Alcmena bring
Assistance, and secure that she bring forth
Two children, mine and his, at a single birth.
I ordered Mercury to attend me close
If I should want him; now I'll speak to her.

ACT III, SCENE II

(*Enter Alcmena from the house*)

ALCMENA (*to herself*): I cannot rest within the house, accused
Of wrong, adultery, and foul disgrace,
By my own husband; he declares these things
Which happened are not so; what never was,
Which I have ne'er admitted, does affirm;
And thinks that under this I will sit down,
Nor care at all, but that's impossible.
I'll not endure to be thus falsely charged.
Either I'll leave him, or he makes it clear
And swears as well that he is sorry for
The charge which he has made against me thus.
JUPITER (*aside*): I certainly must do as she demands
If I would bring this mad woman to herself.
Since what I did annoyed Amphitryon,

And this poor lady's come in grievous trouble
By reason of my love, I must expect
His anger and ill feeling against her
Will turn on me.

ALCMENA (aside):   Ah, there he is, the man
Who accuses me of immodesty and shame.

JUPITER: I wish to speak with you. Why turn you from
me?

ALCMENA: It is my nature; I have always loathed
To look upon my foes.

JUPITER: Your foes!

ALCMENA: Yes, so it is—
Unless you argue that is false as well.

JUPITER: You are too angry.

ALCMENA: Nay, keep off your hands.
For surely if you're wise or know at all
The woman whom you say and think immodest,
With her you'd have no conversation, or
In joke or earnest, unless indeed you are
The greatest fool that lives.

JUPITER: And if I did
Say so, it surely does not make you so
A whit the more, nor do I think you such.
And I returned to clear myself of this;
For nothing ever did annoy me more
Than when I heard that you were vexed with me.
"Why said you so?" you ask. I will explain.
I did not think that you were e'er immodest;
I tried your disposition, how you'd bear it;
I said those things in joke for a little fun.

ALCMENA: But why not bring my kinsman Naucrates,
As you did promise me, to prove you were
Not here?

JUPITER: If aught were said by way of joke,
It is not fair to treat it seriously.

ALCMENA: I know how much those words have grieved
    my heart.
JUPITER: By your right hand I pray, Alcmena dear,
Forgive me—pardon; be not vexed with me.
ALCMENA: My virtue makes your words of none effect;
And now, since I abstained from unchaste deeds,
I wish to avoid all unchaste words as well.
Farewell; keep all you have; return me mine;
And bid these women to accompany me.
JUPITER: But are you mad?
ALCMENA: I'll go, at any rate;
My chastity shall bear me company.
JUPITER: Oh, stay! At your discretion I'll propose
This oath: that I do not believe my wife
To be immodest; if I fail in that,
Then, mighty Jupiter, I pray that you
Will on Amphitryon let your anger fall.
ALCMENA: Propitious rather may he be!
JUPITER: I trust he will.
For I have sworn a sincere oath to you.
You are not angry now?
ALCMENA: I'm not.
JUPITER: 'Tis well;
For in the life of man there often happen
Things of this sort; they meet with pleasure first,
And then with pain; quarrels occur ofttime
And reconciliation takes their place;
And if perchance angry disputes occur,
There comes return of kindly feeling; so
They're greater friends than e'er they were before.
ALCMENA: 'Tis well at first to avoid such words at all;
But if you so apologise for them
Then I must be content.
JUPITER: Now bid, I pray,
The sacred vessels here to be prepared

To celebrate with fitting rites the vows
Which I when with the army vowed to pay,
If I returned home safe; I'd pay them now!
ALCMENA: I'll see to it.
JUPITER: Call Sosia hither now.
And let him summon Blepharo the pilot,
Who was on board with me, to dine today;
(*Aside*) But he himself, undined, shall be befooled,
And I will take Amphitryon by the neck
And put him out.
ALCMENA (*aside*): 'Tis strange he speaks apart.
But the door opens; Sosia arrives.

ACT III, SCENE III

(*Enter Sosia*)

SOSIA: Amphitryon, I'm here; and, if you will,
Command me what you want.
JUPITER: I'm glad to see you.
SOSIA: And peace, I hope, is now restored to you?
I'm glad to see you happy and rejoice.
It is a servant's place to conform himself
To what his master is, to arrange his face
According to his master's; is he sad,
Let him be sad as well, and is he merry,
Let him rejoice. But come now, answer me,
Are you once more in amity again?
JUPITER: You laugh; you know I only spoke in joke.
SOSIA: A joke was it? I thought, indeed, you were
In sober earnest.
JUPITER: I've apologised,
And peace is made.
SOSIA: That is the best of news.
JUPITER: I'll make an offering within, as I

Have promised.

SOSIA: Yes, I think you should at once.

JUPITER: And call the pilot Blepharo from the ship,
That, service over, he may dine with me.

SOSIA: I will be there before you think me gone.

JUPITER: Return at once. (*Sosia departs*)

ALCMENA: Should I not go within
In the first place, and see that all is ready?

JUPITER: By all means, go and bid them be prepared.

ALCMENA: Come when you wish inside; I'll see to it
That there is no delay. (*Alcmena goes into the house.*)

JUPITER (*calling after her*): Rightly you speak,
And as a good and careful housewife should.

(*To himself*) These two, both slave and mistress, are mistaken
In that they think that I'm Amphitryon.

(*To the absent Mercury*) But thou, my Sosia in godlike form,
Be here; hear what I say though you're not present;
And, when Amphitryon comes, see that you keep
Him from the house, whatever way you can.
I wish him to be mocked, while I amuse
Myself a little with this borrowed wife.
Have all things done according to my wish,
And help me while I offer to myself.

(*Jupiter goes into the house.*)

ACT III, SCENE IV

(*Enter Mercury running*)

MERCURY (*to imaginary passers-by*): Out of the way,
out of the way, all you good people, out of the way!
He's a bold man who'd venture to stay
When I bid him to go; I'm a god, and can threaten

The people as much as a slave who is beaten,
In comedies often; they come in and tell
That the ship has arrived in port safe and well;
Or some angry old gentleman is come on the scene.
I am the servant of Jove, and so long have been;
I obey his behests, so why shouldn't I make
All you people depart to make room for my sake.
The father, he summons, I come at his call,
As good son should do, I obey him in all;
I flatter and fawn, assist, humour his whim,
Give advice and joy with him; what's pleasant to him
Is always the greatest of pleasures to me.
Does he love? He is wise and as right as can be;
And wherever he follows his own inclination,
As all men should do if within moderation,
He does well; he would like this Amphitryon to gull,
And gulled he shall be, in your sight to the full.
A wreath now I'll wear on my head, and pretend
That I am quite drunk; and then I will wend
Upstairs, and will watch him and see what I see.
I'll make him as drunk as a lord although he
Has not tasted a drop; and, if Sosia appear,
Most certainly he will the penalty bear
Of all that I've done; and he'll say it was he
Who has done all the mischief that rested with me.
What matters to me? I must always obey
My master's commands, and fall in with his way.
And, look here, here's Amphitryon; now for the fun,
If you'll only wait here, you'll see how it's done.
And now I'll go in, dress myself as I should,
And forbid him to enter his house if he would.

(He goes into the house)

Act IV, Scene I

(*Enter Amphitryon*)

AMPHITRYON (*to himself*): This Naucrates I wished was
    not on board;
Nor in the city could I find a man
Who'd seen him, nor within the house; I've scoured
The squares, gymnasiums, the barbers' shops,
The mart, the shambles, and the wrestling school,
The forum, and the street where doctors dwell,
The perfume-sellers, all the sacred shrines,
I'm wearied with the quest, but Naucrates
I cannot find. Now I'll go home and try
To find out from my wife who it has been
Who has dishonoured her; I'd rather die
Than not pursue this matter to the end.
The doors are closed; 'tis just like all the rest.
I'll knock. Pray open! Open now the door.

Act IV, Scene II

(*Mercury appears on the roof*)

MERCURY: Who's there?
AMPHITRYON: Why, I.
MERCURY: What I?
AMPHITRYON: Well, I who speak!
MERCURY: Well, Jupiter and all the gods are vexed with
    you
For breaking thus the door!
AMPHITRYON: Pray tell me, how?
MERCURY: That all your life you'll be a wretched man.
AMPHITRYON: Now, Sosia!
MERCURY: Yes, I am he, unless
You think that I've forgot my name.

What do you want?

AMPHITRYON: You villain, do you ask
Me what I want?

MERCURY: I do indeed; almost
You've broken off the hinges of the doors.
D'ye think we get them at the public charge?
Why look at me, fool! Tell me who you are,
And what you want!

AMPHITRYON: You ask me what I want,
You scoundrel, you who have destroyed more rods
Than Acheron souls; and for those words of yours
This very day I'll warm you with the scourge.

MERCURY: Ah, yes, in your young days you must have
    been
A prodigal.

AMPHITRYON: How's that?

MERCURY: Because ev'n now
In your old age you ask a thrashing from me.

AMPHITRYON: These words you pour so glibly forth will
    bring
A heavy punishment on you today.

MERCURY: I'll pay my sacrifices to you.

AMPHITRYON: Why?

MERCURY: Because I've cursed you with bad luck today.

[*At this point there is a gap in the manuscripts. The gap
may be filled somewhat as follows: The present scene
concludes with Mercury emptying a pail of water over
Amphitryon. Alcmena comes out and has a dispute with
her husband; she returns to the house, convinced that
he is mad. Sosia appears with Blepharo. Jupiter enters,
and husband and lover abuse each other. Blepharo is
completely puzzled and is unable to decide which is
the real Amphitryon. Here the play resumes.*]

Act IV, Scene III

(Blepharo, Amphitryon, and Jupiter are on the stage)

BLEPHARO: And now arrange yourself in parties as
You choose; I go; my business is done.
Nor have I ever seen such strange things happen.
AMPHITRYON: Nay, Blepharo, do not go; assist me now;
And be my advocate.
BLEPHARO: What use of me,
Who do not even know which side I'm on!
                              (Blepharo departs.)
JUPITER: I go within; Alcmena's taken ill.
                              (Jupiter goes inside)
AMPHITRYON *(to himself)*: Ah! Woe for me, when all
    my advocates
And friends desert me; never sure will I
Be mocked by this man, and be unavenged.
I'll go direct before the king, and tell him
All that has taken place; yes, I will punish
This sorcerer of Thessaly, who has
Unstrung the mind of all my family.
But where is he? He went in to my wife;
Was ever there more wretched man at Thebes,
Whom every one at will ignores and laughs at?
I'll burst into the house, and there straightway
Whoe'er I see, or maid, or slave, or wife,
Sire, or grandsire, or this adulterer,
I will destroy; nor Jupiter nor all
The gods ev'n if they will will hinder me
In what I am resolved. And now I go!
*(As he rushes to the door, there is a peal of thunder;
    Amphitryon falls motionless)*

Act V, Scene I

(Enter Bromia from the house)

BROMIA *(to herself)*: Now all my hopes and means of
    life lie wrecked
And gone; my heart has failed; nor does remain
One spark of courage; all things, sea and land,
And heaven itself, do wish to drag me down
And slay me; what to do I cannot tell.
Such wondrous things have happened in the house.
I'm faint! Oh, for a little water now!
I am exhausted and my strength is gone!
My head is sick! I neither see nor hear!
Nor is there one who is or does appear
More wretched than myself! Such things have chanced
My lady here today; her hour has come;
She straight invokes the gods. What voices come,
What noise, what flashes, how the thunder pealed,
How frequently! And every one fell flat
Just where he was; then with a mighty voice
Some one exclaimed: "Alcmena, help is nigh,
Be not afraid; for he who dwells on high,
Comes both to you and yours with kindly aid.
Rise up," he says, "who've fallen to the ground
In terror and alarm." Then where I lay
I rose; I thought the house was all on fire
Such flashes were there; then Alcmena cries
For me to come; and that brings fresh alarm.
Fear for my mistress is my first concern.
I go to see what she may wish, and there
I see two sons are born, nor any know
When they came forth, or did suspect their birth.
But what is this? And who is this old man,
Who lies before our door? Has he been struck

By Jupiter? 'Twould seem as if he had,
He lies as still as if he were quite dead.
I'll go and search out who he is; it is
My master; 'tis Amphitryon himself.
Amphitryon!

AMPHITRYON: I'm dead!

BROMIA: I pray thee rise!

AMPHITRYON: Nay, all is over.

BROMIA: See, take now my hand.

AMPHITRYON: Who holds me?

BROMIA: 'Tis your maid, 'tis Bromia!

AMPHITRYON: I'm full of fear; for Jove has thundered so!
Nor is it otherwise than just as if
I was in Hell. But why have you come out?

BROMIA: Why, the same things that filled your heart
    with dread
Alarmed us too; I never saw such sights;
Alas! Amphitryon, my mind gives way!

AMPHITRYON: Be quick; art sure I am Amphitryon?

BROMIA: I am.

AMPHITRYON: Quite sure? Look once again!

BROMIA: I am.

AMPHITRYON: Alone of all my household she retains
Her senses.

BROMIA: Nay, my lord, we all are sane.

AMPHITRYON: And yet my wife has made me to be mad
By her foul deeds.

BROMIA: But I will make you tell
Another tale, Amphitryon; you shall know
Your wife is good and faithful; in few words
The reasons and the arguments for that I'll tell.
And first of all Alcmena's borne two sons.

AMPHITRYON: Two sons?

BROMIA: Yes, two.

AMPHITRYON: The gods preserve me now!

BROMIA: Permit me now to speak that you may know
The gods are all propitious to your wife and you.
AMPHITRYON: Speak then.
BROMIA: Well, when her labour first began,
She invoked the immortal gods to give her aid
With washen hands and covered head. There came
A sudden thunderclap with constant crashing.
We thought the house was coming to the ground.
The whole house flashed as if 'twere made of gold.
AMPHITRYON: I pray you let me go, you've fooled
       enough.
What happened then?
BROMIA: While this proceeded, none
Of us did hear her either groan or cry;
It passed without a pain.
AMPHITRYON: Of that I'm glad,
Whatever her deserts towards me.
BROMIA: Pass on,
And hear my words. When she had brought forth boys,
She bade us wash them; we began to do so;
But the boy I washed, how large and strong
He was; we could not bind him in his cot.
AMPHITRYON: Too strange your tale! And if these things
       are true,
I do not doubt that help came from on high.
BROMIA: Still greater things remain, as you will say.
For after he was put into his cot
Two crested snakes of awful size come down
Into the tank for rain; and straightway both
Upraised their heads.
AMPHITRYON: Alas! Alas!
BROMIA: Fear not!
The snakes looked all around, and when they saw
The boys, they fly towards the cot. I then,
Retreating backward, draw them back as well,

Fearing for them, and for myself the while.
But when that one of whom I spoke saw them,
Immediately he jumped out of the cot
And made straight for the snakes; each with one hand
He seizes in a fatal grasp of death.
AMPHITRYON: Strange is your tale; too terrible to hear,
And horror seizes on me as you speak.
And say, what happened next?
BROMIA: The boy killed both;
And while this passes, one with clear loud voice
Calls out your wife's name.
AMPHITRYON: Tell me who was that?
BROMIA: The king of gods and men, the mighty Jove.
He said he was the consort of Alcmena,
And that the son who slew the snakes was his;
The other yours.
AMPHITRYON: Indeed, then, I'm content,
To divide this happiness with Jove. Go home,
And bid your vessels to be straight made fit,
That I with many offerings may seek
The kindly will of Jove. (*To himself, as Bromia goes
inside*) Meanwhile I'll ask
Counsel and help from seer Tiresias.
But what is this? How loud the thunder rolls!
Gods, I beseech your help.

ACT V, SCENE II

(*Jupiter appears above*)

JUPITER: Be of good cheer, Amphitryon. I am
The friend of you and yours; dismiss, I pray,
Your seers and soothsayers; the future I
Will tell you better far than they can do.
And, first of all, I borrowed for a time
Your wife, Alcmena, and so had a son;

You too had got one when you left to join
The army; both were born together at one birth.
That which is mine shall bring immortal fame
To you by his achievements; so return
Into your ancient friendship with your wife.
She has done nothing to deserve your blame,
She was compelled by me. I go to Heaven.

(*Jupiter disappears*)

ACT V, SCENE III

AMPHITRYON: It shall be as you wish; and see that you
Your promises perform. I'll go within
To see my wife, and leave Tiresias.
(*To the audience*) And now, spectators, clap for mighty
    Jove,
And give applause for him that reigns above.

➵➵❋❬❬❬

TERENCE
(Publius Terentius Afer, 190? B.C.–?159 B.C.)

❋

Phormio
Anonymous Translation, Published at London, 1734

CHARACTERS

CHREMES   ⎫
DEMIPHO   ⎬ *brothers*
PHÆDRIA, *Chremes's son*
ANTIPHO, *Demipho's son*
PHORMIO, *a parasite*
DORIO, *a bawd*
GETA, *Demipho's servant*
DAVUS, *a crony of Geta's*
HEGIO   ⎫
CRATINUS   ⎬ *lawyers*
CRITO   ⎭
NAUSISTRATA, *Chremes's wife*
SOPHRONA, *a nurse*

SCENE—*Athens*

PROLOGUE

Since the old bard can not provoke our poet
To leave the muse, and sit hereafter idle,
He new invectives now prepares, in hopes
To terrify him that he'll write no more:

75

His former plays, maliciously he crys,
Are lightly scribled, and the style is poor:
This he reports, because our poet never
Brought on the stage a frantic youth that saw
A hind in flight, and by the hounds pursued,
Her case lamenting, and imploring aid:
But was he conscious that his play's success
Was thro' the actor's merit, not his own,
He wou'd not, as he now offends, offend,
And then his plays wou'd meet with greater favour.
If any now shall say, or can suppose,
That, had not the old poet first provok'd
The young one to abuse him in return,
This had not known what prologues to have wrote,
Our poet answers thus; the prize to all
The servants of the muses is propos'd.
He strove to drive our poet from his studies,
And to subject him to the hand of need:
This strives to answer him, not to provoke:
Had his contention been in gentle words,
He, in return, had gently been reprov'd:
But let him think that, which he brought, repay'd:
Henceforward I shall cease to speak of him,
Since he continues to expose himself.
  Now kindly to my humble suit attend:
I here present to ye a play that's new;
This comedy *Phormio* the Latins call,
And *Epidicazomenos* the Greeks:
Phormio 'tis call'd from the chief character,
The parasite, who shall the bus'ness guide,
If in the poet's favour ye're inclin'd.
  Silent attend with an impartial ear,
That the same fortune now we may not meet,
Which we before had, when our company
Was by the tumult from their places drove;

Which, by the actor's excellence, have since,
Assisted by your goodness, been restor'd.

Act I, Scene I

(Davus)

DAVUS: My good friend and countryman Geta came
to me yesterday: I had a little money of his in my hands
on an old account; which he desir'd me to make up; I
have made it up, and am carrying it up to him. I hear
that his master's son is marry'd; I believe this is scrap'd
together for a present to his bride. How unjust it is,
that they who have but little shou'd be always adding
something to the wealth of the rich! All that this poor
fellow has sav'd, by little and little, out of his wages,
cheating his belly at the same time for't, must go at
once to her, who does not think with what difficulty
'twas got: besides Geta will be struck for another sum
when his mistress is brought to bed, and for another
when the son's birthday comes about next year, at which
time he'll be initiated: all this goes to the mother, tho
the boy's the pretence: but isn't that Geta I see?

Act I, Scene II

(Geta and Davus)

GETA: If a red-hair'd man should enquire for me—
DAVUS: Say no more, he's at your elbow.
GETA: O! Davus, I was just coming to you.
DAVUS: Here, take it; 'tis all good; there's exactly what
I owe you. (*He gives the money to Geta*)
GETA: I love you, and thank you for not neglecting me.
DAVUS: Especially as times go now; things are come
to such a pass, that if a man pays what he owes, his
creditor's to say he's much oblig'd to him: but why are
you melancholly?

GETA: I? You don't know what tribulation and danger I'm in.

DAVUS: What's the matter?

GETA: I'll tell you, if you can be secret.

DAVUS: Away, you fool: are you afraid to trust him with words that you've found faithful in money? What interest have I in betraying you?

GETA: Well, hear me.

DAVUS: I'm attentive.

GETA: Do you know Chremes, Davus, our old man's elder brother?

DAVUS: Know him? Yes.

GETA: Do you? And his son Phædria?

DAVUS: As well as I know you.

GETA: The old men both took a journey at one time, he that I've been speaking of to Lemnos, our old gentleman to Cilicia to an old acquaintance there: this same acquaintance tempted our old man over by letters, promising him mountains of gold, and what not?

DAVUS: To one so rich, and whom has more than he knows what to do with?

GETA: Hold your tongue: 'tis his temper.

DAVUS: O! If I was what I ought to be, I shou'd be a king.

GETA: When the old men went from hence, they both left me as governor over their sons.

DAVUS: O! Geta, 'tis a hard task you've taken on yourself.

GETA: That I know by experience: I am sure my genius was angry, or I had not been left with such a charge. I began at first to oppose 'em: in short, while I was faithful to the old men, my shoulders smarted: I consider'd, that 'tis folly to kick against the pricks: I then devoted myself entirely to my young masters, and did ev'ry thing they'd have me.

DAVUS: You knew how to make your market.

GETA: Our spark did not fly into any mischief at first; but Phædria was not long before he got his music-girl; and he became desperately fond of her; she was in the hands of a sordid rascal of a cock-bawd; and their fathers had taken care that they shou'd not have it in their pow'r to give anything: in the meanwhile he cou'd do nothing with her but feed his eyes, and dangle after her, and lead her to school and back again. We at our leisure gave Phædria our attendance: over against the school where this girl was educated was a barber's shop: there we usually waited till she came from school to go home: as we were sitting there, a young man came crying to us: we were surpris'd: we asked him what's the matter: "Poverty," says he, "never seem'd to me so sad and heavy a burden as it did just now. I have just seen a poor unhappy maid in the neighbourhood here, lamenting over her departed mother: she was plac'd against her, without any kind friend, acquaintance, or relation, excepting one old woman, to assist her in the funeral: it griev'd my heart, to see such beauty in distress!" In short, he mov'd us all: then says Antipho immediately, "Shall we go and see her?" "Yes," says one, "let us go— pray shew us the way." We walk on, we come to the place, we behold her: fair she was indeed, and the more so, because she had no help from art to her beauty: loose was her hair, and bare her feet, she was dirty, ill dress'd, and all in tears, so that, had there not been a native force of beauty in her charms, they had been extinguish'd here. The spark that lov'd the music-girl only say'd, "She's pretty enough," but our—

DAVUS: I easily guess: he was wounded.

GETA: But can you guess how deeply? Observe the consequence. The next day he goes directly to the old woman; he intreats her to let him possess the girl: she refuses, and tells him 'tis unjust to do it, that she's a citizen of Athens, of a good character, and good parentage, if he has a mind to marry her, that he may lawfully do; he had a strong inclination to marry her, but was afraid of his father who's abroad.

DAVUS: Wou'd not his father give him leave, if he was come home?

GETA: He give him leave to marry a wench of no birth or fortune? Never.

DAVUS: What's come of it at last?

GETA: What's come of it? There's a certain parasite, one Phormio, a fellow of an undaunted assurance, who, the devil take him for it—

DAVUS: What has he done?

GETA: —Gave him the following counsel: " 'Tis a law," says he, "that young women, who are orphans, shall be marry'd to their nearest relations, and this same law obliges the men to marry them: I'll say you are her kinsman, and I'll be your prosecutor: I'll pretend to be her father's friend: we'll bring it before the judges: who her father was, who her mother, and how she's related to you, leave to my management, I'll have all ready, to carry it to my own advantage and in favor of me: when you disprove none of these articles, I shall gain my cause. Your father will come home: he'll have a pull with me: what then? We shall secure our woman."

DAVUS: A humourous piece of impudence!

GETA: He prevail'd on the young man: they set about it: they come into court: he marry'd her.

DAVUS: What's that you say?

GETA: 'Tis just as I tell you.

DAVUS: O! Geta, what will become of you?

GETA: I can't tell, by Hercules: this I know, whatever fortune lays upon me, I'll bear it patiently.

DAVUS: I'm glad to hear you say so: 'tis what we all ought to do.

GETA: All my hope is in myself.

DAVUS: I commend you.

GETA: Suppose I get one to intercede for me, this perhaps will be his speech—"pray forgive him now, but if he does so again, I'll not speak a word for him." 'Tis well if he don't add, "when I'm gone, e'en hang him."

DAVUS: What of the music-girl's hero? What exploit has he in hand?

GETA: Nothing worth speaking of.

DAVUS: Perhaps he has it not in his pow'r to give much.

GETA: He can give nothing but hope.

DAVUS: Is his father come home, or not?

GETA: Not yet.

DAVUS: Well, when d'y' expect your old man?

GETA: I don't know certainly; but I hear'd just now that there's a letter come from him, and left at the port: I'll go for it.

DAVUS: Have you any more to say to me, Geta?

GETA: Nothing, but that I wish you well. (*Davus goes*) Here boy. Will nobody come out? (*A boy comes*) Take this, and give it to Dorcius. (*He gives the money to the boy and goes*)

ACT I, SCENE III

(*Antipho and Phædria*)

ANTIPHO: That it shou'd come to this, Phædria, that I shou'd be afraid of my father when I do but think of his return, of a father who wishes me so well! Had I not been an inconsiderate fool, I might have expected him as I ought.

PHÆDRIA: What's the matter?

ANTIPHO: Is that a question for you to ask, who was my confidant in so bold an enterprise? O! that it had never enter'd into Phormio's head to persuade me to it, and that he had not drove me in my fit of love on what has prov'd the source of my misfortunes! If I had not obtain'd her, then I shou'd have been uneasy some few days; but I shou'd have escap'd this perplexity of mind, which ev'ry day torments me—

PHÆDRIA: I hear you.

ANTIPHO: —While I'm ev'ry moment in expectation of his return, who will force me from the arms of my belov'd.

PHÆDRIA: 'Tis a grievance to some that they can't have what they love; satiety's the root of your complaint. Antipho, you're too rich in love; for such, by Hercules, is your situation, 'tis worth our warmest wishes and endeavours. By heav'n cou'd I possess my love so long, I'd purchase it with death, nor think it dear: do but consider, what I endure amidst my present want, and what you gather from your plenteous store; not to mention your good fortune, in having gain'd, according to your will, an honest wellbred wife, whose character has never been stain'd: you're a happy man, if you had but this one thing, a mind to bear your fortune as you ought; you'd feel how 'tis, if you had to do with such a cockbawd as I have: but 'tis in the nature of us all to murmur at our own condition.

ANTIPHO: But, on the contrary, Phædria, you are the fortunate man in my eye now; in whom is lodg'd the pow'r without constraint of consulting what pleases you best, to keep her, love her, or to leave her: I'm unhappily fall'n into such a strait, that I have no right to turn her off, nor pow'r to keep her—but what's here? Isn't that Geta that comes running hither? 'Tis he himself:

I'm afraid, lest he shou'd bring some news now that wo'n't please me.

Act I, Scene IV

(Geta, Antipho, and Phædria)

GETA *(to himself, not seeing them)*: Thou'rt undone, Geta, unless thy invention can relieve thee soon, so many sudden misfortunes hang over thy head now when thou'rt ill prepar'd for 'em; which I know neither how to ward against, nor to get myself out of; for the boldness of our proceedings can't be a secret long; which, if not cunningly guarded against, will fall heavily on me or my master.

ANTIPHO *(to Phædria)*: What's the meaning of his confusion here?

GETA *(to himself)*: Then I've scarcely a minute to turn myself about in, my master's so near.

ANTIPHO: What mischief's forwards?

GETA *(still not seeing them)*: Which when he shall hear of, how shall I oppose his anger? Suppose I pretend to speak? I shall enrage him: what, if I say nothing? I shall provoke him: how if I attempt to clear myself? 'Twill be labour in vain. Alas! what an unhappy fellow I am! While I tremble for myself, I am as much on the rack for Antipho; I am concern'd for him; I fear on his account; 'tis he that detains me; for, was it not for him, I shou'd have taken care enough of myself, and have been reveng'd on the old man's anger; I shou'd have scrap'd up something for my journey, and have march'd off directly.

ANTIPHO *(to Phædria)*: What journey is he making, or what is he scraping up?

GETA *(to himself)*: But where shall I find Antipho? Or where shall I look for him?

PHÆDRIA (*to Antipho*): He names you.

ANTIPHO (*to Phædria*): I'm afraid he's the messenger of some very ill news, tho I don't know what.

PHÆDRIA (*to Antipho*): Ah! Have you loss'd your senses?

GETA (*to himself*): I'll make the best of my way homewards: 'tis most likely he's there.

PHÆDRIA (*to Antipho*): Let's call the fellow back.

ANTIPHO (*to Geta*): Stop, you, immediately.

GETA (*hearing, but not seeing him*): Huy, huy! You speak with authority, whoever you are.

ANTIPHO (*aloud*): Geta.

GETA (*seeing him*): 'Tis the very person I wanted to meet.

ANTIPHO (*to Geta*): Pray let us know what you're so full of, and tell us in a word, if you can.

GETA: So I will.

ANTIPHO: Out with it.

GETA: There's now put into port—

ANTIPHO: Who, my father?

GETA: You're right.

ANTIPHO: I'm ruin'd.

PHÆDRIA: Pshaw!

ANTIPHO: What shall I do?

PHÆDRIA (*to Geta*): What say you?

GETA: That I saw his father your uncle.

ANTIPHO: Alas! what remedy shall I find now to this sudden evil? If such my fortune, my dear Phany, that I must be torn from you, let me part with life and you together.

GETA: Therefore as the affair stands, Antipho, you have the more need to look sharp about you: fortune helps the brave.

ANTIPHO: I'm quite confounded.

GETA: But now you've most occasion to exert yourself, Antipho; for if your father perceives you to be afraid, he'll conclude you're in fault.

PHÆDRIA: That's true.

ANTIPHO: I can't change my nature.

GETA: What wou'd you do if you had now a more difficult affair on your hands?

ANTIPHO: Since I can't go thro this, I shou'd be less able to bear that.

GETA: Here's nothing in this, Phædria; let him go. Why do we labour in vain here? I'll be gone.

PHÆDRIA: So will I.

ANTIPHO: Pray now, suppose I put on a countenance, will it do?

GETA: You do but trifle.

ANTIPHO: Look in my face: hum! Will this do?

GETA: No.

ANTIPHO: What say you to this?

GETA: That will almost do.

ANTIPHO: What to this?

GETA: That will do: ay, keep that; and answer him word for word, and give him as good as he brings; and don't let him bluster you out of countenance in his passion.

ANTIPHO: Very well.

GETA: Say you was forc'd, against your will, by the law, and decree of the court: do you understand me? But what old man's that, which I see at the farther end of the street?

ANTIPHO: 'Tis he himself: I can't stand my ground.

GETA: Ah! what are you doing? Where are you going, Antipho? Stay I say.

ANTIPHO: I know myself and my offence: I leave my Phany and my life to your care. (*Antipho goes*)

Act I, Scene V

(Phædria and Geta)

PHÆDRIA: What's to be done now, Geta?

GETA: You'll have a chiding now; but hanging will be my lot, if I'm not mistaking: but what we just now here advis'd Antipho to do, we must do ourselves, Phædria.

PHÆDRIA: Leave out *must;* and command me what to do.

GETA: Do you remember what you say'd, at the beginning of this enterprise, as a defence necessary to be made, that their cause was just, plain, binding, and the fairest that could be?

PHÆDRIA: I remember.

GETA: Ah! now we have need of it indeed, or, if we cou'd have it, a better, and more subtle one.

PHÆDRIA: I'll take care about it.

GETA: Now go you up to him first: I'll lie ready to relieve you, if you shall happen to want auxiliaries.

PHÆDRIA: Come on.

Act I, Scene VI

(Demipho, Geta, and Phædria)

DEMIPHO *(to himself, not seeing them)*: Is it so, is Antipho marry'd without my consent? Shou'd not my authority—but I wave authority—shou'd not he have fear'd my displeasure at least? Is he not asham'd? Audacious act! O! Geta, thou tutor!

GETA *(aside to Phædria)*: He's out at last.

DEMIPHO *(to himself, not seeing them)*: I wonder what they'll say to me, or what excuse they'll find.

GETA *(aside to Phædria)*: I've found one already: look you for another.

DEMIPHO (*to himself, not seeing them*): Will he ex-cuse himself by saying, "I did it against my will, the law compell'd me?" I hear him, and allow it to be so.

GETA (*aside*): Well say'd.

DEMIPHO (*to himself*): But knowingly, without speaking a word, to give up his cause to his adversaries! Did the law compel him to that too?

PHÆDRIA (*aside to Geta*): That strikes home.

GETA (*aside to Phædria*): I'll find an excuse for that: leave it to me.

DEMIPHO (*to himself*): I know not what to do, because this has happen'd, beyond my expectation or belief: I'm so provok'd, that I am scarcely capable of thinking: ev'ry one therefore, in the heighth of his prosperity, should then think within himself how he cou'd bear adversity; let him always, as he returns home, consider thus, I may meet with dangers, losses, a disobedient son, a dead wife, or a sick daughter, and these are misfortunes common to all men, there's nothing new or strange in either of them, therefore whatever happens beyond his expectation he should account as gain.

GETA (*aside to Phædria*): O! Phædria, 'tis scarcely to be believ'd how much wiser I am than my master: I have consider'd of all the inconveniences which can happen to me, if my master shou'd return, I concluded that I should be condemn'd to perpetual imprisonment to grind there, to be well drubbed, to be fettered, or sentenced to work in the fields; neither of which wou'd be new or strange to me; therefore whatever happens beyond my expectation I shall account as gain: but why don't you go up to the old gentleman, and speak him fair?

DEMIPHO (*to himself*): There's Phædria my brother's son, I see, coming this way.

PHÆDRIA: Uncle, your servant.

DEMIPHO: Your servant: but where's Antipho?

PHÆDRIA: I'm glad to see you safe return'd.

DEMIPHO: I believe you: but give me an answer to what I ask.

PHÆDRIA: He's very well; and he's not far off; but are all things as you'd have 'em?

DEMIPHO: I wish they were.

PHÆDRIA: What's the matter?

DEMIPHO: Do you ask, Phædria? Ye've patch'd up a fine marriage here in my absence.

PHÆDRIA: O, what, are you angry with him for that?

GETA (to himself): He manages him dextrously!

DEMIPHO: Ought I not to be angry with him? I wish he'd come into my presence, that he may see now how he has provok'd a good-natured father by his offence.

PHÆDRIA: But he has done nothing, uncle, to merit your displeasure.

DEMIPHO: See how they hang together; they're all alike; know one, you know all.

PHÆDRIA: Indeed you mistake us.

DEMIPHO: Let one commit a fault, and the other's ready to defend him; if one's here, the other's not far off; so they help one another.

GETA (to himself): The old man has spoke the truth of them without knowing it.

DEMIPHO: For if it was not so, you wou'd not stand up for him, Phædria.

PHÆDRIA: Uncle, if Antipho had been so much his own enemy as to have been guilty of any fault, contrary to his interest or honour, I would not open my lips in his behalf, but give him over to what he might deserve; but supposing any one, by his malicious stratagems, has lay'd a snare for us youth, and has caught us in it, are we to be blam'd or the judges, who often thro envy take from the rich, and as often thro pity add to the poor?

GETA (*aside*): If I did not know the affair, I shou'd believe what he's saying to be true.

DEMIPHO: How should any judge know your right, when you don't speak a word for yourself, as he did not?

PHÆDRIA: He behav'd like a gentleman; when he came before the judges, he was unable to utter what he had premeditated, his modesty and fear so confounded him.

GETA: Well defended: but why don't I go directly up to the old man? (*To himself*) Your servant, Sir: I'm glad to see you safe return'd.

DEMIPHO: Oh! thou excellent guardian, your servant, thou prop of our family, to whose care I committed my son when I went from hence.

GETA: I hear you have been accusing us all undeservedly, and me most undeservedly of all; for what wou'd you have me do for you in this affair? The laws don't allow a servant to plead, nor is his evidence taken.

DEMIPHO: Well, be it so: grant besides that the young man was foolishly fearful, I allow it, you're but a servant; however, if she was ever so near related, there was no occasion for him to marry her; but, as the law requires, you shou'd have giv'n her a portion; and she might look out for another husband: what reason had he to take a beggar home?

GETA: We did not want reason, but money.

DEMIPHO: He shou'd have borrow'd it anywhere.

GETA: Anywhere? Nothing more easily said.

DEMIPHO: If he cou'd not borrow it on other terms, he shou'd have took it up on interest.

GETA: Huy! that's well said: as if any one would lend him money, while you are alive.

DEMIPHO: No, no, it must not be so, it never can: shall I suffer her to live with him one day? There's no temptation for it. I wish that fellow was brought before me, or that I knew where he lives.

GETA: You mean Phormio.

DEMIPHO: The woman's friend.

GETA: I'll bring him here presently.

DEMIPHO: Where's Antipho now?

GETA: Within.

DEMIPHO: Go, Phædria, look for him, and bring him hither.

PHÆDRIA: I'll go directly.

GETA (aside): Yes, to Pamphila.

(Phædria and Geta go)

ACT I, SCENE VII

(Demipho)

DEMIPHO: I'll go home and thank the Gods for my return; then I'll go to the market, and summons some of my friends to be present in this affair, that I may not be unprovided if Phormio comes.

ACT II, SCENE I

(Phormio and Geta)

PHORMIO: Say you so, is he gone, and afraid to shew his face to his father?

GETA: 'Tis even so.

PHORMIO: And is Phanium left to herself, say you?

GETA: Neither better nor worse.

PHORMIO: And is the old man in a rage?

GETA: Yes, and in a great one.

PHORMIO: The burden, Phormio, must lie on your shoulders: you've a hard crust to mumble; you must down with it: set about it.

GETA: Pray do.

PHORMIO: Suppose he should question me about—

GETA: Our hope is in you.

PHORMIO: Ay, but consider, what if he replies?

GETA: You forced us.

PHORMIO: Well, I think that's right.

GETA: Come, give us your assistance.

PHORMIO: Let the old man come; I'll warrant you I am provided for him.

GETA: What do you intend?

PHORMIO: What, but secure Phanium's marriage, and free Antipho from what he's accused of, and take all the old man's anger on myself?

GETA: You've a stout heart of your own, and we are much oblig'd to you: but I'm very much afraid, Phormio, lest you draw the string till it breaks at last.

PHORMIO: Ah! there's no danger of that; I'm experienc'd in those things; I tread sure. How many men d'y' think I have worried to death, strangers and citizens? The oftener I've try'd, the more my hand's in. Tell me now, did you ever hear of an action of battery against me?

GETA: How have you escap'd?

PHORMIO: Because the net is never spread for such birds as the hawk or the kite, which are mischievous to us, but for such as do us no harm; because these are precious morsels, the other are not worth the labour: so they who have anything to lose are most in danger; they know I've nothing: but they'll commit you to prison, say you; to which I answer they do not chuse to maintain such a devouring fellow as I am; and, in my opinion, they'll shew their wisdom, in not doing me so good an office in return for a bad one.

GETA: He can never thank you enough for your favour.

PHORMIO: O! nobody can thank a prince enough for

his royal favour. Is it not pleasant for you to come at free cost, anointed, and fresh from the bath, with an easy mind, while another has the trouble and expense? While you have what you chuse, he's fretting himself, you laugh, drink the first cup, and take the first place, when the dubious entertainment is serv'd up.

GETA: Dubious, why dubious?

PHORMIO: Because you're doubtful what to eat of most:—when you consider how delicious and dear these things are, does not the master of the feast appear a very God to you?

GETA: Here comes the old man: be on your guard: the first onset's the fiercest; if you sustain that, you may wind him about as you will afterwards.

ACT II, SCENE II

(Demipho, Geta, Phormio, Hegio, Cratinus, and Crito)

DEMIPHO (*to the advocates*): Did ye ever hear of any one being more injuriously used than I am in this? Pray assist me.

GETA (*aside to Phormio*): He's in a passion.

PHORMIO (*aside to Geta*): Do you but mind your cue; I'll rouse him presently. (*Aloud to Geta*) Good Gods! does Demipho deny that Phanium's related to him? Does Demipho deny it?

GETA (*aloud*): He does deny it.

DEMIPHO (*to the advocates*): This is he, I think, that I've to do with. Keep close to me.

PHORMIO (*aloud to Geta*): And that he does not know who her father was?

GETA (*aloud*): He denies it.

PHORMIO (*aloud to Geta*): Nor who Stilpho was?

GETA (*aloud*): He knows nothing of him.

PHORMIO (*aloud to Geta*): Because she was left destitute, poor girl, her father's not known, and she's slighted: see, what avarice can make some people do!

GETA (*aloud to Phormio*): If you reflect upon my master for avarice, I'll give you your own.

DEMIPHO (*aside to the advocates*): The impudence of the fellow! Does he come on purpose to accuse me?

PHORMIO (*aloud to Geta*): There's no reason to be angry with the young man, if he had no great knowledge of him; for the poor man was old, and liv'd by his labour, almost confining himself to the country: where he farm'd a piece of ground of my father: the old man has often told me that this kinsman of his slighted him; but what a man did he slight? The best man that I ever saw in my life.

GETA (*aloud to Phormio*): See that you say no more than you can prove of yourself and him.

PHORMIO (*aloud to Geta*): Go hang yourself; if I did not think as well of him as I report him, I'd never get such ill will to our family as I do for her sake that he so ungenerously slights now.

GETA (*aloud to Phormio*): Do you still abuse my master in his absence, you villain?

PHORMIO (*aloud to Geta*): 'Tis no more than he deserves.

GETA (*aloud to Phormio*): Say, you so, you jailbird?

DEMIPHO: Geta.

GETA (*aloud to Phormio, pretending not to hear Demipho*): You're an invader of other people's rights, a perverter of the laws.

DEMIPHO: Geta.

PHORMIO (*aside to Geta*): Answer him.

GETA: Who's that? O! is't you, Sir?

DEMIPHO: Don't talk to him.

GETA: He has been abusing you behind your back, without ceasing, in such a manner as you don't deserve, though he does.

DEMIPHO (*to Geta*): Well, say no more. (*To Phormio*) First, young man, if you'll vouchsafe me an answer, I desire to know, with your good leave, who that friend of yours was, and how he claim'd relation to me.

PHORMIO: So you examine me, as if you did not know.

DEMIPHO: I know?

PHORMIO: Yes.

DEMIPHO: I deny it; you, who affirm it, rub up my memory.

PHORMIO: Huy, huy, as if you did not know your first cousin!

DEMIPHO: You kill me: tell me his name.

PHORMIO: His name?

DEMIPHO: To be sure. Why don't you tell it?

PHORMIO (*aside*): I'm ruin'd, by Hercules, I've forgot his name.

DEMIPHO: Ha, what's that you say?

PHORMIO (*aside to Geta*): Geta, if you remember the name I told you just now, tell it me. (*To Demipho*) I'll not tell you, as if you did not know! You come to try me.

DEMIPHO: I try you?

GETA (*aside to Phormio*): Stilpho.

PHORMIO: What is't to me? 'Tis Stilpho.

DEMIPHO: What's his name, say you?

PHORMIO: Stilpho, I say, you knew him.

DEMIPHO: I knew no such person, nor was any of that name related to me.

PHORMIO: Can you say so? Aren't you asham'd of this? But if he had left an estate of ten talents—

DEMIPHO: The Gods confound you.

PHORMIO: —You'd have been the first to have trac'd your family from generation to generation.

DEMIPHO: It may be so; then, if I had gone about it, I could have told how she was related to me: now do you the same: tell me how she's my relation.

GETA (to Demipho): Well said, master. (To Phormio) You, Sir, take care of yourself.

PHORMIO: I made it appear plain enough, where I ought, before the judges: if it was false, why did not your son then refute it?

DEMIPHO: What tell you me of my son, whose folly can't be sufficiently expressed?

PHORMIO: But do you, who are so very wise, make your appearance in court, and get the same cause tried over again, since you are sovereign here, and you only can obtain a second decree in the same cause.

DEMIPHO: Though I'm much injured, yet, rather than follow lawsuits, or hear you prate, I'll give you fifteen guineas with her, which is the portion that is requir'd by law supposing she was my relation.

PHORMIO: Ha, ha, ha, a pretty sort of a man.

DEMIPHO: What's the matter? Is there anything unreasonable in what I propose? Can't I obtain this, which is common justice?

PHORMIO: Is it come to that, pray, does the law require, after you have used a citizen like a whore, that you should pay her and turn her off? Is it not otherwise, is it not requir'd, to prevent her from bringing shame on herself through poverty, that she should be married to her next relation, that she may have to do only with him, which you are against?

DEMIPHO: Yes, to her next relation; but what have we to do with that? Why must we be concerned?

PHORMIO: O, O, 'tis all over, as they say, you can't try it again.

DEMIPHO: I'll not try it again: yet I'll not drop it till I have gone thro with it.

PHORMIO: Words, words.

DEMIPHO: See if I don't make 'em good.

PHORMIO: In short, Demipho, I've nothing to do with you; 'tis your son that's cast, not you; for you are a little too old for a young bride.

DEMIPHO: Imagine that 'tis he that says all which I now say to you, or I'll thrust him and his wife out of doors.

GETA (*aside to Phormio*): He's nettled.

PHORMIO: You'll think better on't.

DEMIPHO: Are you so provided to do all you can against me, you unlucky knave?

PHORMIO (*aside to Geta*): He's afraid of us, though he endeavours so earnestly to conceal it.

GETA (*aside to Phormio*): You have begun successfully.

PHORMIO: Why don't you bear what can't be avoided like a man? 'Twill be more to your advantage, if you end it amicably with us.

DEMIPHO: Amicably with you? Why shou'd I see you, or hear your impertinence?

PHORMIO: If you and she can agree, you'll have a comfort to your old age: have some regard to your years.

DEMIPHO: Do you take her for a comfort.

PHORMIO: Be not in such a passion.

DEMIPHO: Observe me: we have had words enough; unless you take the wench away quickly, I'll turn her out: I have said it, Phormio.

PHORMIO (*aloud to Demipho*): If you offer to handle her otherwise than becomes a gentlewoman, I'll bring a heavy action against you: I have said it, Demipho. (*Aside to Geta*) If you want me, you'll find me at home.

GETA: I understand you.　　　　　(*Phormio goes*)

Act II, Scene III

(Demipho, Geta, Hegio, Cratinus, and Crito)

DEMIPHO *(to Geta)*: What care and anxiety my son brings upon me, by intangling himself and me in this marriage! and he does not come near me, that I may know at least what he has to say for himself, or what his sentiments are now.—Go you, and see if he isn't come home yet.

GETA: I will.   *(Geta goes)*

Act II, Scene IV

(Demipho, Hegio, Cratinus, and Crito)

DEMIPHO: Ye see how this affair stands: what must I do? Your opinion, Hegio.

HEGIO: Whose, mine? Let Cratinus speak first, if you think fit.

DEMIPHO: Your opinion, Cratinus.

CRATINUS: Mine?

DEMIPHO: Yes.

CRATINUS: I'd have you do what is most to your interest in this affair: I think that what your son did in your absence ought in justice and equity to be made void: and that's what you'll obtain: I've given my opinion.

DEMIPHO: Now, Hegio, your opinion.

HEGIO: I believe he has spoke his best; but so it is, so many men so many minds; ev'ry one has his way: I think what the law has done can't be revoked; and 'tis scandalous to attempt it.

DEMIPHO: Crito, your opinion.

CRITO: I think it requires more time to consider of it: 'tis a weighty affair.

HEGIO: Do you want any more with us?

DEMIPHO: Ye've done enough—(*The Advocates go*)
I am now more at a loss than I was before.

ACT II, SCENE V

(*Geta and Demipho*)

GETA: He's not come home, they say.

DEMIPHO: I wait for my brother, whose advice I'll
follow in this affair: I'll go and enquire at the waterside,
to learn what tidings I can of him.   (*Demipho goes*)

GETA: And I'll look out for Antipho, that I may inform
him of what's done here: but here he comes just as I
want him.

ACT II, SCENE VI

(*Antipho and Geta*)

ANTIPHO (*to himself, not seeing Geta*): Indeed, An-
tipho, your want of courage is much to be blamed; could
you go away, and leave your life and safety in the hands
of other persons? Did you believe other people would
be more careful of your affairs than yourself? However
other things went, you ought certainly to consider her
that you left at home, and not let her suffer any harm,
and be deceived through her confidence in you, whose
hope, poor creature, and all whose interest, now depend
on you alone.

GETA: And indeed, master, we did not spare you in
your absence for going from us.

ANTIPHO: I was looking for you.

GETA: But we were never the more negligent for that.

ANTIPHO: Pray tell me how my interests and my for-
tunes stand: has my father any suspicion?

GETA: Not yet.

ANTIPHO: Is there any hope left?

GETA: I don't know.

ANTIPHO: How!

GETA: But Phædria did all he could for you.

ANTIPHO: There's nothing new in that.

GETA: Then Phormio has been as hearty and as active in this as in other affairs.

ANTIPHO: What has he done?

GETA: He was too hard for the old gentleman as angry as he was.

ANTIPHO: O! brave Phormio.

GETA: I did what I could too.

ANTIPHO: My Geta, I love ye all.

GETA: The first conference was as I tell you: the affair's in a good situation at present; and your father now waits for your uncle's arrival, before he proceeds any farther.

ANTIPHO: What does he wait for him for?

GETA: He said that he'd be directed by his advice in this affair.

ANTIPHO: How I dread my uncle's return now, Geta! For by his sentence only, as you tell me, I must live or die.

GETA: Here comes Phædria.

ANTIPHO: Where?

GETA: See, he's coming from his usual place of exercise.

ACT II, SCENE VII

(Phædria, Dorio, Antipho, and Geta)

PHÆDRIA *(not seeing Antipho and Geta)*: Prithee hear me, Dorio.

DORIO: Not I.

PHÆDRIA: A little.

DORIO: Don't trouble me.

PHÆDRIA: Hear what I have to say.

DORIO: But 'tis tiresome to hear the same a thousand times over and over.

PHÆDRIA: But you'll be pleas'd with what I'm going to say now.

DORIO: Well, let's hear.

PHÆDRIA: Can't I prevail on you to stay three days longer? Where are you going?

DORIO: I should wonder if you had offered anything new to me.

ANTIPHO (*aside to Geta*): The bawd, I fear, is drawing an old house over his head.

GETA (*aside to Antipho*): I fear so too.

PHÆDRIA: You do not believe me.

DORIO: There you're right.

PHÆDRIA: Upon my credit.

DORIO: Mere flams.

PHÆDRIA: You'll have no reason to repent, you'll confess so afterwards.

DORIO: Words, words.

PHÆDRIA: Believe me, you'll be glad of it; 'tis true, by Hercules.

DORIO: 'Tis all a dream.

PHÆDRIA: Do but try, 'tis not long.

DORIO: The same story over again.

PHÆDRIA: I'll acknowledge you for a kinsman, a father, a friend, a—

DORIO: 'Tis all but talk.

PHÆDRIA: That you can be so hardened and inexorable, to be moved neither by pity nor entreaty!

DORIO: That you can be so inconsiderate and ignorant, Phædria, to think by your fine speeches to wheedle me out of what's my own for nothing!

ANTIPHO (*aside to Geta*): I pity him.

PHÆDRIA (*to himself*): Ah! what he says is too true.

GETA (*aside to Antipho*): How they both keep to their characters!

PHÆDRIA: When Antipho is in full possession of his love, that I should have this plague!

ANTIPHO: Ah! Phædria, what's the matter?

PHÆDRIA: O! fortunate Antipho!

ANTIPHO: I fortunate?

PHÆDRIA: Yes, in having what you love at home, and in not having to do with such a villain as this.

ANTIPHO: What I love at home? Yes, as the saying is, I have a wolf by the ears; for I know not how to let her go, nor how to keep her.

DORIO: That's my case with this spark.

ANTIPHO (*to the bawd*): O! brave bawd, don't depart from your character. (*To Phædria*) What has he done at last?

PHÆDRIA: Done? Like an inhuman fellow, he has sold my Pamphila.

GETA: What? Sold her?

ANTIPHO: Sold her, say you?

PHÆDRIA: He has sold her.

DORIO: A horrid crime, to sell a wench that I paid for!

PHÆDRIA (*to Antipho*): I can't persuade him to break off with the other, and stay three days, till I get the money which my friends promis'd. (*To the bawd*) If I don't give it you then, don't stay an hour longer.

DORIO: You stun me.

ANTIPHO: 'Tis but a little time that he requires, Dorio: be prevail'd upon: he'll make it doubly up to you, and you'll deserve it.

DORIO: These are but words.

ANTIPHO (*to Phædria*): Will you endure that Pamphila should be carried from this town? (*To the bawd*) Can you be so hardhearted as to tear these lovers from one another?

DORIO: 'Tis neither I, nor you, that do it.

GETA: May the Gods deny you nothing that you deserve.

DORIO: I have, contrary to my disposition, indulged you many months, you've promised, and whimpered, but never performed anything; now I have found one that proceeds in quite a different strain, who can pay without sniveling; give place to your betters.

ANTIPHO (*to the bawd*): Certainly, if I remember rightly, there was a day fixed formerly, in which you were to let him have her.

PHÆDRIA: There was so.

DORIO: Do I deny it?

ANTIPHO: Is that day pass'd?

DORIO: No, but this is come before it.

ANTIPHO: Aren't you ashamed of your roguery?

DORIO: Not when 'tis to my advantage.

GETA: Dirty rascal!

PHÆDRIA: Dorio, d'y' think you do as you ought?

DORIO: 'Tis my custom, if you like me, use me.

ANTIPHO: Do you impose upon him thus?

DORIO: Rather, Antipho, he imposes upon me; for he knew me to be such a person; I thought him another sort of a man; he has deceived me; I am just the same with him that I always was: but yet, however the affair stands, I'll do this; the captain promised to bring me the money early to-morrow; if you bring it before he does, Phædria, I'll keep up my custom, and prefer the first comer: so adieu. (*Dorio goes*)

Act II, Scene VIII

(*Phædria, Antipho, and Geta*)

PHÆDRIA: What shall I do? How shall I now, that am not worth a straw, raise the money for him so suddenly? If he could but have been prevailed upon to stay three days, I was promised it then.

ANTIPHO: Shall we forsake him, Geta, in his distress, that, according to your own report, assisted me so friendly just now? Rather let us try to return the favor, now there's occasion.

GETA: I know it is but just that we should.

ANTIPHO: Set about it therefore, you are the only man that can save him.

GETA: What can I do?

ANTIPHO: Raise the money.

GETA: With all my heart; but tell me how.

ANTIPHO: My father's at hand.

GETA: I know that; but what then?

ANTIPHO: Pshaw, a word to the wise is enough.

GETA: Say you so?

ANTIPHO: Yes.

GETA: Very fine advice, by Hercules! Why don't you go about it? Shan't I have reason to triumph, if I escape on the account of your marriage, but you must now insist on my bringing one misfortune on the back of another over my head, for his sake too?

ANTIPHO: What he says is true.

PHÆDRIA: What? Do you look upon me as a stranger, Geta?

GETA: By no means; but is it of no consideration, now we have enraged the old man against us all, whether we provoke him so that no room can be left for entreaty?

PHÆDRIA: Shall another man bear her from my eyes

to an unknown land? Alas! Speak to me, Antipho, and consider me, while you may, and while I'm with ye.

ANTIPHO: Why? What are you about now? Tell me.

PHÆDRIA: Whatever part of the world she's carried to, I'm resolved to follow her, or to perish.

GETA: Good luck go with you; yet I'd advise you not to be in a hurry.

ANTIPHO: See if you can assist him, do.

GETA: Assist him? How?

ANTIPHO: Pray try, lest he should more or less, Geta, than we'd wish, and which we shou'd be sorry for afterwards.

GETA: I'm trying. He's secure, I believe; but I'm afraid that I shall suffer for't.

ANTIPHO: Don't be afraid: we'll share your fortune with you, be it good or bad.

GETA (to Phædria): How much money d'y' want? Tell me.

PHÆDRIA: But little more than ninety guineas.

GETA: Ninety guineas? Ah! she's very dear, Phædria.

PHÆDRIA: She's very cheap at that price.

GETA: Well, well, I'll get 'em.

PHÆDRIA (hugging Geta): There's a good fellow!

GETA: Let me go, hands off.

PHÆDRIA: I want the money now.

GETA: You shall have it presently; but I must have Phormio's assistance.

ANTIPHO: He's ready; lay what burden on him you will, and he'll bear it: he's of all men truest to his friend.

GETA: Therefore let us hasten to him.

ANTIPHO: Have ye any farther occasion for me?

GETA: No; but go home, and comfort that poor creature, who is now, I know, quite dispirited with fear. Why d'y' stay?

ANTIPHO: There's nothing that I can do with so good a will.

PHÆDRIA: How do you propose doing that?

GETA: I'll tell you as we go; but make haste from hence.

ACT III, SCENE I

(*Demipho and Chremes*)

DEMIPHO: Why, what did you go to Lemnos for, Chremes? Have you brought your daughter with you?

CHREMES: No.

DEMIPHO: How so?

CHREMES: Her mother, seeing that I stayed here longer than ordinary, and that the girl was of an age that required a husband, is reported to have come here with all her family in search of me.

DEMIPHO: Pray what detained you so long there then, after you had heard it?

CHREMES: A disease.

DEMIPHO: How did you get it? Or what was it?

CHREMES: There's a question! Old age itself is a disease: but the captain who brought them over told me that they arrived safe.

DEMIPHO: Have you heard what has happened to my son in my absence, Chremes?

CHREMES: 'Tis that which now makes me uncertain what to do; for if I should marry her to a stranger, I must tell him how she's my daughter, and who's her mother: I know that you wish me as well as I do myself; but if one who was no relation before should marry her, he'll be silent as long as there's a good understanding betwixt us; but if he begins to have no value for me, I shall wish he did not know so much of me: and I'm afraid it should come to my wife's knowledge; and should it, I've nothing to do but to brush off, and leave my house; for I'm the only friend I have at home.

DEMIPHO: I know it; and that's what troubles me; nor will I desist, till I have performed all that I've promised you.

ACT III, SCENE II

(Geta, Chremes, and Demipho)

GETA (to himself, not seeing Chremes and Demipho): Surely there never was a cunninger fellow than Phormio: I went to him, to inform him that money must be had, and how it might be got: he understood me before I had spoke half what I had to say: he rejoiced, commended me, enquired after the old man, and thanked the Gods that he had an opportunity to shew himself as much Phædria's friend as Antipho's: I bade him wait for me at the market, where I would bring the old man to him: but here he is: who is that behind him? Egad, 'tis Phædria's father: but why, like a beast, should I be afraid? Because I have two in my power now to choose instead of one? 'Tis better, I think, to have two strings to a bow: I'll set upon him that I first proposed; if I get it from him, 'tis well; if I make nothing of him, then I must attack this newcomer.

ACT III, SCENE III

(Antipho, Geta, Chremes, and Demipho)

ANTIPHO (to himself): I expect Geta here:—but surely that's my uncle standing with my father there: Death! I'm in pain to know what effect his arrival will have on my father in my affair!

GETA (*to himself*): I'll go up to 'em. (*Aloud*) Welcome home, Master Chremes.

CHREMES: How is't, Geta?

GETA: I'm glad to see you safe returned.

CHREMES: I believe you.

GETA: How go affairs?

CHREMES: I meet with many alterations here, according to custom.

GETA: True: have you heard what has happened to Antipho?

CHREMES: Yes, all.

GETA (*to Demipho*): Have you informed him? What a shameful thing 'tis, Chremes, to be so imposed upon!

DEMIPHO: That's what I was talking to him about now.

GETA: By Hercules, as I was thinking seriously of it with myself, I believe I found a remedy to this evil.

CHREMES: What is it, Geta?

DEMIPHO: What remedy?

GETA: As I went from you, I happened to meet Phormio.

CHREMES: Who, Phormio?

GETA: The same that took the young woman's part.

CHREMES: I know whom you mean.

GETA: I thought it proper to pump him first. I take him aside: "Phormio," quoth I, "why don't we see and make an end of this business by fair means rather than by foul? My master's a generous man, and hates strife; I can assure you that all his friends have unanimously advised him to turn her out."

ANTIPHO (*to himself*): What is the fellow about, or what will this come to at last?

GETA: Do you think he's in any danger from the laws, if he should turn her out? He has had counsel about that; pshaw, you'll have enough to do, if you go to law with him, he does not want words: but suppose you should cast him, he won't lose his life, a little money will bring him off." When I perceived that what I had said had took down his courage, "We are now alone here," continued I; "hark y', what would you expect down to drop this suit, to have her sent back, and to let us be no more troubled with you?—"

ANTIPHO (*to himself*): Is the devil in him?

GETA: "—I very well know, if you should make a proposal any way just and reasonable, that he's so good a man, you will not have three words to a bargain."

DEMIPHO: By what authority did you say so?

CHREMES: He could not bring about what we want better.

ANTIPHO (*to himself*): I'm ruined!

CHREMES: Go on.

GETA: At first the fellow raved.

DEMIPHO: Why, what does he ask?

GETA: Ask? Too much.

CHREMES: Tell what he demands.

GETA: He talked of no less than a great talent.

DEMIPHO: Hang the rascal: isn't he ashamed?

GETA: I said as much to him. What, continued I, could he do more, if he was going to portion out an only daughter of his own? At that rate he has not gain'd much by not bringing one up, if another is found that he must give a fortune to: to be short, and passing over his impertinences, this was his final answer; I would, says he, at first have marry'd my friend's daughter, as 'twas reasonable I should; for I considered what inconveniences she would be subjected to, poor creature, by marrying into a rich family to be made a slave of: but, to be plain with you now, I wanted one that could bring in something to pay the little that I owe; therefore now, if Demipho will give as much with her, as I am to have with this that I'm engag'd to, I don't know one in the world that I would sooner choose for a wife than her.

ANTIPHO (*to himself*): I can't tell whether 'tis folly or malice that makes him talk thus, whether he does it designedly or not.

DEMIPHO: What is't to us if he owes his soul to any one?

GETA: He mortgaged a piece of ground, he says, for thirty guineas.

DEMIPHO: Well, well, let him marry her; I'll give him as much.

GETA: And a house for thirty more.

DEMIPHO: Huy, huy! that's too much.

CHREMES: Silence: you shall have these thirty from me.

GETA: A maid must be bought for his wife; then some more furniture is wanted; and the expense of the wedding is to be defrayed: these, says he, will require thirty more.

DEMIPHO: I'll sooner bear six hundred actions against me; I'll give nothing; shall I make myself a laughing-stock to the rogue?

CHREMES: Pray be quiet, I'll pay the money; only do you prevail on your son to marry the woman we'd have him.

ANTIPHO (*to himself*): Ah! Geta, thou hast ruined me by thy treachery.

CHREMES: 'Tis on my account she's turned off; 'tis but just therefore that I should defray the expense.

GETA: Let me know as soon as you can, says he, that if they think fit to let me marry her, I may rid myself of the other, and not remain in an uncertainty; for they've appointed to pay me the fortune directly.

CHREMES: He shall have the money immediately; let him break off with the other, and marry this.

DEMIPHO: And ill luck go with him.

CHREMES: I have very seasonably brought money with me now, the rents of my wife's farms at Lemnos; I'll make use of part of that; and I'll tell my wife that you wanted it.   (*Chremes and Demipho go.*)

ACT III, SCENE IV

(*Antipho and Geta*)

ANTIPHO: Geta.

GETA: Ha!

ANTIPHO: What have you done?

GETA: I have cleanly chous'd the old men of the money.

ANTIPHO: Is that sufficient?

GETA: That I can't tell, but I've done no more than I was ordered.

ANTIPHO: I'll drub you; won't you answer me to the purpose?

GETA: What d'y' mean?

ANTIPHO: What can I mean? You might as well giv'n me a halter as have done what you have. Heav'n and hell confound you for an example to such rascals! If any one wants to be brought out of a calm into a storm, I'd recommend him to you. What could you have done worse than have touched on this sore, or named my wife? You have giv'n my father hopes of his being able to turn her away. Prithee tell me now, if Phormio accepts the portion, he must marry her, what must be done then?

GETA: But he'll not marry her.

ANTIPHO: I grant it: but when they demand the

money of him back, our cause will be much the better
I suppose.

GETA: There's nothing, Antipho, but may be spoiled
in the telling: the good you omit here; but you mention
the bad: now hear me; if he takes the money, he must
marry her, as you say; I admit it; but there must be a
little time allow'd to prepare for the wedding, to invite
friends, and to sacrifice: in the meanwhile the other will
get the money which his friends promised him, and
he may return it out of that.

ANTIPHO: How can that be? Or what excuse will he
make?

GETA: Would you know? What strange prodigies, he
may say, have happened to me since the agreement! A
strange black dog came into my house, a snake fell off
the tiles through the spout into my yard, my hen crowed,
the soothsayer warned me, the fortune-teller forbad me
to enter on any new business before winter; there can't
be better excuses: these will do.

ANTIPHO: Would they may.

GETA: They will; depend on me. Your father's coming.
Go, tell Phædria he shall have the money.

(Antipho goes)

ACT III, SCENE V

(Demipho, Geta, and Chremes)

DEMIPHO: Be easy, I say; I'll take care that he sha'n't
impose upon us: I'll never part with this rashly, but I'll
have witnesses present, when I give it; and I'll have a
memorandum taken of the occasion of my giving it.

GETA (to himself): How wary he is, where there is
no reason!

CHREMES: 'Tis necessary you should do so; and make

haste, while he is in this same humor; for if that other woman insists on the contract, he may leave us perhaps in the lurch.

GETA: Well thought of.

DEMIPHO: Therefore show me to him.

GETA: As soon as you will.

CHREMES: When you have done this, go to my wife, that she may talk to her before she goes away: let her tell her that, to prevent any resentment on her side, we have agreed to marry her to Phormio, he being a proper match for her, being more intimate with her, that we have done our duty, having consented to give him as large a portion as he desired.

DEMIPHO: What have you to do with that?

CHREMES: A great deal. Demipho.

DEMIPHO: Is it not enough for you to do your duty, without being publicly applauded for it?

CHREMES: I'd have her consent to what we do, that she mayn't say we force her away.

DEMIPHO: I can manage that myself.

CHREMES: Not so well as one woman can with another.

DEMIPHO: I'll ask your wife to do it.

CHREMES (*to himself*): I am considering where I shall find those women now.   (*They go*)

ACT IV, SCENE I

(*Sophrona and Chremes*)

SOPHRONA (*to herself, not seeing Chremes*): What shall I do? Where shall I find a friend in my distress? Or to whom can I relate my tale? Or where apply for aid? I'm afraid my mistress will suffer undeservedly for following my advice, I hear the young gentleman's father is so enraged at what is done.

CHREMES (*to himself*): What old woman's this, that comes panting from my brother's?

SOPHRONA (*to herself*): Necessity compelled me to what I did (though I knew the match was not good), that I might contrive how to preserve her from want.

CHREMES (*to himself*): Certainly, if I don't mistake, or if I'm not blind, that's my daughter's nurse I see there.

SOPHRONA (*to herself*): And her father—

CHREMES (*to himself*): What's to be done?

SOPHRONA (*to herself*): —is not to be found—

CHREMES (*to himself*): Shall I go to her, or wait and hear what more she has to say?

SOPHRONA (*to herself*): —but if I can find him now, I shall not have any occasion to fear.

CHREMES (*to himself*): 'Tis she: I'll speak to her.

SOPHRONA (*to herself, hearing Chremes*): Whose voice is that?

CHREMES: Sophrona.

SOPHRONA (*to herself*): And he names me!

CHREMES: Look this way.

SOPHRONA (*aloud*): Good Gods, is not this Stilpho?

CHREMES: No.

SOPHRONA: Do you deny your name?

CHREMES: Pray come a little this way from that door, Sophrona: and don't call me by that name any more.

SOPHRONA: How? Are not you the person you always said you was?

CHREMES: St.

SOPHRONA: Why are you afraid of this door?

CHREMES: I have a shrew of a wife shut up here: therefore I gave myself that wrong name formerly, lest any of ye should unadvisedly blab out my right name, and be the occasion of my wife's knowing the affair.

SOPHRONA: That's the reason we poor wretches could never find you out here.

CHREMES: Hark y', tell me what business you have with that family from whence you came now? And where are your mistresses?

SOPHRONA: Alas! alas!

CHREMES: Ah, What's the matter? Are they alive?

SOPHRONA: Your daughter is: but her poor mothei died with grief.

CHREME: O! sad!

SOPHRONA: I, who am a forsaken, poor, ignorant, old woman, did all I could to marry your daughter to the young gentleman of this house.

CHREMES: To whom? To Antipho?

SOPHRONA: To the very same I assure you.

CHREMES: What? Has he two wives?

SOPHRONA: No, I beseech you; he has none but her.

CHREMES: What's the other that they said was his kinswoman?

SOPHRONA: This is she.

CHREMES: What say you?

SOPHRONA: 'Twas done with a design, that, as he was in love with her, he might marry her without a portion.

CHREMES: Good Gods, how things often happen accidentally which we have not courage to wish for! I have found, upon my arrival, my daughter married to the person I would have had her married to, and all as I could have wished: what we both took the greatest pains to bring about, this old woman has alone accomplished by her own great care, without any help from us.

SOPHRONA: Consider now what is necessary to be done: here comes the young gentleman's father; and they say he's very angry at this marriage.

CHREMES: There's no danger: but in the names of Heaven and Earth, don't let any one know she's mine.

SOPHRONA: Nobody shall know from me.

CHREMES: Follow me: you shall hear the rest within.

(*They go*)

ACT IV, SCENE II
(*Demipho and Geta*)

DEMIPHO: 'Tis our own fault that people get by being dishonest, while we study to be thought over punctual and generous: never run into extremes, as the saying is: was it not enough to bear his imposition, but we must give him more than was expected, to put it in his power to support himself, till he can contrive some other mischief?

GETA: You're very right.

DEMIPHO: They are rewarded now, who turn right into wrong.

GETA: 'Tis too true.

DEMIPHO: How foolishly we managed the affair with him!

GETA: If he performs his agreement, and marries her, 'tis well enough.

DEMIPHO: Is that to be doubted?

GETA: Considering what sort of a man he is, I don't know, by Hercules, but he may change his mind.

DEMIPHO: How! change his mind?

GETA: I don't know; but, if it should be so, I say.

DEMIPHO: I'll follow my brother's advice; I'll bring his wife hither to talk with her: go you, Geta, and give her notice of her coming.   (*Demipho goes.*)

ACT IV, SCENE III
(*Geta*)

GETA: The money's procured for Phædria; and no words are made about it: and care's taken that she mayn't stir from hence at present: what more now? What's to be done? You're as deep in the mire as before, you'll pay all with interest, Geta, you only put off a beating to another day, you'll have the more lashes, if you don't look about you: now I'll go home, and instruct Phanium, that she mayn't be afraid of marrying Phormio, nor frighted of what Nausistrata will say to her. (*He goes*)

Act IV, Scene IV

(*Demipho and Nausistrata*)

DEMIPHO: Come, Nausistrata, use some of your art now; and manage her so that she may do as we would have her, and at the same time let it be with her own consent.

NAUSISTRATA: I'll do my best.

DEMIPHO: Assist me now with your labour, as you've done before with your money.

NAUSISTRATA: 'Tis in my inclination; but 'tis less in my power than it ought to be, through my husband's mismanagement.

DEMIPHO: How so?

NAUSISTRATA: Because the estate which came by my father is very ill looked after; he made two talents a year with ease of those farms: ah! what a difference there is betwixt man and man!

DEMIPHO: Two talents, say you?

NAUSISTRATA: Yes, two talents, and in much worse seasons.

DEMIPHO: Indeed!

NAUSISTRATA: What, does this seem strange?

DEMIPHO: Yes, truly.

NAUSISTRATA: I wish I'd been born a man, I'd show him—

DEMIPHO: That you would.

NAUSISTRATA: —how—

DEMIPHO: Don't heat yourself, that you may be able to engage the young woman, and she mayn't run you down.

NAUSISTRATA: I'll do as you direct me: but my husband, I see, is coming from your house.

ACT IV, SCENE V

(*Chremes, Demipho, and Nausistrata*)

CHREMES: O! Demipho, has he had the money yet?

DEMIPHO: I paid it him directly.

CHREMES (*to Demipho*): I wish you had not. (*Aside*) Ah! here's my wife: I'd almost blabbed too much.

DEMIPHO: Why d'y' wish I had not, Chremes?

CHREMES: 'Tis very well.

DEMIPHO: What have you done? Have you told her the occasion of your wife's coming to her?

CHREMES: I went through it.

DEMIPHO: What says she to it?

CHREMES: She can't go.

DEMIPHO: How can't?

CHREMES: Because their affection is mutual.

DEMIPHO: What have we to do with that?

CHREMES: A great deal: besides, I've discovered her to be related to us.

DEMIPHO: What, are you mad?

CHREMES: So it is; I don't speak without foundation; I have recollected myself.

DEMIPHO: Are you in your senses?

NAUSISTRATA: Ah! pray see you don't injure a kinswoman.

DEMIPHO: She's no kinswoman.

CHREMES: Don't deny her; her father went by another name, 'tis that breeds this mistake in you.

DEMIPHO: Did not she know her father?

CHREMES: Yes, yes.

DEMIPHO: Why did he go by another name?

CHREMES (*aside to Demipho*): Will you never yield to what I say, nor understand me?

DEMIPHO: I don't know what you talk of; how should I understand you?

CHREMES (*aside to Demipho*): You ruin all.

NAUSISTRATA: I wonder what's the meaning of all this.

DEMIPHO: By Hercules, I don't know.

CHREMES: Shall I tell you? As I hope to be saved, she has not a nearer relation in the world than you and I are.

DEMIPHO: Good Gods! Let us all go together to her; I'll know whether 'tis so or not.

CHREMES: Ah!

DEMIPHO: What's the matter?

CHREMES: Is my credit so little with you?

DEMIPHO: Would you have me take what you've said for granted? Would you have me seek no farther into it? Well, be it so: but consider, what's to be done with our friend's daughter?

CHREMES: She'll do very well.

DEMIPHO: Must we dismiss her at last?

CHREMES: Why not?

DEMIPHO: And let her stay that is here?

CHREMES: Yes.

DEMIPHO: Then you may go home again, Nausistrata.

NAUSISTRATA: By Pollux, I think your last resolution best, that she should stay here; for she seemed, when I saw her, to be very much of a gentlewoman.

(*Nausistrata goes*)

Act IV, Scene VI

(Demipho and Chremes)

DEMIPHO: What is this business?

CHREMES: Has she shut the door yet?

DEMIPHO: Yes.

CHREMES: O! Jupiter! the Gods are certainly our friends; 'tis my daughter, I find, that is married to your son.

DEMIPHO: Ah! how came that to pass?

CHREMES: 'Tis not safe to tell you here.

DEMIPHO: Go in then.

CHREMES: Hark y', I would not have our sons know of this. (*They go.*)

Act V, Scene I

(Antipho)

ANTIPHO: I am glad, however my own affairs go, that my brother's succeed to his desire. How prudent it is for a man to entertain such appetites as he may easily satisfy when things run cross! As soon as he received the money, he rid himself of his care; but I can find no remedy to my troubles; for if this business continues a secret, I shall be in fear, and, if 'tis discovered, I shall be disgraced: and I should have no heart to go home now, unless I'd some hope of keeping her: but where can I find Geta, that I may consult him about a proper time to meet my father?

Act V, Scene II

(Phormio and Antipho)

PHORMIO (*to himself*): I've received the money, given it to the bawd, brought away the woman, and put

Phædria in possession of her; for she's no longer a slave: now one thing still remains, which I must bring about, that is to get leave of the old men to go and tipple a little; for I'm resolved to enjoy myself these few days.

ANTIPHO (*to himself*): But here's Phormio. —Well, what say you?

PHORMIO: Of what?

ANTIPHO: What's Phædria about now? How does he propose to have his fill of love?

PHORMIO: He's going, in his turn, to act your part.

ANTIPHO: What part?

PHORMIO: To avoid his father: he entreats you again to appear for him, and plead his cause; for he's going to take a glass at my house. I'll tell the old men that I'm going to Sunium to the fair, to buy a girl that Geta spoke of a little while ago, lest, when they miss me here, they should believe that I'm consuming their money: but your door creaks.

ANTIPHO: See who's coming out.

PHORMIO: 'Tis Geta.

ACT V, SCENE III

(Geta, Antipho, and Phormio)

GETA (*to himself, not seeing them*): O! fortune! O! propitious fortune, what unexpected favors have you this day heap'd on my Master Antipho!

ANTIPHO (*to Phormio*): What is he talking of to himself?

GETA (*to himself*): And how have you freed us his friends from fear! But this is no time to loiter, I should throw my cloak cross my shoulder, and run to find him, that I may tell him what has happened.

ANTIPHO (*to Phormio*): Do you understand what he says?

PHORMIO: Do you?

ANTIPHO: Not a word.

PHORMIO: Nor I.

GETA (*to himself*): I'll go directly to the bawd's; they are there now.

ANTIPHO: Soho, Geta.

GETA (*hearing, but not seeing him*): See there! Is there anything wonderful or new in being called back, when a man's going forwards?

ANTIPHO: Geta.

GETA: Again? By Hercules, you may bawl as long as you will, but you shall never bring me back.

ANTIPHO: Won't you stay?

GETA: Go on and be drubbed.

ANTIPHO: That's what you shall be soon, if you don't stay, you Bridewell-cur.

GETA (*aside*): This should be one that's very well acquainted with me, he is so free with his threats: but is it he that I'm in search of, or not?—The very man.

PHORMIO (*to Antipho*): Go up to him immediately.

ANTIPHO (*to Geta*): Well, how go our affairs?

GETA: O! 'tis impossible there can be a more fortunate man living than yourself, for, without dispute, you're the only favorite of Heaven, Antipho.

ANTIPHO: I should be glad of that; but I wish you would give me some reason to believe it.

GETA: Is it not sufficient if I plunge you all over in joy?

ANTIPHO: You kill me.

PHORMIO: Don't keep us in suspense, but out with what you have to tell.

GETA: Oh! are you here too, Phormio?

PHORMIO: Yes; but why are you so tedious?

GETA (*to Phormio*): Well, I'll tell you. As soon as we gave you the money at the marketplace, we went

directly home; (*to Antipho*)—then my master sends
me to your wife.

ANTIPHO: For what?

GETA: I'll omit that; because it signifys nothing to this
affair, Antipho. As I was going to her apartment, her
boy Mida runs to me; he takes hold on my cloak behind,
and pulls me back; I turn my head, and ask him why
he stops me; there are orders, says he, that nobody
should go in to my mistress; Sophrona, continues he,
carried our old gentleman's brother, Chremes, in just
now, and he's with 'em there at this time; as soon as I
heard this, I crept on tiptoes softly to the door; I went
to it, and there I stood; I held my breath, put my ear
close to the door, and fixed myself in this manner to
hear.

ANTIPHO: Well done, Geta.

GETA: There I heard the finest story, that made me
almost cry out for joy, by Hercules.

ANTIPHO: What was it?

GETA: What d'y' think?

ANTIPHO: I don't know.

GETA: The most surprising! Your uncle is discovered
to be your wife's, your Phany's, father.

ANTIPHO: How! What say you?

GETA: He had formerly a private correspondence with
her mother at Lemnos.

PHORMIO: He dreams: how could she be ignorant of
her own father?

GETA: Depend upon it Phormio, there's some reason
for it: but do you imagine that I, who was without,
could understand all that was doing among themselves
within?

ANTIPHO: By Hercules, I've heard the same too.

GETA: I'll give you farther reasons to believe it: in
the meanwhile your uncle goes out; and not long after

he returns with your father and goes in with him; and they both said you're at liberty to keep your wife: at last I was sent to find you and bring you thither.

ANTIPHO: Carry me to them immediately: why d'y' loiter?

GETA: I'll go with you.

ANTIPHO: Adieu, my Phormio.

PHORMIO: Antipho, adieu: 'tis very lucky, as I hope for happiness.

(*Antipho and Geta go*)

ACT V, SCENE IV

(*Phormio*)

PHORMIO: I'm rejoiced at the good fortune that has happened to them so unexpectedly. Here's a fine occasion offered to me now to chouse the old men, and to rid Phædria of the care that he's under for money, that he mayn't lay himself under an obligation to any of his friends for it; for this same money, however 'tis given, will be given with an ill will to him: I have found out a way how I shall surely get it. I must now put on a new face, and a new behavior: but I'll retire into the next alley; and when they come out, I'll shew myself to 'em. I shall not go to the fair as I pretended I should.

ACT V, SCENE V

(*Demipho, Phormio, and Chremes*)

DEMIPHO (*to Chremes, not seeing Phormio*): The Gods deserve my thanks, and they have 'em, since these things have proved so fortunate to us, brother. Let us find Phormio as soon as we can, that we may get our ninety pieces from him before he has consumed 'em.

PHORMIO (*to himself, pretending not to see them*): I'll go and see if Demipho's at home, that I may—

DEMIPHO: We were coming to you, Phormio.

PHORMIO: On this same affair perhaps.

DEMIPHO: On the very same, by Hercules.

PHORMIO: So I thought: but why did you give your-selves the trouble? What a jest that is! Are ye afraid that I should not be so good as my word? Notwithstanding I'm so very poor, I have hitherto taken care of one thing, I've preserved my credit.

CHREMES (to Demipho): Isn't she a genteel girl?

DEMIPHO: Indeed she is.

PHORMIO: Therefore I was coming to ye, Demipho, to tell ye I'm ready: I'll marry her when ye will; for I've laid aside all other business, as I ought, since I saw ye were so earnest for my having her.

DEMIPHO: But my brother here has advised me not to let you have her: "For what will the people say, if you should do so," says he? "When you could have dis-posed of her before with honor, then you neglected it; it would be base now to make a widow of her, and turn her out." He made all the same objections which you did to me before.

PHORMIO: You insult me at your pleasure.

DEMIPHO: How so?

PHORMIO: Is that a question? Because I can't marry the other now; for with what face can I go back to her that I've cast off?

CHREMES (aside to Demipho): Besides, I see that Antipho's unwilling to part with her, say.

DEMIPHO: Besides I see that my son is unwilling to part with her: therefore go to the market, Phormio, and order that money to be paid me back.

PHORMIO: How can that be, when I've paid it to my creditors?

DEMIPHO (aside to Chremes): What's to be done now?

PHORMIO: If you'll give me the wife you promised, I'll marry her; but if you'd rather keep her to yourselves, let me keep the portion, Demipho; for 'tis unjust that I should be disappointed on your account, when for your honor I broke off from the other, who had as good a portion.

DEMIPHO: Go and be hanged, you blust'ring vagabond; d'y' think now we don't know you or your pranks?

PHORMIO: This is provoking.

DEMIPHO: Would you marry her, if you might?

PHORMIO: Try me.

DEMIPHO: Your scheme then was that my son should have her at your house.

PHORMIO: What's that you say, pray?

DEMIPHO: Give me back the money.

PHORMIO: Do you give me my wife.

DEMIPHO: Come before a judge.

PHORMIO: Before a judge? Really if you continue being so troublesome—

DEMIPHO: What will you do?

PHORMIO: Do? Perhaps ye think that I've only beggars under my protection, but you'll find I've others.

CHREMES: What's that to us?

PHORMIO: Nothing: but I know a certain gentlewoman here, whose husband had—

CHREMES (aside): Ah!

DEMIPHO (aside to Chremes): What's the matter?

PHORMIO: —another wife at Lemnos—

CHREMES (aside): I'm a dead man.

PHORMIO: —by whom he had a daughter; which he brings up privately.

CHREMES (aside): I'm buried.

PHORMIO: I'll go this instant and tell the gentlewoman this.

CHREMES: Pray don't.

PHORMIO: Why, was you the man?

DEMIPHO: What a jest he makes of us!

CHREMES: We'll let you go.

PHORMIO: That's all pretence.

CHREMES: What would you have? We give you leave to keep the money that you have.

PHORMIO: I hear you: but why do ye trifle thus shamefully with me, with your foolish childish speeches? I won't, I will, I will, I won't again, take it, give it back; said, and unsaid; a bargain and no bargain.

CHREMES (*to Demipho*): How or where did he come to the knowledge of this?

DEMIPHO (*to Chremes*): I can't tell; but I'm sure I told nobody of it.

CHREMES (*aside to Demipho*): As I hoped to be saved, 'tis next to a miracle.

PHORMIO (*to himself*): I've graveled them.

DEMIPHO (*aside to Chremes*): Zooks, shall he carry off such a sum from us, and laugh at us so openly too? By Hercules I'd sooner lose my life: bear up, man, with courage. You see that this slip of thine is no secret abroad, therefore it can't be long concealed from your wife: now 'tis better for ourselves to tell her what she'll soon hear from other persons, we shall more easily make our peace if we do: then we may revenge ourselves at our pleasure on this villain.

PHORMIO (*to himself*): Body o' me! If I don't look out sharp, I shall be filed, they make towards me with such terrible looks.

CHREMES (*aside to Demipho*): But I'm afraid she will not be easily reconciled.

DEMIPHO (*aside to Chremes*): Have a good heart: I'll bring you into favor again, depend upon it, Chremes, since she's dead by whom you had this daughter.

PHORMIO (*to both*): Do ye deal thus with me? Ye

set upon me very cunningly. (*To Demipho*) By Hercules, Demipho, you don't consult his good in provoking me. (*To Chremes*) Do you think, when you've been following your pleasures abroad, without paying any regard to this worthy gentlewoman here, but offering a strange indignity to her, to come now and wash away your offence by entreatys? I'll so fire her for you by a relation of these pranks, that you shan't be able to quench her, though you melt into tears.

DEMIPHO: May all the Gods and Goddesses confound him: that any man should be possessed of so much impudence! Don't this villain deserve to be transported by the public into some desert?

CHREMES: He has reduced me to such a situation, that I don't know what to do with him.

DEMIPHO: I know; let us go before a judge.

PHORMIO: Before a judge? Yes, in here, if you will.

DEMIPHO: Follow him, and hold him, till I call the servants hither.

CHREMES: I can't alone; come and help me.

PHORMIO (*to Demipho*): I've an action against you.

CHREMES: Do your worst then.

PHORMIO: And another against you, Chremes.

DEMIPHO (*to the servants*): Away with him.

PHORMIO: Are ye at that sport? Then I must use my voice: Nausistrata, come hither.

CHREMES (*to the servants*): Stop his mouth.

DEMIPHO: See how strong the villain is.

PHORMIO: Nausistrata, I say.

CHREMES: Won't you hold your tongue?

PHORMIO: Hold my tongue?

DEMIPHO: If he won't follow, punch your fist in his belly.

PHORMIO: If you tear my eyes out, I shall find a time to be sufficiently revenged on ye.

Act V, Scene VI

(Nausistrata, Chremes, Phormio, and Demipho)

NAUSISTRATA: Who calls me?

CHREMES *(aside)*: Ah!

NAUSISTRATA: Pray, husband, what's this disturbance here?

PHORMIO *(to Chremes)*: Ah! what, are you thunderstruck now?

NAUSISTRATA *(to Chremes)*: Who is this fellow? Don't you answer me?

PHORMIO: How should he answer you, who don't know where himself is?

CHREMES *(to Nausistrata)*: Take care how you believe him.

PHORMIO: Go and feel him, if he is not all over in a cold fit, kill me.

CHREMES: That's nothing.

NAUSISTRATA: Then let me know what it is he has to say?

PHORMIO: That you shall; do but hear me.

CHREMES: Do you resolve to believe him?·

NAUSISTRATA: How should I believe one that has said nothing?

PHORMIO: Fear has took the poor man's senses away.

NAUSISTRATA *(to Chremes)*: By Pollux, you are not thus fearful for nothing?

CHREMES: I fearful?

PHORMIO: Very well truly; since you're afraid of nothing, and what I have to say signifys nothing, do you tell it.

DEMIPHO: Must he tell at your bidding, rascal?

PHORMIO: Well said, you do well to stand up for your brother.

NAUSISTRATA: Won't you tell me, husband?

CHREMES: Why—

NAUSISTRATA: What—why?

CHREMES: 'Tis of no consequence to tell you.

PHORMIO (*to Chremes*): You think so; but 'tis of great consequence to this lady. (*To Nausistrata*) In Lemnos—

CHREMES: Ah? What are you about?

DEMIPHO: Will you not hold your tongue?

PHORMIO (*to Nausistrata*): Unknown to you—

CHREMES (*aside*): I'm ruined!

PHORMIO: —he married another woman.

NAUSISTRATA: Husband, Heaven forbid.

PHORMIO: 'Tis even so.

NAUSISTRATA: What an unhappy undone woman am I!

PHORMIO: And he had a daughter by her, while you dreamed nothing of it.

CHREMES (*to Demipho*): What must we do now?

NAUSISTRATA: Immortal Gods, what an unworthy and injurious act is this!

DEMIPHO: 'Tis done and can't be recalled.

NAUSISTRATA: Was there ever so unworthy an act? When they come to their wives, then they are old. Demipho, I apply myself to you, for it's irksome to me to speak to him: were these his frequent journies, and long continuance at Lemnos? Was this the cheapness of provisions that lowered our rents?

DEMIPHO: Nausistrata, I don't deny that he deserves blame in this affair, but 'tis such as may be pardon'd—

PHORMIO (*aside*): She's deaf to what he says.

DEMIPHO: —for it was not through any neglect or hatred of you he did it; but, being in liquor about fifteen years since, he happened to have an intrigue with the woman by whom he had this daughter; and he never touched her afterwards; she's dead now; the objection in this affair is now removed: therefore, pray, exert your usual good nature, and bear it patiently.

NAUSISTRATA: What should I bear patiently? I wish I was rid of this troublesome affair; but what can I hope? Have I any reason to think age will make him better? He was old enough then, if age would have preserved his modesty: have my years and beauty more temptations in 'em now than before, Demipho? What can you advance to make me expect or hope that 'twill be no more so?

PHORMIO: They who have a mind to be at Chremes's funeral come now, now is the time; I'll give it him home: come on now, and provoke Phormio who dares; he shall meet with the same fate. He may get into favor again; I've had revenge enough; she has something to ring in his ear as long as he lives.

NAUSISTRATA: Can I believe that I've deserved such usage? Why, Demipho, should I repeat how faithful I have been to him in every particular?

DEMIPHO: I know all that as well as yourself.

NAUSISTRATA: Do you think I've deserved this?

DEMIPHO: Nobody less; but, since your reproaches can't undo what is done, forgive him: he asks your pardon, acknowledges his fault, and excuses himself; what would you have more?

PHORMIO (aside): But before she pronounces his pardon, I must take care of myself and Phædria. (To Nausistrata) Hark y', Nausistrata, hear me before you answer him without consideration.

NAUSISTRATA: What have you to say?

PHORMIO: I chous'd him of ninety pieces by a stratagem; which I gave to your son; which he gave to the bawd for his mistress.

CHREMES: Ah! what's that you say?

NAUSISTRATA: Do you think it such a crime, that your son, who is a young man, should have one mistress, while you have two wives? Aren't you ashamed? With what face can you reprove him? answer me.

DEMIPHO: He'll do what you will.

NAUSISTRATA: Well, that you may know my resolution now, I'll neither forgive, nor promise anything, nor answer, till I see my son; I'll be determined by his judgement; I'll do what he desires.

PHORMIO: You are a woman of judgement, Nausistrata.

NAUSISTRATA: Do you approve of it?

PHORMIO: Yes indeed, I'm come well off, and beyond my expectation.

NAUSISTRATA: Tell me your name.

PHORMIO: My name? Phormio, a friend to your family, but more especially to Phædria.

NAUSISTRATA: By Castor, Phormio, from this time forwards I'll serve you in whatever you ask of me, to the utmost of my power, in word and deed.

PHORMIO: You're very good.

NAUSISTRATA: By Pollux, you deserve it.

PHORMIO: First now will you do that, Nausistrata, which will please me, and make your husband's eyes ache?

NAUSISTRATA: With all my heart.

PHORMIO: Invite me to supper.

NAUSISTRATA: By Pollux, I do invite you.

DEMIPHO: Now let us go in.

NAUSISTRATA: We will; but where's Phædria our judge?

PHORMIO (*to Nausistrata*): I'll bring him immediately. (*To the spectators*) Farewell, and give us your applause.

⇜❋⇝

LUCRETIUS

(Titus Lucretius Carus, 96? B.C.–55 B.C.)

❋

From On the Nature of Things*

Translated by William Ellery Leonard

❋

Book I

PROEM

Mother of Rome, delight of Gods and men,
Dear Venus that beneath the gliding stars
Makest to teem the many-voyagèd main
And fruitful lands—for all of living things
Through thee alone are evermore conceived,
Through thee are risen to visit the great sun—
Before thee, Goddess, and thy coming on,
Flee stormy wind and massy cloud away,
For thee the daedal Earth bears scented flowers,
For thee the waters of the unvexèd deep
Smile, and the hollows of the sérene sky
Glow with diffusèd radiance for thee!
For soon as comes the springtime face of day,
And procreant gales blow from the West unbarred,
First fowls of air, smit to the heart by thee,
Foretoken thy approach, O thou Divine,
And leap the wild herds round the happy fields

* Everyman's Library, E. P. Dutton & Co., Inc.

132

Or swim the bounding torrents. Thus amain,
Seized with the spell, all creatures follow thee
Whithersoever thou walkest forth to lead,
And thence through seas and mountains and swift
    streams,
Through leafy homes of birds and greening plains,
Kindling the lure of love in every breast,
Thou bringest the eternal generations forth,
Kind after kind. And since 'tis thou alone
Guidest the Cosmos, and without thee naught
Is risen to reach the shining shores of light,
Nor aught of joyful or of lovely born,
Thee do I crave co-partner in this verse
Which I presume on Nature to compose
For Memmius mine, whom thou hast willed to be
Peerless in every grace at every hour—
Wherefore indeed, Divine one, give my words
Immortal charm. Lull to a timely rest
On sea and land the savage works of war,
For thou alone hast power with public peace
To aid mortality; since he who rules
The savage works of battles, puissant Mars,
How often to thy bosom flings his strength
Overmastered by the eternal wound of love,
And there, with eyes and full throat backward
    thrown,
Gazing, my Goddess, open-mouthed at thee,
Pastures on love his greedy sight, his breath
Hanging upon thy lips. Him thus reclined
Fill with thy holy body, round, above!
Pour from those lips soft syllables to win
Peace for the Romans, glorious Lady, peace!
For in a season troublous to the state
Neither may I attend this task of mine
With thought untroubled, nor mid such events

The illustrious scion of the Memmian house
Neglect the civic cause.
                              Whilst human kind
Throughout the lands lay miserably crushed
Before all eyes beneath Religion—who
Would show her head along the region skies,
Glowering on mortals with her hideous face—
A Greek it was who first opposing dared
Raise mortal eyes that terror to withstand,
Whom nor the fame of Gods nor lightning's stroke
Nor threatening thunder of the ominous sky
Abashed; but rather chafed to angry zest
His dauntless heart to be the first to rend
The crossbars at the gates of Nature old.
And thus his will and hardy wisdom won;
And forward thus he fared afar, beyond
The flaming ramparts of the world, until
He wandered the unmeasurable All.
Whence he to us, a conqueror, reports
What things can rise to being, what cannot,
And by what law to each its scope prescribed,
Its boundary stone that clings so deep in Time.
Wherefore religion now is under foot,
And us his victory now exalts to heaven.

   I know how hard it is in Latian verse
To tell the dark discoveries of the Greeks,
Chiefly because our pauper-speech must find
Strange terms to fit the strangeness of the thing;
Yet worth of thine and the expected joy
Of thy sweet friendship do persuade me on
To bear all toil and wake the clear nights through,
Seeking with what of words and what of song
I may at last most gloriously uncloud
For thee the light beyond, wherewith to view
The core of being at the centre hid.

And for the rest, summon to judgments true,
Unbusied ears and singleness of mind
Withdrawn from cares; lest these my gifts, arranged
For thee with eager service, thou disdain
Before thou comprehendest: since for thee
I prove the súpreme law of Gods and sky,
And the primordial germs of things unfold,
Whence Nature all creates, and multiplies
And fosters all, and whither she resolves
Each in the end when each is overthrown.
This ultimate stock we have devised to name
Procreant atoms, matter, seeds of things,
Or primal bodies, as primal to the world.

I fear perhaps thou deemest that we fare
An impious road to realms of thought profane;
But 'tis that same religion oftener far
Hath bred the foul impieties of men:
As once at Aulis, the elected chiefs,
Foremost of heroes, Danaan counsellors,
Defiled Diana's altar, virgin queen,
With Agamemnon's daughter, foully slain.
She felt the chaplet round her maiden locks
And fillets, fluttering down on either cheek,
And at the altar marked her grieving sire,
The priests beside him who concealed the knife,
And all the folk in tears at sight of her.
With a dumb terror and a sinking knee
She dropped; nor might avail her now that first
'Twas she who gave the king a father's name.
They raised her up, they bore the trembling girl
On to the altar—hither led not now
With solemn rites and hymeneal choir,
But sinless woman, sinfully foredone,
A parent felled her on her bridal day,

Making his child a sacrificial beast
To give the ships auspicious winds for Troy:
Such are the crimes to which religion leads.

And there shall come the time when even thou,
Forced by the soothsayer's terror-tales, shalt seek
To break from us. Ah, many a dream even now
Can they concoct to rout thy plans of life,
And trouble all thy fortunes with base fears.
I own with reason: for, if men but knew
Some fixèd end to ills, they would be strong
By some device unconquered to withstand
Religions and the menacings of seers.
But now nor skill nor instrument is theirs,
Since men must dread eternal pains in death.
For what the soul may be they do not know,
Whether 'tis born, or enter in at birth,
And whether, snatched by death, it die with us,
Or visit the shadows and the vasty caves
Of Orcus, or by some divine decree
Enter the brute herds, as our Ennius sang,
Who first from lovely Helicon brought down
A laurel wreath of bright perennial leaves,
Renowned forever among the Italian clans.
Yet Ennius too in everlasting verse
Proclaims those vaults of Acheron to be,
Though thence, he said, nor souls nor bodies fare,
But only phantom figures, strangely wan,
And tells how once from out those regions rose
Old Homer's ghost to him and shed salt tears
And with his words unfolded Nature's source.
Then be it ours with steady mind to clasp
The purport of the skies—the law behind
The wandering courses of the sun and moon;
To scan the powers that speed all life below;

But most to see with reasonable eyes
Of what the mind, of what the soul is made,
And what it is so terrible that breaks
On us asleep, or waking in disease,
Until we seem to mark and hear at hand
Dead men whose bones earth bosomed long ago.

Lines 1-145

SUBSTANCE IS ETERNAL

This terror, then, this darkness of the mind,
Not sunrise with its flaring spokes of light,
Nor glittering arrows of morning can disperse,
But only Nature's aspect and her law,
Which, teaching us, hath this exordium:
Nothing from nothing ever yet was born.
Fear holds dominion over mortality
Only because, seeing in land and sky
So much the cause whereof no wise they know,
Men think Divinities are working there.
Meantime, when once we know from nothing still
Nothing can be create, we shall divine
More clearly what we seek: those elements
From which alone all things created are,
And how accomplished by no tool of Gods.
Suppose all sprang from all things: any kind
Might take its origin from any thing,
No fixèd seed required. Men from the sea
Might rise, and from the land the scaly breed,
And fowl full fledged come bursting from the sky;
The hornèd cattle, the herds and all the wild
Would haunt with varying offspring tilth and waste;
Nor would the same fruits keep their olden trees,
But each might grow from any stock or limb
By chance and change. Indeed, and were there not
For each its procreant atoms, could things have

Each its unalterable mother old?
But, since produced from fixèd seeds are all,
Each birth goes forth upon the shores of light
From its own stuff, from its own primal bodies.
And all from all cannot become, because
In each resides a secret power its own.
Again, why see we lavished o'er the lands
At spring the rose, at summer heat the corn,
The vines that mellow when the autumn lures,
If not because the fixèd seeds of things
At their own season must together stream,
And new creations only be revealed
When the due times arrive and pregnant earth
Safely may give unto the shores of light
Her tender progenies? But if from naught
Were their becoming, they would spring abroad
Suddenly, unforeseen, in alien months,
With no primordial germs, to be preserved
From procreant unions at an adverse hour.
Nor on the mingling of the living seeds
Would space be needed for the growth of things
Were life an increment of nothing: then
The tiny babe forthwith would walk a man,
And from the turf would leap a branching tree—
Wonders unheard of; for, by Nature, each
Slowly increases from its lawful seed,
And through that increase shall conserve its kind.
Whence take the proof that things enlarge and feed
From out their proper matter. Thus it comes
That earth, without her seasons of fixed rains,
Could bear no produce such as makes us glad,
And whatsoever lives, if shut from food,
Prolongs its kind and guards its life no more.
Thus easier 'tis to hold that many things
Have primal bodies in common (as we see

The single letters common to many words)
Than aught exists without its origins.
Moreover, why should Nature not prepare
Men of a bulk to ford the seas afoot,
Or rend the mighty mountains with their hands,
Or conquer Time with length of days, if not
Because for all begotten things abides
The changeless stuff, and what from that may spring
Is fixed forevermore? Lastly we see
How far the tilled surpass the fields untilled
And to the labour of our hands return
Their more abounding crops; there are indeed
Within the earth primordial germs of things,
Which, as the ploughshare turns the fruitful clods
And kneads the mould, we quicken into birth.
Else would ye mark, without all toil of ours,
Spontaneous generations, fairer forms.
Confess then, naught from nothing can become,
Since all must have their seeds, wherefrom to grow,
Wherefrom to reach the gentle fields of air.

Hence too it comes that Nature all dissolves
Into their primal bodies again, and naught
Perishes ever to annihilation.
For, were aught mortal in its every part,
Before our eyes it might be snatched away
Unto destruction; since no force were needed
To sunder its members and undo its bands.
Whereas, of truth, because all things exist,
With seed imperishable, Nature allows
Destruction nor collapse of aught, until
Some outward force may shatter by a blow,
Or inward craft, entering its hollow cells,
Dissolve it down. And more than this, if Time,
That wastes with eld the works along the world,

Destroy entire, consuming matter all,
Whence then may Venus back to light of life
Restore the generations kind by kind?
Or how, when thus restored, may daedal Earth
Foster and plenish with her ancient food,
Which, kind by kind, she offers unto each?
Whence may the water-springs, beneath the sea,
Or inland rivers, far and wide away,
Keep the unfathomable ocean full?
And out of what does Ether feed the stars?
For lapsèd years and infinite age must else
Have eat all shapes or mortal stock away:
But be it the Long Ago contained those germs,
By which this sum of things recruited lives,
Those same infallibly can never die,
Nor nothing to nothing evermore return.
And, too, the selfsame power might end alike
All things, were they not still together held
By matter eternal, shackled through its parts,
Now more, now less. A touch might be enough
To cause destruction. For the slightest force
Would loose the weft of things wherein no part
Were of imperishable stock. But now
Because the fastenings of primordial parts
Are put together diversly and stuff
Is everlasting, things abide the same
Unhurt and sure, until some power comes on
Strong to destroy the warp and woof of each:
Nothing returns to naught; but all return
At their collapse to primal forms of stuff.
Lo, the rains perish which Ether-father throws
Down to the bosom of Earth-mother; but then
Upsprings the shining grain, and boughs are green
Amid the trees, and trees themselves wax big
And lade themselves with fruits; and hence in turn

The race of man and all the wild are fed;
Hence joyful cities thrive with boys and girls;
And leafy woodlands echo with new birds;
Hence cattle, fat and drowsy, lay their bulk
Along the joyous pastures whilst the drops
Of white ooze trickle from distended bags;
Hence the young scamper on their weakling joints
Along the tender herbs, fresh hearts afrisk
With warm new milk. Thus naught of what so seems
Perishes utterly, since Nature ever
Upbuilds one thing from other, suffering naught
To come to birth but through some other's death.

. . . .[1]

And now, since I have taught that things cannot
Be born from nothing, nor the same, when born,
To nothing be recalled, doubt not my words,
Because our eyes no primal germs perceive;
For mark those bodies which, though known to be
In this our world, are yet invisible:
The winds infuriate lash our face and frame,
Unseen, and swamp huge ships and rend the clouds,
Or eddying wildly down, bestrew the plains
With mighty trees, or scour the mountain tops
With forest-crackling blasts. Thus on they rave
With uproar shrill and ominous moan. The winds,
'Tis clear, are sightless bodies sweeping through
The sea, the lands, the clouds along the sky,
Vexing and whirling and seizing all amain;
And forth they flow and pile destruction round,
Even as the water's soft and supple bulk
Becoming a river of abounding floods,
Which a wide downpour from the lofty hills

[1] Dots denote a break in the Latin, not an editor's or
translator's expurgation.—*W.E.L.*

Swells with big showers, dashes headlong down
Fragments of woodland and whole branching trees;
Nor can the solid bridges bide the shock
As on the waters whelm: the turbulent stream,
Strong with a hundred rains, beats round the piers,
Crashes with havoc, and rolls beneath its waves
Down-toppled masonry and ponderous stone,
Hurling away whatever would oppose.
Even so must move the blasts of all the winds,
Which, when they spread, like to a mighty flood,
Hither or thither, drive things on before
And hurl to ground with still renewed assault,
Or sometimes in their circling vortex seize
And bear in cones of whirlwind down the world:
The winds are sightless bodies and naught else—
Since both in works and ways they rival well
The mighty rivers, the visible in form.
Then too we know the varied smells of things
Yet never to our nostrils see them come;
With eyes we view not burning heats, nor cold,
Nor are we wont men's voices to behold.
Yet these must be corporeal at the base,
Since thus they smite the senses: naught there is
Save body, having property of touch.
And raiment, hung by surf-beat shore, grows moist,
The same, spread out before the sun, will dry;
Yet no one saw how sank the moisture in,
Nor how by heat off-driven. Thus we know,
That moisture is dispersed about in bits
Too small for eyes to see. Another case:
A ring upon the finger thins away
Along the under side, with years and suns;
The drippings from the eaves will scoop the stone;
The hooked ploughshare, though of iron, wastes
Amid the fields insidiously. We view

The rock-paved highways worn by many feet;
And at the gates the brazen statues show
Their right hands leaner from the frequent touch
Of wayfarers innumerable who greet.
We see how wearing-down hath minished these,
But just what motes depart at any time,
The envious nature of vision bars our sight.
Lastly whatever days and nature add
Little by little, constraining things to grow
In due proportion, no gaze however keen
Of these our eyes hath watched and known. No more
Can we observe what's lost at any time,
When things wax old with eld and foul decay,
Or when salt seas eat under beetling crags.
Thus nature ever by unseen bodies works.

Lines 146-328

The Void

But yet creation's neither crammed nor blocked
About by body: there's in things a void—
Which to have known will serve thee many a turn,
Nor will not leave thee wandering in doubt,
Forever searching in the sum of all,
And losing faith in these pronouncements mine.
There's place intangible, a void and room.
For were it not, things could in nowise move;
Since body's property to block and check
Would work on all and at all times the same.
Thus naught could evermore push forth and go,
Since naught elsewhere would yield a starting place.
But now through oceans, lands, and heights of heaven,
By divers causes and in divers modes,
Before our eyes we mark how much may move,
Which, finding not a void, would fail deprived
Of stir and motion; nay, would then have been

Nowise begot at all, since matter, then,
Had staid at rest, its parts together crammed.
Then too, however solid objects seem,
They yet are formed of matter mixed with void:
In rocks and caves the watery moisture seeps,
And beady drops stand out like plenteous tears;
And food finds way through every frame that lives;
The trees increase and yield the season's fruit
Because their food throughout the whole is poured,
Even from the deepest roots, through trunks and boughs;
And voices pass the solid walls and fly
Reverberant through shut doorways of a house;
And stiffening frost seeps inward to our bones.
Which but for voids for bodies to go through
'Tis clear could happen in nowise at all.
Again, why see we among objects some
Of heavier weight, but no bulkier size?
Indeed, if in a ball of wool there be
As much of body as in lump of lead,
The two should weigh alike, since body tends
To load things downward, while the void abides,
By contrary nature, the imponderable.
Therefore, an object just as large but lighter
Declares infallibly its more of void;
Even as the heavier more of matter shows,
And how much less of vacant room inside.
That which we're seeking with sagacious quest
Exists, infallibly, commixed with things—
The void, the invisible inane.

       Right here
I am compelled a question to expound,
Forestalling something certain folk suppose,
Lest it avail to lead thee off from truth:
Waters (they say) before the shining breed
Of the swift scaly creatures somehow give,

And straightway open sudden liquid paths,
Because the fishes leave behind them room
To which at once the yielding billows stream.
Thus things among themselves can yet be moved,
And change their place, however full the Sum—
Received opinion, wholly false forsooth.
For where can scaly creatures forward dart,
Save where the waters give them room? Again,
Where can the billows yield a way, so long
As ever the fish are powerless to go?
Thus either all bodies of motion are deprived,
Or things contain admixture of a void
Where each thing gets its start in moving on.

Lastly, where after impact two broad bodies
Suddenly spring apart, the air must crowd
The whole new void between those bodies formed;
But air, however it stream with hastening gusts,
Can yet not fill the gap at once—for first
It makes for *one* place, ere diffused through *all*.
And then, if haply any think this comes,
When bodies spring apart, because the air
Somehow condenses, wander they from truth:
For then a void is formed, where none before;
And, too, a void is filled which was before.
Nor can air be condensed in such a wise;
Nor, granting it could, without a void, I hold,
It still could not contract upon itself
And draw its parts together into one.
Wherefore, despite demur and counter-speech,
Confess thou must there is a void in things.

And still I might by many an argument
Here scrape together credence for my words.
But for the keen eye these mere footprints serve,
Whereby thou mayest know the rest thyself.

As dogs full oft with noses on the ground,
Find out the silent lairs, though hid in brush,
Of beasts, the mountain-rangers, when but once
They scent the certain footsteps of the way,
Thus thou thyself in themes like these alone
Can hunt from thought to thought, and keenly wind
Along even onward to the secret places
And drag out truth. But, if thou loiter loth
Or veer, however little, from the point,
This I can promise, Memmius, for a fact:
Such copious drafts my singing tongue shall pour
From the large well-springs of my plenished breast
That much I dread slow age will steal and coil
Along our members, and unloose the gates
Of life within us, ere for thee my verse
Hath put within thine ears the stores of proofs
At hand for one soever question broached.

Lines 329-417

NOTHING EXISTS PER SE EXCEPT ATOMS AND THE VOID

But, now again to weave the tale begun,
All nature, then, as self-sustained, consists
Of twain of things: of bodies and of void
In which they're set, and where they're moved around.
For common instinct of our race declares
That body of itself exists: unless
This primal faith, deep-founded, fail us not,
Naught will there be whereunto to appeal
On things occult when seeking aught to prove
By reasonings of mind. Again, without
That place and room, which we do call the inane,
Nowhere could bodies then be set, nor go
Hither or thither at all—as shown before.
Besides, there's naught of which thou canst declare

It lives disjoined from body, shut from void—
A kind of third in nature. For whatever
Exists must be a somewhat; and the same,
If tangible, however light and slight,
Will yet increase the count of body's sum,
With its own augmentation big or small;
But, if intangible and powerless ever
To keep a thing from passing through itself
On any side, 'twill be naught else but that
Which we do call the empty, the inane.
Again, whate'er exists, as of itself,
Must either act or suffer action on it.
Or else be that wherein things move and be:
Naught, saving body, acts, is acted on;
Naught but the inane can furnish room. And thus,
Beside the inane and bodies, is no third
Nature amid the number of all things—
Remainder none to fall at any time
Under our senses, nor be seized and seen
By any man through reasonings of mind.
Name o'er creation with what names thou wilt,
Thou'lt find but properties of those first twain,
Or see but accidents those twain produce.

A property is that which not at all
Can be disjoined and severed from a thing
Without a fatal dissolution: such,
Weight to the rocks, heat to the fire, and flow
To the wide waters, touch to corporal things,
Intangibility to the viewless void.
But state of slavery, pauperhood, and wealth,
Freedom, and war, and concord, and all else
Which come and go whilst nature stands the same,
We're wont, and rightly, to call accidents.
Even time exists not of itself; but sense

Reads out of things what happened long ago,
What presses now, and what shall follow after:
No man, we must admit, feels time itself,
Disjoined from motion and repose of things.
Thus, when they say there "is" the ravishment
Of Princess Helen, "is" the siege and sack
Of Trojan Town, look out, they force us not
To admit these acts existent by themselves,
Merely because those races of mankind
(Of whom these acts were accidents) long since
Irrevocable age has borne away:
For all past actions may be said to be
But accidents, in one way, of mankind,—
In other, of some *region* of the world.
Add, too, had been no matter, and no room
Wherein all things go on, the fire of love
Upblown by that fair form, the glowing coal
Under the Phrygian Alexander's breast,
Had ne'er enkindled that renownèd strife
Of savage war, nor had the wooden horse
Involved in flames old Pergama, by a birth
At midnight of a brood of the Hellenes.
And thus thou canst remark that every act
At bottom exists not of itself, nor is
As body is, nor has like name with void;
But rather of sort more fitly to be called
An accident of body, and of place
Wherein all things go on.

Lines 418-482

CHARACTER OF THE ATOMS

Bodies, again,
Are partly primal germs of things, and partly
Unions deriving from the primal germs.

And those which are the primal germs of things
No power can quench; for in the end they conquer
By their own solidness; though hard it be
To think that aught in things has solid frame;
For lightnings pass, no less than voice and shout,
Through hedging walls of houses, and the iron
White-dazzles in the fire, and rocks will burn
With exhalations fierce and burst asunder.
Totters the rigid gold dissolved in heat;
The ice of bronze melts conquered in the flame;
Warmth and the piercing cold through silver seep,
Since, with the cups held rightly in the hand,
We oft feel both, as from above is poured
The dew of waters between their shining sides:
So true it is no solid form is found.
But yet because true reason and nature of things
Constrain us, come, whilst in few verses now
I disentangle how there still exist
Bodies of solid, everlasting frame—
The seeds of things, the primal germs we teach,
Whence all creation around us came to be.
First since we know a twofold nature exists,
Of things, both twain and utterly unlike—
Body, and place in which all things go on—
Then each must be both for and through itself,
And all unmixed: where'er be empty space,
There body's *not;* and so where body bides,
There not at all exists the void inane.
Thus primal bodies are solid, without a void.
But since there's void in all begotten things,
All solid matter must be round the same;
Nor, by true reason canst thou prove aught hides
And holds a void within its body, unless
Thou grant what holds it be a solid. Know,

That which can hold a void of things within
Can be naught else than matter in union knit.
Thus matter, consisting of a solid frame,
Hath power to be eternal, though all else,
Though all creation, be dissolved away.
Again, were naught of empty and inane,
The world were then a solid; as, without
Some certain bodies to fill the places held,
The world that is were but a vacant void.
And so, infallibly, alternate-wise
Body and void are still distinguishèd,
Since nature knows no wholly full nor void.
There are, then, certain bodies, possessed of power
To vary forever the empty and the full;
And these can nor be sundered from without
By beats and blows, nor from within be torn
By penetration, nor be overthrown
By any assault soever through the world—
For without void, naught can be crushed, it seems,
Nor broken, nor severed by a cut in twain,
Nor can it take the damp, or seeping cold
Or piercing fire, those old destroyers three;
But the more void within a thing, the more
Entirely it totters at their sure assault.
Thus if first bodies be, as I have taught,
Solid, without a void, they must be then
Eternal; and, if matter ne'er had been
Eternal, long ere now had all things gone
Back into nothing utterly, and all
We see around from nothing had been born—
But since I taught above that naught can be
From naught created, nor the once begotten
To naught be summoned back, these primal germs
Must have an immortality of frame.
And into these must each thing be resolved,

When comes its súpreme hour, that thus there be
At hand the stuff for plenishing the world.

. . . .

So primal germs have solid singleness
Nor otherwise could they have been conserved
Through aeons and infinity of time
For the replenishment of wasted worlds.
    Once more, if nature had given a scope for things
To be forever broken more and more,
By now the bodies of matter would have been
So far reduced by breakings in old days
That from them nothing could, at season fixed,
Be born, and arrive its prime and top of life.
For, lo, each thing is quicker marred than made;
And so what'er the long infinitude
Of days and all fore-passèd time would now
By this have broken and ruined and dissolved,
That same could ne'er in all remaining time
Be builded up for plenishing the world.
But mark: infallibly a fixèd bound
Remaineth stablished 'gainst their breaking down;
Since we behold each thing soever renewed,
And unto all, their seasons, after their kind,
Wherein they arrive the flower of their age.

    Again, if bounds have not been set against
The breaking down of this corporeal world,
Yet must all bodies of whatever things
Have still endured from everlasting time
Unto this present, as not yet assailed
By shocks of peril. But because the same
Are, to thy thinking, of a nature frail,
It ill accords that thus they could remain
(As thus they do) through everlasting time,

Vexed through the ages (as indeed they are)
By the innumerable blows of chance.

So in our programme of creation, mark
How 'tis that, though the bodies of all stuff
Are solid to the core, we yet explain
The ways whereby some things are fashioned soft—
Air, water, earth, and fiery exhalations—
And by what force they function and go on:
The fact is founded in the void of things.
But if the primal germs themselves be soft,
Reason cannot be brought to bear to show
The ways whereby may be created these
Great crags of basalt and the during iron;
For their whole nature will profoundly lack
The first foundations of a solid frame.
But powerful in old simplicity,
Abide the solid, the primeval germs;
And by their combinations more condensed,
All objects can be tightly knit and bound
And made to show unconquerable strength.
Again, since all things kind by kind obtain
Fixed bounds of growing and conserving life;
Since nature hath inviolably decreed
What each can do, what each can never do;
Since naught is changed, but all things so abide
That ever the variegated birds reveal
The spots or stripes peculiar to their kind,
Spring after spring: thus surely all that is
Must be composed of matter immutable.
For if the primal germs in any wise
Were open to conquest and to change, 'twould be
Uncertain also what could come to birth
And what could not, and by what law to each
Its cope prescribed, its boundary stone that clings

So deep in Time. Nor could the generations
Kind after kind so often reproduce
The nature, habits, motions, ways of life,
Of their progenitors.
     And then again,
Since there is ever an éxtreme bounding point

. . . .

Of that first body which our senses now
Cannot perceive: That bounding point indeed
Exists without all parts, a minimum
Of nature, nor was e'er a thing apart,
As of itself—nor shall hereafter be,
Since 'tis itself still parcel of another,
A first and single part, whence other parts
And others similar in order lie
In a packed phalanx, filling to the full
The nature of first body: being thus
Not self-existent, they must cleave to that
From which in nowise they can sundered be.
So primal germs have solid singleness,
Which tightly packed and closely joined cohere
By virtue of their minim particles—
No compound by mere union of the same;
But strong in their eternal singleness,
Nature, reserving them as seeds for things,
Permitteth naught of rupture or decrease.

 Moreover, were there not a minimum,
The smallest bodies would have infinites,
Since then a half-of-half could still be halved,
With limitless division less and less.
Then what the difference 'twixt the sum and least?
None: for however infinite the sum,
Yet even the smallest would consist the same

Of infinite parts. But since true reason here
Protests, denying that the mind can think it,
Convinced thou must confess such things there are
As have no parts, the minimums of nature.
And since these are, likewise confess thou must
That primal bodies are solid and eterne.
Again, if Nature, creatress of all things,
Were wont to force all things to be resolved
Unto least parts, then would she not avail
To reproduce from out them anything;
Because whate'er is not endowed with parts
Cannot possess those properties required
Of generative stuff—divers connections,
Weights, blows, encounters, motions, whereby things
Forevermore have being and go on.

Lines 483-634

CONFUTATION OF OTHER PHILOSOPHERS

And on such grounds it is that those who held
The stuff of things is fire, and out of fire
Alone the cosmic sum is formed, are seen
Mightily from true reason to have lapsed.
Of whom, chief leader to do battle, comes
That Heraclitus, famous for dark speech
Among the silly, not the serious Greeks
Who search for truth. For dolts are ever prone
That to bewonder and adore which hides
Beneath distorted words, holding that true
Which sweetly tickles in their stupid ears,
Or which is rouged in finely finished phrase.
For how, I ask, can things so varied be,
If formed of fire, single and pure? No whit
'Twould help for fire to be condensed or thinned,
If all the parts of fire did still preserve
But fire's own nature, seen before in gross.

The heat were keener with the parts compressed,
Milder, again when severed or dispersed—
And more than this thou canst conceive of naught
That from such causes could become; much less
Might earth's variety of things be born
From any fires soever, dense or rare.
This too: if they suppose a void in things,
Then fires can be condensed and still left rare;
But since they see such opposites of thought
Rising against them, and are loath to leave
An unmixed void in things, they fear the steep
And lose the road of truth. Nor do they see,
That, if from things we take away the void,
All things are then condensed, and out of all
One body made, which has no power to dart
Swiftly from out itself not anything—
As throws the fire its light and warmth around,
Giving thee proof its parts are not compact.
But if perhaps they think, in other wise,
Fires through their combinations can be quenched
And change their substance, very well: behold,
If fire shall spare to do so in no part,
Then heat will perish utterly and all,
And out of nothing would the world be formed.
For change in anything from out its bounds
Means instant death of that which was before;
And thus a somewhat must persist unharmed
Amid the world, lest all return to naught,
And, born from naught, abundance thrive anew.
Now since indeed there are those surest bodies
Which keep their nature evermore the same,
Upon whose going out and coming in
And changèd order things their nature change,
And all corporeal substances transformed,
'Tis thine to know those primal bodies, then,

Are not of fire. For 'twere of no avail
Should some depart and go away, and some
Be added new, and some be changed in order,
If still all kept their nature of old heat:
For whatsoever they created then
Would still in any case be only fire.
The truth, I fancy, this: bodies there are
Whose clashings, motions, order, posture, shapes
Produce the fire and which, by order changed,
Do change the nature of the thing produced,
And are thereafter nothing like to fire
Nor whatso else has power to send its bodies
With impact touching on the senses' touch.

Again, to say that all things are but fire
And no true thing in number of all things
Exists but fire, as this same fellow says,
Seems crazèd folly. For the man himself
Against the senses *by* the senses fights,
And hews at that through which is all belief,
Through which indeed unto himself is known
The thing he calls the fire. For, though he thinks
The senses truly can perceive the fire,
He thinks they cannot as regards all else,
Which still are palpably as clear to sense—
To me a thought inept and crazy too.
For whither shall we make appeal? for what
More certain than our senses can there be
Whereby to mark asunder error and truth?
Besides, why rather do away with all,
And wish to allow heat only, than deny
The fire and still allow all else to be?—
Alike the madness either way it seems.
Thus whosoe'er have held the stuff of things
To be but fire, and out of fire the sum,

And whosoever have constituted air
As first beginning of begotten things,
And all whoever have held that of itself
Water alone contrives things, or that earth
Createth all and changes things anew
To divers natures, mightily they seem
A long way to have wandered from the truth.

Add, too, whoever make the primal stuff
Twofold, by joining air to fire, and earth
To water; add who deem that things can grow
Out of the four—fire, earth, and breath, and rain;
As first Empedocles of Acragas,
Whom that three-cornered isle of all the lands
Bore on her coasts, around which flows and flows
In mighty bend and bay the Ionic seas,
Splashing the brine from off their gray-green waves.
Here, billowing onward through the narrow straits,
Swift ocean cuts her boundaries from the shores
Of the Italic mainland. Here the waste
Charybdis; and here Ætna rumbles threats
To gather anew such furies of its flames
As with its force anew to vomit fires,
Belched from its throat, and skyward bear anew
Its lightnings' flash. And though for much she seem
The mighty and the wondrous isle to men,
Most rich in all good things, and fortified
With generous strength of heroes, she hath ne'er
Possessed within her aught of more renown,
Nor aught more holy, wonderful, and dear
Than this true man. Nay, ever so far and pure
The lofty music of his breast divine
Lifts up its voice and tells of glories found,
That scarce he seems of human stock create.

Yet he and those forementioned (known to be
So far beneath him, less than he in all),
Though, as discoverers of much goodly truth,
They gave, as 'twere from out of the heart's own shrine,
Responses holier and soundlier based
Than ever the Pythia pronounced for men
From out of the tripod and the Delphian laurel,
Have still in matter of first-elements
Made ruin of themselves, and, great men, great
Indeed and heavy there for them the fall:
First, because, banishing the void from things,
They yet assign them motion, and allow
Things soft and loosely textured to exist,
As air, dew, fire, earth, animals, and grains,
Without admixture of void amid their frame.
Next, because, thinking there can be no end
In cutting bodies down to less and less
Nor pause established to their breaking up,
They hold there is no minimum in things;
Albeit we see the boundary point of aught
Is that which to our senses seems its least,
Whereby thou mayst conjecture, that, because
The things thou canst not mark have boundary points,
They surely have their minimums. Then, too,
Since these philosophers ascribe to things
Soft primal germs, which we behold to be
Of birth and body mortal, thus, throughout,
The sum of things must be returned to naught,
And, born from naught, abundance thrive anew—
Thou seest how far each doctrine stands from truth.
And, next, these bodies are among themselves
In many ways poisons and foes to each,
Wherefore their congress will destroy them quite
Or drive asunder as we see in storms
Rains, winds, and lightnings all asunder fly.

Thus too, if all things are create of four,
And all again dissolved into the four,
How can the four be called the primal germs
Of things, more than all things themselves be thought,
By retroversion, primal germs of them?
For ever alternately are both begot,
With interchange of nature and aspèct
From immemorial time. But if percase
Thou think'st the frame of fire and earth, the air,
The dew of water can in *such* wise meet
As not by mingling to resign their nature,
From them for thee no world can be create—
No thing of breath, no stock or stalk of tree:
In the wild congress of this varied heap
Each thing its proper nature will display,
And air will palpably be seen mixed up
With earth together, únquenched heat with water.
But primal germs in bringing things to birth
Must have a latent, unseen quality,
Lest some outstanding alien element
Confuse and minish in the thing create
Its proper being.
                         But these men begin
From heaven, and from its fires; and first they feign
That fire will turn into the winds of air,
Next, that from air the rain begotten is,
And earth created out of rain, and then
That all, reversely, are returned from earth—
The moisture first, then air, thereafter heat—
And that these same ne'er cease in interchange,
To go their ways from heaven to earth, from earth
Unto the stars of the æthereal world—
Which in no wise at all the germs can do.
Since an immutable somewhat still must be,
Lest all things utterly be sped to naught;

For change in anything from out its bounds
Means instant death of that which was before.
Wherefore, since *those* things, mentioned heretofore,
Suffer a changèd state, they must derive
From others ever unconvertible,
Lest all things utterly return to naught.
Then why not rather presuppose there be
Bodies with such a nature furnished forth
That, if perchance they have created fire,
Can still (by virtue of a few withdrawn,
Or added few, and motion and order changed)
Fashion the winds of air, and thus all things
Forevermore be interchanged with all?
　　"But facts in proof are manifest," thou sayest,
"That all things grow into the winds of air
And forth from earth are nourished, and unless
The season favour at propitious hour
With rains enough to set the trees a-reel
Under the soak of bulking thunderheads,
And sun, for its share, foster and give heat,
No grains, nor trees, nor breathing things can grow."
True—and unless hard food and moisture soft
Recruited man, his frame would waste away,
And life dissolve from out his thews and bones;
For out of doubt recruited and fed are we
By certain things, as other things by others.
Because in many ways the many germs
Common to many things are mixed in things,
No wonder 'tis that therefore divers things
By divers things are nourished. And, again,
Often it matters vastly with *what* others,
In *what* positions the primordial germs
Are bound together, and *what* motions, too,
They give and get among themselves; for these
Same germs do put together sky, sea, lands,

Rivers, and sun, grains, trees, and breathing things,
But yet commixed they are in divers modes
With divers things, forever as they move.
Nay, thou beholdest in our verses here
Elements many, common to many words,
Albeit thou must confess each verse, each word
From one another differs both in sense
And ring of sound—so much the elements
Can bring about by change of order alone.
But those which are the primal germs of things
Have power to work more combinations still,
Whence divers things can be produced in turn.

Now let us also take for scrutiny
The homéomería of Anaxagoras,
So called by Greeks, for which our pauper-speech
Yieldeth no name in the Italian tongue,
Although the thing itself is not o'erhard
For explanation. First, then, when he speaks
Of this homéomería of things, he thinks
Bones to be sprung from littlest bones minute,
And from minute and littlest flesh all flesh,
And blood created out of drops of blood,
Conceiving gold compact of grains of gold,
And earth concreted out of bits of earth,
Fire made of fires, and water out of waters,
Feigning the like with all the rest of stuff.
Yet he concedes not any void in things,
Nor any limit to cutting bodies down.
Wherefore to me he seems on both accounts
To err no less than those we named before.
Add too: these germs he feigns are far too frail—
If they be germs primordial furnished forth
With but same nature as the things themselves,
And travail and perish equally with those,

And no rein curbs them from annihilation.
For which will last against the grip and crush
Under the teeth of death? the fire? the moist?
Or else the air? which then? the blood? the bones?
No one, methinks, when every thing will be
At bottom as mortal as whate'er we mark
To perish by force before our gazing eyes.
But my appeal is to the proofs above
That things cannot fall back to naught, nor yet
From naught increase. And now again, since food
Augments and nourishes the human frame,
'Tis thine to know our veins and blood and bones
And thews are formed of particles unlike
To them in kind; or if they say all foods
Are of mixed substance having in themselves
Small bodies of thews, and bones, and also veins
And particles of blood, then every food,
Solid or liquid, must itself be thought
As made and mixed of things unlike in kind—
Of bones, of thews, of ichor and of blood.
Again, if all the bodies which upgrow
From earth, are first within the earth, then earth
Must be compound of alien substances
Which spring and bloom abroad from out the earth.
Transfer the argument, and thou may'st use
The selfsame words: if flame and smoke and ash
Still lurk unseen within the wood, the wood
Must be compound of alien substances
Which spring from out the wood.

                                   Right here remains
A certain slender means to skulk from truth,
Which Anaxagoras takes unto himself,
Who holds that all things lurk commixed with all
While *that* one only comes to view, of which
The bodies exceed in number all the rest,

And lie more close to hand and at the fore—
A notion banished from true reason far.
For then 'twere meet that kernels of the grains
Should oft, when crunched between the might of stones,
Give forth a sign of blood, or of aught else
Which in our human frame is fed; and that
Rock rubbed on rock should yield a gory ooze.
Likewise the herbs ought oft to give forth drops
Of sweet milk, flavoured like the uddered sheep's;
Indeed we ought to find, when crumbling up
The earthy clods, there herbs, and grains, and leaves,
All sorts dispersed minutely in the soil;
Lastly we ought to find in cloven wood
Ashes and smoke and bits of fire there hid.
But since fact teaches this is not the case,
'Tis thine to know things are not mixed with things
Thuswise; but seeds, common to many things,
Commixed in many ways, must lurk in things.

"But often it happens on skiey hills," thou sayest,
"That neighbouring tops of lofty trees are rubbed
One against other, smote by the blustering south,
Till all ablaze with bursting flower of flame."
Good sooth—yet fire is not ingraft in wood,
But many are the seeds of heat, and when
Rubbing together they together flow,
They start the conflagrations in the forests,
Whereas if flame, already fashioned, lay
Stored up within the forests, then the fires
Could not for any time be kept unseen,
But would be laying all the wildwood waste
And burning all the boscage. Now dost see
(Even as we said a little space above)
How mightily it matters with *what* others,
In *what* positions these same primal germs

Are bound together? And *what* motions, too,
They give and get among themselves? how, hence,
The same, if altered 'mongst themselves, can body
Both igneous and ligneous objects forth—
Precisely as these words themselves are made
By somewhat altering their elements,
Although we mark with name indeed distinct
The igneous from the ligneous. Once again,
If thou suppose whatever thou beholdest,
Among all visible objects, cannot be,
Unless thou feign bodies of matter endowed
With a like nature—by thy vain device
For thee will perish all the germs of things:
'Twill come to pass they'll laugh aloud, like men,
Shaken asunder by a spasm of mirth,
Or moisten with salty tear-drops cheeks and chins.

Lines 635-920

The Infinity of the Universe

Now learn of what remains! More keenly hear!
And for myself, my mind is not deceived
How dark it is: But the large hope of praise
Hath strook with pointed thyrsus through my heart;
On the same hour hath-strook into my breast
Sweet love of the Muses, wherewith now instinct,
I wander afield, thriving in sturdy thought,
Through unpathed haunts of the Pierides,
Trodden by step of none before. I joy
To come on undefilèd fountains there,
To drain them deep; I joy to pluck new flowers,
To seek for this my head a signal crown
From regions where the Muses never yet
Have garlanded the temples of a man:
First, since I teach concerning mighty things,
And go right on to loose from round the mind

The tightened coils of dread religiôn;
Next, since, concerning themes so dark, I frame
Songs so pellucid, touching all throughout
Even with the Muses' charm—which, as 'twould seem,
Is not without a reasonable ground:
But as physicians, when they seel: to give
Young boys the nauseous wormwood, first do touch
The brim around the cup with the sweet juice
And yellow of the honey, in order that
The thoughtless age of boyhood be cajoled
As far as the lips, and meanwhile swallow down
The wormwood's bitter draught, and, though befooled,
Be yet not merely duped, but rather thus
Grow strong again with recreated health:
So now I too (since this my doctrine seems
In general somewhat woeful unto those
Who've had it not in hand, and since the crowd
Starts back from it in horror) have desired
To expound our doctrine unto thee in song
Soft-speaking and Pierian, and, as 'twere,
To touch it with sweet honey of the Muse—
If by such method haply I might hold
The mind of thee upon these lines of ours,
Till thou see through the nature of all things,
And how exists the interwoven frame.

But since I've taught that bodies of matter, made
Completely solid, hither and thither fly
Forevermore unconquered through all time,
Now come, and whether to the sum of them
There be a limit or be none, for thee
Let us unfold; likewise what has been found
To be the wide inane, or room, or space
Wherein all things soever do go on,
Let us examine if it finite be

All and entire, or reach unmeasured round
And downward an illimitable profound.

Thus, then, the All that is is limited
In no one region of its onward paths,
For then 'tmust have forever its beyond.
And a beyond 'tis seen can never be
For aught, unless still further on there be
A somewhat somewhere that may bound the same—
So that the thing be seen still on to where
The nature of sensation of that thing
Can follow it no longer. Now because
Confess we must there's naught beside the sum,
There's no beyond, and so it lacks all end.
It matters nothing where thou post thyself,
In whatsoever regions of the same;
Even any place a man has set him down
Still leaves about him the unbounded all
Outward in all directions; or, supposing
A moment the all of space finite to be,
If some one farthest traveller runs forth
Unto the éxtreme coasts and throws ahead
A flying spear, is't then thy wish to think
It goes, hurled off amain, to where 'twas sent
And shoots afar, or that some object there
Can thwart and stop it? For the one or other
Thou must admit and take. Either of which
Shuts off escape for thee, and does compel
That thou concede the all spreads everywhere,
Owning no confines. Since whether there be
Aught that may block and check it so it comes
Not where 'twas sent, nor lodges in its goal,
Or whether borne along, in either view
'Thas started not from any end. And so
I'll follow on, and whereso'er thou set

The éxtreme coasts, I'll query, "What becomes
Thereafter of thy spear?" 'Twill come to pass
That nowhere can a world's-end be, and that
The chance for further flight prolongs forever
The flight itself. Besides, were all the space
Of the totality and sum shut in
With fixéd coasts, and bounded everywhere,
Then would the abundance of world's matter flow
Together by solid weight from everywhere
Still downward to the bottom of the world,
Nor aught could happen under cope of sky,
Nor could there be a sky at all or sun—
Indeed, where matter all one heap would lie,
By having settled during infinite time.
But in reality, repose is given
Unto no bodies 'mongst the elements,
Because there is no bottom whereunto
They might, as 'twere, together flow, and where
They might take up their undisturbed abodes.
In endless motion everything goes on
Forevermore; out of all regions, even
Out of the pit below, from forth the vast,
Are hurtled bodies evermore supplied.
The nature of room, the space of the abyss
Is such that even the flashing thunderbolts
Can neither speed upon their courses through,
Gliding across eternal tracts of time,
Nor, further, bring to pass, as on they run,
That they may bate their journeying one whit:
Such huge abundance spreads for things around—
Room off to every quarter, without end.
Lastly, before our very eyes is seen
Thing to bound thing: air hedges hill from hill,
And mountain walls hedge air; land ends the sea,
And sea in turn all lands; but for the All

Truly is nothing which outside may bound.
That, too, the sum of things itself may not
Have power to fix a measure of its own,
Great nature guards, she who compels the void
To bound all body, as body all the void,
Thus rendering by these alternates the whole
An infinite; or else the one or other,
Being unbounded by the other, spreads,
Even by its single nature, ne'ertheless
Immeasurably forth. . . .
Nor sea, nor earth, nor shining vaults of sky,
Nor breed of mortals, nor holy limbs of gods
Could keep their place least portion of an hour:
For, driven apart from out its meetings fit,
The stock of stuff, dissolvèd, would be borne
Along the illimitable inane afar,
Or rather, in fact, would ne'er have once combined
And given a birth to aught, since, scattered wide,
It could not be united. For of truth
Neither by counsel did the primal germs
'Stablish themselves, as by keen act of mind,
Each in its proper place; nor did they make,
Forsooth, a compact how each germ should move;
But since, being many and changed in many modes
Along the All, they're driven abroad and vexed
By blow on blow, even from all time of old,
They thus at last, after attempting all
The kinds of motion and conjoining, come
Into those great arrangements out of which
This sum of things established is create,
By which, moreover, through the mighty years,
It is preserved, when once it has been thrown
Into the proper motions, bringing to pass
That ever the streams refresh the greedy main
With river-waves abounding, and that earth,

Lapped in warm exhalations of the sun,
Renews her broods, and that the lusty race
Of breathing creatures bears and blooms, and that
The gliding fires of ether are alive—
What still the primal germs nowise could do,
Unless from out the infinite of space
Could come supply of matter, whence in season
They're wont whatever losses to repair.
For as the nature of breathing creatures wastes,
Losing its body, when deprived of food:
So all things have to be dissolved as soon
As matter, diverted by what means soever
From off its course, shall fail to be on hand.
Nor can the blows from outward still conserve,
On every side, whatever sum of a world
Has been united in a whole. They can
Indeed, by frequent beating, check a part,
Till others arriving may fulfil the sum;
But meanwhile often are they forced to spring
Rebounding back, and, as they spring, to yield,
Unto those elements whence a world derives,
Room and a time for flight, permitting them
To be from off the massy union borne
Free and afar. Wherefore, again, again:
Needs must there come a many for supply;
And also, that the blows themselves shall be
Unfailing ever, must there ever be
An infinite force of matter all sides round.

And in these problems, shrink, my Memmius, far
From yielding faith to that notorious talk:
That all things inward to the centre press;
And thus the nature of the world stands firm
With never blows from outward, nor can be
Nowhere disparted—since all height and depth
Have always inward to the centre pressed

(If thou art ready to believe that aught
Itself can rest upon itself); or that
The ponderous bodies which be under earth
Do all press upwards and do come to rest
Upon the earth, in some ways upside down,
Like to those images of things we see
At present through the waters. They contend,
With like procedure, that all breathing things
Head downward roam about, and yet cannot
Tumble from earth to realms of sky below,
No more than these our bodies wing away
Spontaneously to vaults of sky above;
That, when those creatures look upon the sun,
We view the constellations of the night;
And that with us the seasons of the sky
They thus alternately divide, and thus
Do pass the night coequal to our days,
But in vain [error has given][1] these [dreams] to fools,
What they've embraced [with reasoning perverse].
For centre none can be [where world is still]
Boundless, nor yet, if now a centre were,
Could aught take there a fixed position [more]
Than for some other cause ['tmight be dislodged].
For all of room and space we call [the void]
[Must] both through centre and non-centre yield
Alike to weights where'er their motions tend.
Nor is there any place, where, when they've come,
Bodies can be at standstill in the void,
Deprived of force of weight; nor yet may void
Furnish support to any—nay, it must,
True to its bent of nature, still give way.
Thus in such manner not at all can things

[1] Brackets denote an attempt to supply a short lacuna.
—W.E.L.

Be held in union, as if overcome
By craving for a centre.
                 But besides,
Seeing they feign that not all bodies press
To centre inward, rather only those
Of earth and water (liquid of the sea,
And the big billows from the mountain slopes,
And whatsoever are encased, as 'twere,
In earthen body), contrariwise, they teach
How the thin air, and with it the hot fire,
Is borne asunder from the centre, and how,
For this all ether quivers with bright stars,
And the sun's flame along the blue is fed
(Because the heat, from out the centre flying,
All gathers there), and how, again, the boughs
Upon the tree-tops could not sprout their leaves,
Unless, little by little, from out the earth
For each were nutriment . . .

.   .   .   .

Lest, after the manner of the wingèd flames,
The ramparts of the world should flee away,
Dissolved amain throughout the mighty void,
And lest all else should likewise follow after,
Aye, lest the thundering vaults of heaven should burst
And splinter upward, and the earth forthwith
Withdraw from under our feet, and all its bulk,
Among its mingled wrecks and those of heaven,
With slipping asunder of the primal seeds,
Should pass, along the immeasurable inane,
Away forever, and, that instant, naught
Of wrack and remnant would be left, beside
The desolate space, and germs invisible.
For on whatever side thou deemest first

The primal bodies lacking, lo, that side
Will be for things the very door of death:
Wherethrough the throng of matter all will dash,
Out and abroad.

> These points, if thou wilt ponder,
Then, with but paltry trouble led along . . .

.   .   .   .

For one thing after other will grow clear,
Nor shall the blind night rob thee of the road,
To hinder thy gaze on nature's Farthest-forth.
Thus things for things shall kindle torches new.

Lines 921-1109

Book III

PROEM

O thou who first uplifted in such dark
So clear a torch aloft, who first shed light
Upon the profitable ends of man,
O thee I follow, glory of the Greeks,
And set my footsteps squarely planted now
Even in the impress and the marks of thine—
Less like one eager to dispute the palm,
More as one craving out of very love
That I may copy thee!—for how should swallow
Contend with swans or what compare could be
In a race between young kids with tumbling legs
And the strong might of the horse? Our father thou,
And finder-out of truth, and thou to us
Suppliest a father's precepts; and from out
Those scriven leaves of thine, renownèd soul,

(Like bees that sip of all in flowery wolds),
We feed upon thy golden sayings all—
Golden, and ever worthiest endless life.
For soon as ever thy planning thought that sprang
From god-like mind begins its loud proclaim
Of nature's courses, terrors of the brain
Asunder flee, the ramparts of the world
Dispart away, and through the void entire
I see the movements of the universe.
Rises to vision the majesty of gods,
And their abodes of everlasting calm
Which neither wind may shake nor rain-cloud splash,
Nor snow, congealèd by sharp frosts, may harm
With its white downfall: ever, unclouded sky
O'er roofs, and laughs with far-diffusèd light.
And nature gives to them their all, nor aught
May ever pluck their peace of mind away.
But nowhere to my vision rise no more
The vaults of Acheron, though the broad earth
Bars me no more from gazing down o'er all
Which under our feet is going on below
Along the void. O, here in these affairs
Some new divine delight and trembling awe
Takes hold through me, that thus by power of thine
Nature, so plain and manifest at last,
Hath been on every side laid bare to man!

    And since I've taught already of what sort
The seeds of all things are, and how, distinct
In divers forms, they flit of own accord,
Stirred with a motion everlasting on,
And in what mode things be from them create,
Now, after such matters, should my verse, meseems,
Make clear the nature of the mind and soul,
And drive that dread of Acheron without,

Headlong, which so confounds our human life
Unto its deeps, pouring o'er all that is
The black of death, nor leaves not anything
To prosper—a liquid and unsullied joy.
For as to what men sometimes will affirm:
That more than Tartarus (the realm of death)
They fear diseases and a life of shame,
And know the substance of the soul is blood,
Or rather wind (if haply thus their whim),
And so need naught of this our science, then
Thou well may'st note from what's to follow now
That more for glory do they braggart forth
Than for belief. For mark these very same:
Exiles from country, fugitives afar
From sight of men, with charges foul attaint,
Abased with every wretchedness, they yet
Live, and where'er the wretches come, they yet
Make the ancestral sacrifices there,
Butcher the black sheep, and to gods below
Offer the honours, and in bitter case
Turn much more keenly to religiòn.
Wherefore, it's surer testing of a man
In doubtful perils—mark him as he is
Amid adversities; for then alone
Are the true voices conjured from his breast,
The mask off-stripped, reality behind.
And greed, again, and the blind lust of honours
Which force poor wretches past the bounds of law,
And, oft allies and ministers of crime,
To push through nights and days with hugest toil
To rise untrammelled to the peaks of power—
These wounds of life in no mean part are kept
Festering and open by this fright of death.
For ever we see fierce Want and foul Disgrace
Dislodged afar from sécure life and sweet,

Like huddling Shapes before the doors of death.
And whilst, from these, men wish to scape afar,
Driven by false terror, and afar remove,
With civic blood a fortune they amass,
They double their riches, greedy, heapers-up
Of corpse on corpse they have a cruel laugh
For the sad burial of a brother-born,
And hatred and fear of tables of their kin.
Likewise, through this same terror, envy oft
Makes them to peak because before their eyes
That man is lordly, that man gazed upon
Who walks begirt with honour glorious,
Whilst they in filth and darkness roll around;
Some perish away for statues and a name,
And oft to that degree, from fright of death,
Will hate of living and beholding light
Take hold on humankind that they inflict
Their own destruction with a gloomy heart—
Forgetful that this fear is font of cares,
This fear the plague upon their sense of shame,
And this that breaks the ties of comradry
And oversets all reverence and faith,
Mid direst slaughter. For long ere today
Often were traitors to country and dear parents
Through quest to shun the realms of Acheron.
For just as children tremble and fear all
In the viewless dark, so even we at times
Dread in the light so many things that be
No whit more fearsome than what children feign,
Shuddering, will be upon them in the dark.
This terror, then, this darkness of the mind,
Not sunrise with its flaring spokes of light,
Nor glittering arrows of morning can disperse,
But only nature's aspect and her law.

Lines 1-93

NATURE AND COMPOSITION OF THE MIND

First, then, I say, the mind which oft we call
The intellect, wherein is seated life's
Counsel and regimen, is part no less
Of man than hand and foot and eyes are parts
Of one whole breathing creature. [But some hold]
That sense of mind is in no fixed part seated,
But is of body some one vital state,—
Named "harmony" by Greeks, because thereby
We live with sense, though intellect be not
In any part: as oft the body is said
To have good health (when health, however, 's not
One part of him who has it), so they place
The sense of mind in no fixed part of man.
Mightily, diversly, meseems they err.
Often the body palpable and seen
Sickens, while yet in some invisible part
We feel a pleasure; oft the other way,
A miserable in mind feels pleasure still
Throughout his body—quite the same as when
A foot may pain without a pain in head.
Besides, when these our limbs are given o'er
To gentle sleep and lies the burdened frame
At random void of sense, a something else
Is yet within us, which upon that time
Bestirs itself in many a wise, receiving
All motions of joy and phantom cares of heart.
Now, for to see that in man's members dwells
Also the soul, and body ne'er is wont
To feel sensation by a "harmony,"
Take this in chief: the fact that life remains
Oft in our limbs, when much of body's gone;
Yet that same life, when particles of heat,

Though few, have scattered been, and through the
    mouth
Air has been given forth abroad, forthwith
Forever deserts the veins, and leaves the bones.
Thus mayst thou know that not all particles
Perform like parts, nor in like manner all
Are props of weal and safety: rather those—
The seeds of wind and exhalations warm—
Take care that in our members life remains.
Therefore a vital heat and wind there is
Within the very body, which at death
Deserts our frames. And so, since nature of mind
And even of soul is found to be, as 'twere,
A part of man, give over "harmony"—
Name to musicians brought from Helicon,—
Unless themselves they filched it otherwise,
To serve for what was lacking name till then.
Whate'er it be, they're welcome to it—thou,
Hearken my other maxims.

                    Mind and soul,
I say, are held conjoinèd one with other,
And form one single nature of themselves;
But chief and regnant through the frame entire
Is still that counsel which we call the mind,
And that cleaves seated in the midmost breast.
Here leap dismay and terror; round these haunts
Be blandishments of joys; and therefore here
The intellect, the mind. The rest of soul,
Throughout the body scattered, but obeys—
Moved by the nod and motion of the mind.
This, for itself, sole through itself, hath thought;
This for itself hath mirth, even when the thing
That moves it, moves nor soul nor body at all.
And as, when head or eye in us is smit

By assailing pain, we are not tortured then
Through all the body, so the mind alone
Is sometimes smitten, or livens with a joy,
Whilst yet the soul's remainder through the limbs
And through the frame is stirred by nothing new.
But when the mind is moved by shock more fierce,
We mark the whole soul suffering all at once
Along man's members: sweats and pallors spread
Over the body, and the tongue is broken,
And fails the voice away, and ring the ears,
Mists blind the eyeballs, and the joints collapse—
Aye, men drop dead from terror of the mind.
Hence, whoso will can readily remark
That soul conjoinèd is with mind, and, when
'Tis strook by influence of the mind, forthwith
In turn it hits and drives the body too.

And this same argument establisheth
That nature of mind and soul corporeal is:
For when 'tis seen to drive the members on,
To snatch from sleep the body, and to change
The countenance, and the whole state of man
To rule and turn,—what yet could never be
Sans contact, and sans body contact fails—
Must we not grant that mind and soul consist
Of a corporeal nature?—And besides
Thou markst that likewise with this body of ours
Suffers the mind and with our body feels.
If the dire speed of spear that cleaves the bones
And bares the inner thews hits not the life,
Yet follows a fainting and a foul collapse,
And, on the ground, dazed tumult in the mind,
And whiles a wavering will to rise afoot.
So nature of mind must be corporeal, since
From stroke and spear corporeal 'tis in throes.

Now, of what body, what components formed
Is this same mind I will go on to tell.
First, I aver, 'tis superfine, composed
Of tiniest particles—that such the fact
Thou canst perceive, if thou attend, from this:
Nothing is seen to happen with such speed
As what the mind proposes and begins;
Therefore the same bestirs itself more swiftly
Then aught whose nature's palpable to eyes.
But what's so agile must of seeds consist
Most round, most tiny, that they may be moved,
When hit by impulse slight. So water moves,
In waves along, at impulse just the least—
Being create of littre shapes that roll;
But, contrariwise, the quality of honey
More stable is, its liquids more inert,
More tardy its flow; for all its stock of matter
Cleaves more together, since, indeed, 'tis made
Of atoms not so smooth, so fine, and round.
For the light breeze that hovers yet can blow
High heaps of poppy-seed away for thee
Downward from off the top; but, contrariwise,
A pile of stones or spiny ears of wheat
It can't at all. Thus, in so far as bodies
Are small and smooth, is their mobility;
But, contrariwise, the heavier and more rough,
The more immovable they prove. Now, then,
Since nature of mind is movable so much,
Consist it must of seeds exceeding small
And smooth and round. Which fact once known to thee,
Good friend, will serve thee opportune in else.
This also shows the nature of the same,
How nice its texture, in how small a space
'Twould go, if once compacted as a pellet:
When death's unvexed repose gets hold on man

And mind and soul retire, thou markest there
From the whole body nothing ta'en in form,
Nothing in weight. Death grants ye everything,
But vital sense and exhalation hot.
Thus soul entire must be of smallmost seeds,
Twined through the veins, the vitals, and the thews,
Seeing that, when 'tis from whole body gone,
The outward figuration of the limbs
Is unimpaired and weight fails not a whit.
Just so, when vanished the bouquet of wine,
Or when an unguent's perfume delicate
Into the winds away departs, or when
From any body savour's gone, yet still
The thing itself seems minished naught to eyes,
Thereby, nor aught abstracted from its weight—
No marvel, because seeds many and minute
Produce the savours and the redolence
In the whole body of the things. And so,
Again, again, nature of mind and soul
'Tis thine to know created is of seeds
The tiniest ever, since at flying-forth
It beareth nothing of the weight away.

　　Yet fancy not its nature simple so.
For an impalpable aura, mixed with heat,
Deserts the dying, and heat draws off the air;
And heat there's none, unless commixed with air:
For, since the nature of all heat is rare,
Athrough it many seeds of air must move.
Thus nature of mind is triple; yet those all
Suffice not for creating sense—since mind
Accepteth not that aught of these can cause
Sense-bearing motions, and much less the thoughts
A man revolves in mind. So unto these
Must added be a somewhat, and a fourth;
That somewhat's altogether void of name;

Than which existeth naught more mobile, naught
More an impalpable, of elements
More small and smooth and round. That first transmits
Sense-bearing motions through the frame, for that
Is roused the first, composed of little shapes;
Thence heat and viewless force of wind take up
The motions, and thence air, and thence all things
Are put in motion; the blood is strook, and then
The vitals all begin to feel, and last
To bones and marrow the sensation comes—
Pleasure or torment. Nor will pain for naught
Enter so far, nor a sharp ill seep through,
But all things be perturbed to that degree
That room for life will fail, and parts of soul
Will scatter through the body's every pore.
Yet as a rule, almost upon the skin
These motions all are stopped, and this is why
We have the power to retain our life.

Now in my eagerness to tell thee how
They are commixèd, through what unions fit
They function so, my country's pauper-speech
Constrains me sadly. As I can, however,
I'll touch some points and pass. In such a wise
Course these primordials 'mongst one another
With inter-motions that no one can be
From other sundered, nor its agency
Perform, if once divided by a space;
Like many powers in one body they work.
As in the flesh of any creature still
Is odour and savour and a certain warmth,
And yet from all these one bulk of body
Is made complete, so, viewless force of wind
And warmth and air, commingled, do create
One nature, by that mobile energy

Assisted which from out itself to them
Imparts initial motion, whereby first
Sense-bearing motion along the vitals springs.
For lurks this essence far and deep and under,
Nor in our body is aught more shut from view,
And 'tis the very soul of all the soul.
And as within our members and whole frame
The energy of mind and power of soul
Is mixed and latent, since create it is
Of bodies small and few, so lurks this fourth,
This essence void of name, composed of small,
And seems the very soul of all the soul,
And holds dominion o'er the body all.
And by like reason wind and air and heat
Must function so, commingled through the frame,
And now the one subside and now another
In interchange of dominance, that thus
From all of them one nature be produced,
Lest heat and wind apart, and air apart,
Make sense to perish, by disseverment.
There is indeed in mind that heat it gets
When seething in rage, and flashes from the eyes
More swiftly fire; there is, again, that wind,
Much, and so cold, companion of all dread,
Which rouses the shudder in the shaken frame;
There is no less that state of air composed,
Making the tranquil breast, the sérene face.
But more of hot have they whose restive hearts,
Whose minds of passion quickly seethe in rage—
Of which kind chief are fierce abounding lions,
Who often with roaring burst the breast o'erwrought,
Unable to hold the surging wrath within;
But the cold mind of stags has more of wind,
And speedier through their inwards rouses up
The icy currents which make their members quake.

But more the oxen live by tranquil air,
Nor e'er doth smoky torch of wrath applied,
O'erspreading with shadows of a darkling murk,
Rouse them too far; nor will they stiffen stark,
Pierced through by icy javelins of fear;
But have their place half-way between the two—
Stags and fierce lions. Thus the race of men:
Though training make them equally refined,
It leaves those pristine vestiges behind
Of each mind's nature. Nor may we suppose
Evil can e'er be rooted up so far
That one man's not more given to fits of wrath,
Another's not more quickly touched by fear,
A third not more long-suffering than he should.
And needs must differ in many things besides
The varied natures and resulting habits
Of humankind—of which not now can I
Expound the hidden causes, nor find names
Enough for all the divers shapes of those
Primordials whence this variation springs.
But this meseems I'm able to declare:
Those vestiges of natures left behind
Which reason cannot quite expel from us
Are still so slight that naught prevents a man
From living a life even worthy of the gods.

So then this soul is kept by all the body,
Itself the body's guard, and source of weal;
For they with common roots cleave each to each,
Nor can be torn asunder without death.
Not easy 'tis from lumps of frankincense
To tear their fragrance forth, without its nature
Perishing likewise: so, not easy 'tis
From all the body nature of mind and soul
To draw away, without the whole dissolved.

With seeds so intertwinèd even from birth,
They're dowered conjointly with a partner-life;
No energy of body or mind, apart,
Each of itself without the other's power,
Can have sensation; but our sense, enkindled
Along the vitals, to flame is blown by both
With mutual motions. Besides the body alone
Is nor begot nor grows, nor after death
Seen to endure. For not as water at times
Gives off the alien heat, nor is thereby
Itself destroyed, but unimpaired remains—
Not thus, I say, can the deserted frame
Bear the dissevering of its joinèd soul,
But, rent and ruined, moulders all away.
Thus the joint contact of the body and soul
Learn from their earliest age the vital motions,
Even when still buried in the mother's womb;
So no dissevering can hap to them,
Without their bane and ill. And thence mayst see
That, as conjoinèd is their source of weal,
Conjoinèd also must their nature be.

If one, moreover, denies that body feel,
And holds that soul, through all the body mixed,
Takes on this motion which we title "sense,"
He battles in vain indubitable facts:
For who'll explain what body's feeling is,
Except by what the public fact itself
Has given and taught us? "But when soul is parted,
Body's without all sense." True!—loses what
Was even in its life-time not its own
And much beside it loses, when soul's driven
Forth from that life-time. Or, to say that eyes
Themselves can see no thing, but through the same
The mind looks forth, as out of opened doors,

Is—a hard saying; since the feel in eyes
Says the reverse. For this itself draws on
And forces into the pupils of our eyes
Our consciousness. And note the case when often
We lack the power to see refulgent things,
Because our eyes are hampered by their light—
With a mere doorway this would happen not;
For, since it is our very selves that see,
No open portals undertake the toil.
Besides, if eyes of ours but act as doors,
Methinks that, were our sight removed, the mind
Ought then still better to behold a thing—
When even the door-posts have been cleared away.

Herein in these affairs nowise take up
What honoured sage, Democritus, lays down—
That proposition, that primordials
Of body and mind, each super-posed on each,
Vary alternately and interweave
The fabric of our members. For not only
Are the soul-elements smaller far than those
Which this our body and inward parts compose,
But also are they in their number less,
And scattered sparsely through our frame. And thus
This canst thou guarantee: soul's primal germs
Maintain between them intervals as large
At least as are the smallest bodies, which,
When thrown against us, in our body rouse
Sense-bearing motions. Hence it comes that we
Sometimes don't feel alighting on our frames
The clinging dust, or chalk that settles soft;
Nor mists of night, nor spider's gossamer
We feel against us, when, upon our road,
Its net entangles us, nor on our head
The dropping of its withered garmentings;

Nor bird-feathèrs, nor vegetable down,
Flying about, so light they barely fall;
Nor feel the steps of every crawling thing.
Nor each of all those footprints on our skin
Of midges and the like. To that degree
Must many primal germs be stirred in us
Ere once the seeds of soul that through our frame
Are intermingled 'gin to feel that those
Primordials of the body have been strook,
And ere, in pounding with such gaps between,
They clash, combine and leap apart in turn.

But mind is more the keeper of the gates,
Hath more dominion over life than soul.
For without intellect and mind there's not
One part of soul can rest within our frame
Least part of time; companioning, it goes
With mind into the winds away, and leaves
The icy members in the cold of death.
But he whose mind and intellect abide
Himself abides in life. However much
The trunk be mangled, with the limbs lopped off,
The soul withdrawn and taken from the limbs,
Still lives the trunk and draws the vital air.
Even when deprived of all but all the soul,
Yet will it linger on and cleave to life—
Just as the power of vision still is strong,
If but the pupil shall abide unharmed,
Even when the eye around it's sorely rent—
Provided only thou destroyest not
Wholly the ball, but, cutting round the pupil,
Leavest that pupil by itself behind—
For more would ruin sight. But if that centre,
That tiny part of eye, be eaten through,
Forthwith the vision fails and darkness comes,
Though in all else the unblemished ball be clear.

'Tis by like compact that the soul and mind
Are each to other bound forevermore.

Lines 94-416

THE SOUL IS MORTAL

Now come: that thou mayst able be to know
That minds and the light souls of all that live
Have mortal birth and death, I will go on
Verses to build meet for thy rule of life,
Sought after long, discovered with sweet toil.
But under one name I'd have thee yoke them both;
And when, for instance, I shall speak of soul,
Teaching the same to be but mortal, think
Thereby I'm speaking also of the mind—
Since both are one, a substance inter-joined.

First, then, since I have taught how soul exists
A subtle fabric, of particles minute,
Made up from atoms smaller much than those
Of water's liquid damp, or fog, or smoke,
So in mobility it far excels,
More prone to move, though strook by lighter cause
Even moved by images of smoke or fog—
As where we view, when in our sleeps we're lulled,
The altars exhaling steam and smoke aloft—
For, beyond doubt, these apparitions come
To us from outward. Now, then, since thou seest,
Their liquids depart, their waters flow away,
When jars are shivered, and since fog and smoke
Depart into the winds away, believe
The soul no less is shed abroad and dies
More quickly far, more quickly is dissolved
Back to its primal bodies, when withdrawn
From out man's members it has gone away.
For, sure, if body (container of the same

Like as a jar), when shivered from some cause,
And rarefied by loss of blood from veins,
Cannot for longer hold the soul, how then
Thinkest thou it can be held by any air—
A stuff much rarer than our bodies be?

Besides we feel that mind to being comes
Along with body, with body grows and ages.
For just as children totter round about
With frames infirm and tender, so there follows
A weakling wisdom in their minds; and then,
Where years have ripened into robust powers,
Counsel is also greater, more increased
The power of mind; thereafter, where already
The body's shattered by master-powers of eld,
And fallen the frame with its enfeebled powers,
Thought hobbles, tongue wanders, and the mind gives
        way;
All fails, all's lacking at the selfsame time.
Therefore it suits that even the soul's dissolved,
Like smoke, into the lofty winds of air;
Since we behold the same to being come
Along with body and grow, and, as I've taught,
Crumble and crack, therewith outworn by eld.
    Then, too, we see, that, just as body takes
Monstrous diseases and the dreadful pain,
So mind its bitter cares, the grief, the fear;
Wherefore it tallies that the mind no less
Partaker is of death; for pain and disease
Are both artificers of death—as well
We've learned by the passing of many a man ere now.
Nay, too, in diseases of body, often the mind
Wanders afield; for 'tis beside itself,
And crazed it speaks, or many a time it sinks,
With eyelids closing and a drooping nod,

In heavy drowse, on to eternal sleep;
From whence nor hears it any voices more,
Nor able is to know the faces here
Of those about him standing with wet cheeks
Who vainly call him back to light and life.
Wherefore mind too, confess we must, dissolves,
Seeing, indeed, contagions of disease
Enter into the same. Again, O why,
When the strong wine has entered into man,
And its diffusèd fire gone round the veins,
Why follows then a heaviness of limbs,
A tangle of the legs as round he reels,
A stuttering tongue, an intellect besoaked,
Eyes all aswim, and hiccups, shouts, and brawls
And whatso else is of that ilk?—Why this?—
If not that violent and impetous wine
Is wont to confound the soul within the body?
But whatso can confounded be and balked,
Gives proof, that if a hardier cause got in,
'Twould hap that it would perish then, bereaved
Of any life thereafter. And, moreover,
Often will some one in a sudden fit,
As if by stroke of lightening, tumble down
Before our eyes, and sputter foam, and grunt,
Blither, and twist about with sinews taut,
Gasp up in starts, and weary out his limbs
With tossing round. No marvel, since distract
Through frame by violence of disease . . .

.   .   .   .

Confounds, he foams, as if to vomit soul,
As on the salt sea boil the billows round
Under the master might of winds. And now
A groan's forced out, because his limbs are griped
But, in the main, because the seeds of voice

Are driven forth and carried in a mass
Outwards by mouth, where they are wont to go,
And have a builded highway. He becomes
Mere fool, since energy of mind and soul
Confounded is, and, as I've shown, to-riven,
Asunder thrown, and torn to pieces all
By the same venom. But, again, where cause
Of that disease has faced about, and back
Retreats sharp poison of corrupted frame
Into its shadowy lairs, the man at first
Arises reeling, and gradually comes back
To all his senses and recovers soul.
Thus, since within the body itself of man
The mind and soul are by such great diseases
Shaken, so miserably in labour distraught,
Why, then, believe that in the open air,
Without a body, they can pass their life,
Immortal, battling with the master winds?
And, since we mark the mind itself is cured,
Like the sick body, and restored can be
By medicine, this is forewarning too
That mortal lives the mind. For proper it is
That whosoe'er begins and undertakes
To alter the mind, or meditates to change
Any another nature soever, should add
New parts, or readjust the order given,
Or from the sum remove at least a bit.
But what's immortal willeth for itself
Its parts be nor increased, nor rearranged,
Nor any bit soever flow away:
For change of anything from out its bounds
Means instant death of that which was before.
Ergo, the mind, whether in sickness fallen,
Or by the medicine restored, gives signs,
As I have taught, of its mortality.

So surely will a fact of truth make head
'Gainst errors' theories all, and so shut off
All refuge from the adversary, and rout
Error by two-edged confutatiòn.

   And since the mind is of a man one part,
Which in one fixèd place remains, like ears,
And eyes, and every sense which pilots life;
And just as hand, or eye, or nose, apart,
Severed from us, can neither feel nor be,
But in the least of time is left to rot,
Thus mind alone can never be, without
The body and the man himself, which seems,
As 'twere the vessel of the same—or aught
Whate'er thou'lt feign as yet more closely joined:
Since body cleaves to mind by surest bonds.

   Again, the body's and the mind's live powers
Only in union prosper and enjoy;
For neither can nature of mind, alone of itself
Sans body, give the vital motions forth;
Nor, then, can body, wanting soul, endure
And use the senses. Verily, as the eye,
Alone, up-rended from its roots, apart
From all the body, can peer about at naught,
So soul and mind it seems are nothing able,
When by themselves. No marvel, because, commixed
Through veins and inwards, and through bones and
    thews,
Their elements primordial are confined
By all the body, and own no power free
To bound around through interspaces big,
Thus, shut within these confines, they take on
Motions of sense, which, after death, thrown out
Beyond the body to the winds of air,

Take on they cannot—and on this account,
Because no more in such a way confined.
For air will be a body, be alive,
If in that air the soul can keep itself,
And in that air enclose those motions all
Which in the thews and in the body itself
A while ago 'twas making. So for this,
Again, again, I say confess we must,
That, when the body's wrappings are unwound,
And when the vital breath is forced without,
The soul, the senses of the mind dissolve—
Since for the twain the cause and ground of life
Is in the fact of their conjoined estate.

Once more, since body's unable to sustain
Division from the soul, without decay
And obscene stench, how canst thou doubt but that
The soul, uprisen from the body's deeps,
Has filtered away, wide-drifted like a smoke,
Or that the changèd body crumbling fell
With ruin so entire, because, indeed,
Its deep foundations have been moved from place,
The soul out-filtering even through the frame,
And through the body's every winding way
And orifice? And so by many means
Thou'rt free to learn that nature of the soul
Hath passed in fragments out along the frame,
And that 'twas shivered in the very body
Ere ever it slipped abroad and swam away
Into the winds of air. For never a man
Dying appears to feel the soul go forth
As one sure whole from all his body at once,
Nor first come up the throat and into mouth;
But feels it failing in a certain spot,
Even as he knows the senses too dissolve

Each in its own location in the frame.
But were this mind of ours immortal mind,
Dying 'twould scarce bewail a dissolution,
But rather the going, the leaving of its coat,
Like to a snake. Wherefore, when once the body
Hath passed away, admit we must that soul,
Shivered in all that body, perished too.
Nay, even when moving in the bounds of life,
Often the soul, now tottering from some cause,
Craves to go out, and from the frame entire
Loosened to be; the countenance becomes
Flaccid, as if the súpreme hour were there;
And flabbily collapse the members all
Against the bloodless trunk—the kind of case
We see when we remark in common phrase,
"That man's quite gone," or "fainted dead away";
And where there's now a bustle of alarm,
And all eager to get some hold upon
The man's last link of life. For then the mind
And all the power of soul are shook so sore,
And these so totter along with all the frame,
That any cause a little stronger might
Dissolve them altogether.—Why, then, doubt
That soul, when once without the body thrust,
There in the open, an enfeebled thing,
Its wrappings stripped away, cannot endure
Not only through no everlasting age,
But even, indeed, through not the least of time?

Then, too, why never is the intellect,
The counselling mind, begotten in the head,
The feet, the hands, instead of cleaving still
To one sole seat, to one fixed haunt, the breast,
If not that fixèd places be assigned
For each thing's birth, where each, when 'tis create,
Is able to endure, and that our frames

Have such complex adjustments that no shift
In order of our members may appear?
To that degree effect succeeds to cause,
Nor is the flame once wont to be create
In flowing streams, nor cold begot in fire.

Besides, if nature of soul immortal be,
And able to feel, when from our frame disjoined,
The same, I fancy, must be thought to be
Endowed with senses five—nor is there way
But this whereby to image to ourselves
How under-souls may roam in Acheron.
Thus painters and the elder race of bards
Have pictured souls with senses so endowed.
But neither eyes, nor nose, nor hand, alone
Apart from body can exist for soul,
Nor tongue nor ears apart. And hence indeed
Alone by self they can nor feel nor be.

And since we mark the vital sense to be
In the whole body, all one living thing,
If of a sudden a force with rapid stroke
Should slice it down the middle and cleave in twain,
Beyond a doubt likewise the soul itself,
Divided, dissevered, asunder will be flung
Along with body. But what severed is
And into sundry parts divides, indeed
Admits it owns no everlasting nature.
We hear how chariots of war, areek
With hurly slaughter, lop with flashing scythes
The limbs away so suddenly that there,
Fallen from the trunk, they quiver on the earth,
The while the mind and powers of the man
Can feel no pain, for swiftness of his hurt,
And sheer abandon in the zest of battle:

With the remainder of his frame he seeks
Anew the battle and the slaughter, nor marks
How the swift wheels and scythes of ravin have dragged
Off with the horses his left arm and shield;
Nor other how his right has dropped away,
Mounting again and on. A third attempts
With leg dismembered to arise and stand,
Whilst, on the ground hard by, the dying foot
Twitches its spreading toes. And even the head,
When from the warm and living trunk lopped off,
Keeps on the ground the vital countenance
And open eyes, until 'thas rendered up
All remnants of the soul. Nay, once again:
If, when a serpent's darting forth its tongue,
And lashing its tail, thou gettest chance to hew
With axe its length of trunk to many parts,
Thou'lt see each severed fragment writhing round
With its fresh wound, and spattering up the sod,
And there the fore-part seeking with the jaws
After the hinder, with bite to stop the pain.
So shall we say that these be souls entire
In all those fractions?—but from that 'twould follow
One creature'd have in body many souls.
Therefore, the soul, which was indeed but one,
Has been divided with the body too:
Each is but mortal, since alike is each
Hewn into many parts. Again, how often
We view our fellow going by degrees,
And losing limb by limb the vital sense;
First nails and fingers of the feet turn blue,
Next die the feet and legs, then o'er the rest
Slow crawl the certain footsteps of cold death.
And since this nature of the soul is torn,
Nor mounts away, as at one time, entire,
We needs must hold it mortal. But perchance

If thou supposest that the soul itself
Can inward draw along the frame, and bring
Its parts together to one place, and so
From all the members draw the sense away,
Why, then, that place in which such stock of soul
Collected is, should greater seem in sense.
But since such place is nowhere, for a fact,
As said before, 'tis rent and scattered forth,
And so goes under. Or again, if now
I please to grant the false, and say that soul
Can thus be lumped within the frames of those
Who leave the sunshine, dying bit by bit,
Still must the soul as mortal be confessed;
Nor aught it matters whether to wrack it go,
Dispersed in the winds, or, gathered in a mass
From all its parts, sink down to brutish death,
Since more and more in every region sense
Fails the whole man, and less and less of life
In every region lingers.
                              And besides,
If soul immortal is, and winds its way
Into the body at the birth of man,
Why can we not remember something, then,
Of life-time spent before? why keep we not
Some footprints of the things we did of old?
But if so changed hath been the power of mind,
That every recollection of things done
Is fallen away, at no o'erlong remove
Is that, I trow, from what we mean by death.
Wherefore 'tis sure that what hath been before
Hath died, and what now is is now create.

Moreover, if after the body hath been built
Our mind's live powers are wont to be put in,
Just at the moment that we come to birth,
And cross the sills of life, 'twould scarcely fit

For them to live as if they seem to grow
Along with limbs and frame, even in the blood,
But rather as in a cavern all alone.
(Yet all the body duly throngs with sense.)
But public fact declares against all this:
For soul is so entwinèd through the veins,
The flesh, the thews, the bones, that even the teeth
Share in sensation, as proven by dull ache,
By twinge from icy water, or grating crunch
Upon a stone that got in mouth with bread.
Wherefore, again, again, souls must be thought
Nor void of birth, nor free from law of death;
Nor, if, from outward, in they wound their way,
Could they be thought as able so to cleave
To these our frames, nor, since so interwove,
Appears it that they're able to go forth
Unhurt and whole and loose themselves unscathed
From all the thews, articulations, bones.
But, if perchance thou thinkest that the soul,
From outward winding in its way, is wont
To seep and soak along these members ours,
Then all the more 'twill perish, being thus
With body fused—for what will seep and soak
Will be dissolvèd and will therefore die.
For just as food, dispersed through all the pores
Of body, and passed through limbs and all the frame,
Perishes, supplying from itself the stuff
For other nature, thus the soul and mind,
Though whole and new into a body going,
Are yet, by seeping in, dissolved away,
Whilst, as through pores, to all the frame there pass
Those particles from which created is
This nature of mind, now ruler of our body,
Born from that soul which perished, when divided
Along the frame. Wherefore it seems that soul

Hath both a natal and a funeral hour.

   Besides are seeds of soul there left behind
In the breathless body, or not? If there they are,
It cannot justly be immortal deemed,
Since, shorn of some parts lost, 'thas gone away:
But if, borne off with members uncorrupt,
'Thas fled so absolutely all away
It leaves not one remainder of itself
Behind in body, whence do cadavers, then,
From out their putrid flesh exhale the worms,
And whence does such a mass of living things,
Boneless and bloodless, o'er the bloated frame
Bubble and swarm? But if perchance thou thinkest
That souls from outward into worms can wind,
And each into a separate body come,
And reckonest not why many thousand souls
Collect where only one has gone away,
Here is a point, in sooth, that seems to need
Inquiry and a putting to the test:
Whether the souls go on a hunt for seeds
Of worms wherewith to build their dwelling places,
Or enter bodies ready-made, as 'twere.
But why themselves they thus should do and toil
'Tis hard to say, since, being free of body,
They flit around, harassed by no disease,
Nor cold nor famine; for the body labours
By more of kinship to these flaws of life,
And mind by contact with that body suffers
So many ills. But grant it be for them
However useful to construct a body
To which to enter in, 'tis plain they can't.
Then, souls for self no frames nor bodies make,
Nor is there how they once might enter in
To bodies ready-made—for they cannot
Be nicely interwoven with the same,

And there'll be formed no interplay of sense
Common to each.

               Again, why is't there goes
Impetuous rage with lion's breed morose,
And cunning with foxes, and to deer why given
The ancestral fear and tendency to flee,
And why in short do all the rest of traits
Engender from the very start of life
In the members and mentality, if not
Because one certain power of mind that came
From its own seed and breed waxes the same
Along with all the body? But were mind
Immortal, were it wont to change its bodies,
How topsy-turvy would earth's creatures act!
The Hyrcan hound would flee the onset oft
Of antlered stag, the scurrying hawk would quake
Along the winds of air at the coming dove,
And men would dote, and savage beasts be wise;
For false the reasoning of those that say
Immortal mind is changed by change of body—
For what is changed dissolves, and therefore dies.
For parts are re-disposed and leave their order;
Wherefore they must be also capable
Of dissolution through the frame at last,
That they along with body perish all.
But should some say that always souls of men
Go into human bodies, I will ask:
How can a wise become a dullard soul?
And why is never a child's a prudent soul?
And the mare's filly why not trained so well
As study strength of steed? We may be sure
They'll take their refuge in the thought that mind
Becomes a weakling in a weakling frame.
Yet be this so, 'tis needful to confess
The soul but mortal, since, so altered now

Throughout the frame, it loses the life and sense
It had before. Or how can mind wax strong
Coequally with body and attain
The cravèd flower of life, unless it be
The body's colleague in its origins?
Or what's the purport of its going forth
From agèd limbs?—fears it, perhaps, to stay,
Pent in a crumbled body? Or lest its house,
Outworn by venerable length of days,
May topple down upon it? But indeed
For an immortal perils are there none.

    Again, at parturitions of the wild
And at the rites of Love, that souls should stand
Ready hard by seems ludicrous enough—
Immortals waiting for their mortal limbs
In numbers innumerable, contending madly
Which shall be first and chief to enter in!—
Unless perchance among the souls there be
Such treaties stablished that the first to come
Flying along, shall enter in the first,
And that they make no rivalries of strength!

    Again, in ether can't exist a tree,
Nor clouds in ocean deeps, nor in the fields
Can fishes live, nor blood in timber be,
Nor sap in boulders: fixèd and arranged
Where everything may grow and have its place.
Thus nature of mind cannot arise alone
Without the body, nor exist afar
From thews and blood. But if 'twere possible,
Much rather might this very power of mind
Be in the head, the shoulders or the heels,
And, born in any part soever, yet
In the same man, in the same vessel abide.

But since within this body even of ours
Stands fixèd and appears arrangèd sure
Where soul and mind can each exist and grow,
Deny we must the more that they can have
Duration and birth, wholly outside the frame.
For, verily, the mortal to conjoin
With the eternal, and to feign they feel
Together, and can function each with each,
Is but to dote: for what can be conceived
Of more unlike, discrepant, ill-assorted,
Than something mortal in a union joined
With an immortal and a secular
To bear the outrageous tempests?

                              Then, again,
Whatever abides eternal must indeed
Either repel all strokes, because 'tis made
Of solid body, and permit no entrance
Of aught with power to sunder from within
The parts compact—as are those seeds of stuff
Whose nature we've exhibited before;
Or else be able to endure through time
For this: because they are from blows exempt,
As is the void, the which abides untouched,
Unsmit by any stroke; or else because
There is no room around, whereto things can,
As 'twere, depart in dissolution all—
Even as the sum of sums eternal is,
Without or place beyond whereto things may
Asunder fly, or bodies which can smite,
And thus dissolve them by the blows of might.

  But if perchance the soul's to be adjudged
Immortal, mainly on ground 'tis kept secure
In vital forces—either because there come
Never at all things hostile to its weal,

Or else because what come somehow retire,
Repelled or ere we feel the harm they work,

.   .   .   .

For, lo, besides that, when the frame's diseased,
Soul sickens too, there cometh, many a time,
That which torments it with the things to be,
Keeps it in dread, and wearies it with cares;
And even when evil acts are of the past,
Still gnaw the old transgressions bitterly.
Add, too, that frenzy, peculiar to the mind,
And that oblivion of the things that were;
Add its submergence in the murky waves
Of drowse and torpor.

Lines 417-827

FOLLY OF THE FEAR OF DEATH

Therefore death to us
Is nothing, nor concerns us in the least,
Since nature of mind is mortal evermore.
And just as in the ages gone before
We felt no touch of ill, when all sides round
To battle came the Carthaginian host,
And the times, shaken by tumultuous war,
Under the aery coasts of arching heaven
Shuddered and trembled, and all humankind
Doubted to which the empery should fall
By land and sea, thus when we are no more,
When comes that sundering of our body and soul
Through which we're fashioned to a single state,
Verily naught to us, us then no more,
Can come to pass, naught move our senses then—
No, not if earth confounded were with sea,
And sea with heaven. But if indeed do feel
The nature of mind and energy of soul,

After their severance from this body of ours,
Yet nothing 'tis to us who in the bonds
And wedlock of the soul and body live,
Through which we're fashioned to a single state.
And, even if time collected after death
The matter of our frames and set it all
Again in place as now, and if again
To us the light of life were given, O yet
That process too would not concern us aught,
When once the self-succession of our sense
Has been asunder broken. And now and here,
Little enough we're busied with the selves
We were aforetime, nor, concerning them,
Suffer a sore distress. For shouldst thou gaze
Backwards across all yesterdays of time
The immeasurable, thinking how manifold
The motions of matter are, then couldst thou well
Credit this too: often these very seeds
(From which we are to-day) of old were set
In the same order as they are today—
Yet this we can't to consciousness recall
Through the remembering mind. For there hath been
An interposèd pause of life, and wide
Have all the motions wandered everywhere
From these our senses. For if woe and ail
Perchance are toward, then the man to whom
The bane can happen must himself be there
At that same time. But death precludeth this,
Forbidding life to him on whom might crowd
Such irk and care; and granted 'tis to know:
Nothing for us there is to dread in death,
No wretchedness for him who is no more,
The same estate as if ne'er born before,
When death immortal hath ta'en the mortal life.

  Hence, where thou seest a man to grieve because

When dead he rots with body laid away,
Or perishes in flames or jaws of beasts,
Know well: he rings not true, and that beneath
Still works an unseen sting upon his heart,
However he deny that he believes
His shall be aught of feeling after death.
For he, I fancy, grants not what he says,
Nor what that presupposes, and he fails
To pluck himself with all his roots from life
And cast that self away, quite unawares
Feigning that some remainder's left behind.
For when in life one pictures to oneself
His body dead by beasts and vultures torn,
He pities his state, dividing not himself
Therefrom, removing not the self enough
From the body flung away, imagining
Himself that body, and projecting there
His own sense, as he stands beside it: hence
He grieves that he is mortal born, nor marks
That in true death there is no second self
Alive and able to sorrow for self destroyed,
Or stand lamenting that the self lies there
Mangled or burning. For if it an evil is
Dead to be jerked about by jaw and fang
Of the wild brutes, I see not why 'twere not
Bitter to lie on fires and roast in flames,
Or suffocate in honey, and, reclined
On the smooth oblong of an icy slab,
Grow stiff in cold, or sink with load of earth
Down-crushing from above.

"Thee now no more
The joyful house and best of wives shall welcome,
Nor little sons run up to snatch their kisses
And touch with silent happiness thy heart.
Thou shalt not speed in undertakings more,

Nor be the warder of thine own no more.
Poor wretch," they say, "one hostile hour hath ta'en
Wretchedly from thee all life's many guerdons,"
But add not, "yet no longer unto thee
Remains a remnant of desire for them."
If this they only well perceived with mind
And followed up with maxims, they would free
Their state of man from anguish and from fear.
"O even as here thou art, aslumber in death,
So shalt thou slumber down the rest of time,
Released from every harrying pang. But we,
We have bewept thee with insatiate woe,
Standing beside whilst on the awful pyre
Thou wert made ashes; and no day shall take
For us the eternal sorrow from the breast."
But ask the mourner what's the bitterness
That man should waste in an eternal grief,
If, after all, the thing's but sleep and rest?
For when the soul and frame together are sunk
In slumber, no one then demands his self
Or being. Well, this sleep may be forever,
Without desire of any selfhood more,
For all it matters unto us asleep.
Yet not at all do those primordial germs
Roam round our members, at that time, afar
From their own motions that produce our senses—
Since, when he's startled from his sleep, a man
Collects his senses. Death is, then, to us
Much less—if there can be a less than that
Which is itself a nothing: for there comes
Hard upon death a scattering more great
Of the throng of matter, and no man wakes up
On whom once falls the icy pause of life.
  This too, O often from the soul men say,
Along their couches holding of the cups,

With faces shaded by fresh wreaths awry:
"Brief is this fruit of joy to paltry man,
Soon, soon departed, and thereafter, no,
It may not be recalled."—As if, forsooth,
It were their prime of evils in great death
To parch, poor tongues, with thirst and arid drought,
Or chafe for any lack.

      Once more, if Nature
Should of a sudden send a voice abroad,
And her own self inveigh against us so:
"Mortal, what hast thou of such grave concern
That thou indulgest in too sickly plaints?
Why this bemoaning and beweeping death?
For if thy life aforetime and behind
To thee was grateful, and not all thy good
Was heaped as in sieve to flow away
And perish unavailingly, why not,
Even like a banqueter, depart the halls,
Laden with life? why not with mind content
Take now, thou fool, thy unafflicted rest?
But if whatever thou enjoyed hath been
Lavished and lost, and life is now offence,
Why seekest more to add—which in its turn
Will perish foully and fall out in vain?
O why not rather make an end of life,
Of labour? For all I may devise or find
To pleasure thee is nothing: all things are
The same forever. Though not yet thy body
Wrinkles with years, nor yet the frame exhausts
Outworn, still things abide the same, even if
Thou goest on to conquer all of time
With length of days, yea, if thou never diest"—
What were our answer, but that Nature here
Urges just suit and in her words lays down
True cause of action? Yet should one complain,

Riper in years and elder, and lament,
Poor devil, his death more sorely than is fit,
Then would she not, with greater right, on him
Cry out, inveighing with a voice more shrill:
"Off with thy tears, and choke thy whines, buffoon!
Thou wrinklest—after thou hast had the sum
Of the guerdons of life; yet, since thou cravest ever
What's not at hand, contemning present good,
That life has slipped away, unperfected
And unavailing unto thee. And now,
Or ere thou guessed it, death beside thy head
Stands—and before thou canst be going home
Sated and laden with the goodly feast.
But now yield all that's alien to thine age—
Up, with good grace! make room for sons: thou must."
Justly, I fancy, would she reason thus,
Justly inveigh and gird: since ever the old
Outcrowded by the new gives way, and ever
The one thing from the others is repaired.
Nor no man is consigned to the abyss
Of Tartarus, the black. For stuff must be,
That thus the after-generations grow—
Though these, their life completed, follow thee;
And thus like thee are generations all—
Already fallen, or some time to fall.
So one thing from another rises ever;
And in fee-simple life is given to none,
But unto all mere usufruct.

        Look back:
Nothing to us was all fore-passèd eld
Of time the eternal, ere we had a birth.
And nature holds this like a mirror up
Of time-to-be when we are dead and gone.
And what is there so horrible appears?
Now what is there so sad about it all?

Is't not serener far than any sleep?
    And, verily, those tortures said to be
In Acheron, the deep, they all are ours
Here in this life. No Tantalus, benumbed
With baseless terror, as the fables tell,
Fears the huge boulder hanging in the air:
But, rather, in life an empty dread of Gods
Urges mortality, and each one fears
Such fall of fortune as may chance to him.
Nor eat the vultures into Tityus
Prostrate in Acheron, nor can they find,
Forsooth, throughout eternal ages, aught
To pry around for in that mighty breast.
However hugely he extend his bulk—
Who hath for outspread limbs not acres nine,
But the whole earth—he shall not able be
To bear eternal pain nor furnish food
From his own frame forever. But for us
A Tityus is he whom vultures rend
Prostrate in love, whom anxious anguish eats,
Whom troubles of any unappeased desires
Asunder rip. We have before our eyes
Here in this life also a Sisyphus
In him who seeketh of the populace
The rods, the axes fell, and evermore
Retires a beaten and a gloomy man.
For to seek after power—an empty name,
Nor given at all—and ever in the search
To endure a world of toil, O this it is
To shove with shoulder up the hill a stone
Which yet comes rolling back from off the top,
And headlong makes for levels of the plain.
Then to be always feeding an ingrate mind,
Filling with good things, satisfying never—
As do the seasons of the year for us,

When they return and bring their progenies
And varied charms, and we are never filled
With the fruits of life—O this, I fancy, 'tis
To pour, like those young virgins in the tale,
Waters into a sieve, unfilled forever.

.   .   .   .

Cerberus and Furies, and that Lack of Light

.   .   .   .

Tartarus, out-belching from his mouth the surge
Of horrible heat—the which are nowhere, nor
Indeed can be: but in this life is fear
Of retributions just and expiations
For evil acts: the dungeon and the leap
From that dread rock of infamy, the stripes,
The executioners, the oaken rack,
The iron plates, bitumen, and the torch.
And even though these are absent, yet the mind,
With a fore-fearing conscience, plies its goads
And burns beneath the lash, nor sees meanwhile
What terminus of ills, what end of pine
Can ever be, and feareth lest the same
But grow more heavy after death. Of truth,
The life of fools is Acheron on earth.
   This also to thy very self sometimes
Repeat thou mayst: "Lo, even good Ancus left
The sunshine with his eyes, in divers things
A better man than thou, O worthless hind;
And many other kings and lords of rule
Thereafter have gone under, once who swayed
O'er mighty peoples. And he also, he—
Who whilom paved a highway down the sea,
And gave his legionaries thoroughfare
Along the deep, and taught them how to cross

The pools of brine afoot, and did contemn,
Trampling upon it with his cavalry,
The bellowings of ocean—poured his soul
From dying body, as his light was ta'en.
And Scipio's son, the thunderbolt of war,
Horror of Carthage, gave his bones to earth,
Like to the lowliest villein in the house.
Add finders-out of sciences and arts;
Add comrades of the Heliconian dames,
Among whom Homer, sceptered o'er them all,
Now lies in slumber sunken with the rest.
Then, too, Democritus, when ripened eld
Admonished him his memory waned away,
Of own accord offered his head to death.
Even Epicurus went, his light of life
Run out, the man in genius who o'er-topped
The human race, extinguishing all others,
As sun, in ether arisen, all the stars.
Wilt thou, then, dally, thou complain to go?—
For whom already life's as good as dead,
Whilst yet thou livest and lookest?—who in sleep
Wastest thy life—time's major part, and snorest
Even when awake, and ceasest not to see
The stuff of dreams, and bearest a mind beset
By baseless terror, nor discoverest oft
What's wrong with thee, when, like a sotted wretch,
Thou'rt jostled along by many crowding cares,
And wanderest reeling round, with mind aswim."
     If men, in that same way as on the mind
They *feel* the load that wearies with its weight,
Could also *know* the causes whence it comes,
And why so great the heap of ill on heart,
O not in this sort would they live their life,
As now so much we see them, knowing not
What 'tis they want, and seeking ever and ever

A change of place, as if to drop the burden.
The man who sickens of his home goes out,
Forth from his splendid halls, and straight—returns,
Feeling i'faith no better off abroad.
He races, driving his Gallic ponies along,
Down to his villa, madly—as in haste
To hurry help to a house afire.—At once
He yawns, as soon as foot has touched the threshold,
Or drowsily goes off in sleep and seeks
Forgetfulness, or maybe bustles about
And makes for town again. In such a way
Each human flees himself—a self in sooth,
As happens, he by no means can escape;
And willy-nilly he cleaves to it and loathes,
Sick, sick, and guessing not the cause of ail.
Yet should he see but *that*, O chiefly then,
Leaving all else, he'd study to divine
The nature of things, since here is in debate
Eternal time and not the single hour,
Mortal's estate in whatsoever remains
After great death.

               And too, when all is said,
What evil lust of life is this so great
Subdues us to live, so dreadfully distraught
In perils and alarms? one fixèd end
Of life abideth for mortality;
Death's not to shun, and we must go to meet.
Besides we're busied with the same devices,
Ever and ever, and we are at them ever,
And there's no new delight that may be forged
By living on. But whilst the thing we long for
Is lacking, that seems good above all else;
Thereafter, when we've touched it, something else
We long for; ever one equal thirst of life
Grips us agape. And doubtful 'tis what fortune

The future times may carry, or what be
That chance may bring, or what the issue next
Awaiting us. Nor by prolonging life
Take we the least away from death's own time,
Nor can we pluck one moment off, whereby
To minish the aeons of our state of death.
Therefore, O man, by living on, fulfil
As many generations as thou may:
Eternal death shall there be waiting still;
And he who died with light of yesterday
Shall be no briefer time in death's No-more
Than he who perished months or years before.

Lines 828-1092

✦✦✦✻✦✦✦

CAESAR

(Gaius Julius Cæsar, 100? B.C.–44 B.C.}

✻

From The Gallic War

Translated by H. J. Edwards

✻

The First Expedition to Britain

ONLY a small part of the summer was left, and in
these regions, as all Gaul has a northerly aspect,
the winters are early; but for all this Cæsar was intent
upon starting for Britain. He understood that in almost
all the Gallic campaigns succours had been furnished for
our enemy from that quarter; and he supposed that if
the season left no time for actual campaigning, it would
still be of great advantage to him merely to have
entered the island, observed the character of the natives,
and obtained some knowledge of the localities, the har-
bours, and the landing-places; for almost all these mat-
ters were unknown to the Gauls. In fact, nobody except
traders journeys thither without good cause; and even
traders know nothing except the sea-coast and the dis-
tricts opposite Gaul. Therefore, although he summoned
to his quarters traders from all parts, he could discover
neither the size of the island, nor the number or the
strength of the tribes inhabiting it, nor their manner of
warfare, nor the ordinances they observed, nor the har-
bours suitable for a number of large ships.

213

To gain such knowledge before he made the venture, Cæsar thought Gaius Volusenus a proper person to send on in advance with a ship of war. His orders were to spy out everything and to return to him at once. He himself with all his forces started for the territory of the Morini, from which was the shortest passage across to Britain. He commanded the general concentration here of ships from the neighbouring districts, and of the fleet which he had built in the previous summer for the Venetian campaign. Meanwhile his purpose had become known and had been reported through traders to the Britons, and deputies came to him from several states in the island with promises to give hostages and to accept the empire of Rome. He heard them, and made them a generous promise, encouraging them to keep their word; then he sent them back home, and along with them he sent Commius, whom he himself, after subduing the Atrebates, had made king over them. Cæsar approved his courage and discretion, and believed him loyal to himself; and his influence was reckoned to be of great account in those parts. Him he commanded to visit what states he could, to exhort them to seek the protection of Rome, and to announce his own speedy advent thither. Volusenus observed all the country so far as was possible for an officer who did not dare to disembark and entrust himself to the rough natives, and on the fifth day returned to Cæsar, and reported his observations in Britain.

While Cæsar tarried where he was to fit out his ships, deputies came to him from a great part of the Morini to make excuse for their policy of the previous season, when in their barbarism and ignorance of our usage they had made war against Rome, and to promise that they would carry out his commands. Cæsar thought this overture exceedingly opportune. He did not wish to leave an enemy in his rear, nor had he a chance of carrying out a campaign because of the lateness of the season; nor did he think the settlement of such trivialities should take precedence of Britain. He therefore ordered them to furnish a large number of hostages; and when they brought these he received them under his protection. When about eight transports—enough, in his opinion, to carry two legions across—had been collected and concentrated, he distributed all the ships of war he had over between his quartermaster-general, lieutenant-generals, and commandants. To the total stated eighteen transports should be added, which were detained eight miles off by the wind, and prevented from entering the port of concentration; these he allotted to the cavalry. The rest of the army he handed over to Quintus Titurius Sabinus and Lucius Aurunculeius Cotta, lieutenant-generals, to be led against the Menapii and against those cantons of the Morini from which no deputies had come to him. He commanded Publius Sulpicius Rufus, lieutenant-general, with a garrison he considered sufficient, to hold the port.

These arrangements made, he caught a spell of fair weather for sailing, and weighed anchor about the third watch: he ordered the cavalry to proceed to the further harbour, embark, and follow him. They took somewhat too long to despatch the business; he himself reached Britain about the fourth hour of the day, and there beheld the armed forces of the enemy displayed on all the cliffs. Such was the nature of the ground, so steep the heights which banked the sea, that a missile could be hurled from the higher levels on to the shore. Thinking this place to be by no means suitable for disembarkation, he waited at anchor till the ninth hour for the rest of the flotilla to assemble there. Meanwhile he summoned together the lieutenant-generals and tribunes, to inform them what he had learnt from Volusenus, and what he wished to be done; and he warned them that, to meet the requirements of tactics and particularly of navigation —with its liability to movements as rapid as they were irregular—they must do everything in the nick of time at a hint from him. He then dismissed them; and catching at one and the same moment a favourable wind and tide, he gave the signal, and weighed anchor, and moving on about seven miles from that spot, he grounded his ships where the shore was even and open.

The natives, however, perceived the design of the Romans. So they sent forward their cavalry and charioteers—an arm which it is their regular custom to employ in fights—and following up with the rest of their forces, they sought to prevent our troops from disembarking. Disembarkation was a matter of extreme difficulty, for the following reasons. The ships, on account of their size, could not be run ashore, except in deep water; the troops—though they did not know the ground, had not their hands free, and were loaded with the great and grievous weight of their arms—had nevertheless at one and the same time to leap down from the vessels, to stand firm in the waves, and to fight the enemy. The enemy, on the other hand, had all their limbs free, and knew the ground exceedingly well; and either standing on dry land or advancing a little way into the water, they boldly hurled their missiles, or spurred on their horses, which were trained to it. Frightened by all this, and wholly inexperienced in this sort of fighting, our troops did not press on with the same fire and force as they were accustomed to show in land engagements.

When Cæsar remarked this, he commanded the ships of war (which were less familiar in appearance to the natives, and could move more freely at need) to remove a little from the transports, to row at speed, and to bring up on the exposed flank of the enemy; and thence to drive and clear them off with slings, arrows, and artillery. This movement proved of great service to our troops; for the natives, frightened by the shape of the ships, the motion of the oars, and the unfamiliar type of the artillery, came to a halt, and retired, but only for a little space. And then, while our troops still hung back, chiefly on account of the depth of the sea, the eagle-bearer of the Tenth Legion, after a prayer to heaven to bless the legion by his act, cried: "Leap down, soldiers, unless you wish to betray your eagle to the enemy; it shall be told that I at any rate did my duty to my country and my general." When he had said this with a loud voice, he cast himself forth from the ship, and began to bear the eagle against the enemy. Then our troops exhorted one another not to allow so dire a disgrace, and leapt down from the ship with one accord. And when the troops on the nearest ships saw them, they likewise followed on, and drew near to the enemy.

The fighting was fierce on both sides. Our troops, however, because they could not keep rank, nor stand firm, nor follow their proper standards—for any man from any ship attached himself to whatever standard he chanced upon—were in considerable disorder. But the enemy knew all the shallows, and as soon as they had observed from the shore a party of soldiers disembarking one by one from a ship, they spurred on their horses and attacked them while they were in difficulties, many surrounding few, while others hurled missiles into a whole party from the exposed flank. Cæsar noticed this; and causing the boats of the warships, and likewise the scout-vessels, to be manned with soldiers, he sent them to support any parties whom he had observed to be in distress. The moment our men stood firm on dry land, they charged with all their comrades close behind, and put the enemy to rout; but they could not pursue very far, because the cavalry had not been able to hold on their course and make the island. This one thing was lacking to complete the wonted success of Cæsar.

So the enemy were overcome in the fight; and as soon as they had recovered from the rout they at once sent deputies to Cæsar to treat for peace, promising that they would give hostages and do what he commanded. Together with these deputies came Commius the Atrebatian, who, as shown above, had been sent forward by Cæsar into Britain. When Commius disembarked and delivered Cæsar's messages to the Britons in the character of an ambassador, they had seized him and thrown him into chains; but now, after the fight, they sent him back. In their entreaty for peace they cast the blame of the misdeed upon the multitude, and sought pardon in consideration of their ignorance. Cæsar complained that though of their own motion they had sent deputies on to the Continent to seek peace from him, they had now begun war on him without cause; but he agreed to pardon their ignorance, and required hostages. Part of these they gave at once, part they said they would summon from the more distant parts and give in a few days. Meanwhile they ordered their own folk to get back to their fields; and the chiefs began to assemble from every quarter, and to deliver themselves and their states to Cæsar.

Peace was thus established. Four days after the arrival in Britain the eighteen ships above mentioned, which had embarked the cavalry, weighed anchor, in a gentle breeze, from the upper port. When they were nearing Britain, and in view of the camp, so fierce a storm suddenly arose that none of them could hold on its course; some were carried back to the selfsame port whence they had started, others were driven away, with great

peril to themselves, to the lower, that is, to the more
westerly, part of the island. None the less, they cast
anchor; but when they began to fill with the waves they
were obliged to stand out to sea in a night of foul
weather, and made for the Continent.

That same night, as it chanced, the moon was full,
the day of the month which usually makes the highest
tides in the Ocean, a fact unknown to our men. There-
fore the tide was found to have filled the warships, in
which Cæsar had caused his army to be conveyed
across, and which he had drawn up on dry land; and
at the same time the storm was buffeting the trans-
ports, which were made fast to anchors. Nor had our
troops any chance of handling them or helping. Several
ships went to pieces; and the others, by loss of cordage,
anchors, and the rest of their tackle, were rendered
useless for sailing. This, as was inevitable, caused great
dismay throughout the army. For there were no other
ships to carry them back; everything needful for the
repair of ships was lacking; and, as it was generally
understood that the army was to winter in Gaul, no corn
had been provided in these parts against the winter.

When they became aware of this, the British chiefs
who had assembled at Cæsar's headquarters after the
fight took counsel together. As they knew that the
Romans lacked cavalry, ships, and corn, and perceived
the scantiness of the army from the smallness of the
camp (it was straitened even more by the fact that
Cæsar had brought the legions over without baggage),
they thought that the best thing to do was to renew the
war, cut off our corn and other supplies, and prolong
the business into the winter; for they were confident
that when the present force was overcome or cut off
from return no one thereafter would cross over into
Britain to make war upon them. Therefore they con-

spired together anew, and departing a few at a time from the camp, they began secretly to draw in their followers from the fields.

Although Cæsar had not yet learnt their designs, yet the misfortune of his ships and the fact that the chiefs had broken off the surrender of hostages led him to suspect that events would turn out as they did; and therefore he prepared means to meet any emergency. He collected corn daily from the fields into the camp, and he utilised the timber and bronze of the ships which had been most severely damaged to repair the rest, and ordered the necessary gear for that purpose to be brought from the Continent. The work was most zealously carried out by the troops; and thus, though twelve ships had been lost, he was able to render the rest tolerably seaworthy.

Meanwhile one legion, called the Seventh, had been sent as usual to collect corn; nor as yet had any suspicion of hostilities intervened, since part of the people remained in the fields, and part were actually frequent visitors to the camp. Then the outposts on duty before the gates of the camp reported to Cæsar that a greater dust than usual was to be seen in that quarter to which the legion had marched. Cæsar suspected the truth—that some fresh design had been started by the natives—and ordered the cohorts which were on outpost to proceed with him to the quarter in question, two of the others to relieve them on outpost, and the rest to arm and follow him immediately. When he had advanced some little way from the camp, he found that his troops were being hard pressed by the enemy and were holding their ground with difficulty: the legion was crowded together, while missiles were being hurled from all sides. The fact was that when the corn had been cut from the rest of the neighbourhood one part remained, and the enemy, supposing that our troops would come hither, had hidden by night in the woods; then, when the men were scattered and, having grounded arms, were engaged in cutting corn, they had suddenly attacked them. They had killed a few, throwing the rest into confusion before they could form up, and at the same time surrounding them with horsemen and chariots.

Their manner of fighting from chariots is as follows. First of all they drive in all directions and hurl missiles, and so by the mere terror that the teams inspire and by the noise of the wheels they generally throw ranks into confusion. When they have worked their way in between the troops of cavalry, they leap down from the chariots and fight on foot. Meanwhile the charioteers retire gradually from the combat, and dispose the chariots in such fashion that, if the warriors are hard pressed by the host of the enemy, they may have a ready means of retirement to their own side. Thus they show in action the mobility of cavalry and the stability of infantry; and by daily use and practice they become so accomplished that they are ready to gallop their teams down the steepest of slopes without loss of control, to check and turn them in a moment, to run along the pole, stand on the yoke, and then, quick as lightning, to dart back into the chariot.

When our troops were thrown into confusion in this fashion by the novel character of the fighting, Cæsar brought assistance in the very nick of time; for his arrival caused the enemy to halt, and enabled our men to recover from their fear. This done, he deemed the moment unsuitable for provoking and engaging in a combat; he therefore stood to his own ground and, after a brief interval, led the legions back to camp. In the course of these events all our troops were busily occupied, and the natives who remained in the fields withdrew. Then for several days on end storms ensued, severe enough to keep our men in camp and to prevent the enemy from fighting. Meanwhile the natives despatched messengers in every direction, to tell of the scanty numbers of our troops and to show how great a chance was given of getting booty and of liberating themselves for ever by driving the Romans out of their camp. By this means they speedily collected a great host of footmen and horsemen, and came on towards the camp.

Cæsar saw that the result would be the same as on the previous days—that the enemy, if repulsed, would use their speed to escape from danger; nevertheless, as he had got about thirty horsemen, whom Commius, the Atrebatian before mentioned, had brought over with him, he formed the legions in line before the camp. When battle was joined the enemy, unable to endure for long the attack of our troops, turned and fled. The Romans followed after, as far as their speed and strength enabled, and slew not a few of them; then, after setting on fire all buildings far and wide, they retired to camp.

On the same day deputies sent by the enemy came to Cæsar to treat of peace. For them Cæsar doubled the number of hostages previously commanded, and ordered them to be brought to the Continent, because the equinox was close at hand, and with a damaged flotilla he did not think it right to subject his crossing to the hazard of winter storms. He himself, taking advantage of a spell of fair weather, weighed anchor a little after midnight, and all the ships came safe to the Continent; but two of the transports were unable to make the same port as the rest, and were carried a little lower down the coast.

When about three hundred men had been landed from these vessels and were marching rapidly to camp, the Morini, who had been left by Cæsar in a state of peace when he set out for Britain, were fired by the hope of booty, and surrounded the troops, at first with no very large number of their own folk, bidding them lay down their arms if they did not wish to be killed. The Romans formed square and defended themselves, and at the noise of shouting some six thousand men speedily came about them. Upon report of this Cæsar sent the whole of the cavalry from the camp to assist his men. Meanwhile our troops withstood the enemy's assault, and fought with the greatest gallantry for more than four hours: they received but a few wounds, and slew a good many of the enemy. Howbeit, as soon as our cavalry came in sight, the enemy threw down their arms and fled, and a great number of them were slain.

Book IV, Chapters 20-37

The Germans

The Germans have no Druids to regulate divine worship, no zeal for sacrifices. They reckon among the gods those only whom they see and by whose offices they are openly assisted—to wit, the Sun, the Fire-god, and the Moon; of the rest they have learnt not even by report. Their whole life is composed of hunting expeditions and military pursuits; from early boyhood they are zealous for toil and hardship. Those who remain longest in chastity win greatest praise among their kindred; some think that stature, some that strength and sinew are fortified thereby. Further, they deem it a most disgraceful thing to have had knowledge of a woman before the twentieth year; and there is no secrecy in the matter, for both sexes bathe in the rivers and wear skins or small cloaks of reindeer hide, leaving great part of the body bare.

For agriculture they have no zeal, and the greater part of their food consists of milk, cheese, and flesh. No man has a definite quantity of land or estate of his own: the magistrates and chiefs every year assign to tribes and clans that have assembled together as much land and in such place as seems good to them, and compel the tenants after a year to pass on elsewhere. They adduce many reasons for that practice—the fear that they may be tempted by continuous association to substitute agriculture for their warrior zeal; that they may become zealous for the acquisition of broad territories, and so the more powerful may drive the lower sort from their holdings; that they may build with greater care to avoid the extremes of cold and heat; that some passion for money may arise to be the parent of parties and of quarrels. It is their aim to keep common people in contentment, when each man sees that his own wealth is equal to that of the most powerful.

Their states account it the highest praise by devastating their borders to have areas of wilderness as wide as possible around them. They think it the true sign of valour when the neighbours are driven to retire from their lands and no man dares to settle near, and at the same time they believe they will be safer thereby, having removed all fear of a sudden inroad. When a state makes or resists aggressive war officers are chosen to direct the same, with the power of life and death. In time of peace there is no general officer of state, but the chiefs of districts and cantons do justice among their followers and settle disputes. Acts of brigandage committed outside the borders of each several state involve no disgrace; in fact, they affirm that such are committed in order to practice the young men and to diminish sloth. And when any of the chiefs has said in public assembly that he will be leader, "Let those who will follow declare it," then all who approve the cause and the man rise together to his service and promise their own assistance, and win the general praise of the people. Any of them who have not followed, after promise, are reckoned as deserters and traitors, and in all things afterwards trust is denied to them. They do not think it right to outrage a guest; men who have come to them for any cause they protect from mischief and regard as sacred; to them the houses of all are open, with them is food shared.

Now there was a time in the past when the Gauls were superior in valour to the Germans and made aggressive war upon them, and because of the number of their people and the lack of land they sent colonies across the Rhine. And thus the most fertile places of Germany round the Hercynian forest (which I see was known by report to Eratosthenes and certain Greeks, who call it the Orcynian forest) were seized by the Volcæ Tectosages, who settled there, and the nation maintains itself to this day in those settlements, and enjoys the highest reputation for justice and for success in war. At the present time, since they abide in the same condition of want, poverty, and hardship as the Germans, they adopt the same kind of food and bodily training. Upon the Gauls, however, the neighbourhood of our provinces and acquaintance with oversea commodities lavishes many articles of use or luxury; little by little they have grown accustomed to defeat, and after being conquered in many battles they do not even compare themselves in point of valour with the Germans.

The breadth of this Hercynian forest, above mentioned, is as much as a nine days' journey for an unencumbered person; for in no other fashion can it be determined, nor have they means to measure journeys.

It begins in the borders of the Helvetii, the Nemetes, and the Rauraci, and, following the direct line of the river Danube, it extends to the borders of the Daci and the Anartes; thence it turns leftwards, through districts apart from the river, and by reason of its size touches the borders of many nations. There is no man in the Germany we know who can say that he has reached the edge of that forest, though he may have gone forward a sixty days' journey, or who has learnt in what place it begins. It is known that many kinds of wild beasts not seen in any other places breed therein, of which the following are those that differ most from the rest of the animal world and appear worthy of record.

There is an ox shaped like a stag, from the middle of whose forehead between the ears stands forth a single horn, taller and straighter than the horns we know. From its top branches spread out just like open hands. The main features of female and of male are the same, the same the shape and the size of the horns.

There are also elks so-called. Their shape and dappled skin are like unto goats, but they are somewhat larger in size and have much blunted horns. They have legs without nodes or joints, and they do not lie down to sleep, nor, if any shock has caused them to fall, can they raise or uplift themselves. Trees serve them as couches; they bear against them, and thus, leaning but a little, take their rest. When hunters have marked by their tracks the spot to which they are wont to betake themselves, they either undermine all the trees in that spot at the roots or cut them so far through as to leave them just standing to outward appearance. When the elks lean against them after their fashion, their weight bears down the weakened trees and they themselves fall along with them.

A third species consists of the ure-oxen so-called. In

size these are somewhat smaller than elephants; in appearance, colour, and shape they are as bulls. Great is their strength and great their speed, and they spare neither man nor beast once sighted. These the Germans slay zealously, by taking them in pits; by such work the young men harden themselves and by this kind of hunting train themselves, and those who have slain most of them bring the horns with them to a public place for a testimony thereof, and win great renown. But even if they are caught very young, the animals cannot be tamed or accustomed to human beings. In bulk, shape, and appearance their horns are very different from the horns of our own oxen. The natives collect them zealously and encase the edges with silver, and then at their grandest banquets use them as drinking-cups.

Book VI, Chapters 21-28

❊

CICERO

(Marcus Tullius Cicero, 106 B.C.–43 B.C.)

❊

From the Orations

❊

First Oration Against Catiline

Translated by Louis E. Lord

IN HEAVEN'S name, Catiline, how long will you abuse our patience? How long will that madness of yours mock us? To what limit will your unbridled audacity vaunt itself? Is it nothing to you that the Palatine has its garrison by night, nothing to you that the city is full of patrols, nothing that the populace is in a panic, nothing that all honest men have joined forces, nothing that the senate is convened in this stronghold, is it nothing to see the looks on all the faces? Do you not know that your plans are disclosed? Do you not see that your conspiracy is bound hand and foot by the knowledge of all these men? Who of us do you think is ignorant of what you did last night, what you did the night before, where you were, whom you called together, what plan you took? What an age! What morals! The senate knows these things, the consul sees them. Yet this man lives. Lives, did I say? Nay, more, he walks into the senate, he takes part in the public counsel. He singles out and marks with his glance each one of us for murder. But we, brave men indeed, seem to be doing our duty by the state if we avoid his fury and his shafts. You ought to have been led to death long ago by the consul's order, Catiline. That destruction which for a long time you have been planning for all of us ought to be visited on you yourself. Shall that distinguished man, Publius Scipio, the pontifex maximus, though he was a private citizen, have killed Tiberius Gracchus, who was only slightly undermining the foundations of the state, and shall we, who are consuls, put up with Catiline, who is anxious to destroy the whole world with murder and fire? For I pass over these precedents as too old, that Gaius Servilius Ahala with his own hand killed Spurius Mælius, who was getting up a revolution. There was once, there was indeed in this state such courage that brave men suppressed a traitorous citizen with more severity than the most hated enemy. We have, Catiline, a decree of the senate against you, potent and stern. The state does not lack the approval nor the support of this body. It is we, I say it openly, we, the consuls, who are lacking.

The senate once decreed that Lucius Opimius, the consul, should "take measures that the state might suffer no harm." Not a single night intervened. There was killed because of a vague suspicion of treason Gaius Gracchus, whose father, grandfather, and ancestors were most distinguished men. There was killed with his children Marcus Fulvius, an ex-consul. A similar decree of the senate entrusted the state to Gaius Marius and Lucius Valerius, the consuls. Did death and the vengeance of the state have to wait a day for the punishment of Lucius Saturninus, the tribune of the people, and Gaius Servilius, the prætor? But we have now for twenty days been allowing the edge of our authority to grow dull. For we have a senate's decree of this kind. But it is merely inserted in the records like a sword buried in its sheath. According to this decree of the senate, Catiline, you should have been instantly executed. You are living—and you are living not to repent, but to augment, your effrontery. I wish, Conscript Fathers, to be merciful. I wish not to seem lax when the perils of the state are so great, but now I condemn myself for inaction and remissness. There is in Italy a camp of enemies of the Roman people, situated in the passes of Etruria, their number is increasing daily; but you behold the commander of that camp and the leader of the enemy inside the walls and even in the senate plotting daily from within the city the destruction of the state. But if, Catiline, I shall order you to be seized, to be executed, I shall have to fear, I suppose, not that all respectable people may say I acted too tardily, but that someone may say that I acted too cruelly! But for a special reason I cannot yet bring myself to do what I should have done long ago. Then at last you shall be executed when no one so depraved, so abandoned, so like yourself, can be found who does not admit that this was done justly. As long as anyone exists who will dare defend you, you will live, and live as you live now, surrounded by many competent guards whom I have set so that you may not be able to move against the state. The eyes and the ears of many shall watch you, although you may not know it, as they have done heretofore.

For what is there, Catiline, for you to wait for longer, if neither night with its darkness can hide your criminal assemblies nor a private house with its walls confine the voices of your conspiracy, if they are patent, if all burst into view? Abandon now that foul plan of yours, be persuaded by me, forget your murder and arson. You are encompassed on all sides; all your plans are clearer to us than the light of day. You may now recall them with me. Do you remember that I said in the senate on the twenty-first of October that Gaius Manlius, a tool and a slave of your bold scheme, would be in arms on a particular day and that that day would be the twenty-seventh of October? Was I wrong, Catiline, in asserting a thing so crucial, so criminal, so unbelievable, but, what was much more surprising, was I mistaken in the day? I also said in the senate that you had postponed till the twenty-eighth of October the slaughter of the influential citizens though by that time many of the chief men of the state had fled from Rome, not so much to save themselves, as to thwart your plans. Can you deny that, on that very day, shut in by my guards, and by my foresight, you could not move against the state, when you said that, in spite of the departure of the others, you would still be content with killing us who had remained? When you thought that by a night attack you would seize Præneste actually on the first of November, did you know that that colony was fortified at my command by my guards, my forces, and my troops? You do nothing, you attempt nothing, you think of nothing which I do not hear and see and understand plainly.

Review with me now the events of the night before last. Now you will know that I watch much more vigilantly for the safety of the state than you do for its destruction. I say that the night before last you came into the Street of the Scythe-makers (I will not deal in general terms), you came to the house of Marcus Læca; to the same place came many of your allies animated by the same madness and wickedness. You do not dare to deny it, do you? Why are you silent? I will convict you if you do deny. For I see here in the senate some who were there with you. O ye immortal gods! Where in the world are we? What sort of a commonwealth do we possess? In what city are we living? Here, here in our very midst, Conscript Fathers, in this most sacred and dignified council of the whole world, are men who plan for the destruction of all of us, who plan for the destruction of this city and even the destruction of the whole world! I, the consul, see them and I consult them on affairs of state, and those who ought to have been slain by the sword I do not yet wound even with my voice! You were, then, at the house of Læca on that night, Catiline, you apportioned the parts of Italy, you determined where you wished each man to go, you selected those whom you would leave at Rome, those whom you would take with you, you parcelled out the parts of the city to be burned, you averred that you yourself would go presently, you said that you would be delayed a little while because I still lived. Two Roman knights were found who would relieve you of that anxiety and they promised that they would kill me on my couch that very night a little before dawn. I learned all these things almost before your council was dismissed; I fortified and strengthened my home with more numerous guards, I refused admittance to those whom you had sent to salute me in the morning, for those very men did come whose coming at that hour I had already foretold to many eminent gentlemen.

Since this is the situation, Catiline, go whither you had intended, depart at last from the city; the gates are open; get on your way! That camp you share with Manlius has awaited you, its commander, for all too long a time. Take with you all these friends of yours, if not all, then as many as you can; purge the city. I shall be free from my great fear only if there is a wall between us. You cannot now remain with us longer; I will not bear it, I will not tolerate it, I will not permit it.

Great thanks are due to the immortal gods and especially to Jupiter Stator here, the most ancient custodian of this city, because we have already so often escaped this curse of the state, so foul, so horrible, so deadly. The safety of the state ought not to be imperilled too often by one man. While I was consul-elect, Catiline, and you lay in wait for me, I defended myself, not by a public guard, but by my own caution. When, at the last consular elections, you wished to kill me and your competitors in the Campus Martius, I foiled your wicked attempt by the resources and protection of my friends without arousing any public disturbance; in a word, as often as you threatened me I thwarted you by my own efforts, although I saw that my death would bring a great calamity upon the state. Now you are attacking openly the whole state, you call for the destruction and devastation of the temples of the immortal gods, the dwellings of the city, the lives of all the citizens, and all Italy. Therefore, since I do not as yet dare to do that which is most important and which most befits this government and our traditions, I will do this which is more lenient in point of severity and more useful as regards the common safety. For if I shall have ordered you to be killed, there will remain in the state the rest of your conspirators; but if you leave the city, as I have long been urging, the city will be drained of the abundant and pestilent bilge-water of the state—your accomplices. What is wrong, Catiline? You do not hesitate, do you, to do at my command what you were already about to do of your own accord? The consul bids a public enemy leave the city. You ask me "Is it to be exile?" I do not order that, but if you ask my opinion, I advise it.

For what, Catiline, can please you now in this city where there is no one, except your fellow-conspirators—ruined men—who does not fear you, no one who does not hate you? What stigma of disgrace is not branded on your private life? What dishonour in personal relations does not cling to your ill fame? What lust has not stained your eyes, what crime has not stained your hands, what corruption has not stained your whole body? To what youth whom you had ensnared by the allurements of your seduction have you not furnished a weapon for his crimes or a torch to kindle his lust? What then? When lately you had made room in your home for a new marriage by murdering your former wife, did you not add to this crime another incredible crime? I do not describe this and I am glad to let it be passed in silence, lest it be thought that the enormity of so great a crime has either existed in this state or has escaped punishment. I pass over in silence the complete ruin of your fortune which you will feel threatening you upon the thirteenth of this month; I come to those things which have to do, not with your private scandals and shame, not with the sordid tangle of your personal affairs, but with the highest interests of the state and with the life and safety of us all. Can this light, Catiline, or the breath of this air be pleasing to you when you are aware that all these men know that you, on the last day of December in the consulship of Lepidus and Tullus, took your place in the assembly armed, that you had prepared a band to kill the consuls and the chief citizens of the state, and that no pity nor fear on your part checked your crime and your madness, but the good fortune of the Roman people? But those crimes I do not mention, for they are not unknown and many have been committed since that time:—how often did you attempt to kill me when I was consul-elect and how often after I was consul! How many of your thrusts, so aimed that they seemed unavoidable, I escaped by a slight movement and a dodge, as they call it! You gain nothing, you accomplish nothing, and still you do not cease trying and hoping. How often already has that dagger been struck from your hands, how often has it fallen by some

chance and slipped! Still you cannot bear to be deprived
of it for a single day. I do not know what sacrifices you
made to hallow and consecrate it because you thought
that you must plunge it into the body of a consul!

But now what is this life of yours? For I shall speak to
you, so that men may feel I am swayed, not by hatred, as
I ought to be, but by pity, none of which is due you.
You came a little while ago into the senate. Who among
all your many friends and relatives saluted you? If such
treatment has been accorded to no one within the mem-
ory of man, do you await the condemnation of the
spoken word when you have been crushed by this most
significant verdict of silence? What of the fact that at
your coming all those near-by seats were deserted, that
all the ex-consuls whom you have often marked out for
murder left all that area of seats vacant and unoccupied
as soon as you took your place—with what feelings do
you think you ought to bear this? By Hercules, if my
slaves feared me as your fellow-citizens fear you I should
think I must leave my house; do you not think you
ought to leave the city? If I thought that I was so
grievously suspected even unjustly, and that I was so
offensive to my fellow-citizens, I should prefer not to be
seen by my fellow-citizens rather than to encounter the
hostile eyes of all; *you* know because you are conscious
of your crimes that the hatred of all toward you is just
and long due. Do you hesitate to avoid the eyes and
the presence of those whose minds and sensibilities you
are torturing? If your parents hated and feared you and
you could not be reconciled to them in any way, you
would, I think, withdraw somewhere from their gaze.
Now your native country, the mother of us all, hates you
and fears you and decides that you have had no single
thought for a long time save for her destruction. Will
you neither revere her authority, nor obey her judge-

ments, nor fear her power? She, Catiline, thus confers with you and, as it were, though silent, speaks: "No crime for some years now has come into existence except through you, no outrage without you; you alone have killed many citizens, harried and despoiled the allies, unpunished and free; you have been able not only to neglect the laws and the courts but even to thwart and destroy them. I endured as I could those earlier deeds, although they ought not to have been borne, but now that I should be wholly in fear on account of you alone, that, at the slightest sound, Catiline should be feared, that no plan, it seems, can be undertaken against me uninspired by your villainy, that is not to be borne. Therefore depart and free me from this terror; if it is well founded, that I may not be overwhelmed; if it is false, that now at last I may cease to fear."

If our country speaks to you thus, as I have said, ought she not to obtain her request, even though she cannot use force? What of the fact that you gave your-self into voluntary custody, that you said that you wished to live at the home of Manius Lepidus, to avoid suspicion? When he would not receive you, you dared to come even to me and ask me to protect you in my home. From me also you got the answer that I could in no way be safe within the same house-walls with you, since I was in great peril because we were encompassed by the same city walls, you came to the home of Quintus Metellus, the prætor. When he repulsed you, you moved on to the boon companion of yours, that noble gentleman, Marcus Metellus; because of course you thought that he would be most careful to guard you, most shrewd to suspect others, and most brave to defend you. But how far do you think a man should be away from prison and chains who already judges himself worthy of custody?

Since these things are so, Catiline, do you hesitate, if you cannot die with a mind at ease, to go to some other land and devote that life of yours, rescued from many just and long-deserved penalties, to exile and solitude? Refer the matter, you say, to the senate; for you demand this and if this body votes that you should go into exile you say that you will obey. I will not refer it; that does not accord with my practice, and still I will so act that you may know what these men think of you. Leave the city, Catiline, free the state from fear; into exile, if you are waiting for this word, go. What is it, Catiline? What are you waiting for? Do you notice at all the silence of these men? They approve it; they are silent. Why do you await the spoken word when you see their wish silently expressed? But if I had said this same thing to that excellent youth, Publius Sestius, if I had said it to that bravest of men, Marcus Marcellus, upon me, the consul, the senate with most just cause would have laid violent hands in this very temple. In your case, however, Catiline, when they say nothing they express their approval; their acquiescence is a decree. By their silence they cry aloud. And this is true not only of these men whose authority is, forsooth, dear to you, whose lives are most cheap, but also those most honourable and noble Roman knights, and the other brave citizens who are standing around the senate. You could see the crowd of them, their zeal you could perceive, and their voices you could hear a little while ago. For a long time with difficulty I have kept their hands and their weapons from you; I will easily persuade them to accompany you as far as the city gates when you leave all that you so long have desired to destroy.

And yet why do I talk? As if anything could move you, as if you could ever pull yourself together, as if you had contemplated flight, as if you had any thought of exile! Would that the immortal gods might incline you to that purpose! And yet I see, if, terrified by my threats, you were to be persuaded to go into exile, what a tempest of ill feeling would await me, if not now while the memory of your crimes is still fresh, certainly in after times. But it is worth all that, provided your ruin remains a private affair and is divorced from the dangers to the state. But that you should be dissuaded from your vices, that you should fear the punishment of the laws, that you should yield to the needs of the state, that is a thing not to be asked. For you are not the man, Catiline, ever to be recalled from disgrace by shame, or from danger by fear, or from madness by reason. Wherefore, as I have now often said, go, and if you wish to stir up hatred against me, your enemy, as you call me, go straight into exile; with difficulty shall I bear the criticisms of mankind if you do this; with difficulty shall I sustain the load of that hatred if you shall go into exile at the consul's orders. But if you prefer to minister to my praise and glory, take with you that rascally gang of criminals, take yourself to Manlius, arouse the debauched, separate yourself from the upright, bring war upon your country, exult in impious robbery; then it will appear that you have gone not expelled by me to join aliens but invited to join your friends. And yet why should I urge you, for I know that you have already sent men ahead to await you under arms at Forum Aurelium. I know that you have arranged and appointed a day with Manlius and that you have also sent forward that silver eagle, which I trust will be a cause of ruin and a curse for all your band. For this eagle a shrine of iniquities has been set up in your own home. Is it possible that you could longer be separated from this to which you were wont to pay homage as you set forth to murder, from whose altars you often have lifted that impious right hand of yours for the slaughter of the citizens?

You will go, then, at last where that unbridled and furious greed of yours has long been hurrying you; indeed this does not bring sorrow to you but a certain incredible delight. For this madness nature bore you, your own wish has trained you, fortune has preserved you. You never desired peace, nor war even unless it were a wicked war. You have a band of criminals swept up from those whom all fortune and even all hope have deserted and abandoned. In their company what joy will be yours, what delights, what exultation, how you will revel in debauchery, when among so many of your friends you will neither hear nor see a single upright man! For pursuing a life like that those "labours" of yours, of which men speak, have been good practice: to lie on the bare ground not only to lay siege to the object of your lust, but also to perpetrate crime; to lose sleep not only plotting against the repose of husbands, but plotting also to steal the goods of peaceable citizens. You have an opportunity to show that famous ability you have to endure hunger, cold, a lack of everything: soon you will know that these practices have ruined you. This much I accomplished when I kept you from the consulship: that you might be able to attack the state as an exile rather than to vex it as a consul, and that this undertaking which has been foully conceived by you may be called brigandage rather than war.

And now, that I may prevent our country by entreaty and prayer, Conscript Fathers, from making a complaint that would be almost justified, listen carefully, I pray you, to what I shall say and store it deep in your hearts and minds. For if our country, which is much dearer to me than my life, if all Italy, if all the state should speak to me thus: "Marcus Tullius, what are you doing? This man is a public enemy as you have discovered; he will be the leader of the war, as you see; men are waiting for him to take command in the enemies' camp, as you know: author of a crime, head of a conspiracy, recruiter of slaves and criminals—and you will let him go, in such a way that he will seem to be not cast out of the city by you but let loose against the city! Will you not command him to be cast into chains, to be haled to death, to be punished with the greatest severity? What, pray, hinders you? The custom of our ancestors? But often even private citizens in this state have punished with death dangerous men. Is it the laws which have been enacted regarding the punishment of Roman citizens? But never in this city have those who revolted against the state enjoyed the rights of citizens. Or do you fear the odium of posterity? A fine return you are making to the Roman people who have raised you, a man distinguished only by your own deeds, and by no achievements of your ancestors, so early to the highest office through every grade of honour, if because of the fear of unpopularity or any danger whatever you neglect the safety of your fellow-citizens! But if there is any fear of unpopularity, the unpopularity that comes from sternness and severity is no more greatly to be dreaded than that which comes from laxness and cowardice. Or when Italy shall be devastated by war, when the cities shall be harried, when houses shall be burned, do you not think that then you will be consumed by the fire of unpopularity?"

To this most solemn utterance of the state and of those men who think these same thoughts I will answer briefly. "If I judged that it were best, Conscript Fathers, that Catiline should be put to death, I should not give to that gladiator the enjoyment of a single further hour of life. For if our most noble men and most famous citizens were not stained but even honoured by shedding the blood of Saturninus, and the Gracchi, and Flaccus, and many men of ancient time, certainly I should not have feared that when this murderer of citizens has been slain any unpopularity would attach to me in after time. But if that did seriously threaten me, still I have always believed that unpopularity won by uprightness was glory and not unpopularity. And yet there are some in this body who either do not see the disasters which threaten us or pretend that they do not see them; these have fostered the hopes of Catiline by mild measures and they have strengthened the growing conspiracy by not believing in its existence; under their influence many ignorant men as well as villains would be saying that I acted cruelly and tyrannically if I had punished Catiline. Now I know that if he arrives at Manlius's camp whither he is now making his way, no one will be so stupid as not to see that a conspiracy has been formed, no one will be so depraved as to deny it. But if this man alone is executed, I know that this disease in the state can can be checked for a little time, but it cannot be completely crushed. But if he shall take himself off, if he shall lead out his friends with him and gather together to the same place other derelicts now collected from all sources, not only this plague rampant in the state but even the roots and seeds of all evil will be obliterated and destroyed.

For many a long day, Conscript Fathers, we have lived and moved amid these dangers and snares of conspiracy; but in some strange way all these crimes and this long-standing madness and audacity have come to a head in the time of my consulship. If out of this great crowd of robbers this one man shall be removed, we shall seem perhaps for a brief time to be relieved of care and fear. But the danger will remain, and it will be hidden deep in the veins and vitals of the state. Just as often men sick with a grievous disease and tossed about in a burning fever drink cold water and at first seem to be relieved, but later are much more grievously and violently afflicted, so this disease in the state, though relieved by the punishment of this man, will grow much worse so long as the rest remain alive. Therefore let the wicked depart; let them separate themselves from the good; let them assemble in one place. And finally, as I often said, let them be separated from us by a wall; let them cease to lie in wait for the consul in his own home, to stand around the tribunal of the city prætor, to besiege the senate-house with swords, to prepare fire-spears and fire-brands with which to burn the city; finally, let every man's thoughts of the state be written on his forehead. I promise you this, Conscript Fathers, that there will be such energy in us, the consuls, such authority in you, such courage in the Roman knights, such cordial agreement among all patriotic men, that after the departure of Catiline you will see all things made clear, brought to light, suppressed and punished.

With omens like these, Catiline, go forth to your impious and wicked war, bringing to the state the greatest of benefits, to yourself destruction and annihilation, and to those who have allied themselves with you for all crime and parricide, utter ruin. O Jupiter, thou who wast established by Romulus under the same auspices under which this city was established, rightly called by us the Stayer of this city and empire, thou wilt repel him and his allies from thy temples and from the other temples, from the dwellings of this city and its walls, from the lives and fortunes of all the citizens, and these men, enemies of the upright, foes of the state, plunderers of Italy, who are united by a compact of crime in an abominable association, thou wilt punish living and dead with eternal punishments.

From Concerning Old Age

Translated by *William Armistead Falconer*

O Titus, should some aid of mine dispel
The cares that now within thy bosom dwell
And wring thy heart and torture thee with pain,
What then would be the measure of my gain?

FOR, my dear Atticus, I may fitly speak to you in these self-same lines in which,

> That man
> Of little wealth, but rich in loyalty

speaks to Flamininus. And yet I am perfectly sure that it cannot be said of you, as the poet said of Flamininus,

> You fret and worry, Titus, day and night,

for I know your self-control and the even temper of your mind, and I am aware that you brought home from Athens not only a cognomen but culture and practical wisdom too. Nevertheless I suspect that you, at times, are quite seriously perturbed by the same circumstances which are troubling me; but to find comfort for them is too difficult a task to be undertaken now and must be deferred until another time.

However, at the present, I have determined to write something on old age to be dedicated to you, for I fain would lighten both for you and for me our common burden of old age, which, if not already pressing hard upon us, is surely coming on apace; and yet I have certain knowledge that you, at all events, are bearing and will continue to bear that burden, as you do all others, with a calm and philosophic mind. But when I resolved to write something on this theme you continually came before my mind as worthy of a gift which both of us might enjoy together. To me, at any rate, the composition of this book has been so delightful that it has not only wiped away all the annoyances of old age, but has even made it an easy and a happy state. Philosophy, therefore, can never be praised as much as she deserves, since she enables the man who is obedient to her precepts to pass every season of life free from worry.

Now on other subjects I have said much and shall often have much to say; this book, which I am sending to you, is on old age. But the entire discourse I have attributed, not to Tithonus, as Aristo of Ceos did, (for there would be too little authority in a myth), but, that I might give it greater weight, I have ascribed it to the venerable Marcus Cato; and I represent Lælius and Scipio, while at his house, expressing wonder that he bears his age so well, and Cato replying to them. If it shall appear that he argues more learnedly than he was accustomed to do in his own books, give the credit to Greek literature, of which, as is well known, he was very studious in his later years. But why need I say more? For from now on the words of Cato himself will completely unfold to you my own views on old age.

scipio: When conversing with Gaius Lælius here present, I am frequently wont to marvel, Cato, both at your pre-eminent, nay, faultless, wisdom in matters generally, and especially at the fact that, so far as I have been able to see, old age is never burdensome to you, though it is so vexatious to most old men that they declare it to be a load heavier than Ætna.

CATO: I think, my friends, that you marvel at a thing really far from difficult. For to those who have not the means within themselves of a virtuous and happy life every age is burdensome; and, on the other hand, to those who seek all good from themselves nothing can seem evil that the laws of nature inevitably impose. To this class old age especially belongs, which all men wish to attain and yet reproach when attained; such is the inconsistency and perversity of Folly! They say that it stole upon them faster than they had expected. In the first place, who has forced them to form a mistaken judgement? For how much more rapidly does old age steal upon youth than youth upon childhood? And again, how much less burdensome would old age be to them if they were in their eight-hundredth rather than in their eightieth year? In fact, no lapse of time, however long, once it had slipped away, could solace or soothe a foolish old age.

Wherefore, if you are accustomed to marvel at my wisdom—and would that it were worthy of your estimate and of my cognomen—I am wise because I follow Nature as the best of guides and obey her as a god; and since she has fitly planned the other acts of life's drama, it is not likely that she has neglected the final act as if she were a careless playwright. And yet there had to be something final, and—as in the case of orchard fruits and crops of grain in the process of ripening which comes with time—something shrivelled, as it were, and prone to fall. But this state the wise man should endure with resignation. For what is warring against the gods, as the giants did, other than fighting against Nature?

LÆLIUS: True, Cato, but you will do a thing most

agreeable to us both—assuming that I may speak for Scipio, too—if, since we hope to become old (at least we wish it), you will, long in advance, teach us on what principles we may most easily support the weight of increasing years.

CATO: To be sure I will, Lælius, especially if, as you say, it is going to prove agreeable to you both.

LÆLIUS: Unless it is too much trouble to you, Cato, since you have, as it were, travelled the long road upon which we also must set out, we really do wish to see what sort of a place it is at which you have arrived.

CATO: I will do so, Lælius, as well as I can. For I have often listened to the complaints of my contemporaries (and according to the old adage, "like with like most readily foregathers"), complaints made also by the ex-consuls, Gaius Salinator and Spurius Albinus, who were almost my equals in years, wherein they used to lament, now because they were denied the sensual pleasures without which they thought life not life at all, and now because they were scorned by the people who had been wont to pay them court. But it seemed to me that they were not placing the blame where the blame was due. For if the ills of which they complained were the faults of old age, the same ills would befall me and all other old men: but I have known many who were of such a nature that they bore their old age without complaint, who were not unhappy because they had been loosed from the chains of passion, and who were not scorned by their friends. But as regards all such complaints, the blame rests with character, not with age. For old men of self-control, who are neither churlish nor ungracious, find old age endurable; while on the other hand perversity and an unkindly disposition render irksome every period of life.

LÆLIUS: What you say is true, Cato; but perhaps

some one may reply that old age seems more tolerable to you because of your resources, means, and social position, and that these are advantages which cannot fall to the lot of many.

CATO: There is something in that objection, Lælius, but not everything. For example, there is a story that when, in the course of a quarrel, a certain Seriphian had said to Themistocles, "Your brilliant reputation is due to your country's glory, not your own," Themistocles replied, "True, by Hercules, I should never have been famous if I had been a Seriphian, nor you if you had been an Athenian." The same may be said of old age; for amid utter want old age cannot be a light thing, not even to a wise man; nor to a fool, even amid utmost wealth, can it be otherwise than burdensome.

Undoubtedly, Scipio and Lælius, the most suitable defences of old age are the principles and practice of the virtues, which, if cultivated in every period of life, bring forth wonderful fruits at the close of a long and busy career, not only because they never fail you even at the very end of life—although that is a matter of highest moment—but also because it is most delightful to have the consciousness of a life well spent and the memory of many deeds worthily performed.

I was as fond of Quintus Fabius Maximus, who recovered Tarentum, as if he had been of my own age, though he was old and I was young. For there was in him a dignity tempered with courtesy, and age had not altered his disposition; and yet when I began to cultivate him he was not extremely old, though he was well advanced in life. For he had been consul for the first time the year after I was born; and when he was in his fourth consulship I was a mere lad, and set out as a private soldier with him for Capua, and five years later for Tarentum; then, four years after that I became quæstor, which office I held while Tuditanus and Cethegus were consuls, and he, at that very time, though far advanced in age, made speeches in favour of the Cincian law on fees and gifts. Though quite old he waged war like a young man, and by his patient endurance checked the boyish impetuosity of Hannibal. My friend Ennius admirably speaks of him thus:

> One man's delay alone restored our State:
> He valued safety more than mob's applause;
> Hence now his glory more resplendent grows.

Indeed, with what vigilance, with what skill he recaptured Tarentum! It was in my own hearing that Salinator, who had fled to the citadel after losing the town, remarked to him in a boasting tone: "Through my instrumentality, Q. Fabius, you have recaptured Tarentum." "Undoubtedly," said Fabius, laughing, "for if you had not lost it I should never have recaptured it." But, indeed, he was not more distinguished in war than in civil life. While consul the second time, unaided by his colleague Spurius Carvilius he, as far as he could, opposed the people's tribune Gaius Flaminius who was endeavouring to parcel out the Picene and Gallic lands, contrary to the expressed will of the senate. And, although an augur, he dared to say that whatever was done for the safety of the Republic was done under the best auspices, and that whatever was inimical to the Republic was against the auspices.

Many are the remarkable things I have observed in that great man, but nothing more striking than the manner in which he bore the death of his distinguished son, a former consul. The funeral oration delivered by him on that occasion is in general circulation, and, when we read it, what philosopher does not appear contemptible? Nor was it merely in public and under the gaze of his fellow-citizens that he was great, but he was greater still in the privacy of his home. What conversation! What maxims! What a knowledge of ancient history! What skill in augural law! He had also read much, for a Roman, and knew by heart the entire history, not only of our own wars, but of foreign wars as well. I was, at that time, as eager to profit by his conversation as if I already foresaw what, in fact, came to pass, that, when he was gone, I should have no one from whom to learn.

Why, then, have I said so much about Maximus? Because you surely realize now that it would be monstrous to call unhappy such an old age as his. And yet, not every one can be a Scipio or a Maximus and call to mind the cities he has taken, the battles he has fought on land and sea, the campaigns he has conducted, and the triumphs he has won. But there is also the tranquil and serene old age of a life spent quietly, amid pure and refining pursuits—such an old age, for example, as we are told was that of Plato, who died, pen in hand, in his eighty-first year; such as that of Isocrates, who, by his own statement, was ninety-four when he composed the work entitled *Panathenaicus,* and he lived five years after that. His teacher, Gorgias of Leontini, rounded out one hundred and seven years and never rested from his pursuits or his labours. When some one asked him why he chose to remain so long alive, he answered: "I have no reason to reproach old age." A noble answer and worthy of a scholar!

For, in truth, it is their own vices and their own faults that fools charge to old age; but Ennius, of whom I spoke a while ago, did not do this, for he says:

> He, like the gallant steed that often won
> Olympic trophy in the final lap,
> Now takes his rest when weakened by old age.

He is comparing his old age to that of a brave and victorious horse. You both may recall him distinctly, for it was only nineteen years from his death until the election of the present consuls, Titus Flamininus and Manius Acilius, and he did not pass away until the consulship of Cæpio and Philip (the latter being in his second term), at a time when I, at sixty-five, spoke publicly for the Voconian law, with loud voice and mighty lungs. But he at seventy—for Ennius lived that long—was bearing the two burdens which are considered the greatest—poverty and old age—and was bearing them in such a way that he seemed almost to take a pleasure in them.

And, indeed, when I reflect on this subject I find four reasons why old age appears to be unhappy: first, that it withdraws us from active pursuits; second, that it makes the body weaker; third, that it deprives us of almost all physical pleasures; and, fourth, that it is not far removed from death. Let us, if you please, examine each of these reasons separately and see how much truth they contain.

*   *   *

It remains to consider now the fourth reason—one that seems especially calculated to render my time of life anxious and full of care—the nearness of death; for death, in truth, cannot be far away. O wretched indeed is that old man who has not learned in the course of his long life that death should be held of no account! For clearly death is negligible, if it utterly annihilates the soul, or even desirable, if it conducts the soul to some place where it is to live for ever. Surely no other alternative can be found. What, then, shall I fear, if after death I am destined to be either not unhappy or happy? And yet is there anyone so foolish, even though he is young, as to feel absolutely sure that he will be alive when evening comes? Nay, even youth, much more than old age, is subject to the accident of death; the young fall sick more easily, their sufferings are more intense, and they are cured with greater difficulty. Therefore few arrive at old age, and, but for this, life would be lived in better and wiser fashion. For it is in old men that reason and good judgement are found, and had it not been for old men no state would have existed at all.

But I return to the question of impending death. What fault is this which you charge against old age, when, as you see, it is one chargeable likewise to youth? That death is common to every age has been brought home to me by the loss of my dearest son, and to you, Scipio, by the untimely end of your two brothers, when they were giving promise of attaining to the highest honours in the State. But, you may say, the young man hopes that he will live for a long time and this hope the old man cannot have. Such a hope is not wise, for what is more unwise than to mistake uncertainty for certainty, falsehood for truth? They say, also, that the old man has nothing even to hope for. Yet he is in better case than the young man, since what the latter merely hopes for, the former has already attained; the one wishes to live long, the other has lived long.

But, ye gods! what is there in human nature that is for long? For grant the utmost limit of life; let us hope to reach the age of the Tartessian king—for at Cadiz there was, as I have seen it recorded, a certain Arganthonius, who had reigned eighty and had lived one hundred and twenty years—but to me nothing whatever seems "lengthy" if it has an end; for when that end arrives, then that which was is gone; naught remains but the fruit of good and virtuous deeds. Hours and days, and months and years, go by; the past returns no more, and what is to be we cannot know; but whatever the time given us in which to live, we should therewith be content.

The actor, for instance, to please his audience need not appear in every act to the very end; it is enough if he is approved in the parts in which he plays; and so it is not necessary for the wise man to stay on this mortal stage to the last fall of the curtain. For even if the allotted space of life be short, it is long enough in which to live honourably and well; but if a longer period of years should be granted, one has no more cause to grieve than the farmers have that the pleasant springtime has passed and that summer and autumn have come. For spring typifies youth and gives promise of future fruits; while the other seasons are designed for gathering in those fruits and storing them away.

Now the fruit of old age, as I have often said, is the memory of abundant blessings previously acquired. Moreover, whatever befalls in accordance with Nature should be accounted good; and indeed, what is more consonant with Nature than for the old to die? But the same fate befalls the young, though Nature in their case struggles and rebels. Therefore, when the young die I am reminded of a strong flame extinguished by a torrent; but when old men die it is as if a fire had gone out without the use of force and of its own accord, after the fuel had been consumed; and, just as apples when they are green are with difficulty plucked from the tree, but when ripe and mellow fall of themselves, so, with the young, death comes as a result of force, while with the old it is the result of ripeness. To me, indeed, the thought of this "ripeness" for death is so pleasant, that the nearer I approach death the more I feel like one who is in sight of land at last and is about to anchor in his home port after a long voyage.

But old age has no certain term, and there is good cause for an old man living so long as he can fulfil and support his proper duties and hold death of no account. By this means old age actually becomes more spirited and more courageous than youth. This explains the answer which Solon gave to the tyrant Pisistratus who asked, "Pray, what do you rely upon in opposing me so boldly?" and Solon replied, "Old age." But the most desirable end of life is that which comes while the mind is clear and the faculties are unimpaired, when Nature herself takes apart the work which she has put together. As the builder most readily destroys the ship or the house which he has built, so Nature is the agent best fitted to give dissolution to her creature, man. Now every structure when newly built is hard to pull apart, but the old and weather-beaten house comes easily down.

Hence, it follows that old men ought neither to cling too fondly to their little remnant of life, nor give it up without a cause. Pythagoras bids us stand like faithful sentries and not quit our post until God, our Captain, gives the word. Solon the Wise has a couplet in which he says that he does not want his death to be free from the grief and mourning of his friends. He wishes, no doubt, to make out that he is dear to his friends, but I am inclined to think that Ennius has expressed it better when he says:

> I do not wish the honour of a tear,
> Or any wailing cries about my bier.

He does not think that death, which is followed by eternal life, should be a cause of grief.

Now, there may be some sensation in the process of dying, but it is a fleeting one, especially to the old; after death the sensation is either pleasant or there is none at all. But this should be thought on from our youth up, so that we may be indifferent to death, and without this thought no one can be in a tranquil state of mind. For it is certain that we must die, and, for aught we know, this very day. Therefore, since death threatens every hour, how can he who fears it have any steadfastness of soul? No very extended argument on this point seems necessary when I recall—not the conduct of Lucius Brutus, who was killed in liberating his country; nor that of the two Decii who rode full speed to a voluntary death; nor that of Marcus Atilius Regulus, who set out from home to undergo torture and keep the faith pledged to his foe; nor that of the two Scipios, who with their bodies sought to stay the Punic march; nor that, Scipio, of your grandfather Lucius Paulus who, in the shameful rout at Cannæ, gave his life to atone for his colleague's folly; nor that of Marcus Marcellus, to whom not even his most pitiless foe denied the honours of a funeral—but rather when I recall, as I have noted in my *Antiquities,* how our legions have often marched with cheerful and unwavering courage into situations whence they thought they would never return. Then shall wise old men fear a thing which is despised by youths, and not only by those who are untaught, but by those also who are mere clowns?

Undoubtedly, as it seems to me at least, satiety of all pursuits causes satiety of life. Boyhood has certain pursuits: does youth yearn for them? Early youth has its pursuits: does the matured or so-called middle stage of life need them? Maturity, too, has such as are not even sought in old age, and finally, there are those suitable to old age. Therefore as the pleasures and pursuits of the earlier periods of life fall away, so also do those of old age; and when that happens man has his fill of life and the time is ripe for him to go.

Really I do not see why I should not venture to tell you what I, myself, think of death; for it seems to me that I apprehend it better as I draw nearer to it. It is my belief, Scipio, that your father, and yours, Lælius—both of them most illustrious men and very dear to me—are living yet, and living the only life deserving of the name. For while we are shut up within these frames of flesh we perform a sort of task imposed by necessity and endure grievous labour; for the soul is celestial, brought down from its most exalted home and buried, as it were, in earth, a place uncongenial to its divine and eternal nature. But I believe that the immortal gods implanted souls in human bodies so as to have beings who would care for the earth and who, while contemplating the celestial order, would imitate it in the moderation and consistency of their lives. Nor have I been driven to this belief solely by the force of reason and of argument, but also by the reputation and authority of philosophers of the highest rank.

I used to be told that Pythagoras and his disciples —who were almost fellow-countrymen of ours, inasmuch as they were formerly called "Italian philosophers"—never doubted that our souls were emanations of the Universal Divine Mind. Moreover, I had clearly set before me the arguments touching the immortality of the soul, delivered on the last day of his life by Socrates, whom the oracle of Apollo had pronounced the wisest of men. Why multiply words? That is my conviction, that is what I believe—since such is the lightning-like rapidity of the soul, such its wonderful memory of things that are past, such its ability to forecast the future, such its mastery of many arts, sciences, and inventions, that its nature, which encompasses all these things, cannot be mortal; and since the soul is always active and has no source of motion because it is self-moving, its motion will have no end, because it will never leave itself; and since in its nature the soul is of one substance and has nothing whatever mingled with it unlike or dissimilar to itself, it cannot be divided, and if it cannot be divided it cannot perish. And a strong argument that men's knowledge of numerous things antedates their birth is the fact that mere children, in studying difficult subjects, so quickly lay hold upon innumerable things that they seem not to be then learning them for the first time, but to be recalling and remembering them. This, in substance, is Plato's teaching.

Again, in Xenophon, Cyrus the Elder utters the following words as he is dying: "Think not, my dearest sons, that, when I have left you, I shall cease to be. For while I was with you you did not see my soul, but you knew that it was in this body from the deeds that I performed. Continue to believe, therefore, that it exists as before, even though you see it not. Nor, indeed, would the fame of illustrious men survive their death if the souls of those very men did not cause us to retain their memory longer. I, for my part, could never be persuaded that souls, which lived while they were in human bodies, perished when they left those bodies; nor, indeed, that the soul became incapable of thought when it had escaped from the unthinking corpse, but rather that, when it had been freed from every admixture of flesh and had begun to exist pure and undefiled, then only was it wise. And even when man is dissolved by death it is evident to the sight whither each bodily element departs; for the corporeal returns to the visible constituents from which it came, but the soul alone remains unseen, both when it is present and when it departs. Again, you really see nothing resembling death so much as sleep; and yet it is when the body sleeps that the soul most clearly manifests its divine nature; for when it is unfettered and free it sees many things that are to come. Hence we know what the soul's future state will be when it has been wholly released from the shackles of the flesh. Wherefore, if what I have said be true, cherish me as you would a god. But on the other hand, if my soul is going to perish along with my body, still you, who revere the gods as the guardians and rulers of this beautiful universe, will keep me in loving and sacred memory."

This was the view of the dying Cyrus. Let me, if you please, give my own.

No one, my dear Scipio, will ever convince me that your father Paulus, or your two grandfathers, Paulus and Africanus, or the latter's father and uncle, or many other illustrious men, unnecessary now to name, would have attempted such mighty deeds, to be remembered by posterity, if they had not known that posterity belonged to them. Or, to boast somewhat of myself after the manner of the old, do you think that I should have undertaken such heavy labours by day and by night, at home and abroad, if I had believed that the term of my earthly life would mark the limits of my fame? Would it not have been far better for me to spend a leisured and quiet life, free from toil and strife? But somehow, my soul was ever on the alert, looking forward to posterity, as if it realized that when it had departed from this life, then at last would it be alive. And, indeed, were it not true that the soul is immortal, it would not be the case that it is ever the souls of the best men that strive most for immortal glory. And what of the fact that the wisest men die with the greatest equanimity, the most foolish with the least? Is it not apparent to you that it is because the soul of the one, having a keener and wider vision, sees that it is setting out for a better country, while that of the other, being of duller sight, sees not its path?

Really, Scipio, I am carried away with the desire to see your father, and yours too, Lælius, both of whom I honoured and loved; and, indeed, I am eager to meet not only those whom I have known, but those also of whom I have heard and read and written. And when I shall have set out to join them, assuredly no one will easily draw me back, or boil me up again, as if I were a Pelias. Nay, if some god should give me leave to return to infancy from my old age, to weep once more in my cradle, I should vehemently protest; for, truly, after I have run my race I have no wish to be recalled, as it were, from the goal to the starting-place. For what advantage has life—or, rather, what trouble does it not have? But even grant that it has great advantage, yet undoubtedly it has either satiety or an end. I do not mean to complain of life as many men, and they learned ones, have often done; nor do I regret that I have lived, since I have so lived that I think I was not born in vain, and I quit life as if it were an inn, not a home. For Nature has given us an hostelry in which to sojourn, not to abide.

O glorious day, when I shall set out to join the assembled hosts of souls divine and leave this world of strife and sin! For I shall go to meet not only the men already mentioned, but my Cato, too, than whom no better man, none more distinguished for filial duty, was ever born. His body was burned by me, whereas, on the contrary, it were more fitting that mine had been burned by him; but his soul, not deserting me, but ever looking back, has surely departed for that realm where it knew that I, myself, must come. People think that I have bravely borne my loss—not that I bore it with an untroubled heart, but I found constant solace in the thought that our separation would not be long.

For these reasons, Scipio, my old age sits light upon me (for you said that this has been a cause of wonder to you and Lælius), and not only is not burdensome, but is even happy. And if I err in my belief that the souls of men are immortal, I gladly err, nor do I wish this error which gives me pleasure to be wrested from me while I live. But if when dead I am going to be without sensation (as some petty philosophers think), then I have no fear that these seers, when they are dead, will have the laugh on me! Again, if we are not going to be immortal, nevertheless, it is desirable for a man to be blotted out at his proper time. For as Nature has marked the bounds of everything else, so she has marked the bounds of life. Moreover, old age is the final scene, as it were, in life's drama, from which we ought to escape when it grows wearisome and, certainly, when we have had our fill.

Such, my friends, are my views on old age. May you both attain it, and thus be able to prove by experience the truth of what you have heard from me.

Chapters 1-5, 10-23

※

CATULLUS

(Gaius Valerius Catullus, 84? B.C.–54 B.C.)

*

Poems

*

VIII. Miser Catulle
Translated by R. C. Trevelyan

Thou miserable Catullus, cease from foolishness
And what thou see'st is lost and perished, deem that
  lost.
The sun shone bright and fair upon thee in those days
When thou didst follow wheresoe'er thy mistress led,
She whom you loved as never other shall be loved.
Then all those many blithe and pleasant deeds were
  done
Which you desired; nor did she desire them less.
Verily the sun-shone fair and bright upon thee then.
Now she says nay; thou too, since there's no help, say
  nay.
Pursue not one who flees thee, nor live miserable,
But with a mind grown resolute endure, be stern.
Mistress, farewell. At last Catullus hath grown stern;
He will not seek thee nor entreat thee against thy will.
But thou shalt grieve when no man shall entreat thee
  more.
Alas, poor wretch! What bitter life must now be thine!
Who shall court thee? To whom shalt thou seem beau-
  tiful?

Whom wilt thou love now? By whose name shalt thou
    be called?
Whom shalt thou kiss? Whose lips in fondness wilt thou
    bite?
But thou, Catullus, be thou resolute and stern.

IX. Verani, omnibus e meis amicis
Translated by Hugh Macnaghten

Is it you, my friend of friends, who come,
Dearer to me than a million others,
Veranius, home to your hearth and home,
The aged mother, the loving brothers?
You have come! ah, joy, it is well, it is well.
I shall see you safe, I shall hear you tell
(You best know how) of Hiberian races,
And the deeds they do, and the storied places,
And drawing your neck to my own the while,
I shall kiss the face and the eyes that smile.
Oh! hearts that are happy above the rest,
Is any so happy as I, so blest?

X. Varus me meus
Translated by John Hookham Frere

Varus, whom I chanced to meet
The other evening on the street,
Engaged me there, upon the spot,
To see a mistress he had got.
She seemed, as far as I can gather,

Lively and smart, and handsome rather.
There, as we rested from our walk,
We entered into different talk—
As how much might Bithynia bring?
And had I found it a good thing?
I answered, as it was the fact,
The province had been stripped and sacked,
That there was nothing for the praetors,
And still less for us wretched creatures,
His poor companions and toad-eaters.
"At least," says she, "you bought some fellows
To bear your litter; for they tell us
Our only good ones come from there—"

I choose to give myself an air;—
"Why, truly with my poor estate,
The difference wasn't quite so great
Between a province, good or bad,
That where a purchase could be had,
Eight lusty fellows, straight and tall,
I shouldn't find the wherewithal
To buy them." But it was a lie;
For not a single wretch had I:
No single cripple fit to bear
A broken bedstead or a chair.
She, like a strumpet, pert and knowing,
Said—"Dear Catullus, I am going
To worship at Serapis' shrine:
Do lend me, pray, those slaves of thine!"
I answered—"It was idly said;
They were a purchase Cinna made
(Caius Cinna, my good friend)—
It was the same thing in the end,
Whether a purchase or a loan,
I always used them as my own;

Only the phrase was inexact;
He bought them for himself in fact.
But you have caught the general vice
Of being too correct and nice,
Over curious and precise;
And seizing with precipitation
The slight neglects of conversation."

XXXI. Paene insularum Sirmio
Translated by Andrew Lang

O Sirmio, eye of all the isles and capes,
Which the broad placid-bosomed lakes enfold,
Or on the mighty main the sea-god shakes,
How gladly thee again do I behold.
Scarcely can I believe that the Bithynian plain
Is far—far off, and I behold thee safe again.
For what is better than aside to lay
The cares that bind us, to lay down our load—
And wearied out with wandering far away,
To come again to our beloved abode;
In far-off longed-for couch to sleep a happy sleep,
Taking for weary toils a respite calm and deep.

Hail, happy Sirmio, do thou hail thy lord.
Smile, pleasant waters of the Lydian lake,
Oh, laughter with melodious accord,
Happy home laughter, sweetly sounding wake!

XLVI. Iam ver egelidos

Translated by William A. Aiken

How rapidly the iron gales of March
are melted in the crucible of spring!
Away, Catullus! Swift as swallow, fly
from breathless summer when the sun will parch
Nicæa's fields; fly without faltering
to where in fame and foam great seaside cities lie.

To yearning heart of wanderer give rein
with fervid foot; so bid a long farewell
to that fond band of friends, who once left home
together, but who must return again
from separate paths, through mottled scenes to swell
the ranks that sway along the spidered roads to Rome.

LI. Ille mi par esse deo videtur

Translated by Lord Byron

Equal to Jove that youth must be—
Greater than Jove he seems to me—
Who, free from Jealousy's alarms,
Securely views thy matchless charms.
The cheek, which ever dimpling glows,
That mouth, from whence such music flows,
To him, alike, are always known,
Reserved for him, and him alone.
Ah! Lesbia, though 'tis death to me,
I cannot choose but look on thee;

But, at the sight, my senses fly;
I needs must gaze, but, gazing, die;
Whilst trembling with a thousand fears,
Parched to the throat my tongue adheres,
My pulse beats quick, my breath heaves short,
My limbs deny their slight support,
Cold dews my pallid face o'erspread,
With deadly languor droops my head,
My ears with tingling echoes ring,
And life itself is on the wing;
My eyes refuse the cheering light,
Their orbs are veiled in starless night;
Such pangs my nature sinks beneath,
And feels a temporary death.

LVIII. Caeli, Lesbia nostra
Translated by R. C. Trevelyan

My Lesbia, *that* Lesbia, whom alone Catullus loved
More than himself and all who are most dear to him,
Now in cross-roads and alleys trading her charms
Fleeces the lordly descendants of Remus.

LXI. Collis o Heliconii
Translated by John Hookham Frere

You that from the mother's side
Lead the lingering, blushing bride,
    Fair Urania's son—
Leave awhile the lonely mount,

The haunted grove and holy fount
    Of chilling Helicon.

With myrtle wreaths enweave thy hair—
Wave the torch aloft in air—
    Make no long delay:
With flowing robe and footsteps light,
And gilded buskins glancing bright,
    Hither bend thy way.

Join at once, with airy vigour,
In the dance's varied figure,
    To the cymbal's chime:
Frolic unrestrain'd and free—
Let voice, and air, and verse agree,
    And the *torch* beat time.

Hymen, come, for Julia
Weds with Manlius today,
    And deigns to be a bride.
Such a form as Venus wore
In the contest famed of yore,
    On Mount Ida's side;

Like the myrtle or the bay,
Florid, elegant, and gay,
    With foliage fresh and new,
Which the nymphs and forest maids
Have foster'd in sequester'd shades,
    With drops of holy dew.

Leave then, all the rocks and cells
Of the deep Aonian dells,
    And the caverns hoar;
And the dreary streams that weep

From the stony Thespian steep,
  Dripping evermore.

Haste away to new delights,
To domestic happy rites,
  Human haunts and ways;
With a kindly charm applied,
Soften and appease the bride,
  And shorten our delays.

Bring her hither, bound to move,
Drawn and led with bands of love,
  Like the tender twine
Which the searching ivy plies,
Clinging in a thousand ties
  O'er the clasping vine.

Gentle virgins, you besides,
Whom the like event betides,
  With the coming year;
Call on Hymen! call him now!
Call aloud! A virgin vow
  Best befits his ear.

"Is there any deity
More beloved and kind than he—
  More disposed to bless;
Worthy to be worshipp'd more;
Master of a richer store
  Of wealth and happiness?

"Youth and age alike agree,
Serving and adoring thee,
  The source of hope and care:
Care and hope alike engage

The wary parent sunk in age
And the restless heir.

"She the maiden, half afraid,
Hears the new proposal made,
    That proceeds from Thee;
You resign and hand her over
To the rash and hardy lover
    With a fix'd decree.

"Hymen, Hymen, you preside,
Maintaining honour and the pride
    Of women free from blame,
With a solemn warrant given,
Is there any power in heaven
    That can do the same?

"Love, accompanied by thee,
Passes unreproved and free,
    But without thee, not:
Where on earth, or in the sky,
Can you find a deity
    With a fairer lot?

"Heirship in an honour'd line
Is sacred as a gift of thine,
    But without thee, not:
Where on earth, or in the sky,
Can you find a deity
    With a fairer lot?

"Rule and empire—royalty,
Are rightful, as derived from thee,
    But without thee, not:
Where on earth, or in the sky,

Can you find a deity
  With a fairer lot?"

Open locks! unbar the gate!
Behold the ready troop that wait
    The coming of the bride;
Behold the torches, how they flare!
Spreading aloft their sparkling hair,
    Flashing far and wide.

Lovely maiden! here we waste
The timely moments;—Come in haste!
    Come then. . . . Out, alack!
Startled at the glare and dim,
She retires to weep within,
    Lingering, hanging back.

Bashful honour and regret
For a while detain her yet,
    Lingering, taking leave:
Taking leave and lingering still,
With a slow, reluctant will,
    With grief that does not grieve.

Aurunculeia, cease your tears,
And when tomorrow's morn appears,
    Fear not that the sun
Will dawn upon a fairer face—
Nor in his airy, lofty race
    Behold a lovelier one.

Mark and hear us, gentle bride;
Behold the torches nimbly plied,
    Waving here and there;
Along the street and in the porch,

See the fiery-tressed torch
   Spreads its sparkling hair.

Like a lily, fair and chaste,
Lovely bride, you shall be placed
   In a garden gay,
A wealthy lord's delight and pride;
Come away then, happy bride,
   Hasten, hence away!

Mark and hear us—he your Lord,
Will be true at bed and board,
   Nor ever walk astray,
Withdrawing from your lovely side;
Mark and hear us, gentle bride,
   Hasten, hence away!

Like unto the tender vine,
He shall ever clasp and twine,
   Clinging night and day,
Fairly bound and firmly tied;
Come away then, happy bride,
   Hasten, hence away!

Happy chamber, happy bed,
Can the joys be told or said
   That await you soon;
Fresh renewals of delight,
In the silent fleeting night
   And the summer noon.

Make ready. There I see within
The bride is veil'd; the guests begin
   To muster close and slow:
Trooping onward close about,

Boys, be ready with a shout—
　　"Hymen! Hymen! Ho!"

Now begins the free career—
For many a jest and many a jeer,
　　And many a merry saw;
Customary taunts and gibes,
Such as ancient use prescribes,
　　And immemorial law.

"Some at home, it must be fear'd,
Will be slighted and cashier'd,
　　Pride will have a fall;
Now the favourites' reign is o'er,
Proud enough they were before—
　　Proud and nice withal.

"Full of pride and full of scorn,
Now you see them clipt and shorn,
　　Humbler in array;
Sent away, for fear of harm,
To the village or the farm—
　　Pack'd in haste away.

"Other doings must be done,
Another empire is begun,
　　Behold your own domain!
Gentle bride! Behold it there!
The lordly palace proud and fair:
　　You shall live and reign

"In that rich and noble house,
Till age shall silver o'er the brows,
　　And nod the trembling head,
Not regarding what is meant,

Incessant uniform assent
    To all that's done or said.

"Let the faithful threshold greet,
With omens fair, those lovely feet,
    Lightly lifted o'er;
Let the garlands wave and bow
From the lofty lintel's brow
    That bedeck the door."

See the couch with crimson dress—
Where, seated in the deep recess,
    With expectation warm,
The bridegroom views her coming near—
The slender youth that led her here
    May now release her arm.

With a fix'd intense regard
He beholds her close and hard
    In awful interview:
Shortly now she must be sped
To the chamber and the bed,
    With attendance due.

Let the ancient worthy wives,
That have pass'd their constant lives
    With a single mate,
As befits advised age,
With council and precaution sage
    Assist and regulate.

She the mistress of the band
Comes again with high command,
    "Bridegroom, go your way;
There your bride is in the bower,

Like a lovely lily flower,
  Or a rose in May.

"Ay, and you yourself in truth
Are a goodly comely youth,
    Proper, tall, and fair;
Venus and the Graces too
Have befriended each of you
    For a lovely pair.

"There you go! may Venus bless
Such as you with good success
    In the lawful track;
You that, in an honest way,
Purchase in the face of day
    Whatsoe'er you lack."

Sport your fill and never spare—
Let us have an infant heir
    Of the noble name;
Such a line should ever last,
As it has for ages past,
    Another and the same.

Fear not! with the coming year,
The new Torquatus will be here,
    Him we soon shall see
With infant gesture fondly seek
To reach his father's manly cheek,
    From his mother's knee.

With laughing eyes and dewy lip,
Pouting like the purple tip
    That points the rose's bud;
While mingled with the mother's grace,

Strangers shall recognise the trace
    That marks the Manlian blood.

So the mother's fair renown
Shall betimes adorn and crown
    The child with dignity,
As we read in stories old
Of Telemachus the bold,
    And chaste Penelope.

Now the merry task is o'er
Let us hence and close the door,
    While loud adieux are paid:
"Live in honour, love and truth,
And exercise your lusty youth
    In matches fairly play'd."

LXX. Nulli se dicit

Translated by Sir Philip Sidney

"Unto nobody," my woman saith, "she had rather a wife
    be
Than to myself; not though Jove grew a suitor of hers."
These be her words, but a woman's words to a love that
    is eager,
In wind or water's streame do require to be writ.

LXXXV. Odi et amo
Translated by Hugh Macnaghten

I hate and love. You question "How?" I lack
An answer, but I feel it on the rack.

XCII. Lesbia me dicit
Translated by Jonathan Swift

Lesbia for ever on me rails,
To talk of me, she never fails,
Now, hang me, but for all her art
I find that I have gained her heart.
My proof is this: I plainly see
The case is just the same with me;
I curse her every hour sincerely,
Yet, hang me, but I love her dearly.

CI. Multas per gentes
Translated by Andrew Lang

From wandering through the nations, o'er the waves,
Brother, I come, and stand beside thy tomb
To give thee the death-offering of the grave,
To call thee, vainly, dumb in Hades' gloom.
Oh, weary is the fortune that bereft me,
I give or gave our fathers long ago

The sad fraternal duty that is left me,
The dreary gifts unto the shades below.
Accept them, dewy with a brother's tears;
Accept the sorrow that they cannot tell,
And through the long eternity of years,
Brother, farewell, for ever fare thee well!

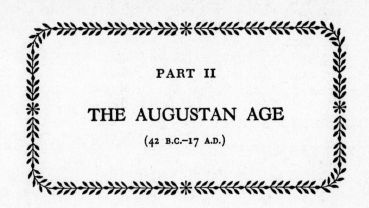

PART II

THE AUGUSTAN AGE

(42 B.C.–17 A.D.)

EDITOR'S NOTE

THE assassination of Julius Cæsar led to another period of chaos, which was brought to an end when Octavius, Julius's nephew and heir, defeated his only remaining rival, Mark Antony, at the Battle of Actium. On his return Octavius was greeted not as the victor in a civil war, but as a sovereign who had crushed a rebellion. And he proceeded to restore, if not the fact, at least the forms, of the Republic. Like Julius Cæsar, he governed through a multiplicity of offices; he was sole consul, re-elected, every year, by an understood agreement, which gave him a position at least equal to that of President; he was governor of all the provinces; he was Commander-in-Chief of the Army, that most important post. In addition, the Senate conferred on him two complimentary titles, which may be said to mark respectively the power which he admitted and that which he actually possessed: the first was Princeps, "First Citizen of the Republic"; the second was Augustus, which means something between "His Majesty" and "His Holiness" (using the words not as conventional titles but in their original meaning). Julius Cæsar had renamed the month Quintilis after himself, July, placing his name among the months dedicated to the gods Janus, Mars, and Maia; he had substituted his image for those of the gods on the coinage. Not to be outdone, Augustus renamed Sextilis, August, and stole a day from February to keep his month from being shorter than his predecessor's. Divine honors were paid to him after his death, though the head of the Roman state was not regarded as a god on earth as yet. Horace indeed speaks of Augustus as a *præsens divus*, a deity among us (contrasted with Jupiter in heaven); but this is in a poem admonishing Augustus as to his duty (not to readmit to citizenship the deserters from Crassus's army who had gone over to the enemy), and is held out as a title consequent on good behavior. "We believe," says Horace, "that Jupiter is in heaven because we hear him thunder; we shall regard Augustus as a deity here present for having added the Britons and the troublesome Parthians to the Empire."

Augustus has been called a constitutional monarch, and so he was, if it is remembered that the constitution was strongly monarchical and that it was not merely unwritten but was supported by no guarantees. The best solution for Roman government might have been a genuine constitutional monarchy, with provision for an imperial council, and, above all, the establishment of the succession to the throne. The absence of a fixed succession was the cause of one of the most important of the reforms by which Diocletian gave the Empire a new lease on life; but such a provision was of course impossible so long as the pretense was maintained that Augustus was the restorer of the Republic. Nevertheless, Augustus did govern through the forms of the Republic, and not only that, but the Senate, the Assembly, and the magistrates had important functions in the state. It was possible to believe that the Republic had in fact been restored and that the extraordinary powers granted to the First Citizen by the Senate would lapse with the passing of the emergency. The ordinary Roman had all the freedom he cared for, and much more than he had had during the irregular dictatorships of the past half-century; he had two things which he greatly valued, law and order; and he had peace.

For almost the first time in history Rome was at peace at home and abroad. It was the beginning of the

Pax Romana, the Roman Peace, which, within the Empire at least, was to endure for centuries. For the first time in their lives men had time to get their breath and look about them; and what they saw was an empire that, as Gibbon said, "comprised the fairest part of the habitable world." They knew that they were living in a great age; they believed that they were on the threshold of a veritable Age of Gold. Virgil's Fourth Eclogue, whose historic meaning is disputed but which probably refers to the birth of an heir to Augustus, salutes so rapturously the child and the age he is to usher in that it was long believed to be a divinely inspired prophecy of the birth of the Messiah, so soon to be born. (That is one reason why Virgil was allowed to guide Dante as far as the Earthly Paradise.)

The writers of the time were moved to celebrate the greatness of Rome, past, present, and to come. The great monument is, of course, Virgil's *Æneid,* which links the foundation of Rome to the fall of Troy, traces the ancestry of Julius Cæsar to the gods, and makes the greatness of Rome the subject of divine intervention and prophecy. If to all moderns (unless they make a special imaginative effort to see Virgil's point of view) Æneas seems a heartless prig when he deserts Dido, he does so because the founding of Rome was a sacred cause, which could demand and justify the breaking of every earthly tie. But Virgil was by no means alone. "*Antiquam exquirite matrem,*" Æneas was charged, "Seek the ancient mother," and the historian Livy was also moved to seek the foundations of Rome's greatness in the heroism and frugality of her early days. Of Livy as a historian, it may be said mildly that he is not reliable, and he has not always been spoken of mildly. Gibbon said of the ancient historians generally, "They said what it would have been meritorious to omit, and omitted what it was essential to say"; and Dr. Arnold of Rugby said, "The use of Livy as an historian is like that of the drunken helot—he shows what history should not be." But Livy was not writing as a historian in the modern sense but almost as a fabulist. He presents his characters as examples of good and evil, as good and bad examples; and he has no doubt that whatever may be the truth of particular stories, the greatness of Rome is in fact founded on *virtus*. He speaks almost in the words of Virgil in declaring that the greatness of Rome was hard-earned. *"Tantæ molis erat Romanam condere gentem,"* says Virgil, "So great a toil it was to found the race of Rome." *"Quanta rerum moles!"* cries Livy, "What a succession of toils!"

The lighter writers share the feeling. That delightful book of fairy-tales for grownups, the *Metamorphoses* of Ovid, manages to hold a fairly chronological course through its labyrinth of wonders, beginning with the shaping of the world out of chaos. It ends with the deification of Julius Cæsar, who shines in heaven as a new star, and with the clear prophecy that his successor will surpass him. In much of his verse Horace deliberately tries to give the impression of an elegant trifler; and one need not compare him with the ardent Catullus to say that in most matters of emotion he is a trifler. He has had affairs with several girls, and his general feeling is, as he says in "Quis multa gracilis," that he is well out of it; or as he says at the beginning of the Fourth Book (written after an interval, when he was older), "Oh, Lord, is *that* beginning again? I thought I was too old!" He can even make fun, in "Integer vitæ," of the sacred Roman concept of virtue, beginning with what is apparently a celebration of virtue and then in a kind of burlesque revealing that the virtue he means is constancy in love—which was to most Romans far less important than *pietas* and *virtus,* and not a virtue for which Horace himself was distinguished. For the rest, he is the poet of strictly rational enjoyments. Let us eat and drink, for we shall soon be dead, and what good will the wine be to us then? But let us not eat and drink too much, or we may have a headache tomorrow. It is sensible and agreeable; it is also, in the magic of Horace's word order, extremely charming; but as an emotional attitude it is apt to seem a little chilly to anyone brought up in a more romantic tradition. The great group of patriotic poems at the beginning of the Third Book, however, the Regulus ode and the rest, show an emotion as deep and intense as anything that poetry can show. It can be said that there were two things that Horace took seriously: Rome and the art of poetry.

Wealth and peace had brought an age in which the art of poetry was cultivated as never before. Lucretius and Catullus, splendid as their diction is, are still chiefly important for what they have to say; they can be read in translation without too great a loss. But much of the matter in the *Odes* of Horace is either the merest platitude or the merest chit-chat, turned into poetry by his *curiosa felicitas,* his choice and arrangement of words. The same thing is true of the greatest lines in Virgil. A. E. Housman has told us that a verse from the Psalms, in the Prayer-Book version, can bring tears to his eyes and make his skin bristle, while the same verse in the King James version leaves him cold. It is the same with such a line as that in Virgil, of the dead souls who cannot pass Lethe: *"Tendebantque manus ripæ ulterioris amore."* What it means is simply: "They stretched out their hands for desire of the farther shore," but that will bring tears to no one's eyes, while the original will —*experto crede.* Those enchantments must be taken on faith; but anyone can enjoy, say, the sheer technical ingenuity, amounting to bravura, with which **Ovid** strings together his stories in the *Metamorphoses*.

It was an age of elegance and urbanity generally, not merely in literature. The *Satires* and *Epistles* of Horace, his verse letters to his friends, have the precise note of the man about town, a note that is hardly struck again until the letters of Horace Walpole. And as in all ages of great urbanity, there was a vogue for country life. Virgil began the pastoral convention. The pastoral indeed begins with the Greek Theocritus, but the pastoral convention with Virgil. Theocritus wrote about the real shepherds and their songs; it is Virgil who first used the figure of a shepherd to mean himself, and a kind employer to mean his patron. But the convention is still not so conventional as it later became; in some of the *Eclogues*, at least, the shepherds might actually be shepherds. In Virgil's *Georgics*, a treatise on farming which is, surprisingly, not merely in verse but in poetry, and in Horace's constant invitations to his Sabine farm, there is real feeling not merely for country life but for simplicity. It is the last time that feeling was to be expressed.

The Romans of the Augustan Age were genuinely interested in the Roman past; but there was another reason for being concerned with it. When Pollio began a history of the First Triumvirate and after, Horace warned him that he was "walking over hidden fires"; he took the warning and stopped at the defeat of the conspirators at Philippi. The past was safe; present events were not. By an arbitrary act of Augustus, Ovid was exiled to the half-Greek, half-barbaric town of Tomi, near the mouth of the Danube, where he spent the rest of his life. For this, Ovid says, there were two reasons. One was the scandal occasioned by his *Ars Amatoria*, though there is nothing in it to shock anyone who has lived to see the release of *Jurgen,* not to mention *Ulysses,* and it is hard to believe that the Romans were more easily scandalized than we. It is true, however, that its tone is cynical, and it unfortunately appeared at the time when Augustus's daughter was involved in a scandal. The other, and probably more important, reason for Ovid's banishment is not known; it apparently involved some offense to Augustus, or to the imperial house, since Augustus's successor Tiberius left Ovid unpardoned. Perhaps the most strongly supported theory is that Ovid was one of the adherents of Tiberius's rivals for the throne, Agrippa or Germanicus. The troubles had begun.

VIRGIL

(Publius Virgilius Maro, 70 B.C.–19 B.C.)

※

From the Eclogues

※

Eclogue I: The Happy Tityrus

Translated by Henry Wadsworth Longfellow

MELIBŒUS

Tityrus, thou in the shade of a spreading beech-tree
  reclining,
Meditatest, with slender pipe, the Muse of the wood-
  lands.
We our country's bounds and pleasant pastures relin-
  quish,
We our country fly; thou, Tityrus, stretched in the
  shadow,
Teachest the woods to resound with the name of the
  fair Amaryllis.

TITYRUS

O Melibœus, a god for us this leisure created,
For he will be unto me a god forever; his altar
Oftentimes shall imbue a tender lamb from our sheep-
  folds.
He, my heifers to wander at large, and myself, as thou
  seest,
On my rustic reed to play what I will, hath permitted.

MELIBŒUS

Truly I envy not, I marvel rather; on all sides
In all the fields is such trouble. Behold, my goats I am
  driving,
Heartsick, further away: this one scarce, Tityrus, lead I;
For having here yeaned twins just now among the dense
  hazels,
Hope of the flock, ah me! on the naked flint she hath left
  them.
Often this evil to me, if my mind had not been insensate,
Oak-trees stricken by heaven predicted, as now I re-
  member;
Often the sinister crow from the hollow ilex predicted.
Nevertheless, who this god may be, O Tityrus, tell me.

TITYRUS

O Melibœus, the city that they call Rome, I imagined,
Foolish I! to be like this of ours, where often we shep-
  herds
Wonted are to drive down of our ewes the delicate off-
  spring.
Thus whelps like unto dogs had I known, and kids to
  their mothers,
Thus to compare great things with small had I been ac-
  customed.
But this among other cities its head as far hath exalted
As the cypresses do among the lissome viburnums.

MELIBŒUS

And what so great occasion of seeing Rome hath pos-
  sessed thee?

TITYRUS

Liberty, which, though late, looked upon me in my inert-
ness,
After the time when my beard fell whiter from me in
shaving—
Yet she looked upon me, and came to me after a long
while,
Since Amaryllis possesses and Galatea hath left me.
For I will even confess that while Galatea possessed me,
Neither care of my flock nor hope of liberty was there.
Though from my wattled folds there went forth many a
victim,
And the unctuous cheese was pressed for the city un-
grateful,
Never did my right hand return home heavy with
money.

MELIBŒUS

I have wondered why sad thou invokedst the gods,
Amaryllis,
And for whom thou didst suffer the apples to hang on
the branches!
Tityrus hence was absent! Thee, Tityrus, even the pine-
trees,
Thee, the very fountains, the very copses, were calling.

TITYRUS

What could I do? No power had I to escape from my
bondage,
Nor had I power elsewhere to recognize gods so propi-
tious.
Here I beheld that youth, to whom each year, Melibœus,
During twice six days ascends the smoke of our altars.
Here first gave he response to me soliciting favor:

"Feed as before your heifers, ye boys, and yoke up your
    bullocks."

MELIBŒUS

Fortunate old man! So then thy fields will be left thee,
And large enough for thee, though naked stone and the
    marish
All thy pasture-lands with the dreggy rush may encom-
    pass.
No unaccustomed food thy gravid ewes shall endanger,
Nor of the neighboring flock the dire contagion infect
    them.
Fortunate old man! Here among familiar rivers
And these sacred founts, shalt thou take the shadowy
    coolness.
On this side, a hedge along the neighboring cross-road,
Where Hyblaean bees ever feed on the flower of the
    willow,
Often with gentle susurrus to fall asleep shall persuade
    thee.
Yonder beneath the high rock, the pruner shall sing to
    the breezes;
Nor meanwhile shall thy heart's delight, the hoarse
    wood-pigeons,
Nor the turtle-dove cease to mourn from aerial elm-trees.

TITYRUS

Therefore the agile stags shall sooner feed in the ether,
And the billows leave the fishes bare on the sea-shore,
Sooner, the border-lands of both overpassed, shall the
    exiled
Parthian drink of the Saone, or the German drink of the
    Tigris,
Than the face of him shall glide away from my bosom!

MELIBŒUS

But we hence shall go, a part to the thirsty Africs,
Part to Scythia come, and the rapid Cretan Oaxes,
And to the Britons from all the universe utterly sundered.
Ah, shall I ever, a long time hence, the bounds of my
    country
And the roof of my lowly cottage covered with greens-
    ward
Seeing, with wonder behold? my kingdoms, a handful of
    wheat-ears!
Shall an impious soldier possess these lands newly cul-
    tured,
And these fields of corn a barbarian? Lo, whither dis-
    cord
Us wretched people hath brought! for whom our fields
    we have planted!
Graft, Melibœus, thy pear-trees now; put in order thy
    vineyards.
Go, my goats, go hence, my flocks so happy aforetime.
Never again henceforth outstretched in my verdurous
    cavern
Shall I behold you afar from the bushy precipice hang-
    ing.
Songs no more shall I sing; not with me, ye goats, as
    your shepherd,
Shall ye browse on the bitter willow or blooming la-
    burnum.

TITYRUS

Nevertheless this night together with me canst thou rest
    thee
Here on the verdant leaves; for us there are mellowing
    apples,

Chestnuts soft to the touch, and clouted cream in
    abundance;
And the high roofs now of the villages smoke in the
    distance,
And from the lofty mountains are falling larger the
    shadows.

Eclogue IV: Pollio

Translated by Charles Stuart Calverley

Muses of Sicily, a loftier song
Wake we! Some tire of shrubs and myrtles low.
Are woods our theme? Then princely be the woods.

Come are those last days that the Sibyl sang:
The ages' mighty march begins anew.
Now comes the virgin, Saturn reigns again:
Now from high heaven descends a wondrous race.
Thou on the newborn babe—who first shall end
That age of iron, bid a golden dawn
Upon the broad world—chaste Lucina, smile:
Now thy Apollo reigns. And, Pollio, thou
Shalt be our prince, when he that grander age
Opens, and onward roll the mighty moons:
Thou, trampling out what prints our crimes have left,
Shalt free the nations from perpetual fear.
While he to bliss shall waken; with the Blest
See the Brave mingling, and be seen of them,
Ruling that world o'er which his father's arm shed peace.

On thee, child, everywhere shall earth, untilled,
Show'r her first baby-offerings, vagrant stems
Of ivy, foxglove, and gay briar, and bean;

Unbid the goats shall come big-uddered home,
Nor monstrous lions scare the herded kine.
Thy cradle shall be full of pretty flowers:
Die must the serpent, treacherous poison-plants
Must die; and Syria's roses spring like weeds.

But, soon as thou canst read of hero-deeds
Such as thy father wrought, and understand
What is true worth: the champaign day by day
Shall grow more yellow with the waving corn;
From the wild bramble purpling then shall hang
The grape; and stubborn oaks drop honeydew.
Yet traces of that guile of older days
Shall linger; bidding men tempt seas in ships,
Gird towns with walls, cleave furrows in the land.
Then a new Tiphys shall arise, to man
New argosies with heroes: then shall be
New wars; and once more shall be bound for Troy
A mightier Achilles. After this,
When thou hast grown and strengthened into man,
The pilot's self shall range the seas no more;
Nor, each land teeming with the wealth of all,
The floating pines exchange their merchandise.
Vines shall not need the pruning-hook, nor earth
The harrow: ploughmen shall unyoke their steers.
Nor then need wool be taught to counterfeit
This hue and that. At will the meadow ram
Shall change to saffron, or the gorgeous tints
Of Tyre, his fair fleece; and the grazing lamb
At will put crimson on. So grand an age
Did those three Sisters bid their spindles spin;
Three, telling with one voice the changeless will of Fate.

Oh draw—the time is all but present—near
To thy great glory, cherished child of heaven,

Jove's mighty progeny! And lo! the world,
The round and ponderous world, bows down to thee;
The earth, the ocean-tracts, the depths of heaven.
Lo! nature revels in the coming age.
Oh! may the evening of my days last on,
May breath be mine, till I have told thy deeds!
Not Orpheus then, not Linus, shall outsing
Me: though each vaunts his mother or his sire,
Calliopea this, Apollo that.
Let Pan strive with me, Arcady his judge;
Pan, Arcady his judge, shall yield the palm.

Learn, tiny babe, to read a mother's smile:
Already ten long months have wearied her.
Learn, tiny babe. Him, who ne'er knew such smiles,
Nor god nor goddess bids to board or bed.

From The Aeneid

Book II
Translated by *John Conington*

Each eye was fixed, each lip compressed,
When thus began the heroic guest:

Too cruel, lady, is the pain
You bid me thus revive again;
How lofty Ilium's throne august
Was laid by Greece in piteous dust,
The woes I saw with these sad eyne,

The deeds whereof large part was mine:
What Argive, when the tale were told,
What Myrmidon of sternest mould,
What foe from Ithaca could hear,
And grudge the tribute of a tear?
Now dews precipitate the night,
And setting stars to rest invite:
Yet, if so keen your zeal to know
In brief the tale of Troy's last woe,
Though memory shrinks with backward start,
And sends a shudder to my heart,
I take the word.

        Worn down by wars,
Long beating 'gainst Fate's dungeon-bars,
    As year kept chasing year,
The Danaan chiefs, with cunning given
By Pallas, mountain-high to heaven
    A giant horse uprear,
And with compacted beams of pine
The texture of its ribs entwine.
A vow for their return they feign:
So runs the tale, and spreads amain.
There in the monster's cavernous side
Huge frames of chosen chiefs they hide,
And steel-clad soldiery finds room
Within that death-producing womb.

An isle there lies in Ilium's sight,
    And Tenedos its name,
While Priam's fortune yet was bright,
    Known for its wealth to fame:
Now all has dwindled to a bay,
Where ships in treacherous shelter stay.
Thither they sail, and hide their host

Along its desolated coast.
We thought them to Mycenæ flown,
And rescued Troy forgets to groan.
Wide stand the gates: what joy to go
    The Dorian camp to see,·
The land disburthened of the foe,
    The shore from vessels free!
There pitched Thessalia's squadron, there
    Achilles' tent was set:
There, drawn on land, their navies were,
    And there the battle met.
Some on Minerva's offering gaze,
And view its bulk with strange amaze:
And first Thymœtes loudly calls
To drag the steed within our walls,
Or by suggestion from the foe,
Or Troy's ill fate had willed it so.
But Capys and the wiser kind
Surmised the snare that lurked behind:
To drown it in the whelming tide,
Or set the fire-brand to its side,
Their sentence is: or else to bore
Its caverns, and their depths explore.
In wild confusion sways the crowd:
Each takes his side and all are loud.

    Girt with a throng of Ilium's sons,
Down from the tower Laocoon runs,
And, "Wretched countrymen," he cries,
"What monstrous madness blinds your eyes?
Think you your enemies removed?
    Come presents without wrong
From Danaans? have you thus approved
    Ulysses, known so long?
Perchance—who knows?—the bulk we see

Conceals a Grecian enemy,
Or 'tis a pile to o'erlook the town,
And pour from high invaders down,
Or fraud lurks somewhere to destroy:
Mistrust, mistrust it, men of Troy!
Whate'er it be, a Greek I fear,
Though presents in his hand he bear."
He spoke, and with his arm's full force
Straight at the belly of the horse
　　His mighty spear he cast:
Quivering it stood: the sharp rebound
Shook the huge monster: and a sound
　　Through all its caverns passed.
And then, had fate our weal designed
Nor given us a perverted mind,
Then had he moved us to deface
The Greeks' accursed lurking-place,
And Troy had been abiding still,
And Priam's tower yet crowned the hill.
Now Dardan swains before the king
With clamorous demonstration bring,
His hands fast bound, a youth unknown,
Across their casual pathway thrown
By cunning purpose of his own,
If so his simulated speech
For Greece the walls of Troy might breach,
Nerved by strong courage to defy
The worst, and gain his end or die.
The curious Trojans round him flock,
With rival zeal a foe to mock.
Now listen while my tongue declares
The tale you ask of Danaan snares,
And gather from a single charge
Their catalogue of crimes at large.
There as he stands, confused, unarmed,

Like helpless innocence alarmed,
His wistful eyes on all sides throws,
And sees that all around are foes.
"What land," he cries, "what sea is left,
To hold a wretch of country reft,
Driven out from Greece while savage Troy
Demands my blood with clamorous joy?"
That anguish put our rage to flight,
And stayed each hand in act to smite:
We bid him name and race declare,
And say why Troy her prize should spare.
Then by degrees he laid aside
His fear, and presently replied:

"Truth, gracious king, is all I speak,
And first I own my nation Greek:
No; Sinon may be Fortune's slave;
She shall not make him liar or knave.
If haply to your ears e'er came
Belidan Palamedes' name,
Borne by the tearful voice of Fame,
Whom erst, by false impeachment sped,
Maligned because for peace he pled,
Greece gave to death, now mourns him dead—
His kinsman I, while yet a boy,
Sent by a needy sire to Troy.
While he yet stood in kingly state,
'Mid brother kings in council great,
I too had power: but when he died,
By false Ulysses' spite belied
(The tale is known), from that proud height
I sank to wretchedness and night,
And brooded in my dolorous gloom
On that my guiltless kinsman's doom
Not all in silence; no, I swore,

Should Fortune bring me home once more,
My vengeance should redress his fate,
And speech engendered cankerous hate.
Thence dates my fall: Ulysses thence
Still scared me with some fresh pretence,
With chance-dropt words the people fired,
Sought means of hurt, intrigued, conspired.
Nor did the glow of hatred cool,
Till, wielding Calchas as his tool—
But why a tedious tale repeat,
To stay you from your morsel sweet?
If all are equal, Greek and Greek,
Enough; your tardy vengeance wreak.
My death will Ithacus delight,
And Atreus' sons the boon requite."

We press, we yearn the truth to know,
Nor dream how doubly base our foe:
He, faltering still and overawed,
Takes up the unfinished web of fraud.
"Oft had we planned to leave your shore,
Nor tempt the weary conflict more.
O, had we done it! sea and sky
Scared us as oft, in act to fly:
But chiefly when completed stood
This horse, compact of maple wood,
Fierce thunders, pealing in our ears,
Proclaimed the turmoil of the spheres.
Perplexed, Eurypylus we send
To question what the fates portend,
And he from Phœbus' awful shrine
Brings back the words of doom divine:
'With blood ye pacified the gales,
    E'en with a virgin slain,
When first ye Danaans spread your sails,

The shores of Troy to gain:
With blood ye your return must buy:
A Greek must at the altar die.'
That sentence reached the public ear,
And bred the dull amaze of fear:
Through every heart a shudder ran,
'Apollo's victim—who the man?'
Ulysses, turbulent and loud,
Drags Calchas forth before the crowd,
And questions what the immortals mean,
Which way these dubious beckonings lean:
E'en then were some discerned my foe,
And silent watch the coming blow.
Ten days the seer, with bated breath,
Restrained the utterance big with death:
O'erborne at last, the word agreed
He speaks, and destines me to bleed.
All gave a sigh, as men set free,
And hailed the doom, content to see
The bolt that threatened each alike
One solitary victim strike.
The death-day came: the priests prepare
Salt cakes, and fillets for my hair;
I fled, I own it, from the knife,
I broke my bands and ran for life,
And in a marish lay that night,
While they should sail, if sail they might.
No longer have I hope, ah me!
My ancient fatherland to see,
Or look on those my eyes desire,
My darling sons, my gray-haired sire:
Perhaps my butchers may requite
On their dear heads my traitorous flight,
And make their wretched lives atone
For this, the single crime I own.

O, by the Gods, who all things view,
And know the false man from the true,
By sacred Faith, if Faith remain
With mortal men preserved from stain,
Show grace to innocence forlorn,
Show grace to woes unduly borne!"

Moved by his tears, we let him live,
And pity crowns the boon we give:
King Priam bids unloose his cords,
And soothes the wretch with kindly words:
"Whoe'er you are, henceforth resign
All thought of Greece: be Troy's and mine:
Now tell me truth, for what intent
This fabric of the horse was meant;
An offering to your heavenly liege?
An engine for assault or siege?"
Then, schooled in all Pelasgian shifts,
His unbound hands to heaven he lifts:
"Ye slumberless, inviolate fires,
And the dread awe your name inspires!
Ye murderous altars, which I fled!
Ye fillets that adorned my head!
Bear witness, and behold me free
To break my Grecian fealty;
To hate the Greeks, and bring to light
The counsels they would hide in night,
Unchecked by all that once could bind,
All claims of country or of kind.
Thou, Troy, remember ne'er to swerve,
Preserved thyself, thy faith preserve,
If true this story I relate,
If these, my prompt returns, be great.
The warlike hopes of Greece were stayed,
E'en from the first, on Pallas' aid:

But since Tydides, impious man,
And foul Ulysses, born to plan,
Dragged with red hands, the sentry slain,
Her fateful image from your fane,
Her chaste locks touched, and stained with gore
The virgin coronal she wore,
Thenceforth the tide of fortune changed,
And Greece grew weak, her queen estranged.
Nor dubious were the signs of ill
That showed the goddess' altered will.
The image scarce in camp was set,
Out burst big drops of saltest sweat
O'er all her limbs: her eyes upraised
With minatory lightnings blazed;
And thrice untouched from earth she sprang
With quivering spear and buckler's clang.
'Back o'er the ocean!' Calchas cries:
'We shall not make Troy's town our prize,
Unless at Argos' sacred seat
Our former omens we repeat,
And bring once more the grace we brought
When first these shores our navy sought.'
So now for Greece they cross the wave,
Fresh blessings on their arms to crave,
Thence to return, so Calchas rules,
Unlooked for, ere your wonder cools.
Premonished first, this frame they planned
In your Palladium's stead to stand,
An image for an image given
To pacify offended Heaven.
But Calchas bade them rear it high
With timbers mounting to the sky,
That none might drag within the gate
This new Palladium of your state.
For, said he, if your hands profaned

The gift for Pallas' self ordained,
Dire havoc—grant, ye powers, that first
That fate be his!—on Troy should burst:
But if, in glad procession haled
By those your hands, your walls it scaled,
Then Asia should our homes invade,
And unborn captives mourn the raid."

Such tale of pity, aptly feigned,
Our credence for the perjurer gained,
And tears, wrung out from fraudful eyes,
Made us, e'en us, a villain's prize,
'Gainst whom not valiant Diomede,
Nor Peleus' Larissæan seed,
Nor ten years' fighting could prevail,
Nor navies of a thousand sail.

But ghastlier portents lay behind,
Our unprophetic souls to bind.
Laocoon, named as Neptune's priest,
Was offering up the victim beast,
When lo! from Tenedos—I quail,
E'en now, at telling of the tale—
Two monstrous serpents stem the tide,
And shoreward through the stillness glide.
Amid the waves they rear their breasts,
And toss on high their sanguine crests:
The hind part coils along the deep,
And undulates with sinuous sweep.
The lashed spray echoes: now they reach
The inland belted by the beach,
And rolling bloodshot eyes of fire,
Dart their forked tongues, and hiss for ire.
We fly distraught: unswerving they
Toward Laocoon hold their way;

First round his two young sons they wreathe,
And grind their limbs with savage teeth:
Then, as with arms he comes to aid,
The wretched father they invade
And twine in giant folds: twice round
His stalwart waist their spires are wound,
Twice round his neck, while over all
Their heads and crests tower high and tall.
He strains his strength their knots to tear,
While gore and slime his fillets smear,
And to the unregardful skies
Sends up his agonizing cries:
A wounded bull such moaning makes,
When from his neck the axe he shakes,
Ill-aimed, and from the altar breaks.
The twin destroyers take their flight
To Pallas' temple on the height;
There by the goddess' feet concealed
They lie, and nestle 'neath her shield.
At once through Ilium's hapless sons
A shock of feverous horror runs:
All in Laocoon's death-pangs read
The just requital of his deed,
Who dared to harm with impious stroke
Those ribs of consecrated oak.
"The image to its fane!" they cry:
"So soothe the offended deity."
Each in the labor claims his share:
The walls are breached, the town laid bare:
Wheels 'neath its feet are fixed to glide,
And round its neck stout ropes are tied:
So climbs our wall that shape of doom,
With battle quickening in its womb,
While youths and maidens sing glad songs
And joy to touch the harness-thongs.

It comes, and, glancing terror down,
Sweeps through the bosom of the town.
O Ilium, city of my love!
O warlike home of powers above!
Four times 'twas on the threshold stayed:
Four times the armor clashed and brayed.
Yet on we press with passion blind,
All forethought blotted from our mind,
Till the dread monster we install
Within the temple's tower-built wall.
E'en then Cassandra's prescient voice
Forewarned us of our fatal choice—
That prescient voice, which Heaven decreed
No son of Troy should hear and heed.
We, careless souls, the city through,
With festal boughs the fanes bestrew,
And in such revelry employ
The last, last day should shine on Troy.

Meantime Heaven shifts from light to gloom,
And night ascends from Ocean's womb,
Involving in her shadow broad
Earth, sky, and Myrmidonian fraud:
And through the city, stretched at will,
Sleep the tired Trojans, and are still.

And now from Tenedos set free
The Greeks are sailing on the sea,
Bound for the shore where erst they lay,
Beneath the still moon's friendly ray:
When in a moment leaps to sight
On the king's ship the signal light,
And Sinon, screened by partial fate,
Unlocks the pine-wood prison's gate.
The horse its charge to air restores,

And forth the armed invasion pours.
Thessander, Sthenelus, the first,
Slide down the rope: Ulysses curst,
Thoas and Acamas are there,
And great Pelides' youthful heir,
Machaon, Menelaus, last
Epeus, who the plot forecast.
They seized the city, buried deep
In floods of revelry and sleep,
Cut down the warders of the gates,
And introduce their banded mates.

It was the hour when Heaven gives rest
To weary man, the first and best:
Lo, as I slept, in saddest guise,
The form of Hector seemed to rise,
Full sorrow gushing from his eyes:
All torn by dragging at the car,
And black with gory dust of war,
As once on earth—his swoln feet bored,
And festering from the inserted cord.
Ah! what a sight was there to view!
How altered from the man we knew,
Our Hector, who from day's long toil
Comes radiant in Achilles' spoil,
Or with that red right hand, which casts
The fires of Troy on Grecian masts!
Blood-clotted hung his beard and hair,
And all those many wounds were there,
Which on his gracious person fell
Around the walls he loved so well.
Methought I first the chief addressed,
With tears like his, and laboring breast:
"O daystar of Dardanian land!
O faithful heart, unconquered hand!

What means this lingering? from what shore
Comes Hector to his home once more?
Ah! since we saw you, many a woe
Has brought your friends, your country low;
And weary eyes and aching brow
Are ours that look upon you now!
What cause has marred that clear calm mien,
Or why those wounds, unclosed and green?"
He answers not, nor recks him aught
Of those the idle quests I sought;
But with a melancholy sigh,
"Ah, goddess-born," he warns me, "fly!
Escape these flames: Greece holds the walls;
Proud Ilium from her summit falls.
Think not of king's or country's claims:
Country and king, alas! are names:
Could Troy be saved by hands of men,
This hand had saved her then, e'en then.
The gods of her domestic shrines
That country to your care consigns:
Receive them now, to share your fate:
Provide them mansions strong and great,
The city's walls, which Heaven has willed
Beyond the seas you yet shall build."
He said, and from the temple brings
Dread Vesta, with her holy things,
Her awful fillets, and the fire
Whose sacred embers ne'er expire.

Meantime throughout the city grow
The agonies of wildering woe:
And more and more, though deep in shade
My father's palace stood embayed,
The tumult rises on the ear,
And clashing armor hurtles fear.

I start from sleep, the roof ascend,
And with quick heed each noise attend.
E'en as, while southern winds conspire,
On standing harvests falls the fire,
Or as a mountain torrent spoils
Field, joyous crop, and oxen's toils,
And sweeps whole woods: the swain spell-bound
Hears from a rock the unwonted sound.
O, then I saw the tale was true:
The Danaan fraud stood clear to view.
Thy halls already, late so proud,
Deiphobus, to fire have bowed:
Ucalegon has caught the light:
Sigeum's waves gleam broad and bright.
Then come the clamor and the blare,
And shouts and clarions rend the air:
I clutch my arms with reeling brain,
But reason whispers, arms are vain:
Yet still I burn to raise a power,
And, rallying, muster at the tower:
Fury and wrath within me rave,
And tempt me to a warrior's grave.

Lo! Panthus, 'scaped from death by flight
Priest of Apollo on the height,
His gods, his grandchild at his side,
Makes for my door with frantic stride—
"Ha! Othrys' son, how goes the fight?
What forces muster at the height?"
I spoke: he heaves a long-drawn breath:
" 'Tis come, our fated day of death.
We have been Trojans: Troy has been:
She sat, but sits no more, a queen:
Stern Jove an Argive rule proclaims:
Greece holds a city wrapt in flames.

There in the bosom of the town
The tall horse rains invasion down,
And Sinon, with a conqueror's pride
Deals fiery havoc far and wide.
Some keep the gates, as vast a host
As ever left Mycenæ's coast:
Some block the narrows of the street,
With weapons threatening all they meet:
The stark sword stretches o'er the way,
Quick-glancing, ready drawn to slay,
While scarce our sentinels resist,
And battle in the flickering mist."
So, stirred by Heaven and Othrys' son,
Forth into flames and spears I run,
Where yells the war-fiend, and the cries
Of slayer and slain invade the skies.
Bold Rhipeus links him to my side,
And Epytus, in arms long tried:
And Hypanis and Dymas hail
And join us in the moonbeam pale,
With young Corœbus, Mygdon's child,
Who came to Troy with yearning wild
　　Cassandra's love to gain,
And, prompt to yield a kinsman's aid,
His troop with Priam's host arrayed:
Ah wretch, whom his demented maid
　　Had warned, but warned in vain!

　　So, when I saw them round me form,
And knew their blood was pulsing warm,
I thus began: "Brave spirits, wrought
To noblest temper, all for nought,
If desperate venture ye desire,
　　Ye see our lost estate:
Gone from each fane, each secret shrine,

Are those who made this realm divine:
The town ẏe aid is wrapped in fire:
  Come, rush we on our fate.
No safety may the vanquished find
Till hope of safety be resigned."
So valour grew to madness. Then,
Like gaunt wolves rushing from their den,
Whom lawless hunger's sullen growl
Drives forth into the night to prowl,
The while, with jaws all parched and black,
Their famished whelps expect them back,
Amid the volley and the foe,
With death before our eyes, we go
On through the town, while darkness spreads
Its hollow covert o'er our heads.
What witness could recount aright
The woes, the carnage of that night,
Or make his tributary sighs
Keep measure with our agonies?
An ancient city topples down
From broad-based heights of old renown:
There in the street confusedly strown
Lie age and helplessness o'erthrown,
Block up the entering of the doors,
And cumber Heaven's own temple-floors.
Nor only Teucrian lives expire:
Sometimes the spark of generous fire
Revives in vanquished hearts again,
And Danaan victors swell the slain.
Dire agonies, wild terrors swarm,
And Death glares grim in many a form.

 First, with a train of Danaan spears,
Androgeos in our path appears:
He deems us comrades of his own,

And hails us thus with friendly tone:
"Bestir you, gallants! why so slack?
See here, while others spoil and sack
The burning town, your tardy feet
But now are coming from the fleet!"
He said: the vague replies we make
Reveal at once his dire mistake:
He sees him fallen among the toils,
And voice and foot alike recoils.
As trampling through the thorny brake
The heedless traveller stirs a snake,
And in a sudden fear retires
From that fierce head, those gathering spires,
E'en so Androgeos at the sight
Was shrinking back in palsied fright.
We mass our arms, and close them round:
Surprised, and ignorant of the ground,
Their scattered ranks we breathless lay,
And Fortune crowns our first essay.
Flashed with wild joy, Corœbus cries,
"See Fortune beckoning from the skies!
When she to safety points the way,
What can be better than obey?
Come, change we bucklers, and advance
Each with a Grecian cognizance.
Who questions, when with foes we deal,
If craft or courage guides the steel?
Themselves shall give us arms to wield."
      He speaks, and from Androgeos tears
His plumy helm and figured shield,
      Girds on an Argive sword, and wears.
And Rhipeus, Dymas, and the rest
Soon in the new-won spoils are dressed.
Mixed with the Greeks, we pass unknown,
'Neath heavenly favors not our own,

Wage many a combat in the gloom,
And many a Greek send down to doom.
Some seek the vessels and the shore:
    Some, smit with fear more low,
Climb the huge horse, and hide once more
    Within the womb they know.
Alas! a mortal may not lean
On Heaven, when Heaven averts its mien.

    Ah see! the Priameian fair,
Cassandra, by her streaming hair,
    Is dragged from Pallas' shrine,
Her wild eyes raised to Heaven in vain;
Her eyes, alas! for cord and chain
    Her tender hands confine.
Corœbus brooked not such a sight,
But plunged infuriate in the fight.
We follow him, as blindly rash,
And, forming, on the spoilers dash:
When from the summit of the fane,
Or ere we deem, a murderous rain
Of Trojan darts our force o'erwhelms,
Misguided by those Argive helms.
Then, groaning deep their prey to lose,
The rallied Danaans round us close:
Fell Ajax and the Atridan pair,
And all Thessalia's host were there:
As when the tempest sounds alarms,
And winds conflicting rush to arms,
Notus and Zephyr join the war,
And Eurus in his orient car:
The lashed woods howl: hoar Nereus raves,
And troubles all his realm of waves.
They too, whom erst in dusk of night
Our cunning practice turned to flight,

Come forth: our lying arms they know,
And in our tones perceive a foe.
At once they crush us, swarm on swarm:
And first beneath Peneleos' arm,
The warlike goddess' shrine before,
Corœbus welters in his gore.
Then Rhipeus dies: no purer son
Troy ever bred, more jealous none
Of sacred right: Heaven's will be done.
Dymas and Hypanis are slain,
By comrades cruelly mista'en;
Nor pious deed, nor Phœbus' wreath,
Could save thee, Panthus, from thy death.
Ye embers of expiring Troy,
Ye funeral flames of all my joy,
Bear witness, in your dying glow,
I shunned nor dart nor fronting foe,
And had it been my fate to bleed
My hand had earned the doom decreed.
Thence forced, to other scenes we flee,
Pelias and Iphitus with me,
This laden with his years and slow,
That halting from Ulysses' blow:
For hark! the growing tumult calls
For rescue to the palace halls.

O, there a giant battle raged!
    Who saw it sure had thought
No war in Troy was elsewhere waged,
    No deaths beside were wrought:
So fierce the fray our eyes that met,
    The Danaans streaming to the roof,
And every gate by foes beset,
    Screened by a penthouse javelin-proof.

Close to the walls the ladders cling:
From step to step the assailants spring,
E'en by the doors: a shield enfolds
Their left: their right a corbel holds.
The Dardans, reckless in despair,
The turrets and the roofs uptear
(E'en to such weapons Fortune drives
Brave patriots, struggling for their lives),
And hurl the gilded beams below,
The pride of ages long ago;
While others on the threshold stand,
And guard the entry, sword in hand,
My heart leaps up, the halls to save,
And help the vanquished to be brave.

A secret postern-gate was there,
Which oped behind a thoroughfare
Through Priam's courts: in happier day
Andromache would pass that way
Alone, to greet the royal pair,
And lead with her her youthful heir.
By this the palace roof I gain,
Whence our poor Trojans, all in vain,
Were showering down their missile rain.
With sheer descent, a turret high
Rose from the roof into the sky,
Whence curious gazers might look down
And see the camp, the fleet, the town:
This, where the flooring timbers join
The stronger stone, we undermine
And tumble o'er: it falls along,
Down crashing on the assailant throng:
But other Danaans fill their place,
And darts and stones still rain apace.

Full in the gate see Pyrrhus blaze,
A meteor, shooting steely rays:
So flames a serpent into light,
    On poisonous herbage fed,
Which late in subterranean night
    Through winter lay as dead:
Now from its ancient weeds undressed
    Invigorate and young,
Sunward it rears its glittering breast
    And darts its three-forked tongue.
There at his side Automedon,
True liegeman both to sire and son,
And giant Periphas, and all
The Seyrian youth assail the wall
    And firebrands roofward dart:
Himself the first with two-edged axe
The brazen-plated doors attacks,
    And makes their hinges start:
Now through the heart of oak he drives
His weapon, and a loophole rives.
There stands revealed the house within,
    Where the long hall retires:
The stately privacy is seen
    Of Priam and his sires,
And on the threshold guards appear
In warlike pomp of shield and spear.

But far within the palace swarms
With tumult and confused alarms:
The deep courts wail with woman's cries:
The clamour strikes the spangled skies.
Pale matrons run from place to place,
And clasp the doors in wild embrace.
Strong as his father, Pyrrhus strains,
Nor bar nor guard his force sustains:

The hacked door reels 'neath blow on blow,
Breaks from its hinges, and lies low.
Force wins her footing: in they rush,
The Danaan hordes, the foremost crush
And deluge with an armed tide
The spacious level far and wide.
Less fierce when, breaking from its bounds,
The water surges o'er the mounds,
Down pours it, tumbling in a heap,
O'er all the fields with headlong sweep,
And whirls before it fold and sheep.
These eyes beheld fell Pyrrhus there
    Intoxicate with gore,
Beheld the curst Atridan pair
    Within the sacred door,
Beheld pale Hecuba, and those
The brides her hundred children chose,
And dying Priam at the shrine
Staining the hearth he made divine.
Those fifty nuptial chambers fair,
That promised many a princely heir.
Those pillared doors in pride erect,
With gold and spoils barbaric decked,
Lie smoking on the ground: the Greek
Is potent, where the fires are weak.

    Perhaps you ask of Priam's fate:
    He, when he sees his town o'erthrown,
Greeks bursting through his palace gate
    And thronging chambers once his own,
His ancient armor, long laid by,
    Around his palsied shoulders throws,
Girds with a useless sword his thigh,
And totters forth to meet his foes.
Within the mansion's central space,

All bare and open to the day,
There stood an altar in its place,
    And, close beside, an aged bay,
That drooping o'er the altar leaned,
And with its shade the home-gods screened.
Here Hecuba and all her train
Were seeking refuge, but in vain,
Huddling like doves by storms dismayed,
And clinging to the gods for aid.
But soon as Priam caught her sight,
Thus in his youthful armor dight,
"What madness," cries she, "wretched spouse,
Has placed that helmet on your brows?
Say, whither fare you? times so dire
Bent knees, not lifted arms require:
Could Hector now before us stand,
No help were in my Hector's hand.
Take refuge here, and learn at length
The secret of an old man's strength:
One altar shall protect us all:
Here bide with us, or with us fall."
She speaks, and guides his trembling feet
To join her in the hallowed seat.

See, fled from murdering Pyrrhus, runs
Polites, one of Priam's sons:
Through foes, through javelins, wounded sore,
He circles court and corridor,
While Pyrrhus follows in his rear
With outstretched hand and levelled spear;
Till just before his parents' eyes,
All bathed in blood, he falls and dies.
With death in view, the unchilded sire
Checked not the utterance of his ire:
"May Heaven. if Heaven be just to heed

Such horrors, render worthy meed,"
He cries, "for this atrocious deed,
Which makes me see my darling die,
And stains with blood a father's eye.
But he to whom you feign you owe
Your birth, Achilles, 'twas not so
He dealt with Priam, though his foe:
He feared the laws of right and truth:
He heard the suppliant's prayer with ruth,
Gave Hector's body to the tomb,
And sent me back in safety home."
So spoke the sire, and speaking threw
A feeble dart, no blood that drew:
The ringing metal turned it back,
And left it dangling, weak and slack.
Then Pyrrhus: "Take the news below,
And to my sire Achilles go:
Tell him of his degenerate seed,
And that and this my bloody deed.
Now die": and to the altar-stone
    Along the marble floor
He dragged the father, sliddering on
    E'en in his child's own gore:
His left hand in his hair he wreathed,
    While with the right he plied
His flashing sword, and hilt-deep sheathed
    Within the old man's side.
So Priam's fortunes closed at last:
So passed he, seeing as he passed
His Troy in flames, his royal tower
Laid low in dust by hostile power,
Who once o'er lands and peoples proud
Sat, while before him Asia bowed:
Now on the shore behold him dead,
A nameless trunk, a trunkless head.

O then I felt, as ne'er before,
Chill horror to my bosom's core.
I seemed my aged sire to see,
Beholding Priam, old as he,
Gasp out his life: before my eyes
Forlorn Creusa seemed to rise,
Our palace, sacked and desolate,
And young Iulus, left to fate.
Then, looking round, the place I eyed,
To see who yet were at my side.
Some by the flames were swallowed: some
Had leapt to earth: the end was come.

I stood alone, when lo! I mark
In Vesta's temple crouching dark
The traitress Helen: the broad blaze
Gives me full light, as round I gaze.
She, shrinking from the Trojan's hate
Made frantic by their city's fate,
Nor dreading less the Danaan sword,
The vengeance of her injured lord—
She, Troy's and Argos' common fiend,
Sat cowering, by the altar screened.
My blood was fired: fierce passion woke
To quit Troy's fall by one sure stroke.
"What? to Mycenæ shall she go,
A conqueress, in a pageant show,
See home, sire, children, spouse again,
With Phrygian menials in her train?
Good Priam slaughtered? Troy no more?
The Dardan plains afloat with gore?
No; though no glory be to gain
From vengeance on a woman ta'en,
Yet he that rids the world of guilt

May claim the praise of blood well spilt:
'Twere joy to satiate righteous ire,
And slake my country's funeral fire."
Thus was I raving, past control,
In aimless turbulence of soul,
When sudden dawning on the night
(Ne'er had I known her face so bright)
My mother flashed upon my sight,
Confessed a goddess, with the mien
And stature that in heaven are seen:
Reproachfully my hand she pressed,
And thus from roseate lips addressed:
"My son, what cruel wrongs excite
Your wrath to such pernicious height?
What mean you by this madness? where
Left you that love to me you bear?
And will you not at least inquire
What fate betides your time-worn sire?
If your Creusa still survive?
If young Ascanius be alive?
All these are trembling as for life,
With Grecian bands around them rife,
And, but for me, had sunk o'erpowered
By flame, or by the sword devoured.
Not the loathed charms of Sparta's dame,
Nor Paris, victim of your blame—
No, 'tis the Gods, the Gods destroy
This mighty realm, and pull down Troy.
Behold! for I will purge the haze
That darkles round your mortal gaze
And blunts its keenness—mark me still,
Nor disobey your mother's will—
Here, where you see huge blocks unfixed,
And dust and smoke in whirlwind mixed,
Great Neptune with his three-forked mace

Upheaves the ramparts from their place,
And rocks the town from cope to base.
Here Juno at the Scæan gates,
Begirt with steel, impatient waits,
And clamorous from the navy calls
Her comrades to the captured walls.
Look back; see Pallas o'er the tower
With cloud and Gorgon redly lower.
E'en Jove to Greece his strength affords,
And fights from heaven 'gainst Dardan swords.
Then fly, and give the struggle o'er;
Myself will guard you, till once more
You stand before your father's door."
She spoke, and vanished from my sight,
Lost in the darkness of the night.
Dire presences their forms disclose,
And powers of terror, Ilium's foes.

That vision showed me Neptune's town
In blazing ruin sinking down:
As rustics strive with many a stroke
To fell some venerable oak,
It still keeps nodding to its doom,
Still bows its head, and shakes its plume,
Till, by degrees o'ercome, one groan
It heaves, and on the hill lies prone.
Down from my perilous height I glide,
Safe sheltered by my heavenly guide,
So thread my way through foes and fire:
The darts give place, the flames retire.

But when I gained Anchises' door,
And stood within my home once more,
My sire, whom I had hoped to bear
Safe to the hills with chiefest care,

Refused to lengthen out his span
And live on earth an exiled man.
"You, you," he cries, "bestir your flight,
Whose blood is warm, whose limbs are light:
Had Heaven not willed my life to cease,
Heaven would have kept my home in peace.
Enough, that I have once been saved,
Survivor of a town enslaved.
Now leave me: be your farewell said
To this my corpse, and count me dead.
My hand shall win me death: the foe
Such mercy as I need will show,
Will strip my spoils, and pass for brave.
He lacks not much that lacks a grave.
Long have I lived to curse my birth,
A useless cumberer of the earth,
E'en from the day when Heaven's dread sire
In anger scathed me with his fire."

So talked he, obstinately set:
While we, our eyes with sorrow wet,
All on our knees, wife, husband, boy,
Implore—O let him not destroy
Himself and us, nor lend his weight
To the incumbent load of fate!
He hears not, but refuses still,
Unchanged alike in place and will.
Desperate, again to arms I fly,
And make my wretched choice to die:
For what deliverance now was mine,
What help in fortune or design?
"What? leave my sire behind and flee?
Such words from you? such words to me?
The watch that guards a parent's lip,
Lets it such dire suggestion slip?

If Heaven in truth has willed to spare
No relic of a town so fair,
If you and all wherein you joy
Must burn to feed the flames of Troy,
See there, Death waits you at the door:
See Pyrrhus, steeped in Priam's gore,
Repeats his double crime once more:
The son before his father's eyes,
The father at the altar dies.
O mother! was it then for this
I passed where fires and javelins hiss
Safe in thy conduct, but to see
Foes in my home's dear sanctuary,
All murdered, father, wife, and child,
Each in the other's blood defiled?
My arms! my arms! the fatal day
Calls, and the vanquished must obey;
Return me to the Danaan crew!
Let me the yielded fight renew!
No; one at least these walls contain
Who will not unavenged be slain."

Once more I gird me for the field,
And to my arm make fast my shield,
And issue from the door; when see!
Creusa clings around my knee,
And offers with a tender grace
Iulus to his sire's embrace:
"If but to perish forth you fare,
Take us with you, your fate to share;
But if you hope that help may come
From sword and shield, first guard your home
Think, think to whom you leave your child,
Your sire, and her whom bride you styled."

So cried she, and the tearful sound
Was filling all the chambers round,
When sudden in the house we saw
A sight for wonderment and awe:
Between us while Iulus stands
'Mid weeping eyes and clasping hands,
Lo! from the summit of his head
A lambent flame was seen to spread,
Sport with his locks in harmless play,
And grazing round his temples stray.
We hurrying strive his hair to quench,
And the blest flame with water drench.
But sire Anchises to the skies
In rapture lifts voice, hands, and eyes:
"Vouchsafe this once, almighty Jove,
If prayer thy righteous will can move,
And if our care have earned us thine,
Give aid, and ratify this sign."
Scarce had the old man said, when hark!
It thundered left, and through the dark
A meteor with a train of light
Athwart the sky gleamed dazzling bright.
Right o'er our palace-roof it crossed,
Then in Idæan woods was lost,
Still glittering on: a fiery trail
Succeeds, and sulphurous fumes exhale.
At this my sire his form uprears,
Salutes the Gods, the star reveres:
"Lead on, blest sign! no more I crave:
Gods, save my house, my grandchild save!
You sent this augury of joy;
Where you are present, there is Troy.
I yield, I yield, nor longer shun
To share the exile of my son."

He ceased: and near and yet more near
The loud flame strikes on eye and ear.
"Come, mount my shoulders, dear my sire:
Such load my strength shall never tire.
Now, whether fortune smiles or lowers,
One risk, one safety shall be ours.
My son shall journey at my side,
My wife her steps by mine shall guide,
At distance safe. What next I say,
Attend, my servants, and obey.
Without the city stands a mound
With Ceres' ruined temple crowned:
A cypress spreads its branches near,
Hoar with hereditary fear.
Part we our several ways, to meet
At length beside that hallowed seat.
You, father, in your arms upbear
Troy's household gods with duteous care:
For me, just 'scaped from battle-fray,
On holy things a hand to lay
Were desecration, till I lave
My body in the running wave."
So saying, in a lion's hide
I robe my shoulders, mantling wide,
    And stoop beneath the precious load:
Iulus fastens to my side,
His steps scarce matching with my stride:
    My wife behind me takes her road.
We travel darkling in the shade,
    And I, whom through that fearful night
Nor volleyed javelins had dismayed
    Nor foeman hand to hand in fight,
Now start at every sound, in dread
For him I bore and him I led.

And now the gates I neared at last,
And all the journey seemed o'erpast,
 When trampling feet my ear assail;
My father, peering through the gloom,
Cries "Haste, my son! O haste! they come:
 I see their shields, their glittering mail."
'Twas then, alas! some power unkind
Bereft me of my wildered mind.
While unfrequented paths I thread,
And shun the roads that others tread,
My wife Creusa—did she stray,
Or halt exhausted by the way?
I know not—parted from our train,
Nor ever crossed our sight again.
Nor e'er my eyes her figure sought,
Nor e'er towards her turned my thought,
Till when at Ceres' hallowed spot
We mustered, she alone was not,
And her companions, spouse and son,
Looked round and saw themselves undone.
Ah, that sad hour! whom spared I then,
In my wild grief, of gods and men?
What woe, in all the town o'erthrown,
Thought I more cruel than my own?
My father and my darling boy,
And, last not least, the gods of Troy,
To my retainers I confide
And in the winding valley hide,
While to the town once more I go,
And shining armor round me throw,
Resolved through Troy to measure back
From end to end my perilous track.

First to the city's shadowed gate
I turn me, whence we passed so late,

My footsteps through the darkness trace,
And cast my eyes from place to place.
A shuddering on my spirit falls,
And e'en the silence' self appals.
Then to my palace I repair,
In hope, in hope, to find her there:
In vain, the foes had forced the door,
And flooded all the mansions o'er.
Fanned by the wind, the flame upsoars
Roof-high; the hot blast skyward roars.
Departing thence, I seek the tower,
The ruined seat of Priam's power.
There Phœnix and Ulysses fell
In the void courts by Juno's cell
      Were set the spoil to keep;
Snatched from the burning shrines away,
There Ilium's mighty treasure lay,
Rich altars, bowls of massy gold,
And captive raiment, rudely rolled
      In one promiscuous heap;
While boys and matrons, wild with fear,
In long array were standing near.
With desperate daring I essayed
To send my voice along the shade,
Roused the still streets, and called in vain
Creusa o'er and o'er again.
Thus while in agony I pressed
From house to house the endless quest,
The pale sad spectre of my wife
Confronts me, larger than in life.
I stood appalled, my hair erect,
And fear my tongue-tied utterance checked,
While gently she her speech addressed,
And set my troubled heart at rest:
"Why grieve so madly, husband mine?

Nought here has chanced without design:
Fate and the Sire of all decree
Creusa shall not cross the sea.
Long years of exile must be yours,
Vast seas must tire your laboring oars;
At length Hesperia you shall gain,
Where through a rich and peopled plain
    Soft Tiber rolls his tide:
There a new realm, a royal wife,
Shall build again your shattered life.
Weep not your dear Creusa's fate:
Ne'er through Mycenæ's haughty gate
    A captive shall I ride,
Nor swell some Grecian matron's train,
I, born of Dardan princes' strain,
    To Venus' seed allied:
Heaven's mighty Mother keeps me here:
Farewell, and hold our offspring dear."
Then, while I dewed with tears my cheek,
And strove a thousand things to speak,
    She melted into night:
Thrice I essayed her neck to clasp:
Thrice the vain semblance mocked my grasp,
    As wind or slumber light.
So now, the long, long night o'erpast,
I reach my weary friends at last.
There with amazement I behold
New-mustering comrades, young and old,
Sons, mothers, bound from home to flee,
A melancholy company.
They meet, prepared to brave the seas
And sail with me where'er I please.
Now, rising o'er the heights of Ide,
Shone the bright star, day's orient guide:
The Danaans swarmed at every door,

Nor seemed there hope of safety more:
I yield to fate, take up my sire,
And to the mountain's shade retire.

Book III

Translated by William Morris

Now after it had pleased the Gods on high to overthrow
The Asian weal and sackless folk of Priam, and alow
Proud Ilium lay, and Neptune's Troy was smoldering on
    the ground,
For diverse outlands of the earth and waste lands are we
    bound,
Driven by omens of the Gods. Our fleet we built beneath
Antandros, and the broken steeps of Phrygian Ida's
    heath,
Unwitting whither Fate may drive, or where the Gods
    shall stay.
And there we draw together men.
                      Now scarce upon the way
Was summer when my father bade spread sails to Fate
    at last.
Weeping I leave my father-land, and out of haven
    passed
Away from fields where Troy-town was, an outcast o'er
    the deep,
With folk and son and Household Gods and Greater
    Gods to keep.

Far off a peopled land of Mars lies midst its mighty
    plain,
Tilled of the Thracians; there whilom did fierce Lycur-
    gus reign.

'Twas ancient guesting-place of Troy: our Gods went
    hand in hand
While bloomed our weal: there are we borne, and on the
    hollow strand
I set my first-born city down, 'neath evil fates begun,
And call the folk Æneadæ from name myself had won.

Unto Dione's daughter there, my mother, and the rest,
I sacrificed upon a day to gain beginning blest,
And to the King of Heavenly folk was slaying on the
    shore
A glorious bull: at hand by chance a mound at topmost
    bore
A cornel-bush and myrtle stiff with shafts close set
    around:
Thereto I wend and strive to pluck a green shoot from
    the ground,
That I with leafy boughs thereof may clothe the altars
    well;
When lo, a portent terrible and marvellous to tell!
For the first stem that from the soil uprooted I tear out
Oozes black drops of very blood, that all the earth about
Is stained with gore: but as for me, with sudden horror
    chill
My limbs fall quaking, and my blood with freezing fear
    stands still.
Yet I go on and strive from earth a new tough shoot to
    win,
That I may search out suddenly what causes lurk within;
And once again from out the bark blood followeth as
    before.

I turn the matter in my mind: the Field-Nymphs I adore,
And him, Gradivus, father dread, who rules the Thra-
    cian plain,

And pray them turn the thing to good and make its
    threatenings vain.
But when upon a third of them once more I set my hand,
And striving hard thrust both my knees upon the oppos-
    ing sand—
—Shall I speak now or hold my peace?—a piteous groan
    is heard
From out the mound, and to mine ears is borne a dread-
    ful word:
"Why manglest thou a wretched man? O spare me in my
    tomb!
Spare to beguilt thy righteous hand, Æneas! Troy's own
    womb
Bore me, thy kinsman; from this stem floweth no alien
    gore:
Woe's me! flee forth the cruel land, flee forth the greedy
    shore;
For I am Polydore: pierced through, by harvest of the
    spear
O'ergrown, that such a crop of shafts above my head
    doth bear."

I stood amazed: the wildering fear the heart in me
    down-weighed.
My hair rose up, my frozen breath within my jaws was
    stayed.
Unhappy Priam privily had sent this Polydore,
For fostering to the Thracian king with plenteous golden
    store.
In those first days when he began to doubt the Dardan
    might,
Having the leaguered walls of Troy for ever in his sight.
This king, as failed the weal of Troy and fortune fell
    away,

Turned him about to conquering arms and Agamemnon's
    day.
He brake all right, slew Polydore, and all the gold he got
Perforce: O thou gold-hunger cursed, and whither
    driv'st thou not
The hearts of men?
              But when at length the fear from me did fall,
Unto the chosen of the folk, my father first of all,
I show those portents of the Gods and ask them of their
    will,
All deem it good that we depart that wicked land of ill,
And leave that blighted guesting-place and give our
    ships the breeze.
Therefore to Polydore we do the funeral services,
The earth is heaped up high in mound; the Death-Gods'
    altars stand
Woeful with bough of cypress black and coal-blue holy
    band;
The wives of Ilium range about with due dishevelled
    hair;
Cups of the warm and foaming milk unto the dead we
    bear,
And bowls of holy blood we bring, and lay the soul in
    grave,
And cry a great farewell to him, the last that he shall
    have.
But now, when we may trust the sea and winds the
    ocean keep
Unangered, and the South bids on light whispering to
    the deep,
Our fellows crowd the sea-beach o'er and run the ships
    adown,
And from the haven are we borne, and fadeth field and
    town.

Amid the sea a land there lies, sweet over every thing,
Loved of the Nereids' mother, loved by that Ægean
    king
Great Neptune: this, a-wandering once all coasts and
    shores around,
The Bow-Lord good to Gyaros and high Myconos bound,
And bade it fixed to cherish folk nor fear the wind again:
There come we; and that gentlest isle receives us weary
    men;
In haven safe we land, and thence Apollo's town adore;
King Anius, who, a king of men, Apollo's priesthood
    bore,
His temples with the fillets done and crowned with holy
    bays,
Meets us, and straight Anchises knows, his friend of
    early days.
So therewith hand to hand we join and houseward get
    us gone.

There the God's fane I pray unto, the place of ancient
    stone:
"Thymbræan, give us house and home, walls to the
    weary give,
In folk and city to endure: let Pergamos twice live,
In Troy twice built, left of the Greeks, left of Achilles'
    wrath!
Ah, whom to follow? where to go? wherein our home set
    forth?
O Father, give us augury and sink into our heart!"

Scarce had I said the word, when lo, all doors with sud-
    den start
Fell trembling, and the bay of God, and all the moun-
    tain side,

Was stirred, and in the opened shrine the holy tripod
    cried:
There as a voice fell on our ears we bowed ourselves to
    earth:
"O hardy folk of Dardanus, the land that gave you birth
From root and stem of fathers old, its very bosom kind,
Shall take you back: go fare ye forth, your ancient
    mother find:
There shall Æneas' house be lords o'er every earth and
    sea,
The children of his children's sons, and those that thence
    shall be."

So Phœbus spake, and mighty joy arose with tumult
    mixed,
As all fell wondering where might be that seat of city
    fixed,
Where Phœbus called us wondering folk, bidding us
    turn again.
Thereat my father, musing o'er the tales of ancient men,
Saith: "Hearken, lords, and this your hope a little learn
    of me!
There is an isle of mightiest Jove called Crete amid the
    sea;
An hundred cities great it hath, that most abundant
    place;
And there the hill of Ida is, and cradle of our race.
Thence Teucer our first father came, if right the tale they
    tell,
When borne to those Rhœtean shores he chose a place
    to dwell
A very king: no Ilium was, no Pergamos rose high;
He and his folk abode as then in dales that lowly lie:
Thence came Earth-mother Cybele and Corybantian
    brass,

And Ida's thicket; thence the hush all hallowed came to
    pass,
And thence the lions yoked and tame, the Lady's chariot
    drag.
On then! and led by God's command for nothing let us
    lag!
Please we the winds, and let our course for Gnosian land
    be laid;
Nor long the way shall be for us: with Jupiter to aid,
The third-born sun shall stay our ships upon the Cretan
    shore."

So saying, all the offerings due he to the altar bore,
A bull to Neptune, and a bull to thee, Apollo bright,
A black ewe to the Storm of sea, to Zephyr kind a white.

Fame went that Duke Idomeneus, thrust from his
        fathers' land,
Had gone his ways, and desert now was all the Cretan
    strand,
That left all void of foes to us those habitations lie.
Ortygia's haven then we leave, and o'er the sea we fly
By Naxos of the Bacchus ridge, Donusa's green-hued
    steep,
And Olearon, and Paros white, and scattered o'er the
    deep
All Cyclades; we skim the straits besprent with many a
    folk;
And diverse clamour mid the ships seafarers striving
    woke;
Each eggs his fellow: On for Crete, and sires of time
    agone!
And rising up upon our wake a fair wind followed on.

And so at last we glide along the old Curetes' strand,
And straightway eager do I take the city wall in hand,

And call it Pergamea, and urge my folk that name who
love,
For love of hearth and home to raise a burg their walls
above.

And now the more part of the ships are hauled up high
and dry,
To wedding and to work afield the folk fall presently,
And I give laws and portion steads; when suddenly
there fell
From poisoned heaven a wasting plague, a wretched
thing to tell,
On limbs of men, on trees and fields; and deadly was
the year,
And men must leave dear life and die, or weary sick
must bear
Their bodies on: then Sirius fell to burn the acres dry;
The grass was parched, the harvest sick all victual did
deny.
Then bids my father back once more o'er the twice-
measured main,
To Phœbus and Ortygia's strand, some grace of prayer
to gain:
What end to our outworn estate he giveth? whence will
he
That we should seek us aid of toil; where turn to o'er
the sea?

Night falleth, and all lives of earth doth sleep on bosom
bear,
When lo, the holy images, the Phrygian House-Gods
there,
E'en them I bore away from Troy and heart of burning
town,
Were present to the eyes of me in slumber laid adown,

Clear shining in the plenteous light that over all was
    shed
By the great moon anigh her full through windows
    fashionèd.
Then thus they fall to speech with me, end of my care to
    make:

"The thing that in Ortygia erst the seer Apollo spake
Here telleth he, and to thy doors come we of his good
    will:
Thee and thine arms from Troy aflame fast have we
    followed still.
We 'neath thy care and in thy keel have climbed the
    swelling sea,
And we shall bear unto the stars thy sons that are to be,
And give thy city majesty: make ready mighty wall
For mighty men, nor toil of way leave thou, though long
    it fall.
Shift hence abode; the Delian-born Apollo ne'er made
    sweet
These shores for thee, nor bade thee set thy city down in
    Crete:
There is a place, the Westland called of Greeks in days
    that are,
An ancient land, a fruitful soil, a mighty land of war;
Œnotrian folk tilled the land, whose sons, as rumours
    run,
Now call it nought but Italy, from him who led them
    on.
This is our very due abode: thence Dardanus outbroke,
Iasius our father thence, beginner of our folk.
Come rise, and glad these tidings tell unto thy father
    old,
No doubtful tale: now Corythus, Ausonian field and fold
Let him go seek, for Jupiter banneth Dictæan mead."

All mazed was I with sight and voice of Gods; because
   indeed
This was not sleep, but face to face, as one a real thing
   sees.
I seemed to see their coifèd hair and very visages,
And over all my body too cold sweat of trembling
   flowed.
I tore my body from the bed, and, crying out aloud,
I stretched my upturned hands to heaven and unstained
   gifts I spilled
Upon the hearth, and joyfully that worship I fulfilled.
Anchises next I do to wit and all the thing unlock;
And he, he saw the twi-branched stem, twin fathers of
   our stock,
And how by fault of yesterday through steads of old he
   strayed.

"O son, well learned in all the lore of Ilium's fate," he
   said,
"Cassandra only of such hap woul' sing; I mind me well
Of like fate meted to our folk full oft would she foretell;
And oft would call to Italy and that Hesperian home.
But who believed that Teucrian folk on any day might
   come
Unto Hesperia's shores? or who might trow Cassandra
   then?
Yield we to Phœbus, follow we as better-counselled men
The better part."
                    We, full of joy, obey him with one mind;
From this seat too we fare away and leave a few behind;
With sail abroad in hollow tree we skim the ocean o'er.

But when our keels the deep sea made, nor had we any
   more

The land in sight, but sea around, and sky around was
    spread,
A coal-blue cloud drew up to us that, hanging overhead,
Bore night and storm, and mirky gloom o'er all the
    waters cast:
Therewith the winds heap up the waves, the seas are
    rising fast
And huge; and through the mighty whirl scattered we
    toss about;
The storm-clouds wrap around the day, and wet mirk
    blotteth out
The heavens, and mid the riven clouds the ceaseless
    lightnings live.
So are we blown from out our course, through might of
    seas we drive,
Nor e'en might Palinurus' self the day from night-tide
    sift,
Nor have a deeming of the road atwixt the watery drift.
Still on for three uncertain suns, that blind mists over-
    lay,
And e'en so many starless nights, across the sea we stray;
But on the fourth day at the last afar upon us broke
The mountains of another land, mid curling wreaths of
    smoke.
Then fall the sails, we rise on oars, no sloth hath any
    place,
The eager seamen toss the spray and sweep the blue
    sea's face;
And me first saved from whirl of waves the Strophades
    on strand
Now welcome; named by Greekish name Isles of the
    Sea, they stand
Amid the great Ionian folk: Celæno holds the shores,
And others of the Harpies grim, since shut were Phineus'
    doors

Against them, and they had to leave the tables they had
    won.
No monster woefuller than they, and crueller is none
Of all God's plagues and curses dread from Stygian
    waters sent.
A wingèd thing with maiden face, whose bellies' excre-
    ment
Is utter foul; and hookèd hands, and face for ever pale
With hunger that no feeding stints.

Borne thither, into haven come, we see how every-
    where
The merry wholesome herds of neat feed down the
    meadows fair,
And all untended goatish flocks amid the herbage bite.
With point and edge we fall on them, and all the Gods
    invite,
Yea, very Jove, to share the spoil, and on the curvèd
    strand
We strew the beds, and feast upon rich dainties of the
    land.
When lo, with sudden dreadful rush from out the
    mountains hap
The Harpy folk, and all about their clanging wings they
    flap,
And foul all things with filthy touch as at the food they
    wrench,
And riseth up their grisly voice amid the evilest stench.

Once more then 'neath a hollow rock at a long valley's
    head,
Where close around the boughs of trees their quavering
    shadows shed,
We dight the boards, and once again flame on the altars
    raise.

Again from diverse parts of heaven, from dusky lurking-
    place,
The shrieking rout with hookèd feet about the prey
    doth fly,
Fouling the feast with mouth: therewith I bid my
    company
To arms, that with an evil folk the war may come to
    pass.
They do no less than my commands, and lay along the
    grass
Their hidden swords, and therewithal their bucklers
    cover o'er.
Wherefore, when swooping down again, they fill the
    curvèd shore
With noise, Misenus blows the call from off a watch-
    stead high
With hollow brass; our folk fall on and wondrous battle
    try,
Striving that sea-foul's filthy folk with point and edge
    to spill.
But nought will bite upon their backs, and from their
    feathers still
Glanceth the sword, and swift they flee up 'neath the
    stars of air,
Half-eaten meat and token foul leaving behind them
    there.
But on a rock exceeding high yet did Celæno rest,
Unhappy seer! there breaks withal a voice from out her
    breast:

"What, war to pay for slaughtered neat, war for our
    heifers slain?
O children of Laomedon, the war then will ye gain?
The sackless Harpies will ye drive from their own land
    away?

Then let this sink into your souls, heed well the words
    I say;
The Father unto Phœbus told a tale that Phœbus told
To me, and I the first-born fiend that same to you
    unfold:
Ye sail for Italy, and ye, the winds appeased by prayer,
Shall come to Italy, and gain the grace of haven there:
Yet shall ye gird no wall about the city granted you,
Till famine, and this murder's wrong that ye were fain
    to do,
Drive you your tables gnawed with teeth to eat up
    utterly."

She spake, and through the woody deeps borne off on
    wings did fly.
But sudden fear fell on our folk, and chilled their frozen
    blood;
Their hearts fell down; with weapon-stroke no more
    they deem it good
To seek for peace: but rather now sore prayers and vows
    they will,
Whether these things be goddesses or filthy fowls of
    ill.
Father Anchises on the strand stretched both his hands
    abroad,
And, bidding all their worship due, the Mighty Ones
    adored:
"Gods, bring their threats to nought! O Gods, turn ye
    the curse, we pray!
Be kind, and keep the pious folk!"
                  Then bade he pluck away
The hawser from the shore and slack the warping cable's
    strain:
The south wind fills the sails, we fare o'er foaming waves
    again,

E'en as the helmsman and the winds have will that we
    should fare.

And now amidmost of the flood Zacynthus' woods ap-
    pear,
Dulichium, Samos, Neritos, with sides of stony steep:
Wide course from cliffs of Ithaca, Laertes' land, we
    keep,
Cursing the soil that bore and nursed Ulysses' cruelty.
Now open up Leucata's peaks, that fare so cloudy high
Over Apollo, mighty dread to all seafarers grown;
But weary thither do we steer and make the little town,
We cast the anchors from the bows and swing the sterns
    a-strand.
And therewithal since we at last have gained the longed-
    for land,
We purge us before Jupiter and by the altars pray,
Then on the shores of Actium's head the Ilian plays we
    play.
Anointed with the sleeking oil there strive our fellows
    stripped
In wrestling game of fatherland: it joys us to have
    slipped
By such a host of Argive towns amidmost of the foe.

Meanwhile, the sun still pressing on, the year about doth
    go,
And frosty winter with his north the sea's face rough
    doth wear;
A buckler of the hollow brass of mighty Abas' gear
I set amid the temple-doors with singing scroll thereon,
ÆNEAS HANGETH ARMOUR HERE FROM CONQUERING
    DANAANS WON.
And then I bid to leave the shore and man the thwarts
    again.

Hard strive the folk in smiting sea, and oar-blades brush
    the main.
The airy high Phæacian towers sink down behind our
    wake,
And coasting the Epirote shores Chaonia's bay we make,
And so Buthrotus' city-walls high set we enter in.
There tidings hard for us to trow unto our ears do win,
How Helenus, e'en Priam's son, hath gotten wife and
    crown
Of Pyrrhus come of Æacus, and ruleth Greekish town,
And that Andromache hath wed one of her folk once
    more.
All mazed am I; for wondrous love my heart was
    kindling sore
To give some word unto the man, of such great things
    to learn:
So from the haven forth I fare, from ships and shore
    I turn.

But as it happed Andromache was keeping yearly day,
Pouring sad gifts unto the dead, amidst a grove that lay
Outside the town, by wave that feigned the Simoïs that
    had been,
Blessing the dead by Hector's mound empty and grassy
    green,
Which she with altars twain thereby had hallowed for
    her tears.
But when she saw me drawing nigh with armour that
    Troy bears
About me, senseless, throughly feared with marvels
    grown so great,
She stiffens midst her gaze; her bones are reft of life-
    blood's heat,
She totters, scarce, a long while o'er, this word comes
    forth from her:

"Is the show true, O Goddess-born? com'st thou a mes-
　　senger
Alive indeed? or if from thee the holy light is fled,
Where then is Hector?"
　　　　　　Flowed the tears e'en as the word she said,
And with her wailing rang the place: sore moved I
　　scarce may speak
This word to her, grown wild with grief, in broken voice
　　and weak:
"I live indeed, I drag my life through outer ways of ill;
Doubt not, thou seest the very sooth.
Alas! what hap hath caught thee up from such a man
　　downcast?
Hath any fortune worthy thee come back again at last?
Doth Hector's own Andromache yet serve in Pyrrhus'
　　bed?"

She cast her countenance adown, and in a low voice
　　said:
"O thou alone of Trojan maids that won a little joy,
Bidden to die on foeman's tomb before the walls of Troy!
Who died, and never had to bear the sifting lot's award,
Whose slavish body never touched the bed of victor
　　lord!
We from our burning fatherland carried o'er many a sea,
Of Achillæan offspring's pride the yoke-fellow must be,
Must bear the childbed of a slave: thereafter he, being
　　led
To Leda's child Hermione and that Laconian bed,
To Helenus his very thrall me very thrall gave o'er:
But there Orestes, set on fire by all the love he bore
His ravished wife, and mad with hate, comes on him
　　unaware

Before his father's altar-stead and slays him then and
    there.
By death of Neoptolemus his kingdom's leavings came
To Helenus, who called the fields Chaonian fields by
    name,
And all the land Chaonia, from Chaon of Troy-town;
And Pergamos and Ilian burg on ridgy steep set down.
What winds, what fates gave thee the road to cross the
    ocean o'er?
Or what of Gods hath borne thee on unwitting to our
    shore?
What of the boy Ascanius? lives he and breathes he yet?
Whom unto thee when Troy yet was——
The boy then, of his mother lost, hath he a thought of
    her?
Do him Æneas, Hector gone, father and uncle, stir,
To valour of the ancient days, and great hearts' glorious
    gain?"

Such tale she poured forth, weeping sore, and long she
    wept in vain
Great floods of tears: when lo, from out the city draweth
    nigh
Lord Helenus the Priam-born midst mighty company,
And knows his kin, and joyfully leads onward to his
    door,
Though many a tear 'twixt broken words the while doth
    he outpour.
So on; a little Troy I see feigned from great Troy of
    fame,
A Pergamos, a sandy brook that hath the Xanthus' name,
On threshold of a Scæan gate I stoop to lay a kiss.
Soon, too, all Teucrian folk are wrapped in friendly city's
    bliss,

And them the King fair welcomes in amid his cloisters
broad,
And they amidmost of the hall the bowls of Bacchus
poured,
The meat was set upon the gold, and cups they held in
hand.

So passed a day and other day, until the gales command
The sails aloft, and canvas swells with wind from out the
South:
Therewith I speak unto the seer, such matters in my
mouth:
"O Troy-born, O Gods' messenger, who knowest Phœ-
bus' will,
The tripods and the Clarian's bay, and what the stars
fulfil,
And tongues of fowl, and omens brought by swift fore-
flying wing,
Come, tell the tale! for of my way a happy heartening
thing
All shrines have said, and all the Gods have bid me fol-
low on
To Italy, till outland shores, far off, remote were won:
Alone Celæno, Harpy-fowl, new dread of fate set forth,
Unmeet to tell, and bade us fear the grimmest day of
wrath,
And ugly hunger. How may I by early perils fare?
Or doing what may I have might such toil to overbear?"

So Helenus, when he hath had the heifers duly slain,
Prays peace of Gods, from hallowed nead he doffs the
bands again,
And then with hand he leadeth me, O Phœbus, to thy
door,

My fluttering soul with all thy might of godhead
  shadowed o'er.
There forth at last from God-loved mouth the seer this
  word did send:

"O Goddess-born, full certainly across the sea ye wend
By mightiest bidding, such the lot the King of Gods hath
  found
All fateful; so he rolls the world, so turns its order round.
Few things from many will I tell that thou the outland
  sea
May'st sail the safer, and at last make land in Italy;
The other things the Parcæ still ban Helenus to wot,
Saturnian Juno's will it is that more he utter not.
First, from that Italy, which thou unwitting deem'st
  anigh,
Thinking to make in little space the haven close hereby,
Long is the wayless way that shears, and long the length
  of land;
And first in the Trinacrian wave must bend the rower's
  wand.
On plain of that Ausonian salt your ships must stray
  awhile,
And thou must see the nether meres, Æææan Circe's isle,
Ere thou on earth assured and safe thy city may'st set
  down.
I show thee tokens; in thy soul store thou the tokens
  shown.
When thou with careful heart shalt stray the secret
  stream anigh,
And 'neath the holm-oaks of the shore shalt see ə great
  sow lie,
That e'en now farrowed thirty head of young, long on
  the ground

She lieth white, with piglings white their mother's dugs
    around—

That earth shall be thy city's place, there rest from toil
    is stored.

Nor shudder at the coming curse, the gnawing of the
    board,

The Fates shall find a way thereto; Apollo called shall
    come.

But flee these lands of Italy, this shore so near our home,

That washing of the strand thereof our very sea-tide
    seeks;

For in all cities thereabout abide the evil Greeks.

There now have come the Locrian folk Narycian walls
    to build;

And Lyctian Idomeneus Sallentine meads hath filled

With war-folk; Philoctetes there holdeth Petelia small,

Now by that Melibœan duke fenced round with mighty
    wall.

Moreover, when your ships have crossed the sea, and
    there do stay,

And on the altars raised thereto your vows ashore ye
    pay,

Be veiled of head, and wrap thyself in cloth of purple
    dye,

Lest 'twixt you and the holy fires ye light to God on high

Some face of foeman should thrust in the holy signs to
    spill.

Now let thy folk, yea and thyself, this worship thus
    fulfil,

And let thy righteous sons of sons such fashion ever
    mind.

But when, gone forth, to Sicily thou comest on the wind,

And when Pelorus' narrow sea is widening all away,

Your course for leftward lying land and leftward waters
    lay,

How long soe'er ye reach about: flee righthand shore
and wave.

In time agone some mighty thing this place to wrack
down drave,

So much for changing of the world doth lapse of time
avail.

It split atwain, when heretofore the two lands, saith the
tale,

Had been but one, the sea rushed in and clave with
mighty flood

Hesperia's side from Italy, and field and city stood

Drawn back on either shore, along a sundering sea-race
strait

There Scylla on the right hand lurks, the left insatiate

Charybdis holds, who in her maw all whirling deep
adown

Sucketh the great flood tumbling in thrice daily, which
out-thrown

Thrice daily doth she spout on high, smiting the stars
with brine.

But Scylla doth the hidden hole of mirky cave confine;

With face thrust forth she draweth ships on to that stony
bed;

Manlike above, with maiden breast and lovely fashionèd

Down to the midst, she hath below huge body of a
whale,

And unto maw of wolfish heads is knit a dolphin's tail.

'Tis better far to win about Pachynus, outer ness

Of Sicily, and reach long round, despite the weariness,

Than have that ugly sight of her within her awful den,

And hear her coal-blue baying dogs and rocks that ring
again.

"Now furthermore if Helenus in any thing have skill,

Or aught of trust, or if his soul with sooth Apollo fill,

Of one thing, Goddess-born, will I forewarn thee over
    all,
And spoken o'er and o'er again my word on thee shall
    fall:
The mighty Juno's godhead first let many a prayer seek
    home;
To Juno sing your vows in joy, with suppliant gifts
    o'ercome
That Lady of all Might; and so, Trinacria overpast,
Shalt thou be sped to Italy victorious at the last.
When there thou com'st and Cumæ's town amidst thy
    way hast found,
The Holy Meres, Avernus' woods fruitful of many a
    sound,
There the wild seer-maid shalt thou see, who in a rock-
    hewn cave
Singeth of fate, and letteth leaves her names and tokens
    have:
But whatso song upon those leaves the maiden seer hath
    writ
She ordereth duly, and in den of live stone leaveth it:
There lie the written leaves unmoved, nor shift their
    ordered rows.
But when the hinge works round, and thence a light air
    on them blows,
Then, when the door doth disarray among the frail
    leaves bear,
To catch them fluttering in the cave she never hath a
    care,
Nor will she set them back again nor make the song-
    words meet;
So folk unanswered go their ways and loathe the Sibyl's
    seat.
But thou, count not the cost of time that there thou hast
    to spend;

Although thy fellows blame thee sore, and length of way
    to wend
Call on thy sails, and thou may'st fill their folds with
    happy gale,
Draw nigh the seer, and strive with prayers to have her
    holy tale;
Beseech her sing, and that her words from willing
    tongue go free:
So reverenced shall she tell thee tale of folk of Italy
And wars to come; and how to 'scape, and how to bear
    each ill,
And with a happy end at last thy wandering shall fulfil.
Now is this all my tongue is moved to tell thee lawfully:
Go, let thy deeds Troy's mightiness exalt above the sky!"

So when the seer from loving mouth such words as this
    had said,
Then gifts of heavy gold and gifts of carven tooth he
    bade
Be borne a-shipboard; and our keels he therewithal doth
    stow
With Dodonæan kettle-ware and silver great enow,
A coat of hookèd woven mail and triple golden chain,
A helm with noble towering crest crowned with a flow-
    ing mane,
The arms of Pyrrhus: gifts most meet my father hath
    withal;
And steeds he gives and guides he gives,
Fills up the tale of oars, and arms our fellows to their
    need.

Anchises still was bidding us meanwhile to have a heed
Of setting sail, nor with the wind all fair to make delay;
To whom with words of worship now doth Phœbus'
    servant say:

"Anchises, thou whom Venus' bed hath made so
 glorious,
Care of the Gods, twice caught away from ruin of
 Pergamos,
Lo, there the Ausonian land for thee, set sail upon the
 chase:
Yet needs must thou upon the sea glide by its neighbour-
 ing face.
Far off is that Ausonia yet that Phœbus open lays.
Fare forth, made glad with pious son! why tread I
 longer ways
Of speech, and stay the rising South with words that I
 would tell?"

And therewithal Andromache, sad with the last farewell,
Brings for Ascanius raiment wrought with picturing wool
 of gold,
And Phrygian coat; nor will she have our honour wax
 a-cold,
But loads him with the woven gifts, and such word
 sayeth she:
"Take these, fair boy; keep them to be my hands' last
 memory,
The tokens of enduring love thy younger days did win
From Hector's wife Andromache, the last gifts of thy
 kin.
O thou, of my Astyanax the only image now!
Such eyes he had, such hands he had, such countenance
 as thou,
And now with thee were growing up in equal tale of
 years."

Then I, departing, spake to them amid my rising tears:
"Live happy! Ye with fortune's game have nothing more
 to play,

While we from side to side thereof are hurried swift
    away.
Your rest hath blossomed and brought forth; no sea-field
    shall ye till,
Seeking the fields of Italy that fade before you still.
Ye see another Xanthus here, ye see another Troy,
Made by your hands for better days, mehopes, and
    longer joy:
And soothly less it lies across the pathway of the Greek,
If ever I that Tiber flood and Tiber fields I seek
Shall enter, and behold the walls our folk shall win of
    fate.
Twin cities some day shall we have, and folks confed-
    erate,
Epirus and Hesperia; from Dardanus each came,
One fate had each: then shall we make one city and the
    same,
One Troy in heart: lo, let our sons of sons' sons see to it!"
Past nigh Ceraunian mountain-sides thence o'er the sea
    we flit,
Whence the sea-way to Italy the shortest may be made.
But in the meanwhile sets the sun, the dusk hills lie in
    shade,
And, choosing oaf-wards, down we lie on bosom of the
    land
So wished for: by the water-side and on the dry sea-
    strand
We tend our bodies here and there; sleep floodeth every
    limb.
But ere the hour-bedriven night in midmost orb did
    swim,
Nought slothful Palinurus rose, and wisdom strives to
    win
Of all the winds: with eager ear the breeze he drinketh
    in;

He noteth how through silent heaven the stars soft glid-
    ing fare,
Arcturus, the wet Hyades, and either Northern Bear,
And through and through he searcheth out Orion girt
    with gold.
So when he sees how every thing a peaceful sky foretold,
He bloweth clear from off the poop, and we our camp-
    ment shift,
And try the road and spread abroad our sail-wings to the
    lift.

And now, the stars all put to flight, Aurora's blushes
    grow,
When we behold dim fells afar and long lands lying low
—E'en Italy. Achates first cries out on Italy;
To Italy our joyous folk glad salutation cry.
Anchises then a mighty bowl crowned with a garland
    fair,
And filled it with unwatered wine and called the Gods to
    hear,
High standing on the lofty deck:
"O Gods that rue the earth and sea, and all the tides of
    storm,
Make our way easy with the wind, breathe on us kindly
    breath!"

Then riseth up the long-for breeze, the haven openeth
As nigh we draw, and on the cliff a fane of Pallas shows:
Therewith our fellow-folk furl sail and shoreward turn
    the prows.
Bow-wise the bight is hollowed out by eastward-setting
    flood,
But over-foamed by salt-sea spray thrust out its twin
    horns stood,

While it lay hidden; tower-like rocks let down on either hand
Twin arms of rock-wall, and the fane lies backward from the strand.

But I beheld upon the grass four horses, snowy white,
Grazing the meadows far and wide, first omen of my sight.
Father Anchises seeth and saith: "New land, and bear'st thou war?
For war are horses dight; so these war-threatening herd-beasts are.
Yet whiles indeed those four-foot things in car will well refrain,
And tamed beneath the yoke will bear the bit and bridle's strain,
So there is yet a hope of peace."
                    Then on the might we call
Of Pallas of the weapon-din, first welcomer of all,
And veil our brows before the Gods with cloth of Phrygian dye;
And that chief charge of Helenus we do all rightfully,
And Argive Juno worship there in such wise as is willed.

We tarry not, but when all vows are duly there fulfilled,
Unto the wind our sail-yard horns we fall to turn about,
And leave the houses of the Greeks, and nursing fields of doubt.
And next is seen Tarentum's bay, the Herculean place
If fame tell true; Lacinia then, the house of Gods, we face;
And Caulon's towers, and Scylaceum, of old the ship-man's bane,
Then see we Ætna rise far off above Trinacria's main;

Afar the mighty moan of sea, and sea-cliffs beaten sore,
We hearken, and the broken voice that cometh from the
    shore:
The sea leaps high upon the shoals, the eddy churns the
    sand.

Then saith Anchises: "Lo forsooth, Charybdis is at hand,
Those rocks and stones the dread whereof did Helenus
    foretell.
Save ye, O friends! swing out the oars together now and
    well!"

Nor worser than his word they do, and first the roaring
    beaks
Doth Palinurus leftward wrest; then all the sea-host
    seeks
With sail and oar the waters wild upon the left that lie:
Upheaved upon the tossing whirl we fare unto the sky,
Then down unto the nether Gods we sink upon the
    wave:
Thrice from the hollow-carven rocks great roar the sea-
    cliffs gave;
Thrice did we see the spray cast forth and stars with sea-
    dew done;
But the wind left us weary folk at sinking of the sun,
And on the Cyclops' strand we glide unwitting of the
    way.
Locked from the wind the haven is, itself an ample bay;
But hard at hand mid ruin and fear doth Ætna thunder
    loud;
And while it blasteth forth on air a black and dreadful
    cloud,
That rolleth on a pitchy wreath, where bright the ashes
    mix,

And heaveth up great globes of flame and heaven's high
    star-world licks,
And other whiles the very cliffs, and riven mountain-
    maw
It belches forth; the molten stones together will it draw
Aloft with moan, and boileth o'er from lowest inner vale.
This world of mountain presseth down, as told it is in
    tale,
Enceladus the thunder-scorched; huge Ætna on him
    cast,
From all her bursten furnaces breathes out his fiery
    blast;
And whensoe'er his weary side he shifteth, all the shore
Trinacrian trembleth murmuring, and heaven is smoke-
    clad o'er.

In thicket close we wear the night amidst these marvels
    dread,
Nor may we see what thing it is that all the noise hath
    shed:
For neither showed the planet fires, nor was the heaven
    bright
With starry zenith; mirky cloud hung over all the night,
In midst of dead untimely tide the moon was hidden
    close.

But when from earliest Eastern dawn the following day
    arose,
And fair Aurora from the heaven the watery shades had
    cleared,
Lo, suddenly out of the wood new shape of man ap-
    peared.
Unknown he was, most utter lean, in wretchedest of
    plight:

Shoreward he stretched his suppliant hands; we turn
    back at the sight,
And gaze on him: all squalor there, a mat of beard we
    see,
And raiment clasped with wooden thorns; and yet a
    Greek is he,
Yea, sent erewhile to leaguered Troy in Greekish weed
    of war.
But when he saw our Dardan guise and arms of Troy
    afar,
Feared at the sight he hung aback at first a little space,
But presently ran headlong down into our sea-side place
With tears and prayers:
        "O Teucrian men, by all the stars," he cried,
"By all the Gods, by light of heaven ye breathe, O bear
    me wide
Away from here! to whatso land henceforth ye lead my
    feet
It is enough. That I am one from out the Danaan fleet,
And that I warred on Ilian house erewhile, most true
    it is;
For which, if I must pay so much wherein I wrought
    amiss,
Then strew me on the flood and sink my body in the
    sea!
To die by hands of very men shall be a joy to me."

He spake with arms about our knees, and wallowing
    still he clung
Unto our knees: but what he was and from what blood
    he sprung
We bade him say, and tell withal what fate upon him
    drave.
His right hand with no tarrying then Father Anchises
    gave

Unto the youth, and heartened him with utter pledge of
 peace.
So now he spake when fear of us amid his heart did
 cease:

"Luckless Ulysses' man am I, and Ithaca me bore,
Hight Achemenides, who left that Adamastus poor
My father (would I still were there!) by leaguered Troy
 to be.
Here while my mates aquake with dread the cruel
 threshold flee,
They leave me in the Cyclops' den unmindful of their
 friend;
A house of blood and bloody meat, most huge from end
 to end,
Mirky within: high up aloft star-smiting to behold
Is he himself; such bane, O God, keep thou from field
 and fold!
Scarce may a man look on his face; no word to him is
 good;
On wretches' entrails doth he feed and black abundant
 blood.
Myself I saw him of our folk two hapless bodies take
In his huge hand, whom straight he fell athwart a stone
 to break
As there he lay upon his back; I saw the threshold swim
With spouted blood, I saw him grind each bloody
 dripping limb,
I saw the joints amidst his teeth all warm and quivering
 still.
—He payed therefore, for never might Ulysses bear
 such ill,
Nor was he worser than himself in such a pinch bestead:
For when with victual satiate, deep sunk in wine, his
 head

Fell on his breast, and there he lay enormous through
    the den,
Snorting out gore amidst his sleep, with gobbets of the
    men
And mingled blood and wine; then we sought the great
    Gods with prayer
And drew the lots, and one and all crowded about him
    there,
And bored out with a sharpened pike the eye that used
    to lurk
Enormous lonely 'neath his brow o'erhanging grim and
    mirk,
As great as shield of Argolis, or Phœbus' lamp on high;
And so our murdered fellows' ghosts avenged we joy-
    ously.
—But ye, O miserable men, flee forth! make haste to
    pluck
The warping hawser from the shore!
For even such, and e'en so great as Polypheme in cave
Shuts in the wealth of woolly things and draws the
    udders' wave,
An hundred others commonly dwell o'er these curving
    bights,
Unutterable Cyclop folk, or stray about the heights.
Thrice have the twin horns of the moon fulfilled the
    circle clear
While I have dragged out life in woods and houses of
    the deer,
And gardens of the beasts; and oft from rocky place on
    high
Trembling I note the Cyclops huge, hear foot and voice
    go by.
And evil meat of wood-berries, and cornel's flinty fruit
The bush-boughs give; on grass at whiles I browse, and
    plucked-up root.

So wandering all about, at last I see unto the shore
Your ships a-coming: thitherward my steps in haste I
    bore:
Whate'er might hap enough it was to flee this folk of
    ill;
Rather do ye in any wise the life within me spill."

And scarcely had he said the word ere on the hill above
The very shepherd Polypheme his mountain mass did
    move,
A marvel dread, a shapeless trunk, an eyeless monstrous
    thing,
Who down unto the shore well known his sheep was
    shepherding;
A pine-tree in the hand of him leads on and stays his
    feet;
The woolly sheep his fellows are, his only pleasure sweet,
The only solace of his ill.
But when he touched the waters deep, and mid the
    waves was come,
He falls to wash the flowing blood from off his eye dug
    out;
Gnashing his teeth and groaning sore he walks the sea
    about,
But none the less no wave there was up to his flank
    might win.
Afeard from far we haste to flee, and, having taken in
Our suppliant, who had earned it well, cut cable silently,
And bending to the eager oars sweep out along the
    sea.
He heard it, and his feet he set to follow on the sound;
But when his right hand failed to reach, and therewithal
    he found
He might not speed as fast as fares the Ionian billow
    lithe,

Then clamour measureless he raised, and ocean quaked
  therewith
Through every wave, and inwardly the land was terrified
Of Italy, and Ætna boomed from many-hollowed side.
But all the race of Cyclops stirred from woods and lofty
  hills,
Down rushes to the haven-side and all the haven fills;
And Ætna's gathered brethren there we see; in vain
  they stand
Glowering grim-eyed with heads high up in heaven, a
  dreadful band
Of councillors: they were as when on ridge aloft one
  sees
The oaks stand thick against the sky, and cone-hung
  cypresses,
Jove's lofty woods, or thicket where Diana's footsteps
  stray.

Then headlong fear fell on our folk in whatsoever way
To shake the reefs out, spreading sail to any wind that
  blew;
But Helenus had bid us steer a midmost course and true
'Twixt Scylla and Charybdis, lest to death we sail o'er-
  close:
So safest seemed for backward course to let the sails go
  loose.
But lo, from out Pelorus' strait comes down the northern
  flaw,
And past Pantagia's haven-mouth of living stone we
  draw,
And through the gulf of Megara by Thapsus lying
  low.
Such names did Achemenides, Ulysses' fellow, show,
As now he coasted back again the shore erst wandered
  by.

In jaws of the Sicanian bay there doth an island lie
Against Plemyrium's wavy face; folk called it in old days
Ortygia: there, as tells the tale, Alpheus burrowed ways
From his own Elis 'neath the sea, and now by mouth of
     thine,
O Arethusa, blendeth him with that Sicilian brine.
We pray the isle's great deities, e'en as we bidden were:
And thence we pass the earth o'erfat about Helorus'
     mere;
Then by Pachynus' lofty crags and thrust-forth rocks we
     skim,
And Camarina showeth next a long way off and dim;
Her whom the Fates would ne'er be moved: then comes
     the plain in sight
Of Gela, yea, and Gela huge from her own river hight:
Then Acragas the very steep shows great walls far away,
Begetter of the herds of horse high-couraged on a day.
Then thee, Selinus of the psalms, I leave with happy
     wind,
And coast the Lilybean shoals and tangled skerries blind.

But next the firth of Drepanum, the strand without a joy,
Will have me. There I tost so sore, the tempests' very
     toy,
O woe is me! my father lose, lightener of every care,
Of every ill: me all alone, me weary, father dear,
There wouldst thou leave; thou borne away from perils
     all for nought!
Ah, neither Helenus the seer, despite the fears he taught,
Nor grim Celæno in her wrath, this grief of soul fore-
     bode.
This was the latest of my toils, the goal of all my road,
For me departed thence some God to this your land did
     bear."

So did the Father Æneas, with all at stretch to hear,
Tell o'er the fateful ways of God, and of his wanderings
    teach:
But there he hushed him at the last and made an end of
    speech.

Book IV

Translated by Sir Richard Fanshawe

But she who Love long since had swallowed down,
   Melts with hid fire; her wound doth inward weep:
   The man's much worth, his nation's much renown
   Runs in her mind: his looks and words are deep
   Fixt in her breast: care weans her eyes from sleep.
   The Morn with Phœbus' lamp the earth survey'd
   And drew Heav'n's veil through which moist stars did
      creep,
   When thus to her dear sister, sick, she said,
"Anna, what frightful dreams my wavering soul invade!

"Who is this man that visits our abodes?
   How wise! how valiant! what a face he has!
   Well may he be descended from the gods.
   Fear shows ignoble minds: but he, alas,
   Tost with what fates! through what wars did he pass!
   Were I not well resolv'd never to wed
   Since my first love by death bereft me was:
   Did I not loathe the nuptial torch and bed,
To this one fault perchance, perchance I might be led.

"For since my poor Sychæus' fatal hour
   (Our household gods besmear'd by brother's steel)

This only man, I must confess, had power
To shake my constant faith and make it reel:
The footsteps of that ancient flame I feel.
But first earth swallow me, or, thunder-slain,
Jove nail me to the shades, pale shades of Hell,
And everlasting night, before I stain
Thee, holy chastity, or thy fair rites profane.

"He took my love with him (and let him keep't
Cold in his grave), to whom I first was tied."
This said, her bosom full of tears she wept.
"O dearer than my life!" Anna replied,
"Wilt thou for ever live a dead man's bride?
Nor pretty babes, rewards of Venus, know?
Are ghosts appeas'd, or ashes satisfied
With this, think'st thou? What if before, thy woe
Yet green and fresh, no husbands down with thee
    would go?

"Not Libya's king, Iarbas, scorn'd in Tyre
Before, with other chiefs whom Afric high
In mettle breeds? Wilt thou quench love's sweet fire?
Nor yet consider whom thou'rt planted nigh?
Here, a fierce people, the Gætulians lie,
Bitless Numidian horse, and quicksands dire;
There mad Barceans block thee up, and dry
Deserts. What speak I of the bloodier ire
A wolf turn'd brother breathes, and gathering clouds
    from Tyre!

"Auspicious Heav'ns, and Juno's care of thee
The Trojan navy hither, doubtless, led.
O sister, what a city will this be!
How shalt thou see thy sceptre flourish! wed
To Troy, how will the Punic glory spread!

"Ask but Heav'n's leave, thy guest then, feasting, keep,
    Pretending 'tis unsafe to sail in winter,
    When ships are tost, and Pleiades do weep,
    And ominous skies forbid on seas to venter."
    These words blew love t' a flame, for doubts hope lent
      her
    And stanch'd her blushes. First in solemn wise
    To Phœbus, Bacchus, Ceres, Law's inventor,
    Selected lambs i' th' fane they sacrifice,
But Juno most atone who favours nuptial ties.

The queen herself, more beauteous in those rites,
    Between the crescent of a milk-white cow
    The liquor pours: or passing in their sights
    Unto the gods with reverend grace doth bow,
    Consults the panting lites, and prays her vow.
    Alas, vain mysteries! blind priests aread,
    Which is the sacrifice is offer'd now!
    Soft flames upon the offerer's marrow feed,
And her concealed wound doth freshly inward bleed.

Poor Dido burns, and stung with restless love,
    Runs raving to and fro through every street,
    Runs like a hind, which in some covert grove
    Where she securely graz'd in fruitful Crete,
    A woodman shooting at far distance hit;
    Drunk in her veins the feather'd iron lies,
    Nor he who made the wound doth know of it;
    She through Dictæan woods and pastures hies,
But carries in her side the arrow which she flies.

She takes Aeneas with her up and down,
    And shews him the vast wealth she brought from Tyre,
    The goodly streets and bulwarks of her town.
    No less a thousand times did she desire

To show unto him too her amorous fire;
And oft began, but shame represt her tongue.
At night unto their banquets they retire,
And Troy's sad fall again she must have sung,
And at his charming lips again she fondly hung.

When every one was parted to his rest,
And the dim moon trod on the heels of day,
And setting stars show'd it high time to rest,
She in the empty house languisht away,
And on the couch, which he had pressed, lay:
Absent she sees him whom her thoughts admire,
Him absent hears, or on her lap doth stay
Ascanius, the true picture of his sire,
As if she so could cheat her impotent desire.

All works are at a stand; the youth for war
Provide no forts, nor training exercise;
Huge beams, and arches, which half finisht are,
Hang doubtful in the air, to fall, or rise,
And towers do threat at once both earth and skies.
Whom whenas Jove's dear wife perceiv'd so drown'd
In witchcrafts, and that fame, with loudest cries,
Could not awake her from the pleasing swound,
She thus accosted Venus, and her mind did sound.

"Great glory sure, and goodly spoils ye gain,
You and your boy: a doughty enterprise
Ye have achieved, and worthy to remain
In lasting marble, if two deities
By subtlety one woman do surprise.
Nor am I ignorant, that to defend
Your race from fear of future enemies,
Y' are jealous of my walls. But to what end
Should so near friends as we eternally contend?

"Nay rather let us knit eternal love,
  And bind the peace more strong with Hymen's cord.
  Ye have the thing for which so much ye strove,
  Elissa with Love's fiery shaft is gor'd;
  Then rule we this joint town with one accord,
  And who shall aid it most be now our strife.
  Once let a queen obey a Trojan lord,
  And Tyrians, to preserve a lover's life,
Call thee their patroness, as dowry of his wife."

Venus, who saw her drift was to translate
  To Carthaginians those imperial dues
  Which were reserved to Italy by fate,
  Made this reply. "Who madly would refuse
  So advantageous match, and rather choose
  To war with you? If but the fair event
  According to your wise forecast ensues.
  But fates I fear me, nor will Jove consent
That Tyrians and Trojans in one town be pent.

"And yet, perchance, you lying in his breast
  With a wife's rhetoric may his counsels sway;
  Then break the ice; I'll second the request."
  "Leave that to me," said she, "and for a way
  T' effect our wishes, mark my plot I pray.
  Tomorrow when the sun shall be descried
  To gild the mountains with his earliest ray,
  Æneas and the love-sick queen provide
To have a solemn hunting in the forest wide.

"Now I, when here they beat the coppice, there
  The horsemen flutter, on their heads will pour
  A pitchy cloud, and heaven with thunder tear.
  Their followers, for shelter from the show'r,

By several paths along the plain shall scour;
Mask'd in dead night, unto one cave they two
Shall come: there I will be; and (add your pow'r)
Tie such a knot as only Fates undo;
I'll seal her his. Good Hymen shall be present too."

Venus seems, nodding, to consent; and smiles
To see Dame Juno's craft. Meanwhile the Morn
Arose: and the choice youth, with subtle toils,
Sharp hunting-spears, fleet steeds in Barbary born,
And sure-nos'd hounds tun'd to the bugle-horn,
Are gone before. The lords at door expect
Whilst the Queen stays within herself t' adorn.
Her palfrey stands with gold and scarlet deckt,
And champs the foaming bit, as scorning to be checkt.

At length she comes, with a huge troop: her gown
Of Tyrian dye, border'd with flowers of gold:
A quiver by her comely side hung down,
Gold ribboning her brighter hair enroll'd,
Gold buttons did her purple vesture hold.
The Trojans too and blithe Iulus went:
Above the rest, far goodliest to behold,
Æneas' self his gladding presence lent,
And with his dark'ned train did Dido's train augment.

As when Apollo leaves his winter seats
Of Lycia and Xanthus' floods, to see
His country Delos, and his feast repeats;
About his altar hum confusedly
Cretes, Dryopes, and ruddy Nymphs: but he
On Cynthus rides, and pleating doth enlace
His flowing hair with gold, and his lov'd tree:
His shafts shog at his back. With no less grace
Æneas march'd: such rays display'd his lovely face.

When in the mountains now engag'd they were
   And pathless woods, lo, goats from summits cast
   Run tumbling through the bushes: herds of deer
   Another way come hurrying down as fast,
   And raise a cloud as through the dust they haste;
   Hotspur Iulus on his mettled horse
   Out-cracking all, now these, now those men past,
   And wish'd 'mong those faint beasts, and without
      force,
Some lion or tusk'd boar would cross him in his course.

Meanwhile loud thunder heaven's pavilion tears,
   Making a passage for th' ensuing rain:
   The Trojan youth, and Tyrian followers,
   And Venus' Dardan grandchild through the plain
   Seek several shelters: rivers, like a main,
   Rush from the mountains round. One cave that lord
   Of Troy, and she who did in Carthage reign,
   Lighted upon. Earth gives the signal word,
And Juno, queen of marriage, doth their hands accord.

The guilty Heavens, as blushing to have been
   An instrument this meeting to fulfil,
   With flashing lightning shone: the Nymphs were seen
   To weep with all their streams, and from each hill
   Were heard to murmur the presaged ill.
   That day did utter death, and Dido's shame:
   For now she's arm'd, let men say what they will,
   Nor seeks as erst to hide her amorous flame:
She calls it wedlock, gives her fault an honest name.

Fame straight through Libya's goodly towns doth post,
   Fame, a fleet evil, which none can outfly;

Most strong she is when she hath travel'd most,
First small through fear, but grown so instantly,
That standing on the ground she'll reach the sky.
She was the last birth Mother Earth did bring,
When her proud anger did the gods defy,
The Giants' sister, swift of foot and wing;
A huger never was, nor a more monstrous thing.

Most strange! There's not a plume her body bears,
But under it a watching eye doth peep,
As many tattling tongues, and list'ning ears.
By night 'tween Earth and Heaven she doth sweep
Screeching, nor shuts her lids with balmy sleep.
And all the day time upon castle gates,
Or steeple-tops, she doth strict watches keep,
And frights great cities with her sudden baits,
And with one confidence both truths and lies relates.

She, glad of such a prey whereon to plume,
Through people's minds truths mixt with falsehood
sent:
How one Æneas came from Troy, with whom
Fair Dido deign'd to wed; and how they spent
In revels the long winter, wholly bent
On brutish love, drowning affairs of state:
These things she sow'd in men's rank mouths: then
went
To King Iarbas, and did irritate
His mind with tales, and his old wrath exasperate.

An hundred temples built to Jove had he,
(Who unto Hammon forc'd Gramantis bore)
An hundred altars burning constantly,
The gods' eternal sentinels, each floor

Painted with blood of beasts, with flowers each door:
Who mad with love, and with the bitter news,
Before the altars and the gods before,
Kneeling with hands upheav'd to Jove, doth use
Great supplications, and in this manner sues.

"Jove, to whom Moors rich wine on carpets drink,
  See'st this? Or when thy arm doth lightning shake,
  Giv'st thou false fire t' a cloud to make fools wink?
  And, when it thunders, dost thou only make
  A rumbling o'er our heads at which we quake?
  A stray, to whom ourself (being hither fled)
  Hir'd a small barren plat, for pity sake,
  With some restraints, refus'd with us to wed,
And Don Æneas takes unto her crown and bed.

"And now this Paris, with a coif to stay
  His beard and powder'd locks, and 's beaver train
  Of she-men, gluts himself upon the prey;
  Whilst we with gifts on gifts enrich thy fane,
  And make our person glorious in vain."
  Th' all-powerful heard these prayers, and cast his eye
  On the new walls where th' amorous pair remain
  Careless how desperate sick their fame doth lie,
Then spake, and gave this charge to winged Mercury.

"Go, son, as swift as winds in Carthage light,
  Tell Venus' son, whom loit'ring there thou'lt see
  Unworthy of that fate which he doth slight,
  That his fair mother painted him to me
  Another man, and therefore twice did free
  From Grecian swords; one who with steady rein
  Should manage proud and warlike Italy,
  And prove himself of Teucer's haughty strain,
And the triumphed world under his laws maintain.

"If not at all this him with glory fires,
  Nor care of his own greatness doth he show,
  Why should he grudge his son the Roman spires?
  What makes he here? What seeks he from a foe?
  Latium, and them who there expect to grow
  From him, let him regard. Let him away.
  This is th' effect, from me this let him know."
  At once Jove ended, and the son of May
His greater sire's commands prepar'd himself t' obey.

First golden wings unto his feet he binds,
  Which over lands and over seas that swell
  Bear him aloft, as speedy as the winds;
  Then takes his rod. With this he calls from Hell
  Pale ghosts, sends others in sad shades to dwell,
  Gives sleep and takes it from the drowsy brain,
  And seals up eyes with death. He doth repel
  By power of this the heav'ns which part in twain,
And through the watery cloud he sails as through a
      main.

He soaring the lank sides and crown disclos'd
  Of craggy Atlas, whose neck props the sky,
  Atlas, whose piney head to storms expos'd
  Is bound about with clouds continually.
  Thick on his aged back the snow doth lie,
  And down his dravel'd chin pour plenteous springs,
  His beard in icicles grows horribly.
  Here lights the god pois'd on his hovering wings,
Towards the sea from hence his body headlong flings.

Like to a bird, which round the shores doth glide
  And fishy rocks, skimming along the bay;
  So flies 'tween earth and heaven, and doth divide

The wind and sandy coast of Libya,
Leaving his mother's sire, the son of May.
Who landing where the sheep-cotes lately were,
Sees how Æneas doth the works survey,
Here building towers, and alt'ring turrets there,
He by his side a sword all starr'd with gems did wear.

Upon his shoulder to the air display'd
A robe of Tyrian purple seemed to flame,
Which Dido with her own fair hands had made
And edg'd the seams with gold. "Here do you frame."
Said Hermes, "hind'ring your own crown and fame,
High towers of Carthage, and, uxorious, raise
Fair walls whereof another bears the name?
Mark now what Jove himself, whom Heav'n obeys
And Earth, by his wing'd messenger unto you says.

"What make you here loit'ring in Libya?
If glory of great actions fire not you,
Nor your own interest nor fame you weigh;
Seek your heir's good, Iulus' hopes pursue,
To whom the Latian crown and Rome is due."
This having said, Cyllenius vanish'd quite
From mortal eyes, and back to Heaven flew.
Æneas at the vision shakes with fright,
His tongue cleaves to his jaws, his hair stands bolt up-
        right.

He is on fire to go, and fly that land
Of sweet enchantments, being scar'd away
By no less warning than the gods' command.
But, ah, what shall he do? How dare t' assay
With words the amorous queen? What should he say
For introduction? His swift-beating thought

In doubtful balance thousand things did lay,
　　And this way cast them, and then that way wrought;
At last this seem'd the best when all ways he had
　　　　sought.

He call'd Sergestus, Mnestheus, and the stout
　　Cloanthus, bids them fit immediately
　　Their fleet, and draw their companies about
　　The port, their arms prepar'd, not telling why;
　　Meanwhile himself (when no least jealousy
　　To the good queen should thought of breach betray
　　In so great loves) an entrance would espy,
　　The season of soft speech, and dextrous way.
With readiness and joy they do him all obey.

But Dido found their plot—what's hid from lovers?
　　Herself, who doubts even safe things, first doth see't:
　　And the same tattling Fame to her discovers
　　That Trojans are departing with their fleet.
　　She's mad, stark mad, and runs through every street,
　　Like Bacchus' she-priests, when the god is in,
　　And they to do him furious homage meet,
　　Cithæron yelling with their midnight din:
Then thus t' Æneas speaks, nor stays till he begin.

"Didst thou hope too by stealth to leave my land,
　　And that such treason could be unbetray'd?
　　Nor should my love, nor thy late plighted hand,
　　Nor Dido, who would die, thy flight have stay'd?
　　Must too this voyage be in winter made?
　　Through storms? O, cruel to thyself and me,
　　Didst thou not hunt strange lands and sceptres sway'd
　　By others, if old Troy reviv'd should be,
Should Troy itself be sought through a tempestuous sea?

"Me fly'st thou? By these tears and thy right hand
(Since this is all's now left to wretched me),
By marriage's new joys, and sacred band,
If ought I did could meritorious be,
If ever ought of mine were sweet to thee,
Pity our house, which must with my decay
Give early period to its sovereignty;
And put, I do beseech thee, far away
This cruel mind, if cruel minds hear them that pray.

"For thee the Libyan nations me defy,
The kings of Scythia hate me, and my Tyre:
For thee I lost my shame, and that whereby
Alone I might unto the stars aspire,
The chaster fame which I did once acquire.
To whom, my guest (for husband's out of date),
Dost thou commit me ready to expire?
Why stay I? Till Pygmalion waste my state?
Or on Iarbas' wheels, a captive queen, to wait?

"Yet if before thou fled'st out of this place,
Some child at least I unto thee had borne,
If in my court, resembling but thy face,
Some young Æneas play'd, I should not mourn
As one so quite deluded or forlorn."
Here ceased she. But he, whom Jove had tied
With strict commands, his eyes did no way turn,
But stoutly did his grief suppress and hide
Under his secret heart. Then thus in short replied:

"For me, O Queen, I never will deny
But that I owe you more than you can say,
Nor shall I stick to bear in memory
Elissa's name, whilst breath these limbs doth sway.

But to the point. I never did intend,
Pray charge me not with that, to steal away:
And much less did I wedlock-bands pretend,
Neither to such a treaty ever condescend.

"Would Fates permit me mine own way to take,
And please myself in choosing of a land,
Ilium out of her ashes I would rake,
And glean my earth's sweet relics; Troy should stand,
The vanquish'd troops replanted by my hand,
And Priam's towers again to Heav'n aspire.
But now I have the oracles' command
To seek great Italy; the same require
The Destinies. My country's this; this my desire.

"If you of Tyre with Carthage towers are took,
Why should our seeking Latian fields offend?
May not the Trojans to new mansions look?
As oft as night moist shadows doth extend
Over the earth, and golden stars ascend,
My father's chiding ghost affrights my sleep:
My son, on whom that realm is to descend,
And those dear eyes do freshly seem to weep,
Complaining that from him his destin'd crown I keep.

"And now Jove's son, by both their heads I swear,
Was sent to me, myself the god did see
In open day, and with these ears did hear:
Then vex not with complaints yourself and me,
I go against my will to Italy."
Whilst thus he spake, she look'd at him askew,
Rolling her lightning eyes continually,
And him from head to foot did silent view,
When, being throughly heat, these thund'ring words
        ensue.

"Nor goddess was thy mother, nor the source
 Of thy high blood renowned Dardanus,
 But some Hyrcanian tigress was thy nurse,
 Out of the stony loins of Caucasus
 Descended, cruel and perfidious.
 For with what hopes should I thy faults yet cover?
 Did my tears make thee sigh? Or bend, but thus,
 Thine eyes? Or sadness for my grief discover?
Or if thou couldst not love, to pity yet a lover?

"Whom first accuse I since these loves began?
 Jove is unjust, Juno her charge gives o'er;
 Whom may a woman trust? I took this man
 Homeless, a desperate wrack upon my shore,
 And fondly gave him half the crown I wore:
 His ships rebuilt, t' his men new lives I lent.
 And now the Fates, the oracles, what more?
 (It makes me mad) Jove's son on purpose sent
Brings him forsooth a menace through the firmament.

"As if the gods their blissful rest did break
 With thinking on thy voyages. But I
 Nor stop you, nor confute the words you speak.
 Go, chase on rolling billows realms that fly,
 With fickle waves uncertain Italy.
 Some courteous rock, if Heaven just curses hear,
 Will be revenger of my injury:
 When thou perceiving the sad fate draw near,
Shalt Dido, Dido, call, who surely will be there.

"For when cold death shall part with dreary swoon
 My soul and flesh, my ghost, where'er thou be,
 Shall haunt thee with dim torch, and light thee down
 To thy dark conscience: I'll be Hell to thee,
And this glad news will make Hell Heav'n to me."

Here, falling as far from him as she might,
    She fainted ere her speech was finished:
    Leaving him tossing in his tender spright
    What he should say to her, or leave unsaid,
    Her maids convey her to her ivory bed.
    But good Æneas, though he fain would prove
    To swage her grief, and leave her comforted,
    Pierc'd to the soul with her so ardent love,
Yet goes to view his fleet, obedient unto Jove.

Ay, now the Trojans fall to work for good,
    And hale their vessels down from all the shores;
    The caulk'd ships are on float, and from the wood
    They bring whole oaks unwrought and leavy oars,
    For haste to fly away.
    Through every gate they pack and trudge amain:
    As when the emmets sally through earth's pores
    To sack, for hoard, some barn full-stuff'd with grain,
Rememb'ring barren winter must return again;

The black troops march, and through the meadows bear
    The booty by a narrow path; some hale
    The heavy corns; others bring up the rear,
    And prick them forwards that begun to fail,
    The busy labourers every path engrail.
    What sighs gav'st thou now, Dido, looking out
    From thy high tower? How did thy senses quail
    Seeing the shores so swarm'd, and round about
Hearing confused shoutings of the nautic rout?

O Tyrant Love, how absolute thou art
    In human breasts! Again she's forc'd to fly
    To tears and prayers, and bow her prostrate heart
    To the subduing passion, glad to try

　　All cures before the last, which is to die.
　　"Sister," said she, "thou seest they all repair
　　To th' port, and only for a wind do lie,
　　Inviting it with streamers wav'd i' th' air:
Had I but fear'd this blow, I should not now despair.

"Yet try for me this once; for only thee
　　That perjur'd soul adores, to thee will show
　　His secret thoughts: thou when his seasons be,
　　And where the man's accessible dost know.
　　Go, sister, meekly speak to the proud foe.
　　I was not with the Greeks at Aulis sworn
　　To raze the Trojan name, nor did I go
　　'Gainst Ilium with my fleet, neither have torn
Anchises' ashes up from his profaned urn.

"Why is he deaf to my entreaties? Whither
　　So fast? It is a lover's last desire
　　That he would but forsake me in fair weather
　　And a safe time. I do not now aspire
　　To his broke wedlock-vow, neither require
　　He should fair Latium and a sceptre leave:
　　Poor time I beg, my passions to retire;
　　Truce to my woe; nor pardon, but reprieve;
Till griefs, familiar grown, have taught me how to
　　grieve.

"For sisterhood, for sense of my distress,
　　Let me this last boon, ere I die, obtain."
　　This Dido spake. The sad ambassadress
　　Carries her tears, and brings them back again
　　(As brackish tides post from and to the main).
　　But not an ocean of bitter tears
　　Can alter him, nor will he entertain
　　The flattering force of words: he only hears

The Fates, and Jove's command, which dams up his
    mild ears.

As an old oak, but yet not weak with eld,
    Which showers and blasts to overthrow contend,
    It cracks and, the trunk shook, leaves strow the field,
    That sticks in rocks, whose roots tow'rds Hell descend
    As far as towards Heav'n the boughs ascend:
    So stands the hero, beat with wind and rain;
    His stout heart groans, and his affections bend,
    Shook with their sighs; but his resolves remain
As unremov'd as rocks, tears roll their waves in vain.

Then doth unhappy Dido, given o'er
    By her last hope, desire to die. The light
    Is irksome to her eyes. To confirm more
    Her purpose to embrace eternal night,
    Placing on th' incense-burning altars bright
    Her gifts, the holy water she beheld
    Converted to black ink, portentous sight!
    And the pour'd wine to roaping blood congeal'd;
This thing to none, not to her sister, she reveal'd.

A marble fane too in the house she had,
    Where lay her first lord's ashes, kept among
    Her most adored reliques: 'twas with sad
    Dark yew-tree and the whitest fleeces hung.
    Hence in the night she heard her husband's tongue
    Call her, she thought. And oft the boding owl
    Alone on the house-top harsh dirges sung,
    And with long notes quaver'd a doleful howl,
Besides old prophecies, which terrify her soul.

Cruel Æneas ev'n her sleep torments:
    And still she dreams she's wand'ring all alone

Through a long way with steep and dark descents,
Calling her Tyrians in a land where none
But some pale ghost echoes her with a groan.
As when mad Pentheus troops of furies fright,
Who sees a twofold Thebes and double sun:
Or when Orestes flies his mother's sight,
Hunting his bloody track with hell-hounds by torch-
     light.

Sunk then with grief, possess'd with Furies, bent
On death, she plots the means, and in her eye
A feign'd hope springing, hiding her intent,
Accosts sad Anne. "Partake thy sister's joy;
I've found a way to make him burn as I,
Or turn me cold like him. Near Phœbus' set
At the land's end doth Æthiopia lie,
Where on great Atlas' neck the heav'n thick set
With glorious diamond-stars hangs like a carcanet.

"Of a great sorceress have I been told
There born, who did th' Hesperian temple keep,
The dragon fed, and sacred fruit of gold
Watch'd on the tree which she for dew did steep
In honey, and moist poppy causing sleep.
She undertakes to cure the love-sick breast,
And whom she list to plunge in love as deep,
The water's course in rivers to arrest,
And call down stars from heav'n, and call up ghosts
     from rest.

"Under her tread thou shalt perceive earth groan,
And oaks skip from the hills; I swear to thee,
Calling the gods to record, and thine own
Sweet head, that forc'd to these black arts I flee.

Thou on some tower a stack build secretly,
Lay on it the man's clothes, and sword which lies
Within, and that which prov'd a grave to me,
My wedding bed. So doth the witch advise,
Ev'n that I blot out all the traitor's memories."

This said, grew pale. Yet thinks not Anne that she
With these new rites her funeral doth shade,
Nor fears such monsters or worse ecstasy
Than at Sychæus' death; therefore obey'd.
But Dido, a great pile of wood being made,
The place with flowers and fatal cypress crown'd,
There on his clothes and sword bequeathed laid
His picture on the bed, the mystic ground
Known only to herself. Altars are placed round.

With hair dispread like a black falling storm,
Th' inchantress thunders out three hundred names,
Orcus, and Chaos, Hecate triform,
Which virgin Dian's triple power enseams:
She sprinkled too Avernus' fabulous streams:
And herbs were sought for, sprouting forth ripe bane,
With brazen sickles cropt in the moon's beams;
And pull'd from new-born colt, that lump, which ta'en
From the dam's mouth, no love t' her issue doth remain.

Herself in a loose vest, one foot unshod,
With meal in pious hands near th' altar drew;
"Witness, ye guilty stars, and every god,"
Saith she, "I'm forc'd to die." Invokes them too
Who care of lovers take (if any do)
Unequally. 'Twas night, and conquering sleep
With weari'd bodies the whole earth did strew;

When woods are quiet, and the cruel deep,
When stars are half-way down, when fields still silence
        keep,

And beasts and painted birds, which liquid springs
    Inhabit, or which bushy lands contain,
    Nuzzling their cares beneath sleep's downy wings,
    Do bury the past day's forgotten pain;
    All but the hapless queen, she doth refrain
    From rest, nor takes it at her eyes or heart.
    After long seeming dead, love rose again
    And fought with wrath as when two tides do thwart,
While thus her big thoughts roll and wallow to each
        part.

"What shall I do? Shall I a suitor be
    To my old suitors, scorned by the new,
    And woo those kings so oft despis'd by me?
    What then? Shall I the Ilian fleet pursue,
    And share all this man's fates? Yes, he doth shew
    Such sense of my first aids: or, say I would,
    Whom he hath mock'd, will not his proud ships too
    Reject? Ah, fool, by whom the perjur'd brood
Of false Laomedon is not yet understood!

"Grant they'd admit me, shall I fly alone
    With mariners? Or chase him with the power
    O' th' emptied town, and servants of mine own,
    And whom I scarce from Tyre by the roots uptore,
    Compel to plough the horrid seas once more?
    No, die as thou deserv'st, cure woes with woe.
    Thou sister, first, when I my tears did shower
    To quench these rising flames, thou didst them
        blow
And out of cruel pity sold'st me to the foe.

"Why might not I, alas! have mourn'd away
   My widow'd youth, as well as turtles do?
   Nor twice have made myself misfortune's prey,
   Or to Sychæus' ashes prov'd untrue?"
   These words with sighs out of her bosom flew.
   Æneas slept aboard, all things prepar'd;
   To whom again Jove's son with the same hue
   Divine, so silver-voic'd, so golden-hair'd,
So straight and lovely shap'd, thus rousing him appear'd.

"O goddess-born, now dost thou sleep? nor know
   How many dangers watch to compass thee?
   Nor hear this good wind whispering thee to go?
   Purpos'd to die, great plots and dire broods she,
   Who boils with rage like a high going sea.
   Fly while thou may'st fly. If the morning find
   Thee napping here, the seas will cover'd be
   With ships, the shore with flames; fly with the wind:
Trust that, but do not trust a woman's fickle mind."

This said, he mix'd himself with night: but then
   Æneas, at these visions sore aghast,
   Starts out of sleep and cries, "Up, up, O men,
   Hoist up your sails, fly to your oars, row fast;
   Behold, a god from heaven again bids haste,
   Cutting the wreathed cable. O, whoe'er,
   We follow thee, obey'd as late thou wast
   Most gladly. Aid what thou command'st, and steer
With prosperous stars bespoke as thou fly'st through their sphere."

This said, whipt out his lightning sword, and strook
   The fastening ropes. Like zeal his pattern bred

In all. They snatch'd, they ran, the shores forsook,
Their sails like wings over the waves were spread:
They comb'd with oars great Neptune's curled head.
And now Aurora scattered rosy light
Upon the earth from Tithon's purple bed.
Whom Dido, having scouted all the night,
Discover'd from the watch-tower by her ensigns white.

Seeing the fleet sail smoothly on, she knocks
    Three or four times her breast of ivory,
    And tearing piteously her amber locks;
    "O Jove, but shall he then be gone," said she,
    "And shall a stranger mock my realm and me?
    Shall not my powers pursue him from the shore,
    And my tall galleys mann'd out instantly?
    Arm, arm, ye men of Tyre, bring fire-balls store,
Hoise in a trice the sails, tug stoutly at the oar.

"What talk I? Or where am I? Do I rave?
    Poor Dido, now you see his heart; before
    Could you not see it, when your crown you gave
    To his dispose? Behold the faith he swore,
    Who sav'd his gods and his old father bore!
    I'll strow him on the waves, his men first kill'd,
    And spitted upon swords, and sauc'd in gore,
    Ascanius to him his last meal shall yield,
The father's yearning bowels with his bowels fill'd.

"But this would be a doubtful battle. Be 't,
    What should she fear whose wishes are to die!
    I will blow up the hatches, burn the fleet,
    Son, sire, and nation in one bonfire fry,
    And myself last to crown the tragedy.
    O Sol, the index of whose purging light

Doth all the works of skilful Nature try;
And Juno, cause of this my woeful plight,
And Proserpine, cried through the towns in dead of
     night.

"And your revenging powers, Gods which pertain
    To dying Dido; all of you incline
    Your deities to this my prayer; both deign
    Gently to hear, and lend me your divine
    Assistance, due to such high wrongs as mine.
    If one so clogg'd with perjuries as he
    Must needs attain the port he doth design,
    And swim to shore, because his destiny
So wills, and such is Jove's immutable decree;

"Yet vext by a warlike people, forc'd to fly,
    Torn and divorc'd from his dear son's embrace,
    Let him beg foreign aid, see his men die
    For crimes not theirs, and let him, when a peace
    Shall be concluded by him with disgrace,
    Enjoy nor crown nor life (then seeming good)
    But be cut off in middle of his race,
    And uninterr'd float on the restless flood:
Thus pray I, these last words I pour out with my blood.

"Then you, O Tyrians, breed your children in
    Successive hate, so shall my wrong'd ghost rest;
    Let peace or faith with these be held a sin;
    Some one of ours with fire and sword infest
    The proud Æneiades where'er they nest,
    And through the world once more the stragglers drive;
    Now or hereafter, when your strength serves best;
    Be shores opposed to shores, let our tides strive
With theirs, and our late sons keep endless war alive."

This said, she cast to fly day's loathed beams,
   And called Sychæus' nurse (her own was dead):
   "Good Nurse, go bid my sister, dash'd with streams,
Come straight, and bring the beasts I ordered
For sacrifice: do thou too bind thy head
With holy fillet. I will consummate
Rites well begun to Dis, and fire the bed
Where the man's portrait's laid, t' annihilate
All care." So did she gallop at an old wives' rate.

But Dido, fearing what she wish'd, sad doom,
   Rolling her bloodshot eyes, and in her face
   The paleness of the death that was to come,
With trembling spots, rush'd to that secret place,
And climbing the high pile with furious pace,
   The Dardan sword, not therefore given, unsheath'd.
Spying the clothes and well-known bed, a space
She paus'd, till some few tears she had bequeath'd,
And leaning on that bed her latest speech she breath'd.

"Sweet pledges, whilst the Fates and Jove so will'd,
   Receive this soul, and free me from this woe:
   I liv'd, and my good fortune's circle fill'd,
And now my great ghost to Elysium go:
I built a famous city, saw it grow
   To the perfection which it boasts this day;
Reveng'd my husband on his brother-foe:
   My too much happiness had lack'd allay,
If Ilium's wandering fleet had never pass'd this way."

Then grovelling on the bed, "But shall I die,
   And not reveng'd? Yes, die. What, so present
   Myself to Dis? Even so. Drink with thine eye,
Fierce Trojan, this flame's comet-like portent
And let my death bode thee a dire event."

Here her maids saw her with spread hands fall down
Upon the reeking blade: a shrill cry went
To the high roofs, and through th' astonish'd town,
Swift as a thunderbolt, the raging news was blown.

With sighs, laments, shrieks and a female yell
    Earth sounds, and Heav'n's high battlements resound,
    As if, the foe let in, all Carthage fell,
    Or mother walls of Tyre were brought to ground,
    And fanes and houses one flame did confound.
    Her frighted sister hears the baleful noise:
    She thumps her bosom, and with nails doth wound
    Her face, distracted through the press she flies,
And "Dido, Dido, O my sister Dido," cries.

"Was this the business? Wouldst thou cozen me?
    Those fires, piles, altars, hid they this beneath?
    Scorn'dst thou in fate thy sister's company?
    I might have been invited to thy death;
    One sword and one hour should have reft our breath.
    Must I too build the pile, and Heav'n invoke
    For this? Thy cruel hand extinguisheth
    Thyself and me, senate and common folk,
And thy new-raised town, with one all-murthering
        stroke.

"Tears, bathe her wounds; suck her last breath, my
        lips,
    If any about hers yet hovering stays."
    This said, she passes the high stairs and clips
    Her half-dead sister, whom she fostering lays
    To her warm breasts, and as the breath decays,
    Sighs new, the gore-blood with her garment dried.
    She, striving her eyes' heavy lids to raise,
    Fainted again, her wound's mouth gaping wide

Vents by a nearer way her heart's groans through her
　　side.

Thrice on her arm she did her body stay,
　　Thrice tumbled backward, and with rolling eyes
　　Grop'd for and sigh'd to find the glaring day.
　　Then Juno pitying her long agonies
　　And pangs of death, sent Iris from the skies,
　　Her wrestling soul from twisting limbs t' untwine:
　　For since of age nor malady she dies,
　　But by despair nipt early, Proserpine
Had not yet cut her hair, and said, "This head is mine."

So Iris her great mistress' will obeys,
　　Descending to the earth immediately
　　On curious wings, which the sun's oblique rays
　　With water-colours painted variously:
　　And standing right over her head, said she,
　　"As I am bid, these vowed locks I bear
　　To Hell's black prince, and do pronounce thee free
　　From body's bonds." This said, cut off her hair;
Heat left her, and th' uncaged soul flew through the
　　air.

※※※※※

HORACE

(Quintus Horatius Flaccus, 65 B.C.–8 B.C.)

✳

From the Odes

✳

I:5 Quis multa gracilis

Translated by John Milton

What slender youth, bedew'd with liquid odours,
Courts thee on roses in some pleasant cave,
    Pyrrha? For whom bind'st thou
      In wreaths thy golden hair,

Plain in thy neatness? O how oft shall he
On faith and changed gods complain, and seas
    Rough with black winds, and storms
      Unwonted shall admire!

Who now enjoys thee credulous, all gold,
Who always vacant, always amiable,
    Hopes thee, of fluttering gales
      Unmindful. Hapless they

T'whom thou untried seem'st fair. Me in my vowed
Picture the sacred wall declares to have hung
    My dank and dripping weeds
      To the stern god of sea.

*

I:7 Laudabunt alii

Translated by Lord Dunsany

Others than I will sing of Rhodes' renown,
    Of Mitylene or of Ephesus,
Or Corinth 'twixt her seas, Thebes, Bacchus' town,
    Or Delphi, for Apollo glorious,
Or of Thessalian Tempe. Others sing
    The city of unmated Pallas; long
They sing of it, and before everything
    Gathered from trees they put the olive. Strong
In numbers those are that for Juno's sake
    Give honour most to Argos, where they rear
The horses, or of rich Mycenæ make
    Their eulogies. But not to me so dear
Hard Lacedæmon, or Larissa's plain,
    With all its wealth, as loud Albunea seems,
And headlong Anio, Tibur's woodland fane,
    And orchards watered with swift-running streams.
Often the bright south wind drives clouds away
    From the dark sky; so, wisely, Plancus, end
The cares of life with wine, whether you stay
    Where the camp gleams with ensigns, or where
      bend
The woods above your Tibur. When he fled
    From Salamis and from his father's house
Teucer yet bound for Bacchus round his head
    A wreath of foliage from the poplar's boughs.
To his sad friends, "Where Fortune leads," he said,
    "More kindly than my father, we shall follow.
Never despair with Teucer at your head,
    For we are promised, and by sure Apollo,

In a new land another Salamis
    Like to the old. Brave comrades, who with me
Have often been through things as bad as this,
    Drink now. Tomorrow to the open sea."

✳

I:9 Vides ut alta

Translated by Charles Stuart Calverley

One dazzling mass of solid snow
    Soracte stands; the bent woods fret
    Beneath their load; and, sharpest-set
With frost, the streams have ceased to flow.

Pile on great faggots and break up
    The ice: let influence more benign
    Enter with four-years-treasured wine,
Fetched in the ponderous Sabine cup:

Leave to the gods all else. When they
    Have once bid rest the winds that war
    Over the passionate seas, no more
Gray ash and cypress rock and sway.

Ask not what future suns shall bring.
    Count today gain, whate'er it chance
    To be: nor, young man, scorn the dance,
Nor deem sweet Love an idle thing,

Ere Time thy April youth hath changed
    To sourness. Park and public walk
    Attract thee now, and whispered talk
At twilight meetings prearranged;

Hear now the pretty laugh that tells
In what dim corner lurks thy love;
And snatch a bracelet or a glove
From wrist or hand that scarce rebels.

I:11 Tu ne quaesieris

Translated by Charles Stuart Calverley

Ask not, for thou shalt not find it, what my end, what
thine shall be;
Ask not of Chaldæa's science what God wills, Leuconoë:
Better far, what comes, to bear it. Haply many a wintry
blast
Waits thee still; and this, it may be, Jove ordains to be
thy last,
Which flings now the flagging sea-wave on the obstinate
sandstone reef.
Be thou wise: fill up the wine-cup, shortening, since the
time is brief,
Hopes that reach into the future. While I speak, hath
stol'n away
Jealous Time. Mistrust tomorrow, catch the blossom of
today.

I:22 Integer vitae

Translated by Samuel Johnson

The man, my friend, whose conscious heart
With virtue's sacred ardour glows,
Nor taints with death th' envenomed dart,
Nor needs the guard of Moorish bows:

Though Scythia's icy cliffs he treads,
    Or horrid Afric's faithless sands;
Or where the fam'd Hydaspes spreads
    His liquid wealth o'er barbarous lands;

For while, by Chloë's image charm'd,
    Too far in Sabine woods I stray'd,
Me, singing, careless, and unarm'd,
    A grisly wolf surpris'd and fled.

No savage more portentous stain'd
    Apulia's spacious wilds with gore;
None fiercer Juba's thirsty land,
    Dire nurse of raging lions, bore.

Place me where no soft summer gale
    Among the quivering branches sighs,
Where clouds condens'd for ever veil
    With horrid gloom the frowning skies;

Place me beneath the burning line,
    A clime denied to human race;
I'll sing of Chloë's charms divine,
    Her heavenly voice, and beauteous face.

III:5 Caelo tonantem
Translated by Charles Stuart Calverley

Jove we call King, whose bolts rive heaven:
    Then a god's *presence* shall be felt
    In Cæsar, with whose power the Celt
And Parthian stout in vain have striven.

Could Crassus' men wed alien wives,
    And greet, as sons-in-law, the foe?
    In the foes' land (oh Romans, oh
Lost honour!) end, in shame, their lives,

'Neath the Mede's sway? They, Marsians and
    Apulians—shields and rank and name
    Forgot, and that undying flame—
And Jove still reign, and Rome still stand?

This thing wise Regulus could presage:
    He brooked not base conditions; he
    Set not a precedent to be
The ruin of a coming age:

"No," cried he, "let the captives die,
    Spare not. I saw Rome's ensigns hung
    In Punic shrines; with sabres, flung
Down by Rome's sons ere blood shed. I

"Saw our free citizens with hands
    Fast pinioned; and, through portals now
    Flung wide, our soldiers troop to plough,
As once they trooped to waste, the lands.

" 'Bought by our gold, our men will fight
    But keener.' What? To shame would you
    Add loss? As wool, its natural hue
Once gone, may not be *painted* white;

"True Valour, from her seat once thrust,
    Is not replaced by meaner wares.
    Do stags, delivered from the snares,
Fight? Then shall *he* fight, who did trust

"His life to foes who spoke a lie:
  And *his* sword shatter Carthage yet,
  Around whose arms the cords have met,
A sluggard soul, that feared to die!

"Life, howe'er bought, he treasured: he
  Deemed war a thing of trade. Ah fie!—
  Great art thou, Carthage—towerest high
O'er shamed and ruined Italy!"

As one uncitizen'd—men said—
  He puts his wife's pure kiss away,
  His little children; and did lay
Stern in the dust his manly head:

Till those unequalled words had lent
  Strength to the faltering sires of Rome;
  Then from his sorrow-stricken home
Went forth to glorious banishment.

Yet knew he, what wild tortures lay
  Before him: knowing, put aside
  His kin, his countrymen—who tried
To bar his path, and bade him stay:

He might be hastening on his way,—
  A lawyer freed from business—down
  To green Venafrum, or a town
Of Sparta, for a holiday.

*

III: 9 Donec gratus eram tibi

Translated by Robert Herrick

HORACE

While, Lydia, I was loved of thee,
Nor any was preferred before me
To hug thy whitest neck: than I,
The Persian King lived not more happily.

LYDIA

While thou no other didst affect,
Nor Cloe was of more respect;
Then Lydia, far-famed Lydia,
I flourish't more than Roman Ilia.

HORACE

Now Thracian Cloe governs me,
Skillful with the Harpe, and Melodie:
For whose affection, Lydia, I
(So Fate spares her) am well content to die.

LYDIA

My heart now set on fire is
By Ornithes sonne, young Calais;
For whose commutuall flames here I
(To save his life) twice am content to die.

HORACE

Say our first loves we showed revoke,
And severed, joyne in brazed yoke:
Admit I Cloe put away,
And love again love-cast-off Lydia?

LYDIA
Though mine be brighter than the Star;
Thou lighter than the Cork by far;
Rough as the Adratick sea, yet I
Will live with thee, or else for thee will die.

*

IV:7 Diffugere nives

Translated by A. E. Housman

The snows are fled away, leaves on the shaws
    And grasses in the mead renew their birth,
The river to the river-bed withdraws,
    And altered is the fashion of the earth.

The Nymphs and Graces three put off their fear
    And unapparelled in the woodland play.
The swift hour and the brief prime of the year
    Say to the soul, *Thou wast not born for aye.*

Thaw follows frost; hard on the heel of spring
    Treads summer sure to die, for hard on hers
Comes autumn, with his apples scattering;
    Then back to wintertide, when nothing stirs.

But oh, whate'er the sky-led seasons mar,
    Moon upon moon rebuilds it with her beams:
Come *we* where Tullus and where Ancus are,
    And good Æneas, we are dust and dreams.

Torquatus, if the gods in heaven shall add
    The morrow to the day, what tongue has told?

Feast then thy heart, for what thy heart has had
 The fingers of no heir will ever hold.

When thou descendest once the shades among,
 The stern assize and equal judgment o'er,
Not thy long lineage nor thy golden tongue,
 No, nor thy righteousness, shall friend thee more.

Night holds Hippolytus the pure of stain,
 Diana steads him nothing, he must stay;
And Theseus leaves Pirithoüs in the chain
 The love of comrades cannot take away.

IV:13 Audivere, Lyce

Translated by Charles Stuart Calverley

Lyce, the gods have listened to my prayer:
The gods have listened, Lyce. Thou art grey
 And still would'st thou seem fair;
 Still unshamed drink, and play,

And, wine-flushed, woo slow-answering Love with weak
Shrill pipings. With young Chia He doth dwell,
 Queen of the harp; her cheek
 Is his sweet citadel:

He marked the withered oak, and on he flew
Intolerant; shrank from Lyce grim and wrinkled,
 Whose teeth are ghastly-blue,
 Whose temples snow-besprinkled:

Not purple, not the brightest gem that glows,
Brings back to her the years which, fleeting fast,

Time hath once shut in those
   Dark annals of the Past.

Oh, where is all thy loveliness? soft hue
And motions soft? Oh, what of Her doth rest,
   Her, who breathed love, who drew
     My heart out of my breast?

Fair, and far-famed, and subtly sweet, thy face
Ranked next to Cinara's. But to Cinara fate
   Gave but a few years' grace;
     And lets live, all too late,

Lyce, the rival of the beldam crow:
That fiery youth may see with scornful brow
   The torch that long ago
     Beamed bright, a cinder now.

From the Satires

✳

A Pertinacious Bore and Sycophant

Translated by Alexander Murison

It chanced that I was walking on a day
Along the Sacred Street; as is my way,
Thinking some trifle over, wholly too
Absorbed in it: a man ran up to me—
A man I knew by name alone—and he,
Seizing my hand, cried out: "Ah! how d'ye do,
My dearest friend on earth?" "As times go now,

I'm pretty well," say I; "the same to you."
Close clung he to me, so I said "Good-bye!"
Anticipating him. He made reply:
"You can't but know me: I'm a scholar, I."
"The more," say I, "I'll hold you in esteem."
Sadly impatient to get off from him,
I walked at times apace, and there and here
I stopped and whispered in my lackey's ear,
Whilst to my very heels the sweat did run.
And to myself I said: "O happy one,
Bolanus, for a temper boiling hot!"
While still my man kept chattering Heaven knows what
About the streets, the City. No reply.
Whereon said he: "You're longing mightily
To get away; I saw it some time past;
But 'tis no use; I will to you stick fast;
I'll dog your steps: where are you going, pray?"
"No need for you to wander from your way:
I'm going to see a man unknown to you;
He's ill in bed, beyond the Tiber far,
Near Cæsar's gardens." "I have nought to do;
I walk quite briskly: on, and there we are!"
I hang my head, like sullen ass with pack
He finds too heavy for his youthful back.

He starts again: "If I myself well know,
You will not higher confidence bestow
On Viscus or on Varius as a friend;
For where's the other man that can pretend
To write more verses in the time than I?
Or who can foot a dance more gracefully?
And then I sing so well Hermogenes
May envy me." Then in a word I squeeze:
"Have you a mother? Have you any kin
To take an interest in your precious skin?"

"Not one; for I have laid them all to rest."
"O happy they! Now I am left. 'Twere best
You finish me at once; for my sad doom
Is close at hand, to lay me in the tomb—
The doom that a Sabellian crone foretold,
On shaking duly the divining urn,
I yet a boy: 'This boy nor poisons dire
Nor sword of foe from life shall ever spurn,
Nor pleurisy, nor gout, nor cough nor cold;
A babbler's clack will drive him to expire
One day or other: if the boy have sense,
As soon as he attains adolescence,
When chatterers appear, let him go hence.'"

A quarter of the day already past,
To Vesta's temple had we come at last;
And, as the best of luck would have it, he
Was bound just then to answer to his bail:
Unless he did so, then his case would fail.
"O, as you love me," said he, "stand by me
A moment here." "Nay, on my life," I said,
"I can't stand here; the law I've never read.
Besides, I'm hurrying on to where you know."
"I am in doubt," said he, "what I'm to do—
My case abandon, or abandon you."
"Me, me," said I. Said he: "I won't do so";
And then proceeded on in front to go.
I—for it is not easy to contend
With one that vanquishes you—after wend.
And then he starts again: "Now, tell me true:
What are the terms Mæcenas holds with you?"
"Choice in his friends, a man of sober sense,
No man has used with more intelligence
His chances." "You would have a powerful stay,
Well fit the second part to you to play,

Me would you introduce. Ay, by my fay,
You'd sweep all rivals from your path away."

Then I replied: "Of quite another kind
Our life is there than what you have in mind:
There's not a house where reigns a purer tone;
There such annoyances are never known;
Ne'er jars it on me, has one greater pelf,
Or is more learnèd than I am myself:
We have our several places, every one."
"News marvellous, beyond belief almost!"
"Yet so it is." "You fire my wish to boast
Close friendship with him." "Just you try it—warm:
Your merit's such you'll take him straight by storm;
Moreover, he's a man that may be won,
And this is why approach, when first begun,
Is not so very easy." Then said he:
"No effort on my part shall wanting be:
I'll bribe the slaves; if in my face the door
Be shut today, for that I'll not give o'er;
I'll watch my opportunities—I'll meet
My man about the corners of each street;
I'll wait upon him home and to his haunts:
Without great toil life nought to mortals grants."

While he is this way running on in talk,
Fuscus Aristius meets us in our walk—
Dear friend of mine, and like to know the man.
We stop; exchange "Good day!" then I began
To twitch his robe, and next his arms to seize—
Arms irresponsive; and, to get release,
I nod, I wink. With wit unkind and bland,
He laughed, and feigned he did not understand.
My heart with anger surges. "Sure," quoth I,
"You said you wished to tell me privately

About some matter." "I remember well,
But at a better season I will tell
You all about it: thirtieth Sabbath this;
You would not want to scandalise, ywis,
The circumcisèd Jews?" "For that," say I,
"I have no scruple." "I have, though," says he;
"I'm rather a weak brother—as many be;
You'll pardon me; some opportunity
Will soon occur, when we will talk it o'er."
To think this very day the sun should lower
So dark on me! And off the rascal got,
And left me with the knife upon my throat.

Just then by chance the plaintiff meets my man,
And shouts to him as loud as e'er he can:
"Where are you off to, scoundrel? Do you hear?
May I call you to witness?"—this to me;
And with alacrity I lend my ear.
He drags my man to court; then shouts ring free
This side and that; the crowd keeps gathering fast:
And so Apollo saved me at the last.

Book 1, Chapter 9

*

The Art of Poetry
Translated by Alexander Murison

Suppose a painter should at fancy's beck
Join to a human head a horse's neck,
And, bringing limbs of every beast together,
Stick on them plumes of parti-coloured feather,
So that a woman beautiful and nesh
Should tail off to a shocking ugly fish,
Could you, my friends, admitted to the sight,

Refrain from laughing at the thing outright?
Believe, my Pisos, such a sketch would be
The very moral of a book where we
Should find the ideas vague, unreal, vain,
Like dreams disordered of a sick man's brain,
So neither head nor foot finds proper place
In form precise in any single case.

"Always have painters, yea and poets too,
Been privileged whate'er they like to do."

Ay, true! This privilege the bard demands,
The critic grants it, each at other's hands;
But there's a limit: for one must not bring
A tame in union with a savage thing—
Pair birds and serpents, lambs and tigers join.
Upon a work of weight and promise fine
Are purple patches, brilliant meant to shine,
Ofttimes sewed on, now here now there:
When Dian's grove and Dian's altar fair,
And hurrying waters that meandering twine
Through pleasant fields, or when the river Rhine
Or else the rainbow is portrayed. But now
Was not the time such pictures to bestow.
And maybe you can draw a cypress tree:
But where comes in the use of it, tell me,
If he that paid to have his portrait painted
Is swimming hopeless from a wreck presented?
The thing was first intended for a vase:
Why does it leave the wheel a pitcher base?
Nay, let the subject, be it what it may,
Be simple and a unity alway.

The most of us touched with poetic fire,
Both sire and sons—sons worthy of their sire—

Mistake apparent right for rightness pure.
I labour to be brief, I end obscure;
Pursue the easy, nerves and spirit fail;
Try the sublime, you are bombastical.
If one too cautious is, too timid found
To face the storm, he creeps upon the ground;
If one a monstrous variation craves,
Dolphins in woods he paints, and boars in waves.
To flee from error is in fault to rush,
If skill is lacking to the painter's brush.
Beside the Æmilian school a sculptor great
In bronze will nails express and imitate
Soft hair, yet in the ensemble he will fail
Because he can't dispose the whole to scale.
A man like this, cared I but to compose,
No more I'd be than sport a crookèd nose—
Distinguished with black eyes and with black hair.
All ye that write, material select
That suits your powers, and see you long reflect
What weight your shoulders will refuse to bear,
What strength they have in them. Choose, then, with
    care,
A fitting subject well within your border,
You'll ne'er lack matter nor a lucid order.
The worth and charm of order will be this,
Unless my judgment should be much amiss,
To say just now what just now should be said,
Most things deferred, aside at present laid.
Yea, let the author of the piece in hand
This point prefer, that other point remand.

In planting words too, cautious, using care,
You will express yourself right well indeed
If by an artful junction you suceed
In giving common words a novel air.

And, should it happen that you have to mark
Things that have hitherto lain in the dark,
Then will it fall to you to coin a word
Cethegi with their cinctures never heard;
And licence will be granted if you use
The freedom you have ta'en without abuse.
And words quite novel, words but lately coined,
Will very readily acceptance find,
If taken from the Greek with little change.
Why should the Roman people ever yield
To Plautus and Cæcilius a range
From Virgil and from Varius withheld?
And why should I, if it be in my power
A few such words to gather, grudge incur,
When Cato's, Ennius', language has made rich
By new words introduced our native speech?
It has been lawful, lawful will be ever,
A word with current stamp on't to deliver.
As forests change their leaves as wanes the year,
The earliest fall, so words grown ancient perish,
And words but newly born in vigour flourish,
As flourish men in blooming youth's career.

We all and all our works are due to death.
Whether Neptunus, brought into the land,
Defends our navies from the north-wind's scathe—
A kingly work—or marshy stretch of sand,
Long sterile, fit indeed for oars, yet now
Feeds neighbour towns and feels the heavy plough—
Or river, to a better channel led,
Has changed its course, which oft the crops o'erspread—
All mortal works will perish. Much less, sure,
Can dignity and grace of speech endure.
Revive will many words now fallen away,
And fall away will many prized today,

If such the will of custom, which alone
Decides the laws and rules that speech must own.
Homerus showed the measure for the verse
Meet for the deeds of kings and chiefs, and wars.
Unequal verses in conjunction placed
The feelings of lament at first expressed,
And, later, wishes gratified embraced;
But who the humble elegy put out
The first of all, that critics still dispute,
And still the issue does the judge engage.
Archilochus the poet, armed with rage,
Invented his iambics; then this foot
Adopted both the sock and stately boot
As suited dialogue well to express
And silence clamour of the populace,
And born to fit the action of the stage.
And gods and sons of gods, and such as wage
Victorious battle in the boxing ring,
The horses that run foremost in the race,
The cares of lads and maids alike to sing,
The wines that free the bosom with their fire—
All these the Muse committed to the lyre.

If, then, I am not able to discern
These different distinctions and to learn
The different colouring of works, nor know it,
Why am I greeted with the name of Poet?
Why, with false modesty, do I prefer
Still to be ignorant, to learn not care?
A comic subject tragic verses spurns;
And so the banquet of Thyestes scorns
Narration in the speech of common folk—
Speech very much as suits the humble sock.
Let each particular type in every case
Keep, as it ought to keep, its proper place.

True, Comedy at times her voice upraises,
And angry Chremes rails in swelling phrases;
And oft the tragic poet grieves in prose.
Peleus and Telephus—to name but those—
Exiled and poor, cast off grandiloquence
And words of half a yard of elegance,
If one or other of them is intent
To touch the looker-on with his complaint.

But poems should be more than fine and gay:
They should be tender too, and they should sway
The hearer's soul whatever way they may.
As human faces smile on such as smile,
So weep they too with such as weep the while:
Wouldst have me weep, then first yourself must grieve:
'Tis only then your troubles I'll believe,
Peleus or Telephus; if the role you have
Is given you wrongly, I'll go sleep or laugh.
Sad words become a melancholy face;
An angry face should threatening words address;
Sportive expressions need a playful cheer;
And serious matters call for looks severe.
For Nature forms us from the first within
To Fortune's every mood to show akin:
She drives to rage, she tickles to delight,
She presses us to earth in woeful plight,
And tortures us; and then, the soul thus wrung,
Its feelings she interprets by the tongue.
If words the speaker's station fail to suit,
The Roman knights and commons laugh and hoot;
And wide indeed the difference it will make
Whether a rich man or a hero speak,
An agèd man or man of youthful force,
A noble matron or a fussy nurse,
A merchant wont both near and far to roam

Or tiller of a thriving farm at home,
A Colchian or an Assyrian,
A man of Argos or a native Theban.

Follow tradition, or, if you invent,
See that your characters be congruent.
Put you renowned Achilles on the stage,
As indefatigable let him rage,
Wrathful, inexorable, vehement;
Let him deny that laws for him were framed,
Let him appeal to arms when aught is claimed.
Medea shall be pictured fierce and ruthless,
Ino all pitiful, Ixion truthless,
A wanderer Io, and Orestes spent.
If something new you to the stage deliver,
And venture a new character to draw,
Then see that to the very last it show
Such as it was at first, consistent ever.
'Tis hard to handle things to all bards free
So they consistent, individual, be.
More wise the Iliad to reduce to acts
Than introduce unknown, untreated, facts.
Public material will to private pass
Provided that you deal not with the mass
Of wretched trivial stuff, hold it absurd
All faithfully to render word by word,
Nor imitation land you in a strait
Whence shame or plan of work forbids retreat.
Do not commence your verses to outpour
As did the wretched Cyclic bard of yore:
"I'll sing of Priam and the glorious war."
What will this vaunter worth his vaunt produce?
The mountains labour: lo! a peddling mouse!
How much more rightly starts his poem he
That handles nothing injudiciously:

"Sing me, O Muse, the man, when Troy was ta'en,
That saw the ways and towns of many men."
Not smoke from lightning flash, but light from smoke,
His purpose 'tis at all times to evoke,
So thence he draw his pictures marvellous—
Scylla, Cyclops, Antiphates, Charybdis—
Nor dates he the return of Diomedes
From Meleager's death, nor the Trojan war
From those twin eggs that Leda erstwhile bare.
Always he hastens to the issue; brings
The hearer quickly to the heart of things,
As if the whole were known; and leaves apart
What he despairs to blazon by his art;
And so presents his fictions to the view,
So deftly intermingles feigned and true,
That ne'er the middle with the opening wars
Nor e'er the ending with the middle jars.

List you what I want, what the public sense:
If you would find a friendly audience,
Such as will wait the curtain, keep their seats
Until the player their applause entreats,
Each age's manners must be kept in mind,
And congruous characters must be assigned
To varying dispositions, varying years.
The boy just fit to echo what he hears,
Who prints with steady foot the yielding clay,
Delights with fellows like himself to play,
Gets angry, then gets pleased, capriciously,
And changes humour as the hours go by.
The beardless youth, at length from guidance freed,
Rejoices in his dogs and in his steed
And in the sunny Campus' verdant mead,
As pliable as wax to bend to vice,
Intolerant of admiration wise,

Slow to provide him things of use at all,
Free with his money as a prodigal,
Presumptuous, amorous, and in hasty fashion
Abandoning the objects of his passion.

Our interests changed with age, our manly mind
Seeks wealth and troops of friends for us to find,
Strives eagerly some office to secure,
And cautiously avoids in faults to fall
It presently will labour to recall.
An old man is besieged with troubles, sure,
Either because he seeks to get him gains
And, having got them, wretched man, abstains
From using them, obsessed the while with fear,
Or else because the business he transacts
He always does in cold and timid acts,
Is dilatory, slow to entertain
High hopes, inert, athirst long life to gain,
Morose, and querulous, much given to praise
The good old times that were his boyhood's days,
And castigate and censure younger men.
Advancing years bring with them in their train
Advantages a many: so, too, aye
Declining years a many take away.
That old men's parts may not be given a youth
Nor young men's parts assigned a boy, in sooth
We always must regard with prudence sage
Whate'er belongs to and befits each age.

An action is or shown upon the stage
Or, if performed elsewhere, related there.
The things that make their entrance by the ear
Less vividly the mind's regard engage
Than such as strike upon the faithful eyes
And the spectator for himself descries.

But still you must not bring upon the stage
Things only fit to act behind the flies;
And you must from the public camouflage
A many that a witness' wordy spate
May soon before the audience relate.
Let not Medea in the people's sight
Murder her sons; nor openly be dight
By execrable Atreus' banquet grim
Of human entrails and of human limb;
Nor metamorphose Procne to a bird,
Nor Cadmus change into a snake abhorred.
Whate'er you show me in such fashion dressed
I don't believe, I heartily detest.
A play that would be called for, and, though seen,
Would yet be put upon the boards again
In five acts, neither less nor more, express;
Nor ever let a god come in, unless
A knot that's worthy of a god occur.
Let no fourth character put in his oar.

The chorus? Let it bear an actor's part
And all the duties of such part assert.
Between the acts it shall not sing a note
That fails to help and fit in with the plot.
Let it show favour always to the good,
And friendly counsel to all such impart;
Let it control the passionate of mood,
And give the folk that fear to sin its heart;
Praise short and simple meals; and show
The salutary rule of justice, law,
And peace with gates thrown frankly open wide;
What secrets are entrusted to it hide;
And supplicate the gods and them implore
That Fortune to the hapless hope restore,
And prideful men abandon to their pride.

The flute, not, as 'tis now, bewhipt with brass
And emulous the trumpet to surpass,
But unadorned, charged with less swelling note,
Furnished with stops but few, good service wrought,
Accompanying and supporting still
The chorus, with a tone that served to fill
The seats not yet too crowded, where were blent
An audience, sure, not difficult at all
To number—for as yet it was but small—
Attentive, well-behaved, and reverent.
But, when a folk victorious begun
Their territories to extend, and run
Around their towns a wall of wider sweep,
And when on festal days with drinking deep
Even in the day-time they'd propitiate
Their Genius, nor incur reproof or hate,
The numbers and the measures flowed more free.
For what should be a country bumpkin's taste,
A man unlettered, just from toil released,
When mixed with city men in company—
A yokel mixed with gentlemen confest?
So the musician to the ancient art
Did quicker movement, richer tone, impart,
And trailed behind him, strutting up and down,
Along the stage, his freely flowing gown.
And so were added to the grave-toned lyre
New notes, and speech of bold and rapid fire
Produced a diction hardly known before;
And, too, the sentiments, shrewd, practical,
Yea, and prophetic of events in store,
Struck just the note of Delphi's oracle.

The bard that battled for a paltry goat
Soon naked satyrs of the woodland brought,

And tried to show a rough jocosity
Without a sacrifice of dignity;
For the spectator, fresh from sacred rite,
Well primed with wine, in humour reckless quite,
Had to be kept from leaving by some wile
Attractive, pleasing, and of novel style.
Expedient, though, 'twill be so to commend
The fun and banter that the satyrs lend,
And so to turn the earnest into jest,
That neither god nor hero lately dressed
In purple and in gold, conspicuous each,
Descend to taverns low with vulgar speech;
Nor, while he contact with the ground would spare,
Grasp at the misty clouds and empty air.

Now Tragedy, while scorning trivial chatter,
Will, like a matron on a festal day
To dance commanded, in a shamefast way
Mix even with the saucy satyrs' patter.
Not I, ye Pisos, should I come to write
Satyric dramas, e'er will stoop to choose
Plain literal terms and words alone to use;
Nor shall I strive to deviate, left or right,
So far from tragic style as not to make
A clear distinction whether Davus speak—
And Pythias bold, who Simo gulled, and won
A talent—or Silenus guardian
And of his foster-child divine companion.
Of known material so my play I'll frame
That whosoe'er may hope to do the same
Shall, if he ventures on it, in the end
Much labour and much sweat in vain expend.
So great the power that in arrangement lies
And in connexion of the words; so fair
The grace that common words may come to wear.

The Fauns brought from the forests, I surmise,
Should never in too mincing verses sport
As if they had been born in city court
Or almost in the Forum reared, nor blurt
Unclean remarks and ignominious jests;
For all men are offended at such pests—
All men with steed, with father, with estate—
Nor with content receive and decorate
With laurel crown the wretched quips that please
The purchasers of parchèd nuts and peas.

Two syllables, a short and then a long,
Form an iambus. 'Tis a rapid foot;
And so the name of trimeter bade put
To lines iambic, since, six beats among,
Each foot was an iambus, first to last.
Not long ago, that it not quite so fast
And with more weight might fall upon the ear,
It generously admitted to the sphere
Of its paternal rights steadfast spondees,
On terms, as friends might do, that never these
Should oust it from the fourth and second place.
But the iambus rarely shows its face
In Accius's far-famed trimeters,
And casts the charge on Ennius's verse,
Dumped on the stage o'erloaded with spondees,
Of lack of care and overhastiness,
Or of disgraceful ignorance of his art.

It is not every one can play the part
Of certain judge of inharmonious lines,
And so opinion with opinion joins
An undeserved indulgence to allow
To Roman poets. But am I to bow
To such opinion, and go far astray

And write my lines in this licentious way?
Or am I to assume that every cit
Will see whatever faults I may commit,
And rest secure too cautious to outpace
The furthest limits of the hope of grace?
Nay; then indeed, though censure I should shun,
Yet shall I not a claim to praise have won.

O ye, my Pisos, eager well to write,
Turn o'er the Grecian models day and night.
Your ancestors, 'tis true, they thought it fit
To praise both Plautus' numbers and his wit;
Too tolerantly—nay, but foolishly—
Admiring each of them, if you and I
Can but distinguish boorish drolleries
From witty repartee, and recognize
The cadence true by fingers and by ear.

To Thespis is assigned as being his own
A form of tragedy before unknown.
His plays 'tis said that he conveyed on carts
Whereon the actors sang and played their parts,
Their faces smeared with wine-lees from the cask.
Next Æschylus, the inventor of the mask
And of the stately robe, the stage o'erlaid
With boards some moderate extent outspread,
And taught to speak in a commanding tone
And strut in buskins up the stage and down.
And then the Old Comedy came after these,
And managed fairly well the folk to please;
Its freedom, though, declined into excess
And violence law only could repress:
Accordingly, a law was passed, and straight
The chorus, having lost the right to rate,
Fell into silence, to its deep disgrace.

No form our bards have left untried indeed:
Nor have deserved the smallest honour's meed
Such of them as have ventured to neglect
The footsteps of the Greeks and to affect
Domestic subjects, whether tragedies
They have exhibited or comedies.
Not more impressive would be Latium's charms
By noble deeds or famous feats of arms
Than by its language, but for the recoil
Of all our poets from the exacting toil
And long time spent in using of the file.
Pompilius' descendants, turn away
A poem that has not for many a day
Severe correction borne, and without fail
Been ten times polished to the very nail.
Because Democritus thinks in his heart
That native gift excelleth wretched art,
And off from Helicon severely fences
All poets still considered in their senses,
A goodly part refuse their nails to pare
Or shave their beards; indeed they oft repair
To lonely places; and the baths they shun.
For name and fame of poet they'll have won
Provided they take care not to be lured
To place their heads i' th' hands of Licinus,
The barber—heads that never can be cured
By medicine of three Anticyras.

Ah! what a fool am I, who for the bile
Am purged in springtime! Else, no man the while
Could better poems make. But, after all,
What does it matter? Therefore I will fall
To act the whetstone, which, although it fails
Itself to cut, to sharpen iron avails:

And, though myself nought of the kind I write,
To such as do I'll teach the business quite—
Where plenty matter may be got, what feeds
And forms the bard, what's fitting, what's not right,
And whither skill, and whither error, leads.

Sound sense is the first principle and source
Of writing well. Materials of course
Socratic works will amply you supply.
And, when the subject has been studied close,
The words will follow on spontaneously.
He that has learnt how deep a debt he owes
His country and his friends—the man that knows
What love is due to father, brother, guest,
What duties rest on judge or senator
Or on a general sent forth to war—
Undoubtedly he knows how to present
Each character in its true lineament.
The skilful imitator I'll enjoin
To mark the pattern life and manners show
And thence descriptions to the life to draw.
Sometimes a play, with commonplaces fine,
Expressing manners with exactness meet,
Though void of elegance, of force, of art,
With higher pleasure moves the people's heart
Than tuneful trifles, verses void of meat.

Unto the Greeks—yea, unto all and each—
The Muse gave native power and finished speech—
The Greeks, who cared for nothing but for fame,
To win themselves an everlasting name.
The Roman boys with long sums rend their hearts
To split a pound into a hundred parts.
"Here you, Albinus' son, cudgel your brains:
From ounces five take one, and what remains?

Come, out with it!" . . . "Third of a pound." . . .
    'Well done!
You'll manage well your own affairs, my son.
Now turn the case about, and one ounce add:
What then?" . . . "Why, half a pound." . . . "Good
    lad!"
What! Can we then expect, when day by day
This lust of avarice and slavish greed
Has stamped its taint on people's minds indeed,
That poems will be written such as may
Be rubbed with cedar oil and stored away
In cases of smoothed cypress-wood to stay?

The poets aim to profit and amuse,
Or what in life is pleasant and of use
To say at once. The precepts you lay down,
Let them be brief; so docile minds may soon
Lay hold of them, and faithful them retain.
Superfluous instructions are in vain:
From minds too full they simply overflow.
Whate'er is feigned some pleasure to bestow,
Feign it as near as may be to the truth.
Let not a play e'er claim belief, forsooth,
For every marvel it may choose to feign:
Let it not from a Lamia's stomach draw
A living child when she has staunched her maw.
The centuries of elders damn a play
That nothing that's instructive has to say;
The haughty Ramnes scout the austere alway;
But every vote polls he that knows to blend
The pleasant with the useful, and to lend
The reader counsel and delight together.
Such books for Sosii the money gather;
They make their way across the ocean faem,
And they immortalise the author's name.

Yet faults there are whereat we would not carp:
Not always does the string give back the note
The player's mind, the player's hand, hath sought,
But for a flat there oft returns a sharp;
Nor always bow will hit the mark designed.
So, when the beauties dominant I find,
Rare blemishes I shall not greatly mind—
Such blemishes as rose from lack of care
Or human nature weakly failed to spare.

How stands the case, then? As a copyist
That, howsoever warned, will yet persist
To make the same mistake, finds no excuse,
And as a harpist falling in the use
Of blundering always on the self-same note
Is thus to ridicule most surely brought,
E'en so the poet that falls much a-lee
Becomes another Chœrilus to me,
Whom, though I find him good or here or there,
I marvel at and laugh at; and, whene'er
The good Homerus nods, it grieves me deep—
And yet it is permissible that sleep
Upon a work of vast extent should creep.

As 'tis with painting, 'tis with poesy:
One piece will take you more if near you be,
And others if you stand somewhat away;
One loves the dark, another loves the day,
Not dreading what the keenest judge may say;
One piece has once pleased, and another piece,
If ten times viewed, will ten times also please.

O elder Piso, though you have been trained
To judgment right by teaching of your sire,

And have keen insight of your own engrained,
Yet take to you this saying, nor e'er tire
To bear it well in mind: in certain cases
E'en middling and but passable successes
Are properly allowed. A man of law
And barrister of mediocre power
Is far below the talent and the skill
Of eloquent Messalla and the lore
Cascellius Aulus has in ample store,
And yet the man is held of value still.
But mediocrity in poets, sure,
Nor men nor gods nor bookstalls can endure.

As pleasure at a feast is sadly marred
By music from discordant voices jarred,
By unguents thick and coarse, by poppy blent
With honey from Sardinian meadows sent,
Because they are not needed for the feast,
E'en so a poem for all men's delight
Devised and made, if in the very least
It chances to fall short of merit's height,
Is little better than at bottom quite.

The man that knows not how the games to play
From contests in the Campus keeps away;
The man that has not learnt to play the ball,
The quoit, the hoop, he does not play at all,
For fear the crowded circles at him laugh
While he is helpless to resent their chaff;
And yet a man that nought of verses knows
Adventures boldly verses to compose.
Why not? He's free, and free he saw the light,
Ay, more than that, he's rated as a knight,
And then his character is spotless white.
But nothing either say or do will you,

Piso, but with consideration due:
Such is your judgment, such your disposition.
But, should you ever make a composition,
Submit it to some Mæcius as judge,
Or to your father, or to me; and lay
The copy in your desk, nor let it budge
Until the ninth year shall have passed away.
What you have never published you may blot;
The word you have sent forth returneth not.

Orpheus, the priest, the mouthpiece of the gods,
Deterred wild men from murders and foul foods,
And hence was said to tame the raging moods
Of tigers and of lions; and 'twas said
Amphion, founder of the city Thebes,
Made stones to move with tunes his cithern played
And led them where he willed with gentle art.
In times of yore it was the poet's part—
The part of sapience—to distinguish plain
Between the public and the private things,
Between the sacred things and things profane,
To check the ills that sexual straying brings,
To show how laws for married people stood,
To build the towns, to carve the laws in wood:
And so to bards divine and to their lays
Came honour and renown. In later days
Homerus' and Tyrtæus' verse of charms
Their manly spirit stirred to deeds of arms;
In form of verse were oracles declared;
The path of life to all men's eyes was bared;
In strains Pierian princes' grace was sought,
And festivals were into fashion brought,
Closing the long-drawn labours of the year.
And so you need not feel or shame or fear
To cultivate the Muse skilled with the lyre

And god Apollo, Lord of lyric fire.
A question has been raised: Comes poetry
Deserving praise from nature or from art?
I never have been able, for my part,
To see what can be done by industry
Without a vein of rich poetic tone,
Nor what can untaught genius all alone:
So much does each demand the other's aid,
And both conspire as friends to act as one.
The man that has his mind upmade
To reach the wished-for goal, in early days
Hath much endured and done, borne cold and heat,
Abstained from wine and women; he that plays
The flute at Pythian games first learnt the feat
And bore a master's harshness. Nowadays
Enough to say: "I make fine verses, I;
Deuce take the hindmost; it is shameful—fie!—
For me to lag behind, and to confess
No scrap of what I learnt not to possess."

E'en as a huckster draws to him a crowd
To buy his wares by shouting long and loud,
A poet rich in lands and rich in coin
Put out at interest bids flatterers join
His circle, something as reward to gain;
But, though he be a man can entertain
In proper style, and stand security
For poor and needy men, and set them free
From meshes of vexatious suits at law,
Yet shall I be surprised if—happy man!—
False friend from true friend he distinguish can.
Have you bestowed, or mean you to bestow,
On any one a gift, you'll be to blame
If e'er you show him verses made by you
When he is blithe and gay, for then he'll hail

"Charming!" "Well done!" "First rate!" He'll then turn
    pale
In contemplation of them; e'en the dew
Will from his friendly eyes to drop be found,
Yea, he'll jump up, and stamp upon the ground.

As those that mourn at funerals for hire
Make greater fuss and lamentation dire
That those that in their hearts are sore afflicted,
E'en so the flatterer is more affected
Than those whose admiration is sincere.
With bumper upon bumper, as we hear,
Princes will ply one, so they throughly know
To trust him as a friend or let him go.
If poems you compose, be not deceived
By latent wiles a fox may have conceived.

If you read verses to Quintilius,
"Pray, alter that," he'd say, "and alter this."
If you replied that you could do no more,
For you had tried, yea twice and three times o'er,
But all in vain, he'd bid you "out them score"
And place your ill-turned verses once again
Upon the anvil. But, if you preferred
Your fault not to correct but to maintain,
He would not spend on you another word
Nor waste his efforts, but would leave you there
Yourself to fancy and your verses fair,
Without corrival, by yourself, alone.
An honest and discriminating man
Will censure verses that are weak and tame,
Harsh verses likewise he will mark with blame,
Inelegant with lines of black he'll score,
Pretentious ornaments he'll cut away,
He'll have made clear what was obscure before,

Ambiguous expressions shall not stay,
He'll point the changes that the verses need,
He'll prove an Aristarchus: he'll not say,
"Why with mere trifles should I vex my friend?"
Ah! trifles will to serious troubles lead
A man that once has been befooled indeed
By friends uncandid for a dubious end.

Like one that suffers from a nasty itch,
Or jaundice, or wild frenzy, madness plain,
So men of sense avoid and shrink to touch
A crazy poet: boys torment the man,
And people follow him, a heedless rout.
If he, while head in air he stalks about
And spouts his verses, e'er should chance to fall,
Like to a fowler on his game intent,
Into a well or pit, though loud he call,
"Ho, citizens, help! help!" none would consent,
None would take pains, to help the fellow out;
But, should one take the pains aid to convey
And let him down a rope, then I should say,
"How know you that he did not with intention
Throw himself down, nor wants your intervention?"
And I will tell how a Sicilian poet
Came by his death—already you may know it:
Empedocles, fain to be deemed a god,
Leapt into flaming Ætna in cold blood.
If bards there be that such ambition cherish,
Leave them the right and liberty to perish.
He that would save a man against his will
Is on a par with one that would him kill.
Besides, the man has done the thing before,
Nor, if you rescue him, will he give o'er:
E'en then he'll not become a sober man,
Nor cease for a notorious death to plan.

And why on earth does he so keenly crave
To write? Has he befouled his father's grave?
Or has he with unhallowed feet been found
In impious trespass on polluted ground?
At any rate, he's mad; and, like a bear
That bursts the gates that pen him in his lair,
This merciless reciter puts to flight
Alike the learnèd and the unlearnèd wight;
But, let him catch one, then he holds him fast
And with his verses kills him at the last:
A very leech he is, and won't let go
Till with the captive's blood he fills his maw.

LIVY

(Titus Livius, 59 B.C.–17 A.D.)

✳

From The History of Rome

✳

The War with Lars Porsinna
Translated by B. O. Foster

NEXT Publius Valerius (for the second time) and
Titus Lucretius were made consuls. By this time
the Tarquinii had sought refuge with Lars Porsinna, king
of Clusium. There they mingled advice and entreaty,
now imploring him not to permit them, Etruscans by
birth and of the same blood and the same name as
himself, to suffer the privations of exile, and again even
warning him not to allow the growing custom of ex-
pelling kings to go unpunished. Liberty was sweet
enough in itself. Unless the energy with which nations
sought to obtain it were matched by the efforts which
kings put forth to defend their power, the highest would
be reduced to the level of the lowest; there would be
nothing lofty, nothing that stood out above the rest of
the state; there was the end of monarchy, the noblest
institution known to gods or men. Porsinna, believing
that it was not only a safe thing for the Etruscans that
there should be a king at Rome, but an honour to have
that king of Etruscan stock, invaded Roman territory
with a hostile army. Never before had such fear seized
the senate, so powerful was Clusium in those days, and

429

so great Porsinna's fame. And they feared not only the enemy but their own citizens, lest the plebs should be terror-stricken and, admitting the princes into the City, should even submit to enslavement, for the sake of peace. Hence the senate at this time granted many favours to the plebs. The question of subsistence received special attention, and some were sent to the Volsci and others to Cumæ to buy up corn. Again, the monopoly of salt, the price of which was very high, was taken out of the hands of individuals and wholly assumed by the government. Imposts and taxes were removed from the plebs that they might be borne by the well-to-do, who were equal to the burden: the poor paid dues enough if they reared children. Thanks to this liberality on the part of the Fathers, the distress which attended the subsequent blockade and famine was powerless to destroy the harmony of the state, which was such that the name of king was not more abhorrent to the highest than to the lowest; nor was there ever a man in after years whose demagogic arts made him so popular as its wise governing at that time made the whole senate.

When the enemy appeared, the Romans all, with one accord, withdrew from their fields into the City, which they surrounded with guards. Some parts appeared to be rendered safe by their walls, others by the barrier formed by the river Tiber. The bridge of piles almost afforded an entrance to the enemy, had it not been for one man, Horatius Cocles; he was the bulwark of defence on which that day depended the fortune of the City of Rome. He chanced to be on guard at the bridge when Janiculum was captured by a sudden attack of the enemy. He saw them as they charged down on the run from Janiculum, while his own people behaved like a frightened mob, throwing away their arms and quitting their ranks. Catching hold first of one and then of

another, blocking their way and conjuring them to listen,
he called on gods and men to witness that if they for-
sook their post it was vain to flee; once they had left a
passage in their rear by the bridge, there would soon
be more of the enemy on the Palatine and the Capitol
than on Janiculum. He therefore warned and com-
manded them to break down the bridge with steel, with
fire, with any instrument at their disposal; and promised
that he would himself receive the onset of the enemy,
so far as it could be withstood by a single body. Then,
striding to the head of the bridge, conspicuous amongst
the fugitives who were clearly seen to be shirking the
fight, he covered himself with his sword and buckler
and made ready to do battle at close quarters, confound-
ing the Etruscans with amazement at his audacity. Yet
were there two who were prevented by shame from
leaving him. These were Spurius Larcius and Titus
Herminius, both famous for their birth and their deeds.
With these he endured the peril of the first rush and
the stormiest moment of the battle. But after a while
he forced even these two to leave him and save them-
selves, for there was scarcely anything left of the bridge,
and those who were cutting it down called to them to
come back. Then, darting glances of defiance around
at the Etruscan nobles, he now challenged them in turn
to fight, now railed at them collectively as slaves of
haughty kings, who, heedless of their own liberty, were
come to overthrow the liberty of others. They hesitated
for a moment, each looking at his neighbour to begin
the fight. Then shame made them attack, and with a
shout they cast their javelins from every side against
their solitary foe. But he caught them all upon his shield,
and, resolute as ever, bestrode the bridge and held his
ground; and now they were trying to dislodge him by
a charge, when the crash of the falling bridge and the

cheer which burst from the throats of the Romans, exulting in the completion of their task, checked them in mid-career with a sudden dismay. Then Cocles cried, "O Father Tiberinus, I solemnly invoke thee; receive these arms and this soldier with propitious stream!" So praying, all armed as he was, he leaped down into the river, and under a shower of missiles swam across unhurt to his fellows, having given a proof of valour which was destined to obtain more fame than credence with posterity. The state was grateful for so brave a deed: a statue of Cocles was set up in the comitium, and he was given as much land as he could plough around in one day. Private citizens showed their gratitude in a striking fashion, in the midst of his official honours, for notwithstanding their great distress everybody made him some gift proportionate to his means, though he robbed himself of his own ration.

Porsinna, repulsed in his first attempt, gave up the plan of storming the City, and determined to lay siege to it. Placing a garrison on Janiculum, he pitched his camp in the plain by the banks of the Tiber. He collected ships from every quarter, both for guarding the river, to prevent any corn from being brought into the City, and also to send his troops across for plundering, as the opportunity might present itself at one point or another; and in a short time he made all the territory of the Romans so unsafe that not only were they forced to bring all their other property inside the walls, but even their flocks too, nor did anybody dare to drive them outside the gates. This great degree of licence was permitted to the Etruscans not so much from timidity as design. For Valerius the consul, who was eager for an opportunity of assailing a large number at once, when they should be scattered about and not expecting an attack, cared little to avenge small aggressions, and reserved his punishment for a heavier blow. Accordingly, to lure forth plunderers, he issued orders to his people that on the following day a large number of them should drive out their flocks by the Esquiline Gate, which was the most remote from the enemy, believing that they would hear of it, since the blockade and famine were causing desertions on the part of faithless slaves. And in fact the enemy did hear of it from a deserter's report, and crossed the river in much greater force than usual, in the hope of making a clean sweep of the booty. Consequently Publius Valerius directed Titus Herminius to lie in ambush with a small force two miles out on the Gabinian Way, and Spurius Larcius with a body of light-armed youths to take post at the Colline Gate, until the enemy should pass, and then to throw themselves between him and the river, cutting off his retreat. Of the two consuls, Titus Lucretius went out by the Nævian Gate with several maniples of soldiers, Valerius himself led out some picked cohorts by way of the Cælian Mount. These last were the first to be seen by the enemy. Herminius had no sooner perceived that the skirmish was begun than he rushed in from his ambush and fell upon the rear of the Etruscans, who had turned to meet Valerius. On the right hand and on the left, from the Nævian Gate and from the Colline, an answering shout was returned. Thus the raiders were hemmed in and cut to pieces, for they were no match for the Romans in fighting strength, and were shut off from every line of retreat. This was the last time the Etruscans roamed so far afield.

The blockade went on notwithstanding. The corn was giving out, and what there was cost a very high price, and Porsinna was beginning to have hopes that he would take the City by sitting still, when Gaius Mucius, a young Roman noble, thinking it a shame that although

the Roman People had not, in the days of their servitude
when they lived under kings, been blockaded in a war
by any enemies, they should now, when free, be be-
sieged by those same Etruscans whose armies they had
so often routed, made up his mind that this indignity
must be avenged by some great and daring deed. At
first he intended to make his way to the enemy's camp
on his own account. Afterwards, fearing that if he
should go unbidden by the consuls and without anyone's
knowing it, he might chance to be arrested by the
Roman sentries and brought back as a deserter—a
charge which the state of the City would confirm—
he went before the senate. "I wish," said he, "to cross
the river, senators, and enter, if I can, the enemy's camp
—not to plunder or exact reprisals for their devastations:
I have in mind to do a greater deed, if the gods grant
me their help." The Fathers approved. Hiding a sword
under his dress, he set out. Arrived at the camp, he took
up his stand in the thick of the crowd near the royal
tribunal. It happened that at that moment the soldiers
were being paid; a secretary who sat beside the king,
and wore nearly the same costume, was very busy,
and to him the soldiers for the most part addressed
themselves. Mucius was afraid to ask which was Por-
sinna, lest his ignorance of the king's identity should
betray his own, and following the blind guidance of
Fortune, slew the secretary instead of the king. As he
strode off through the frightened crowd, making a way
for himself with his bloody blade, there was an outcry,
and thereat the royal guards came running in from every
side, seized him and dragged him back before the tri-
bunal of the king. But friendless as he was, even then,
when Fortune wore so menacing an aspect, yet as one
more to be feared than fearing, "I am a Roman citizen,"
he cried; "men call me Gaius Mucius. I am your enemy,

and as an enemy I would have slain you; I can die as resolutely as I could kill: both to do and to endure valiantly is the Roman way. Nor am I the only one to carry this resolution against you: behind me is a long line of men who are seeking the same honour. Gird yourself therefore, if you think it worth your while, for a struggle in which you must fight for your life from hour to hour with an armed foe always at your door. Such is the war we, the Roman youths, declare on you. Fear no serried ranks, no battle; it will be between yourself alone and a single enemy at a time." The king, at once hot with resentment and aghast at his danger, angrily ordered the prisoner to be flung into the flames unless he should at once divulge the plot with which he so obscurely threatened him. Whereupon Mucius, exclaiming, "Look, that you may see how cheap they hold their bodies whose eyes are fixed upon renown!" thrust his hand into the fire that was kindled for the sacrifice. When he allowed his hand to burn as if his spirit were unconscious of sensation, the king was almost beside himself with wonder. He bounded from his seat and bade them remove the young man from the altar. "Do you go free," he said, "who have dared to harm yourself more than me. I would invoke success upon your valour, were that valour exerted for my country; since that may not be, I release you from the penalties of war and dismiss you scathless and uninjured." Then Mucius, as if to requite his generosity, answered, "Since you hold bravery in honour, my gratitude shall afford you the information your threats could not extort: we are three hundred, the foremost youths of Rome, who have conspired to assail you in this fashion. I drew the first lot; the others, in whatever order it falls to them, will attack you, each at his own time, until Fortune shall have delivered you into our hands."

The release of Mucius, who was afterwards known as Scævola, from the loss of his right hand, was followed by the arrival in Rome of envoys from Porsinna. The king had been so disturbed, what with the hazard of the first attack upon his life, from which nothing but the blunder of his assailant had preserved him, and what with the anticipation of having to undergo the danger as many times more as there were conspirators remaining, that he voluntarily proposed terms of peace to the Romans. In these terms Porsinna suggested, but without effect, that the Tarquinii should be restored to power, more because he had been unable to refuse the princes this demand upon their behalf than that he was ignorant that the Romans would refuse it. In obtaining the return of their lands to the Veientes he was successful; and the Romans were compelled to give hostages if they wished the garrison to be withdrawn from Janiculum. On these terms peace was made, and Porsinna led his army down from Janiculum and evacuated the Roman territory. The Fathers bestowed on Gaius Mucius, for his bravery, a field across the Tiber, which was later known as the Mucian Meadows.

Now when courage had been thus distinguished, even the women were inspired to deeds of patriotism. Thus the maiden Clœlia, one of the hostages, eluded the sentinels, when it chanced that the Etruscans had encamped not far from the bank of the Tiber, and heading a band of girls swam the river and, under a rain of hostile darts, brought them all back in safety to their kinsmen in Rome. When this had been reported to the king, he was at first enraged and sent emissaries to Rome to demand that the hostage Clœlia be given up, for he made no great account of the others. Then, admiration getting the better of anger, he asserted that her feat was a greater one than those of Cocles and Mucius, and de-

clared that although in case the hostages were not re-
turned he should regard the treaty as broken, yet if she
were restored to him he would send her back safe and
inviolate to her friends. Both parties kept their word.
The Romans returned the pledge of peace, as the treaty
required; and the Etruscan king not only protected the
brave girl but even honoured her, for after praising her
heroism he said that he would present her with half the
hostages, and that she herself should choose the ones
she wished. When they had all been brought out it is
said that she selected the young boys, because it was
not only more seemly in a maiden, but was unanimously
approved by the hostages themselves, that in delivering
them from the enemy she should give the preference
to those who were of an age which particularly exposed
them to injury. When peace had been established the
Romans rewarded this new valour in a woman with a
new kind of honour, an equestrian statue, which was set
up on the summit of the Sacred Way, and represented
the maiden seated on a horse.

This peaceful departure of the Etruscan king from
Rome is inconsistent with the custom handed down
from antiquity even to our own age, among other for-
malities observed at sales of booty, of proclaiming "the
goods of King Porsinna." Such a practice must either
have arisen during the war and have been retained when
peace was made, or else have had its origin in some
kindlier circumstance than would be suggested by the
notice that an enemy's goods were to be sold. The most
credible of the traditional explanations is that when
Porsinna retired from Janiculum he handed over his
camp, well stocked with provisions brought in from
the neighbouring fertile fields of Etruria, as a gift to
the Romans, who were then in a destitute condition
after the long siege. These supplies were then sold, lest,

if people were given a free hand, they might plunder the camp like an enemy; and they were called the goods of Porsinna rather by way of implying thankfulness for the gift than an auction of the king's property, which was not even in the possession of the Roman People.

On relinquishing his campaign against the Romans, Porsinna was unwilling that he should appear to have led his army into that region to no purpose, and accordingly sent a part of his forces, under his son Arruns, to besiege Aricia. At first the Aricini were paralysed with surprise. Afterwards the auxiliaries whom they called in from the Latin peoples, and also from Cumæ, so encouraged them that they ventured to measure their strength with the enemy in the open field. When the battle began, the attack of the Etruscans was so impetuous that they routed the Aricini at the first charge. The Cumæan levies, employing skill to meet force, swerved a little to one side, and when the enemy had swept by them, faced about and attacked them in the rear, with the result that the Etruscans, caught between two lines, almost in the moment of victory, were cut to pieces. A very small number of them, having lost their leader and finding no nearer refuge, drifted to Rome, unarmed and with all the helplessness and the dejected aspect of suppliants. There they were kindly received and were quartered about among the citizens. When their wounds had healed, some departed for their homes to report the hospitality and kindness they had met with, but many were persuaded to remain in Rome by the affection they felt for their hosts and for the City. To these a place of residence was allotted which was afterwards called the Vicus Tuscus.

Spurius Larcius and Titus Herminius were the next consuls, and after them came Publius Lucretius and Publius Valerius Publicola. In the latter years an em-

bassy was sent to Rome for the last time by Porsinna to
negotiate for the restoration of Tarquinius to power. To
these envoys the senate replied that they would send
representatives to the king, and they forthwith dis-
patched those of the Fathers who were held in the
highest esteem. It would not have been impossible, they
said, to reply shortly that the royal family would not be
received. It was not for that reason that they had pre-
ferred to send chosen members of the senate to him
rather than to give their answer to his ambassadors in
Rome. But they had desired that for all time discussion
of that question might be ended, and that where there
were so great obligations on both sides there might not
be mutual irritation, from the king's seeking that which
was incompatible with the liberty of the Roman people,
while the Romans, unless they were willing to sacrifice
their existence to their good nature, denied the request
of a man whom they would not willingly have denied
anything. The Roman people were not living under a
monarchy, but were free. They had resolved to throw
open their gates to enemies sooner than to kings; in this
prayer they were all united, that the day which saw
the end of liberty in their City might also see the City's
end. They therefore entreated him, if he desired the
welfare of Rome, to permit her to be free. The king,
yielding to his better feelings, made answer: "Since this
is your fixed resolve, I will neither importune you with
repeated insistence upon a hopeless plea, nor will I
deceive the Tarquinii with the hope of aid which it is
not in my power to grant. Let them seek elsewhere,
whether war or peace be their object, for a place of
exile, that nothing may hinder my being at peace with
you." His words were followed by yet more friendly
deeds. The hostages remaining in his hands he returned,
and he gave back the Veientine land which he had taken

from the Romans by the treaty made on Janiculum. Tarquinius, cut off from all hope of returning, departed for Tusculum, to spend his exile in the home of his son-in-law, Mamilius Octavius. The Romans enjoyed an unbroken peace with Porsinna.

Book II, Chapters 9-15

*

Cato on Extravagance

Translated by Cyrus Edmonds

Amid the serious concerns of important wars, either scarcely brought to a close or impending, an incident intervened, trivial indeed to be mentioned, but which, through the zeal of the parties concerned, issued in a violent contest. Marcus Fundanius and Lucius Valerius, plebeian tribunes, proposed to the people the repealing of the Oppian law. This law, which had been introduced by Caius Oppius, plebeian tribune, in the consulate of Quintus Fabius and Tiberius Sempronius, during the heat of the Punic war, enacted that "no woman should possess more than half an ounce of gold, or wear a garment of various colours, or ride in a carriage drawn by horses, in a city, or any town, or any place nearer thereto than one mile; except on occasion of some public religious solemnity." Marcus and Publius Junius Brutus, plebeian tribunes, supported the Oppian law, and declared, that they would never suffer it be repealed; while many of the nobility stood forth to argue for and against the motion proposed. The Capitol was filled with crowds, who favoured or opposed the law; nor could the matrons be kept at home, either by advice or shame, nor even by the commands of their husbands; but beset every street and pass in the city, beseeching the men as they went down to the forum, that in the present flourishing state of the commonwealth, when the private fortune of all was daily increasing, they would suffer the women to have their former ornaments of dress restored. This throng of women increased daily, for they arrived even from the country towns and villages; and they had at length the boldness to come up to the consuls, praetors, and magistrates, to urge their request. One of the consuls, however, they found especially inexorable— Marcus Porcius Cato, who, in support of the law proposed to be repealed, spoke to this effect:

"If, Romans, every individual among us had made it a rule to maintain the prerogative and authority of a husband with respect to his own wife, we should have less trouble with the whole sex. But now, our privileges, overpowered at home by female contumacy, are, even here in the forum, spurned and trodden under foot; and because we are unable to withstand each separately, we now dread their collective body. I was accustomed to think it a fabulous and fictitious tale, that, in a certain island, the whole race of males was utterly extirpated by a conspiracy of the women. But the utmost danger may be apprehended equally from either sex, if you suffer cabals, assemblies, and secret consultations to be held: scarcely, indeed, can I determine, in my own mind, whether the act itself, or the precedent that it affords, is of more pernicious tendency. The latter of these more particularly concerns us consuls, and the other magistrates: the former, yourselves, my fellow-citizens. For, whether the measure proposed to your consideration be profitable to the state or not, is to be determined by you, who are about to go to the vote. As to the outrageous behaviour of these women, whether it be merely an act of their own, or owing to your instigations, Marcus Fundanius and Lucius Valerius, it unquestionably implies culpable conduct in magistrates. I know not whether it reflects greater disgrace on you, tribunes, or on the consuls: on you certainly, if you have, on the present occasion, brought these women hither for the purpose of raising tribunitian seditions; on us, if we suffer laws to be imposed on us by a secession of women, as was done formerly by that of the common people. It was not without painful emotions of shame, that I, just now, made my way into the forum through the midst of a band of women. Had I not been restrained by respect for the modesty and dignity of some individuals among them, rather than of the whole number, and been unwilling that they should be seen rebuked by a consul, I should have said to them, 'What sort of practice is this, of running out into public, besetting the streets, and addressing other women's husbands? Could not each have made the same request to her husband at home? Are your blandishments more seducing in public than in private; and with other women's husbands, than with your own? Although if the modesty of matrons confined them within the limits of their own rights, it did not become you, even at home, to concern yourselves about what laws might be passed or repealed here.' Our ancestors thought it not proper that women should perform any, even private business, without a director; but that they should be ever under the control of parents, brothers, or husbands. We, it seems, suffer them, now, to interfere in the management of state affairs, and to introduce themselves into the forum, into general assemblies, and into assemblies of election. For, what are they doing, at this moment, in your streets and lanes? What, but arguing, some in support of the motion of the plebeian tribunes; others, for the repeal of the law? Will you give the reins to their intractable nature, and their uncontrolled passions, and then expect that themselves should set bounds to their licentiousness, when you have failed to do so? This is the smallest of the injunctions laid on them by usage or the laws, all which women bear with impatience: they long for liberty; or rather, to speak the truth, for unbounded freedom in every particular. For what will they not attempt, if they now come off victorious?

"Recollect all the institutions respecting the sex, by which our forefathers restrained their undue freedom, and by which they subjected them to their husbands; and yet, even with the help of all these restrictions, you can scarcely keep them within bounds. If, then, you suffer them to throw these off one by one, to tear them all asunder, and, at last, to be set on an equal footing with yourselves, can you imagine that they will be any longer tolerable by you? The moment they have arrived at an equality with you, they will have become your superiors. But, forsooth, they only object to any new law being made against them: they mean to deprecate, not justice, but severity. Nay, their wish is, that a law which you have admitted, established by your suffrages, and confirmed by the practice and experience of so many years to be beneficial, should now be repealed; that is, that, by abolishing one law, you should weaken all the rest. No law perfectly suits the convenience of every member of the community: the only consideration is, whether, upon the whole, it be profitable to the greater part. If, because a law proves obnoxious to a private individual, that circumstance should destroy and sweep it away, to what purpose is it for the community to enact general laws, which those, with reference to whom they were passed, could presently repeal? I should like, however, to hear what this important affair is which has induced the matrons thus to run out into public in this excited manner, scarcely restraining from pushing into the forum and the assembly of the people. Is it to solicit that their parents, their husbands, children, and brothers may be ransomed from captivity under Hannibal? By no means: and far be ever from the commonwealth so unfortunate a situation. Yet, even when such was the case, you refused this to their prayers. But it is not duty, nor solicitude for their friends; it is religion that has collected them together. They are about to receive the Idæan Mother, coming out of Phrygia from Pessinus! What motive, that even common decency will allow to be mentioned, is pretended for this female insurrection? Why, say they, that we may shine in gold and purple; that, both on festal and common days, we may ride through the city in our chariots, triumphing over vanquished and abrogated law, after having captured and wrested from you your suffrages; and that there may be no bounds to our expenses and our luxury.

"Often have you heard me complain of the profuse expenses of the women—often of those of the men; and that not only of men in private stations, but of the magistrates: and that the state was endangered by two opposite vices, luxury and avarice; those pests, which have been the ruin of all great empires. These I dread the more, as the circumstances of the commonwealth grow daily more prosperous and happy; as the empire increases; as we have now passed over into Greece and Asia, places abounding with every kind of temptation that can inflame the passions; and as we have begun to handle even royal treasures: so much the more do I fear that these matters will bring us into captivity, rather than we them. Believe me, those statues from Syracuse were brought into this city with hostile effect. I already hear too many commending and admiring the decorations of Athens and Corinth, and ridiculing the earthen images of our Roman gods that stand on the fronts of their temples. For my part I prefer these gods—propitious as they are, and I hope will continue to be, if we allow them to remain in their own mansions. In the memory of our fathers, Pyrrhus, by his ambassador Cineas, made trial of the dispositions, not only of our men, but of our women also, by offers of presents: at that time the Oppian law, for restraining female luxury, had not been made; and yet not one woman accepted a present. What, think you, was the reason? That for which our ancestors made no provision by law on this subject: there was no luxury existing which needed to be restrained. As diseases must necessarily be known before their remedies, so passions come into being before the laws which prescribe limits to them. What called forth the Licinian law, restricting estates to five hundred acres, but the unbounded desire for enlarging estates? What the Cincian law, concerning gifts and presents, but that the plebians had become vassals and tributaries to the senate? It is not therefore in any degree surprising, that no want of the Oppian law, or of any other, to limit the expenses of the women, was felt at that time, when they refused to receive gold and purple that was thrown in their way, and offered to their acceptance. If Cineas were now to go round the city with his presents, he would find numbers of women standing in the public streets to receive them. There are some passions, the causes or motives of which I can no way account for. For that that should not be lawful for you which is permitted to another, may perhaps naturally excite some degree of shame or indignation; yet, when the dress of all is alike, why should any one of you fear, lest she should not be an object of observation? Of all kinds of shame, the worst, surely, is the being ashamed of frugality or of poverty; but the law relieves you with regard to both; since that which you have not it is unlawful for you to possess. This equalization, says the rich matron, is the very thing that I cannot endure. Why do not I make a figure, distinguished with gold and purple? Why is the poverty of others concealed under this cover of a law, so that it should be thought that, if the law permitted, they would have such things as they are not now able to procure? Romans, do you wish to excite among your wives an emulation of this sort, that the rich should wish to have what no other can have; and that the poor, lest they should be despised as such, should extend their expenses beyond their means? Be assured, that when a woman once begins to be ashamed of what she ought not to be ashamed of, she will not be ashamed of what she ought. She who can, will purchase out of her own purse; she who cannot, will ask her husband. Unhappy is the husband, both he who complies with the request, and he who does not; for what he will not give himself, he will see given by another. Now, they openly solicit favours from other women's husbands; and, what is more, solicit a law and votes. From some they obtain them; although, with regard to yourself, your property, or your children, they would be inexorable. So soon as the law shall cease to limit the expenses of your wife, you yourself will never be able to do so. Do not suppose that the matter will hereafter be in the same state in which it was before the law was made on the subject. It is safer that a wicked man should even never be accused, than that he should be acquitted; and luxury, if it had never been meddled with, would be more tolerable than it will be, now, like a wild beast, irritated by having been chained, and then let loose. My opinion is, that the Oppian law ought on no account to be repealed. Whatever determination you may come to, I pray all the gods to prosper it."

Book XXIV, Chapters 1-4

OVID

(Publius Ovidius Naso, 43? B.C.–17 A.D.)

✻

From the Metamorphoses

✻

Book III
Translated by Joseph Addison

When now Agenor had his daughter lost,
He sent his son to search on every coast,
And sternly bid him to his arms restore
The darling maid, or see his face no more,
But live in exile in a foreign clime;
Thus was the father pious to a crime.

The restless youth search'd all the world around;
But how can Jove in his amours be found?
When, tired at length with unsuccessful toil,
To shun his angry sire and native soil,
He goes a suppliant to the Delphic dame;
There asks the god what new appointed home
Should end his wand'rings, and his toil relieve.
The Delphic oracles this answer give:
"Behold among the fields a lonely cow,
Unworn with yokes, unbroken to the plough:
Mark well the place where first she lays her down,
There measure out thy walls, and build thy town;
And from the guide Bœotia call the land,
In which the destined walls and town shall stand."

No sooner had he left the dark abode,
Big with the promise of the Delphic god,
When in the fields the fatal cow he view'd,
Nor gall'd with yokes, nor worn with servitude;
Her gently at a distance he pursued,
And, as he walk'd aloof, in silence pray'd
To the great power whose counsels he obey'd.
Her way through flowery Panope she took,
And now, Cephisus, cross'd thy silver brook,
When to the heavens her spacious front she raised,
And bellow'd thrice, then backward turning gazed
On those behind, till on the destined place
She stoop'd, and couch'd amid the rising grass.

Cadmus salutes the soil, and gladly hails
The new-found mountains and the nameless vales,
And thanks the gods, and turns about his eye
To see his new dominions round him lie;
Then sends his servants to a neighb'ring grove
For living streams, a sacrifice to Jove.
O'er the wide plain there rose a shady wood
Of aged trees, in its dark bosom stood
A bushy thicket, pathless and unworn,
O'errun with brambles, and perplex'd with thorn:
Amidst the brake a hollow den was found,
With rocks and shelving arches vaulted round.

Deep in the dreary den, conceal'd from day,
Sacred to Mars, a mighty dragon lay,
Bloated with poison to a monstrous size;
Fire broke in flashes when he glanced his eyes;
His towering crest was glorious to behold,
His shoulders and his sides were scaled with gold;
Three tongues he brandish'd when he charged his foes,
His teeth stood jaggy in three dreadful rows.
The Tyrians in the den for water sought,
And with their urns explored the hollow vault;

From side to side their empty urns rebound,
And rouse the sleeping serpent with the sound.
Straight he bestirs him, and is seen to rise,
And now with dreadful hissings fills the skies,
And darts his forky tongues, and rolls his glaring eyes.
The Tyrians drop their vessels in the fright,
All pale and trembling at the hideous sight.
Spire above spire uprear'd in air he stood,
And gazing round him overlook'd the wood,
Then floating on the ground in circles roll'd,
Then leap'd upon them in a mighty fold.
Of such a bulk and such a monstrous size
The serpent in the polar circle lies,
That stretches over half the northern skies.
In vain the Tyrians on their arms rely,
In vain attempt to fight, in vain to fly;
All their endeavours and their hopes are vain;
Some die entangled in the winding train;
Some are devour'd, or feel a loathsome death,
Swoln up with blasts of pestilential breath.

And now the scorching sun was mounted high,
In all its lustre, to the noon-day sky,
When, anxious for his friends, and fill'd with cares,
To search the woods the impatient chief prepares.
A lion's hide around his loins he wore,
The well-poised javelin to the field he bore,
Inured to blood, the far destroying dart,
And, the best weapon, an undaunted heart.

Soon as the youth approach'd the fatal place,
He saw his servants breathless on the grass,
The scaly foe amid their corpse he view'd,
Basking at ease and feasting in their blood.

"Such friends," he cries, "deserved a longer date;
But Cadmus will revenge, or share their fate."
Then heaved a stone, and rising to the throw,

He sent it in a whirlwind at the foe;
A tower, assaulted by so rude a stroke,
With all its lofty battlements had shook;
But nothing here the unwieldy rock avails,
Rebounding harmless from the plaited scales,
That, firmly join'd, preserved him from a wound,
With native armour crusted all around.
With more success the dart unerring flew,
Which at his back the raging warrior threw:
Amid the plaited scales it took its course,
And in the spinal marrow spent its force.
The monster hiss'd aloud, and raged in vain,
And writhed his body to and fro with pain;
He bit the dart, and wrench'd the wood away;
The point still buried in the marrow lay;
And now his rage, increasing with his pain,
Reddens his eyes and beats in every vein;
Churn'd in his teeth the foamy venom rose,
Whilst from his mouth a blast of vapours flows,
Such as the infernal Stygian waters cast;
The plants around him wither in the blast.
Now in a maze of rings he lies inroll'd;
Now all unravell'd and without a fold;
Now, like a torrent, with a mighty force
Bears down the forest in his boist'rous course.
Cadmus gave back, and on the lion's spoil
Sustain'd the shock, then forced him to recoil:
The pointed javelin warded off his rage:
Mad with his pains, and furious to engage,
The serpent champs the steel, and bites the spear,
Till blood and venom all the point besmear.
But still the hurt he yet received was slight;

For, whilst the champion with redoubled might
Strikes home the javelin, his retiring foe
Shrinks from the wound, and disappoints the blow.

The dauntless hero still pursues his stroke,
And presses forward, till a knotty oak
Retards his foe, and stops him in the rear;
Full in his throat he plunged the fatal spear,
That in the extended neck a passage found,
And pierced the solid timber through the wound.
Fix'd to the reeling trunk, with many a stroke
Of his huge tail he lash'd the sturdy oak,
Till spent with toil, and lab'ring hard for breath,
He now lay twisting in the pangs of death.
Cadmus beheld him wallow in a flood
Of swimming poison intermix'd with blood,
When suddenly a speech was heard from high
(The speech was heard, nor was the speaker nigh),
"Why dost thou thus with secret pleasure see,
Insulting man! what thou thyself shalt be?"
Astonish'd at the voice, he stood amazed,
And all around, with inward horror, gazed,
When Pallas swift descending from the skies,
Pallas, the guardian of the bold and wise,
Bids him plough up the field, and scatter round
The dragon's teeth o'er all the furrow'd ground;
Then tells the youth how to his wondering eyes
Embattled armies from the field should rise.

He sows the teeth at Pallas's command,
And flings the future people from his hand;
The clods grow warm, and crumble where he sows,
And now the pointed spears advance in rows;
Now nodding plumes appear, and shining crests,
Now the broad shoulders and the rising breasts;
O'er all the field the breathing harvest swarms,
A growing host, a crop of men and arms.

So through the parting stage a figure rears
Its body up, and limb by limb appears
By just degrees, till all the man arise,

And in his full proportion strikes the eyes.

    Cadmus, surprised and startled at the sight
Of his new foes, prepared himself for fight;
When one cried out, "Forbear, fond man, forbear
To mingle in a blind promiscuous war."
This said, he struck his brother to the ground,
Himself expiring by another's wound;
Nor did the third his conquest long survive,
Dying ere scarce he had begun to live.

    The dire example ran through all the field,
Till heaps of brothers were by brothers kill'd;
The furrows swam in blood, and only five
Of all the vast increase were left alive.
Echion one, at Pallas's command,
Let fall the guiltless weapon from his hand,
And with the rest a peaceful treaty makes,
Whom Cadmus as his friends and partners takes.
So founds a city on the promised earth,
And gives his new Bœotian empire birth.

    Here Cadmus reign'd; and now one would have
        guess'd
The royal founder in his exile bless'd:
Long did he live within his new abodes,
Allied by marriage to the deathless gods;
And in a fruitful wife's embraces old,
A long increase of children's children told:
But no frail man, however great or high,
Can be concluded bless'd before he die.

    Actæon was the first of all his race,
Who grieved his grandsire in his borrow'd face,
Condemn'd by stern Diana to bemoan
The branching horns and visage not his own;
To shun his once loved dogs, to bound away,
And from their huntsman to become their prey.
And yet consider why the change was wrought,

You'll find it his misfortune, not his fault;
Or, if a fault, it was the fault of chance:
For how can guilt proceed from ignorance?
   In a fair chase a shady mountain stood,
Well stored with game, and mark'd with trails of blood;
Here did the huntsmen, till the heat of day,
Pursue the stag, and load themselves with prey;
When thus Actæon calling to the rest:
"My friends," said he, "our sport is at the best,
The sun is high advanced, and downward sheds
His burning beams directly on our heads;
Then by consent abstain from further spoils,
Call off the dogs, and gather up the toils,
And ere tomorrow's sun begins his race
Take the cool morning to renew the chase."
They all consent, and in a cheerful train
The jolly huntsmen, loaden with the slain,
Return in triumph from the sultry plain.
   Down in a vale with pine and cypress clad,
Refresh'd with gentle winds, and brown with shade,
The chaste Diana's private haunt, there stood,
Full in the centre of the darksome wood,
A spacious grotto, all around o'ergrown
With hoary moss, and arch'd with pumice-stone.
From out its rocky clefts the waters flow,
And trickling swell into a lake below.
Nature had every where so play'd her part,
That every where she seem'd to vie with art.
Here the bright goddess, toil'd and chafed with heat,
Was wont to bathe her in the cool retreat.
   Here did she now with all her train resort,
Panting with heat, and breathless from the sport;
Her armour-bearer laid her bow aside,
Some loosed her sandals, some her veil untied;
Each busy nymph her proper part undress'd,

While Crocale, more handy than the rest,
Gather'd her flowing hair, and in a noose
Bound it together, whilst her own hung loose;
Five of the more ignoble sort, by turns,
Fetch up the water, and unlade the urns.
   Now all undress'd the shining goddess stood,
When young Actæon wilder'd in the wood,
To the cool grot by his hard fate betray'd,
The fountains fill'd with naked nymphs survey'd.
The frighted virgins shriek'd at the surprise,
(The forest echo'd with their piercing cries)
Then in a huddle round their goddess press'd;
She, proudly eminent above the rest,
With blushes glow'd; such blushes as adorn
The ruddy welkin or the purple morn;
And though the crowding nymphs her body hide,
Half backward shrunk, and view'd him from aside.
Surprised, at first she would have snatch'd her bow,
But sees the circling waters round her flow;
These in the hollow of her hand she took,
And dash'd them in his face, while thus she spoke:
   "Tell, if thou canst, the wondrous sight disclosed,
A goddess naked to thy view exposed."
   This said, the man began to disappear
By slow degrees, and ended in a deer.
A rising horn on either brow he wears,
And stretches out his neck, and pricks his ears;
Rough is his skin, with sudden hairs o'ergrown,
His bosom pants with fears before unknown;
Transform'd at length, he flies away in haste,
And wonders why he flies away so fast.
But, as by chance within a neighb'ring brook,
He saw his branching horns and alter'd look,
Wretched Actæon! in a doleful tone
He tried to speak, but only gave a groan;

And as he wept, within the watery glass
He saw the big round drops, with silent pace,
Run trickling down a savage hairy face.
What should he do? Or seek his old abodes,
Or herd among the deer and skulk in woods?
Here shame dissuades him, there his fear prevails,
And each by turns his aching heart assails.

As he thus ponders, he behind him spies
His op'ning hounds, and now he hears their cries:
A gen'rous pack, or to maintain the chase,
Or snuff the vapour from the scented grass.

He bounded off with fear, and swiftly ran
O'er craggy mountains and the flow'ry plain,
Through brakes and thickets forced his way, and flew
Through many a ring where once he did pursue.
In vain he oft endeavour'd to proclaim
His new misfortune, and to tell his name;
Nor voice, nor words, the brutal tongue supplies,
From shouting men, and horns, and dogs, he flies,
Deafen'd and stunn'd with their promiscuous cries.
When now the fleetest of the pack, that press'd
Close at his heels and sprung before the rest,
Had fasten'd on him, straight another pair
Hung on his wounded haunch, and held him there,
Till all the pack came up, and every hound
Tore the sad huntsman grovelling on the ground,
Who now appear'd but one continued wound.
With dropping tears his bitter fate he moans,
And fills the mountain with his dying groans.
His servants with a piteous look he spies,
And turns about his supplicating eyes.
His servants, ignorant of what had chanced,
With eager haste and joyful shouts advanced,
And call'd their lord, Actæon, to the game;
He shook his head in answer to the name;

He heard, but wish'd he had indeed been gone;
Or only to have stood a looker-on:
But to his grief he finds himself too near,
And feels his ravenous dogs with fury tear
Their wretched master panting in a deer.

Actæon's sufferings, and Diana's rage,
Did all the thoughts of men and gods engage;
Some call'd the evils, which Diana wrought,
Too great and disproportion'd to the fault:
Others, again, esteem'd Actæon's woes
Fit for a virgin goddess to impose.
The hearers into different parts divide,
And reasons are produced on either side.

Juno alone, of all that heard the news,
Nor would condemn the goddess, nor excuse;
She heeded not the justice of the deed,
But joy'd to see the race of Cadmus bleed;
For still she kept Europa in her mind,
And, for her sake, detested all her kind.
Besides, to aggravate her hate, she heard
How Semele, to Jove's embrace preferr'd,
Was now grown big with an immortal load,
And carried in her womb a future god.
Thus, terribly incensed, the goddess broke
To sudden fury, and abruptly spoke:

"Are my reproaches of so small a force?
'Tis time I then pursue another course.
It is decreed the guilty wretch shall die,
If I'm indeed the mistress of the sky;
If rightly styled, among the powers above,
The wife and sister of the thundering Jove
(And none can sure a sister's right deny),
It is decreed the guilty wretch shall die.
She boasts an honour I can hardly claim,
Pregnant she rises to a mother's name;

While proud and vain she triumphs in her Jove,
And shows the glorious tokens of his love:
But if I'm still the mistress of the skies,
By her own lover the fond beauty dies."
This said, descending in a yellow cloud,
Before the gates of Semele she stood.

Old Beroë's decrepit shape she wears,
Her wrinkled visage, and her hoary hairs,
Whilst in her trembling gait she totters on,
And learns to tattle in the nurse's tone.
The goddess thus disguised in age beguiled
With pleasing stories her false foster-child.
Much did she talk of love, and when she came
To mention to the nymph her lover's name,
Fetching a sigh, and holding down her head,
" 'Tis well," says she, "if all be true that's said.
But trust me, child, I'm much inclined to fear
Some counterfeit in this your Jupiter.
Many an honest well-designing maid
Has been by these pretended gods betray'd.
But if he be indeed the thund'ring Jove,
Bid him, when next he courts the rites of love,
Descend triumphant, from the ethereal sky,
In all the pomp of his divinity,
Encompass'd round by those celestial charms
With which he fills the immortal Juno's arms."

The unwary nymph, ensnared with what she said,
Desired of Jove, when next he sought her bed,
To grant a certain gift which she would choose.

"Fear not," replied the god, "that I'll refuse
Whate'er you ask: may Styx confirm my voice,
Choose what you will, and you shall have your choice."
"Then," says the nymph, "when next you seek my arms,
May you descend in those celestial charms
With which your Juno's bosom you inflame,

And fill with transport heaven's immortal dame."
The god, surprised, would fain have stopp'd her voice,
But he had sworn, and she had made her choice.

To keep his promise he ascends, and shrouds
His awful brow in whirlwinds and in clouds;
Whilst all around, in terrible array,
His thunders rattle and his lightnings play;
And yet the dazzling lustre to abate,
He set not out in all his pomp and state,
Clad in the mildest lightning of the skies,
And arm'd with thunder of the smallest size:
Not those huge bolts, by which the giants slain
Lay overthrown on the Phlegrean plain;
'Twas of a lesser mould and lighter weight,
They call it thunder of a second rate;
For the rough Cyclops, who by Jove's command
Temper'd the bolt, and turn'd it to his hand,
Work'd up less flame and fury in its make,
And quench'd it sooner in the standing lake.
Thus dreadfully adorn'd with horror bright,
The illustrious god, descending from his height,
Came rushing on her in a storm of light.

The mortal dame, too feeble to engage
The lightning's flashes and the thunder's rage,
Consumed amidst the glories she desired,
And in the terrible embrace expired.

But to preserve his offspring from the tomb,
Jove took him smoking from his mother's womb,
And, if on ancient tales we may rely,
Inclosed the abortive infant in his thigh.
Here when the babe had all his time fulfill'd,
Ino first took him for her foster-child;
Then the Niseans, in their dark abode,
Nursed secretly with milk the thriving god.

Famed far and near for knowing things to come,

From him the inquiring nations sought their doom.
The fair Liriope his answers tried,
And first the unerring prophet justified.
This nymph the god Cephisus had abused,
With all his winding waters circumfused,
And by the Nereid had a lovely boy,
Whom the soft maids ev'n then beheld with joy.
    The tender dame, solicitous to know
Whether her child should reach old age or no,
Consults the sage Tiresias; who replies,
"If e'er he knows himself he surely dies."
Long lived the dubious mother in suspense,
Till time unriddled all the prophet's sense.
    Narcissus now his sixteenth year began,
Just turn'd of boy, and on the verge of man;
Many a friend the blooming youth caress'd,
Many a love-sick maid her flame confess'd.
Such was his pride, in vain the friend caress'd,
The love-sick maid in vain her flame confess'd.
    Once, in the woods, as he pursued the chase,
The babbling Echo had descried his face,
She, who in other words her silence breaks,
Nor speaks herself but when another speaks.
Echo was then a maid of speech bereft,
Of wonted speech; for though her voice was left,
Juno a curse did on her tongue impose,
To sport with every sentence in the close.
Full often when the goddess might have caught
Jove and her rivals in the very fault,
This nymph with subtile stories would delay
Her coming, till the lovers slipp'd away.
The goddess found out the deceit in time,
And then she cried, "That tongue, for this thy crime,
Which could so many subtile tales produce,
Shall be hereafter but of little use."

Hence 'tis she prattles in a fairer tone,
With mimic sounds and accents not her own.

This love-sick virgin, overjoy'd to find
The boy alone, still follow'd him behind;
When glowing warmly at her near approach,
As sulphur blazes at the taper's touch,
She long'd her hidden passion to reveal
And tell her pains, but had not words to tell;
She can't begin, but waits for the rebound
To catch his voice, and to return the sound.

The nymph, when nothing could Narcissus move,
Still dash'd with blushes for her slighted love,
Lived in the shady covert of the woods,
In solitary caves and dark abodes,
Where pining wander'd the rejected fair,
Till harass'd out and worn away with care,
The sounding skeleton, of blood bereft,
Besides her bones and voice had nothing left.
Her bones are petrified, her voice is found
In vaults, where still it doubles every sound.

Thus did the nymphs in vain caress the boy,
He still was lovely, but he still was coy,
When one fair virgin of the slighted train
Thus pray'd the gods, provoked by his disdain:
"O! may he love like me, and love like me in vain!"
Rhamnusia pitied the neglected fair,
And with just vengeance answer'd to her prayer.

There stands a fountain in a darksome wood,
Nor stain'd with falling leaves, nor rising mud,
Untroubled by the breath of winds it rests,
Unsullied by the touch of men or beasts;
High bowers of shady trees above it grow,
And rising grass and cheerful greens below.
Pleased with the form and coolness of the place,
And overheated by the morning chase,

Narcissus on the grassy verdure lies;
But whilst within the crystal fount he tries
To quench his heat, he feels new heat arise:
For, as his own bright image he survey'd,
He fell in love with the fantastic shade,
And o'er the fair resemblance hung unmoved;
Nor knew, fond youth! it was himself he loved.
The well-turn'd neck and shoulders he descries,
The spacious forehead, and the sparkling eyes,
The hands that Bacchus might not scorn to show,
And hair that round Apollo's head might flow,
With all the purple youthfulness of face,
That gently blushes in the watery glass.
By his own flames consumed the lover lies,
And gives himself the wound by which he dies.
To the cold water oft he joins his lips,
Oft catching at the beauteous shade he dips
His arms, as often from himself he slips.
Nor knows he who it is his arms pursue
With eager clasps, but loves he knows not who.

   What could, fond youth, this helpless passion move?
What kindled in thee this unpitied love?
Thy own warm blush within the water glows,
With thee the colour'd shadow comes and goes,
Its empty being on thyself relies;
Step thou aside and the frail charmer dies.

   Still o'er the fountain's watery gleam he stood,
Mindless of sleep, and negligent of food,
Still view'd his face, and languish'd as he view'd.
At length he raised his head, and thus began
To vent his griefs, and tell the woods his pain:
"You trees," says he, "and thou surrounding grove,
Who oft have been the kindly scenes of love,
Tell me, if e'er within your shades did lie
A youth so tortured, so perplex'd as I?

I, who before me see the charming fair,
Whilst there he stands, and yet he stands not there:
In such a maze of love my thoughts are lost;
And yet no bulwark'd town nor distant coast
Preserves the beauteous youth from being seen,
No mountains rise nor oceans flow between;
A shallow water hinders my embrace,
And yet the lovely mimic wears a face
That kindly smiles, and when I bend to join
My lips to his, he fondly bends to mine.
Hear, gentle youth, and pity my complaint;
Come from thy well, thou fair inhabitant.
My charms an easy conquest have obtain'd
O'er other hearts, by thee alone disdain'd.
But why should I despair? I'm sure he burns
With equal flames, and languishes by turns.
Whene'er I stoop, he offers at a kiss,
And when my arms I stretch, he stretches his;
His eyes with pleasure on my face he keeps,
He smiles my smiles, and when I weep he weeps;
Whene'er I speak his moving lips appear
To utter something, which I cannot hear.
  "Ah, wretched me! I now begin too late
To find out all the long perplex'd deceit;
It is myself I love, myself I see,
The gay delusion is a part of me;
I kindle up the fires by which I burn,
And my own beauties from the well return.
Whom should I court? how utter my complaint?
Enjoyment but produces my restraint,
And too much plenty makes me die for want.
How gladly would I from myself remove!
And at a distance set the thing I love;
My breast is warm'd with such unusual fire,
I wish him absent whom I most desire;

And now I faint with grief, my fate draws nigh,
In all the pride of blooming youth I die.
Death will the sorrows of my heart relieve.
O! might the visionary youth survive,
I should with joy my latest breath resign!
But, oh! I see his fate involved in mine."
   This said, the weeping youth again return'd
To the clear fountain, where again he burn'd.
His tears defaced the surface of the well,
With circle after circle as they fell;
And now the lovely face but half appears,
O'errun with wrinkles and deform'd with tears.
"Ah! whither," cries Narcissus, "dost thou fly?
Let me still feed the flame by which I die;
Let me still see, though I'm no further bless'd."
Then rends his garment off and beats his breast;
His naked bosom redden'd with the blow,
In such a blush as purple clusters show,
Ere yet the sun's autumnal heats refine
Their sprightly juice, and mellow it to wine;
The glowing beauties of his breast he spies,
And with a new redoubled passion dies.
As wax dissolves, as ice begins to run
And trickle into drops before the sun,
So melts the youth, and languishes away,
His beauty withers, and his limbs decay,
And none of those attractive charms remain,
To which the slighted Echo sued in vain.
   She saw him in his present misery,
Whom, spite of all her wrongs, she grieved to see.
She answer'd sadly to the lover's moan,
Sigh'd back his sighs, and groan'd to every groan.
"Ah youth! beloved in vain," Narcissus cries;
"Ah youth! beloved in vain," the nymph replies.
"Farewell." says he; the parting sound scarce fell

From his faint lips, but she replied, "Farewell."
Then on the unwholesome earth he gasping lies,
Till death shuts up those self-admiring eyes.
To the cold shades his flitting ghost retires,
And in the Stygian waves itself admires.

For him the Naiads and the Dryads mourn,
Whom the sad Echo answers in her turn;
And now the sister-nymphs prepare his urn:
When, looking for his corpse, they only found
A rising stalk with yellow blossoms crown'd.

This sad event gave blind Tiresias fame,
Through Greece establish'd in a prophet's name.

The unhallow'd Pentheus only durst deride
The cheated people and their eyeless guide.
To whom the prophet in his fury said,
Shaking the hoary honors of his head,
" 'Twere well, presumptuous man, 'twere well for thee,
If thou wert eyeless too, and blind like me:
For the time comes, nay, 'tis already here,
When the young god's solemnities appear,
Which, if thou dost not with just rites adorn,
Thy impious carcase, into pieces torn,
Shall strew the woods, and hang on every thorn.
Then, then, remember what I now foretell:
And own the blind Tiresias saw too well."

Still Pentheus scorns him, and derides his skill;
But time did all the prophet's threats fulfil.
For now through prostrate Greece young Bacchus rode,
Whilst howling matrons celebrate the god.
All ranks and sexes to his orgies ran,
To mingle in the pomps and fill the train,
When Pentheus thus his wicked rage express'd:
"What madness, Thebans, has your souls possess'd?
Can hollow timbrels, can a drunken shout,
And the lewd clamours of a beastly rout,

Thus quell your courage? Can the weak alarm
Of women's yells those stubborn souls disarm,
Whom nor the sword nor trumpet e'er could fright,
Nor the loud din and horror of a fight?
And you, our sires, who left your old abodes,
And fix'd in foreign earth your country gods,
Will you without a stroke your city yield,
And poorly quit an undisputed field?
But you, whose youth and vigour should inspire
Heroic warmth, and kindle martial fire,
Whom burnish'd arms and crested helmets grace,
Not flowery garlands and a painted face;
Remember him to whom you stand allied;
The serpent for his well of waters died.
He fought the strong, do you his courage show,
And gain a conquest o'er a feeble foe.
If Thebes must fall, O might the Fates afford
A nobler doom from famine, fire, or sword;
Then might the Thebans perish with renown:
But now a beardless victor sacks the town,
Whom nor the prancing steed, nor ponderous shield,
Nor the hack'd helmet, nor the dusty field,
But the soft joys of luxury and ease,
The purple vests, and flowery garlands please.
Stand then aside, I'll make the counterfeit
Renounce his godhead, and confess the cheat.
Acrisius from the Grecian walls repell'd
This boasted power: why then should Pentheus yield?
Go quickly, drag the impostor boy to me,
I'll try the force of his divinity."
Thus did the audacious wretch those rites profane;
His friends dissuade the audacious wretch in vain,
In vain his grandsire urged him to give o'er
His impious threats, the wretch but raves the more.
    So have I seen a river gently glide

In a smooth course and inoffensive tide,
But if with dams its current we restrain,
It bears down all, and foams along the plain.

But now his servants came, besmear'd with blood,
Sent by their haughty prince to seize the god;
The god they found not in the frantic throng,
But dragg'd a zealous votary along.

Him Pentheus view'd with fury in his look,
And scarce withheld his hands, whilst thus he spoke:
"Vile slave! whom speedy vengeance shall pursue
And terrify thy base seditious crew,
Thy country and thy parentage reveal,
And why thou join'st in these mad orgies tell."

The captive views him with undaunted eyes,
And, arm'd with inward innocence, replies:
"From high Mæonia's rocky shores I came,
Of poor descent, Accœtes is my name.
My sire was meanly born; no oxen plough'd
His fruitful fields, nor in his pastures low'd;
His whole estate within the waters lay,
With lines and hooks he caught the finny prey;
His art was all his livelihood, which he
Thus with his dying lips bequeathed to me:
'In streams, my boy, and rivers take thy chance,
There swims,' said he, 'thy whole inheritance.'
Long did I live on this poor legacy,
Till, tired with rocks and my old native sky,
To arts of navigation I inclined,
Observed the turns and changes of the wind,
Learn'd the fit heavens, and began to note
The stormy Hyades, the rainy Goat,
The bright Taygete, and the shining Bears,
With all the sailors' catalogue of stars.
Once, as by chance for Delos I design'd,
My vessel, driven by a strong gust of wind,

Moor'd in a Chian creek; ashore I went,
And all the following night in Chios spent.
When morning rose, I sent my mates to bring
Supplies of water from a neighb'ring spring,
Whilst I the motion of the winds explored;
Then summon'd in my crew and went aboard.
Opheltes heard my summons, and with joy
Brought to the shore a soft and lovely boy,
With more than female sweetness in his look,
Whom straggling in the neighb'ring fields he took.
With fumes of wine the little captive glows,
And nods with sleep, and staggers as he goes.
   "I view'd him nicely, and began to trace
Each heavenly feature, each immortal grace,
And saw divinity in all his face:
'I know not who,' said I, 'this god should be,
But that he is a god I plainly see.
And thou, whoe'er thou art, excuse the force
These men have used; and O befriend our course!'
'Pray not for us,' the nimble Dictys cried,
Dictys, that could the main-top mast bestride,
And down the ropes with active vigour slide.
But, as he plies, each busy arm shrinks in,
And by degrees is fashion'd to a fin.
Another, as he catches at a cord,
Misses his arms, and, tumbling overboard,
With his broad fins and forky tail he laves
The rising surge, and flounces in the waves.
Thus all my crew transform'd around the ship,
Or dive below, or on the surface leap,
And spout the waves, and wanton in the deep.
Full nineteen sailors did the ship convey,
A shole of nineteen dolphins round her play.
I only in my proper shape appear,
Speechless with wonder, and half dead with fear,

Till Bacchus kindly bid me fear no more.
With him I landed on the Chian shore,
And him shall ever gratefully adore."

"This forging slave," says Pentheus, "would prevail
O'er our just fury by a far-fetch'd tale:
Go; let him feel the whips, the swords, the fire,
And in the tortures of the rack expire."
The officious servants hurry him away,
And the poor captive in a dungeon lay.
But, whilst the whips and tortures are prepared,
The gates fly open, of themselves unbarr'd;
At liberty the unfetter'd captive stands,
And flings the loosen'd shackles from his hands.

But Pentheus, grown more furious than before,
Resolved to send his messengers no more,
But went himself to the distracted throng,
Where high Cithæron echo'd with their song.
And as the fiery war-horse paws the ground,
And snorts and trembles at the trumpet's sound,
Transported thus he heard the frantic rout,
And raved and madden'd at the distant shout.

A spacious circuit on the hill there stood,
Level and wide, and skirted round with wood;
Here the rash Pentheus, with unhallow'd eyes,
The howling dames and mystic orgies spies.
His mother sternly view'd him where he stood,
And kindled into madness as she view'd:
Her leafy javelin at her son she cast,
And cries, "The boar that lays our country waste!
The boar, my sisters! Aim the fatal dart,
And strike the brindled monster to the heart."

Pentheus astonish'd heard the dismal sound,
And sees the yelling matrons gathering round;
He sees and weeps at his approaching fate,
And begs for mercy, and repents too late.

"Help! help! my aunt Autonoë," he cried,
"Remember how your own Actæon died."
Deaf to his cries, the frantic matron crops
One stretch'd-out arm, the other Ino lops.
In vain does Pentheus to his mother sue,
And the raw bleeding stumps present to view.
His mother howl'd, and, heedless of his prayer,
Her trembling hand she twisted in his hair,
"And this," she cried, "shall be Agave's share";
When from his neck his struggling head she tore,
And in her hands the ghastly visage bore.
With pleasure all the hideous trunk survey,
Then pull'd and tore the mangled limbs away,
As starting in the pangs of death it lay.
Soon as the wood its leafy honours casts,
Blown off and scatter'd by autumnal blasts,
With such a sudden death lay Pentheus slain,
And in a thousand pieces strow'd the plain.
  By so distinguishing a judgment awed,
The Thebans tremble and confess the god.

From the Epistles

Sappho to Phaon
Translated by Alexander Pope

Say, lovely youth, that dost my heart command,
Can Phaon's eyes forget his Sappho's hand?
Must then her name the wretched writer prove?
To thy remembrance lost, as to thy love!

Ask not the cause that I new numbers choose,
The lute neglected, and the lyric muse;
Love taught my tears in sadder notes to flow,
And tuned my heart to elegies of wo.
I burn, I burn, as when through ripen'd corn
By driving winds, the spreading flames are borne!
Phaon to Ætna's scorching fields retires,
While I consume with more than Ætna's fires!
No more my soul a charm in music finds;
Music has charms alone for peaceful minds:
Soft scenes of solitude no more can please;
Love enters there, and I'm my own disease:
No more the Lesbian dames my passion move,
Once the dear objects of my tender love;
All other loves are lost in only thine,
Ah youth, ungrateful to a flame like mine!
Whom would not all those blooming charms surprise,
Those heavenly looks, and dear deluding eyes?
The harp and bow would you like Phœbus bear,
A brighter Phœbus Phaon might appear;
Would you with ivy wreathe your flowing hair,
Not Bacchus' self with Phaon could compare:
Yet Phœbus loved, and Bacchus felt the flame;
One Daphne warm'd and one the Cretan dame:
Nymphs that in verse no more could rival me,
Than ev'n those gods contend in charms with thee.
The Muses teach me all their softest lays,
And the wide world resounds with Sappho's praise.
Though great Alcæus more sublimely sings,
And strikes with bolder rage the sounding strings,
No less renown attends the moving lyre,
Which Cupid tunes, and Venus does inspire.
To me what Nature has in charms denied
Is well by wit's more lasting charms supplied.
Though short my stature, yet my name extends

To heaven itself, and earth's remotest ends.
Brown as I am, an Ethiopian dame
Inspired young Perseus with a generous flame.
Turtles and doves of differing hues unite,
And glossy jet is pair'd with shining white.
If to no charms thou wilt thy heart resign,
But such as merit, such as equal thine,
By none, alas! by none thou canst be moved,
Phaon alone by Phaon must be loved!
Yet once thy Sappho could thy cares employ,
Once in her arms you centred all your joy:
Still all those joys to my remembrance move,
For oh, how vast a memory has love!
My music, then, you could for ever hear,
And all my words were music to your ear.
You stopp'd with kisses my enchanting tongue,
And found my kisses sweeter than my song.
The fair Sicilians now thy soul inflame;
Why was I born, ye gods, a Lesbian dame?
But ah beware, Sicilian nymphs! nor boast
That wandering heart which I so lately lost;
Nor be with all those tempting words abused;
Those tempting words were all to Sappho used.
And you that rule Sicilia's happy plains,
Have pity, Venus, on your poet's pains!
Shall Fortune still in one sad tenor run,
And still increase the woes so soon begun?
Inured to sorrows from my tender years,
My parent's ashes drank my early tears;
My brother next, neglecting wealth and fame,
Ignobly burn'd in a destructive flame.
An infant daughter late my griefs increased,
And all a mother's cares distract my breast.
Alas, what more could Fate itself impose,
But thee, the last and greatest of my woes?

No more my robes in waving purple flow,
Nor on my hand the sparkling diamonds glow;
No more my locks in ringlets curl'd diffuse
The costly sweetness of Arabian dews;
Nor braids of gold the varied tresses bind,
That fly disorder'd with the wanton wind:
For whom should Sappho use such arts as these;
He's gone, whom only she desired to please!
Cupid's light darts my tender bosom move,
Still is there cause for Sappho still to love:
So from my birth the sisters fix'd my doom,
And gave to Venus all my life to come;
Or while my muse in melting notes complains,
My heart relents, and answers to my strains.
By charms like thine which all my soul have won,
Who might not—ah! who would not be undone?
For those, Aurora Cephalus might scorn,
And with fresh blushes paint the conscious morn.
For those might Cynthia lengthen Phaon's sleep,
And bid Endymion nightly tend his sheep.
Venus for those had rapt thee to the skies,
But Mars on thee might look with Venus' eyes.
O scarce a youth, yet scarce a tender boy!
O useful time for lovers to employ!
Pride of thy age, and glory of thy race,
Come to these arms, and melt in this embrace!
The vows you never will return, receive;
And take at least the love thou wilt not give.
See, while I write, my words are lost in tears;
The less my sense, the more my love appears.
Sure 'twas not much to bid one kind adieu
(At least to feign was never hard to you).
"Farewell, my Lesbian love!" you might have said,
Or coldly thus, "Farewell, O Lesbian maid!"
No tear did you, no parting kiss receive,

Nor knew I then how much I was to grieve.
No gift on thee thy Sappho could confer,
And wrongs and woes were all you left with her.
No charge I gave you, and no charge could give,
But this: "Be mindful of our loves, and live."
Now by the Nine, those powers adored by me,
And Love, the god that ever waits on thee,
When first I heard (from whom I hardly knew)
That you were fled, and all my joys with you,
Like some sad statue, speechless, pale, I stood;
Grief chill'd my breast, and stopp'd my freezing blood;
No sigh to rise, no tear had power to flow;
Fix'd in a stupid lethargy of woe.
But when its way the impetuous passion found,
I rend my tresses, and my breast I wound;
I rave, then weep, I curse, and then complain,
Now swell to rage, now melt in tears again.
Not fiercer pangs distract the mournful dame,
Whose first-born infant feeds the funeral flame.
My scornful brother with a smile appears,
Insults my woes, and triumphs in my tears;
His hated image ever haunts my eyes,
And "Why this grief? thy daughter lives," he cries.
Stung with my love, and furious with despair,
All torn my garments, and my bosom bare,
My woes, thy crimes, I to the world proclaim;
Such inconsistent things are love and shame!
'Tis thou art all my care, and my delight,
My daily longing, and my dream by night:
O night more pleasing than the brightest day,
When fancy gives what absence takes away,
And dress'd in all its visionary charms,
Restores my fair deserter to my arms!
But when with day the sweet delusions fly,
And all things wake to life and joy, but I,

As if once more forsaken, I complain,
And close my eyes, to dream of you again.
Then frantic rise, and like some fury rove
Through lonely plains, and through the silent grove;
As if the silent grove, and lonely plains,
That knew my pleasures, could relieve my pains.
I view the grotto, once the scene of love,
The rocks around, the hanging roofs above,
Which charm'd me more, with native moss o'ergrown,
Than Phrygian marble or the Parian stone.
For thee the fading trees appear to mourn,
And birds defer their songs till thy return:
Night shades the groves, and all in silence lie,
All, but the mournful Philomel and I;
With mournful Philomel I join my strain,
Of Tereus she, of Phaon I complain.

A spring there is, whose silver waters show,
Clear as a glass, the shining sands below;
A flowery lotos spreads its arms above,
Shades all the banks, and seems itself a grove;
Eternal greens the mossy margin grace,
Watch'd by the sylvan genius of the place.
Here as I lay, and swell'd with tears the flood,
Before my sight a watery virgin stood;
She stood and cried: "O you that love in vain!
Fly hence, and seek the far Leucadian main;
There stands a rock from whose impending steep,
Apollo's fane surveys the rolling deep;
There injured lovers, leaping from above,
Their flames extinguish, and forget to love.
Deucalion once with hopeless fury burn'd,
In vain he loved, relentless Pyrrha scorn'd;
But when from hence he plunged into the main,
Deucalion scorn'd, and Pyrrha loved in vain.
Haste, Sappho, haste, from high Leucadia throw

Thy wretched weight, nor dread the deeps below!"
She spoke, and vanish'd with the voice—I rise,
And silent tears fall trickling from my eyes.
I go, ye nymphs! those rocks and seas to prove,
How much I fear, but ah! how much I love!
I go, ye nymphs! where furious love inspires:
Let female fears submit to female fires!
To rocks and seas I fly from Phaon's hate,
And hope from seas and rocks a milder fate.
Ye gentle gales, beneath my body blow,
And softly lay me on the waves below!
And thou, kind Love, my sinking limbs sustain,
Spread thy soft wings, and waft me o'er the main,
Nor let a lover's death the guiltless flood profane!
On Phœbus' shrine my harp I'll then bestow,
And this inscription shall be placed below:
"Here she who sung, to him that did inspire,
Sappho to Phœbus consecrates her lyre;
What suits with Sappho, Phœbus, suits with thee;
The gift, the giver, and the god agree."
    But why, alas, relentless youth! ah why
To distant seas must tender Sappho fly?
Thy charms than those may far more powerful be,
And Phœbus' self is less a god to me.
Ah! canst thou doom me to the rocks and sea,
O far more faithless and more hard than they?
Ah! canst thou rather see this tender breast
Dash'd on sharp rocks, than to thy bosom press'd?
This breast, which once, in vain! you liked so well!
Where the loves play'd, and where the muses dwell—
Alas! the muses now no more inspire:
Untuned my lute, and silent is my lyre;
My languid numbers have forgot to flow,
And Fancy sinks beneath a weight of woe.
Ye Lesbian virgins, and ye Lesbian dames,

Themes of my verse, and objects of my flames,
No more your groves with my glad songs shall ring,
No more these hands shall touch the trembling string:
Since Phaon fled, I all those joys resign,
Wretch that I am, I'd almost call'd him mine!
Return, fair youth, return, and bring along
Joy to my soul, and vigour to my song:
Absent from thee, the poet's flame expires,
But ah! how fiercely burn the lover's fires!
Gods! can no prayers, no sighs, no numbers move
One savage heart, or teach it how to love?
The winds my prayers, my sighs, my numbers bear,
The flying winds have lost them all in air!
O when, alas! shall more auspicious gales
To these fond eyes restore thy welcome sails?
If you return—ah why these long delays?
Poor Sappho dies while careless Phaon stays.
O launch thy bark, nor fear the watery plain,
Venus for thee shall smooth her native main.
O launch thy bark, secure of prosperous gales,
For thee shall Cupid spread the swelling sails.
If you will fly—(yet ah! what cause can be,
Too cruel youth, that you should fly from me?)
If not from Phaon I must hope for ease,
Ah let me seek it from the raging seas:
From thee to those, unpitied, I'll remove,
And either cease to live, or cease to love!

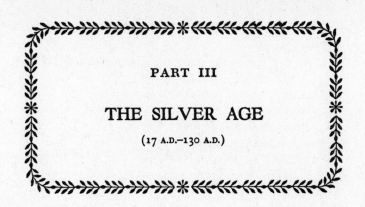

PART III

THE SILVER AGE

(17 A.D.–130 A.D.)

THE argument has been put forward, I believe seriously, by Roman Catholic apologists, that the Papacy must be of divine institution or it could never have survived some of the popes. Dante, who believed that the Roman Empire was a similarly divine institution in the secular sphere, might have supported his view by saying that otherwise it could never have survived the emperors of the Julio-Claudian house. Among them, it has been said, "an arch-dissembler was succeeded by a madman, and a fool by a monster"—Tiberius, Augustus's stepson, by Caligula, and Claudius by Nero. Most of them indulged in what old-fashioned historians liked to call Nameless Excesses (though Suetonius found names for them); and reign by reign they took away more power from the Senate and the other institutions surviving from the Republic. There was still a legal fiction that Rome was a republic, and that the head of the state merely held all the offices for the duration of the emergency, but the pretense was growing more and more threadbare. Everyone knew that at the death of an emperor the supreme power would go to whoever could seize it or persuade the dying emperor to give it to him. The dying emperors generally displayed a positive genius for passing over a promising and closely related kinsman in favor of the worst possible candidate, a genius that reached its peak when Claudius's wife, Agrippina, persuaded him to set aside his own son Britannicus in favor of Nero, her son by a former marriage; after which she poisoned him. Augustus had had the sincere support of practically everyone, as the Savior of Society; but as reign succeeded reign and the emergency showed no signs of ending, the old Republicans tried to oppose the emperor, an opposition which of course provoked countermeasures. Tiberius made it a practice to seek out and punish all literary allusions to himself, real or supposed. It was not an encouraging time for writers. Nor was the succeeding reign, that of Caligula, who interested himself in literature to the extent of proposing to remove from the public libraries the works of Homer, Virgil, and Livy, on critical grounds.

The last of the Julio-Claudian emperors, Nero, fancied himself as a patron of the arts; unfortunately he also fancied himself as a poet, challenging Homer with an epic on the Trojan War, and it did not do to rival him too closely. But by now writers had had time to come to terms with the situation, and there emerged a group who formed the Silver Age, an age whose poetry is less concerned with what is said than with the way of saying it. The Romans had always taken great pleasure in an art they called "rhetoric," an art of pleading—much the same as oratory, except that the productions of the rhetoricians were designed to be read as well as heard. As the actual oratory of the Senate became of less and less importance, the art of the rhetoricians grew in favor and dealt with situations that were more and more farfetched. At this time there was also an increase in the always popular pastime of reading aloud. As good money is driven out by bad, the theater had been unable to withstand the competition of the arena with its actual deaths. Plays were no longer produced, but they were written to be read aloud.

In the plays of Seneca, who was the tutor of Nero, one can see the influence of the rhetoricians, with their verbal points and antitheses. I have seen an edition of Seneca, published in the seventeenth century, which admired him greatly and shared his taste for *sententiæ*, apothegms or epigrammatic sayings; the *sententiæ* in this text are marked in the margin, and there are sometimes a dozen to a page. Seneca's characters converse in this fashion: "Whome'er thou shalt see wretched, know him man." "Whome'er thou shalt see brave, call him not wretched"; or this, between Theseus and his wife Phædra, struck with a guilty love she will not avow: "What is the crime that you would purge by death?" "I live." This sort of thing, though it is not much to the taste of the present day, Seneca could do really well. He could also display, in the general conception of his tragedies, a positively monumental want of taste. One would say that he was trying to outdo the gladiatorial shows on their own ground. He selected for imitation those Greek tragedies which contained the most violent or unnatural situations and piled on the horrors by every possible means. Hippolytus, in Euripides, brought to his death by his father Theseus through a fatal misunderstanding, is brought on dying, and there is a truly beautiful scene of reconciliation. Hippolytus, in Seneca, is brought on not merely dead but in pieces in a basket, and Theseus, who has learned the truth too late, puts him together like a large jigsaw puzzle, saying at one point, "What is this ugly, shapeless piece all covered with wounds? I don't know what part of thee it is, but it is part of thee. Put it down here, not where it belongs, but in an empty space."

There is the same mixture of the old Roman self-reliance, epigrammatically expressed, and a positively Gothic romanticism and exaggeration, in the *Pharsalia*, an epic poem on the civil war between Julius Cæsar and Pompey, by Seneca's nephew Lucan. At a safe distance in history, it laments the beginning of the end of the Republic. It contains the great line "*Victrix causa diis*

placuit, sed victa Catoni" ("The gods the victors, he the
vanquished chose," is Dryden's rendering)—the great
line for all lost causes; Kingsley applied it, with a satiric
twist, to Charles I, Naomi Mitchison to the Gauls. But
Lucan's hyperbole knows neither measure nor restraint;
and he also can fall into the unintentionally humorous, as
in the catalogue of snakes that assail Cato's army; each
bites a soldier, causes death in its peculiar fashion, re-
ceives an appropriate epigram, and falls back for the
next. Of the epic poets of the next reign, Statius, Silius
Italicus, and Valerius Flaccus, it is enough to say that
they are bankrupt through the inflation of the poetic
currency by Lucan.

The Stoic ideals which inspire Lucan's Cato and
Seneca's tragic heroes are better expressed in Seneca's
philosophical writing; and in his death, if not in his life,
Seneca was himself their worthy exemplar. When Nero,
whose favor he had lost some time before, accused him
of conspiracy and ordered him to end his life, he called
his wife and friends about him, opened his veins, and
discoursed to them of virtue as his life ebbed, dying, like
Shakespeare's Cleopatra, "in the high Roman fashion"
that was an example to so many centuries. Yet in reading
his philosophy it is hard not to remember that this praise
of manly independence comes from the man who flat-
tered the Emperor Claudius while he lived, and as soon
as he was dead lampooned him in the *Apocolocyntosis
Claudii,* the *Pumpkinification of Claudius* (an allusion
to Claudius's official deification; the word is a parapros-
dokian for Apotheosis). It is hard not to remember that
this praise of poverty comes from the man who in five
years of Nero's favor became the richest subject in the
Empire, with money at usury (that continuing curse of
the Roman state) as far out as Britain.

The Julio-Claudian emperors, like all unconstitutional

rulers, found their strongest opposition in the aristocracy of the old regime, the old senatorial families; and, like all unconstitutional rulers, they set themselves to create in opposition to it a class of *novi homines*, "new men" of wealth. "*Enrichissez-vous*," Nero might have said to his favorites, as Louis-Philippe did to his *roturiers*. And there never has been a period when it was so possible to enrich oneself with such vast success. The sort of man who had grown rich appears in the episode of "Trimalchio's Dinner," from the *Satyricon* of Petronius. Petronius was also a favorite of Nero, his semi-official arbiter of elegancies—"vices, genuine or assumed," says one historian, "gained him admission to the inner circle of Nero." Like Seneca, he was accused of conspiracy, ordered to die, and did so, if not with Stoic elevation, at least with a cheerfulness which is perhaps more appealing. While his veins were draining "he listened to no disquisitions on the immortality of the soul or the dogmas of philosophy," says Tacitus, "but to entertaining songs and humorous verses." His *Satyricon* is an enormous, rambling novel, a sort of *Gil Blas* or *Peregrine Pickle*, much of which has been lost. The chief part that remains is "Trimalchio's Dinner," which displays the enormous, the inconceivable wealth, the extravagant luxury, and the universal sycophancy of Roman society. It might have borne the title of one of Trollope's best and most neglected novels, written toward the end of his life, when he perceived how far English society was controlled and corrupted by wealth —*The Way We Live Now*.

Tacitus, who wrote of the death of Petronius, also wrote, in his *Annals* and *History*, of the death of Republican freedom. At its beginning the Empire had promised in exchange the peace of Augustus—and, it must be emphasized, in most of the Roman world this promise had been kept. But to men highly placed in the city itself, it had meant conspiracies, assassinations, incriminations under torture, and death at the suspicion of the emperor. It was a world in which a man became famous through his great age, his wealth, and "his wide avoidance of the malignity of so many emperors." Tacitus has no hope of the return of the Republic; no hope, perhaps, for better things for the Roman world. It is this which gives interest to his *Germania,* an account of the Germans of his day. Tacitus has been accused of anticipating Rousseau in the invention of that fraud, the Noble Savage; but this is not fair. Tacitus is quite aware of the characteristic vices of the Germans, their fondness for gambling and drink, their dislike of discipline and hard work. But in Germany, he says, "no one laughs at vice, nor calls mutual corruption fashionable"; in Germany "it does not pay to be childless."

Two other poets show "the way we live now," Juvenal and Martial. Martial wrote twelve books of epigrams— short poems, each with a sting in the tail. The epigram in the Greek anthology had been the vehicle for love, humor, pathos, mourning; it had paid the last tribute to the men of Thermopylæ or bidden the lady drink to the poet only with her eyes. In Martial, not exclusively but most commonly, it is the vehicle of brutal insult. There are some friendly invitations and a few tender epitaphs, but most of them hit off some weakness. And what weaknesses! About one in ten of them must be left, even in these liberal days, in "the decent obscurity of a learned tongue." Among the remainder there are squibs against sycophants, bad poets, sponging guests and stingy hosts, husbands and wives who marry a rich partner for money, and sometimes hurry things when they get tired of waiting for it—all the crew whom we have met in Petronius and are to meet again in Juvenal. It is Juvenal who gives its real meaning to the word satire. The *satura*, a hodgepodge which would hold anything you liked to put into it, had always been used for making fun, as Horace made fun of the bore he met on the Appian Way. But when an eighteenth-century satirist is praised as one "Born to delight at once and lash the age," that conception, that lashing the age was a task for a poet, comes from Juvenal's view of Rome. Juvenal is the last Roman writer of great importance. He is followed by Suetonius, a minor historian, who wrote the lives of the first twelve Cæsars. And though there are no sharp lines in history, though there are always precursors and epigoni, it may be said that, with Juvenal and Suetonius, Roman literature is at an end.

In reading Tacitus and Juvenal we feel that they must have exaggerated. Like the man who comforted himself after the sermon on hell fire with the reflection that "no constitution would stand it," we feel that if half this were true the Roman state must have come to an end far sooner, long before this, whereas it not merely lasted but went on to achieve greater order and prosperity. Halfway through the Silver Age, Nero provoked a revolt, and there followed in rapid succession four emperors by the grace of the Army—Galba, Otho, Vitellius, and Vespasian, representing respectively the Army of Spain, the Household Troops, the Army of the Rhine, and a coalition of the Armies of the Danube and the Euphrates. Now there was no more make-believing in the Republic. For a number of reigns the throne was inherited by a real or adoptive heir (with one or two violent changes of dynasty; the Roman Empire from first to last resembled Gilbert's "Utopia, Ltd.," "a despotism tempered by dynamite," or by the assassination which was its Roman equivalent). The change from pretended First Citizen to avowed Emperor had come about by Tacitus's time; it was because the Republic was unquestionably, irretrievably gone that it was safe to regret it. The Emperor was deified in his lifetime, and the worship of the deified Emperor held together the Roman state. And for some two centuries that state had a succession of strong and able rulers. The period of the Antonine Emperors has been called, for its peace and prosperity, the Golden Age of the Roman Empire. But something had gone out of it, for it produced no more great works. Peace and prosperity are not enough.

SENECA

(Lucius Annæus Seneca, 4? B.C.–65 A.D.)

*

Medea

Translated by Frank Justus Miller

CHARACTERS

MEDEA, *daughter of Æetes, King of Colchis, and wife of Jason*

JASON, *son of Æson, and nephew of Pelias, the usurping king of Thessaly; organizer and leader of the Argonautic expedition to Colchis in quest of the golden fleece*

CREON, *King of Corinth, who had received into his hospitable kingdom Medea and Jason, fugitives from Thessaly, after Medea had plotted the death of Pelias*

NURSE, *of Medea*

MESSENGER

TWO SONS, *of Medea and Jason* (personæ mutæ)

CHORUS OF CORINTHIANS, *friendly to Jason and hostile to Medea*

The time of the play is confined to the single day of the culmination of the tragedy, the day proposed by Creon for the banishment of Medea and marriage of Jason to Creüsa, daughter of Creon.

The scene is in Corinth, in the court of the house of Jason.

487

Act I

MEDEA: Ye gods of wedlock, thou the nuptial couch's
     guard,
Lucina, thou from whom that tamer of the deep,
The Argo's pilot, learned to guide his pristine bark,
And Neptune, thou stern ruler of the ocean's depths,
And Titan, by whose rays the shining day is born,
Thou triformed maiden Hecate, whose conscious beams
With splendour shine upon the mystic worshipers—
Upon ye all I call, the powers of heaven, the gods
By whose divinity false Jason swore; and ye
Whose aid Medea may more boldly claim, thou world
Of endless night, th' antipodes of heavenly realms,
Ye damnèd ghosts, thou lord of hades' dark domain,
Whose mistress was with trustier pledge won to thy
     side—
Before ye all this baleful prayer I bring: Be near!
Be near! Ye crime-avenging furies, come and loose
Your horrid locks with serpent coils entwined, and grasp
With bloody hands the smoking torch; be near as once
Ye stood in dread array beside my wedding couch.
Upon this new-made bride destruction send, and death
Upon the king and all the royal line! But he,
My husband, may he live to meet some heavier doom;
This curse I imprecate upon his head; may he,
Through distant lands, in want, in exile wander, scorned
And houseless. Nay, may he once more my favor woo;
A stranger's threshold may he seek where now he walks
A well-known guest; and—this the blackest curse I
     know—
May children rise to him to emulate their sire,
Their mother's image bear.—Now won is vengeance,
     won!
For I have children borne.—Nay, nay, 'tis empty plaints

And useless words I frame. Shall I not rather rush
Against the foe and dash the torches from their hands,
The light from heaven? Does Father Phœbus suffer this?
Do men behold his face, as, seated in his car,
He rolls along th' accustomed track of sky serene?
Why does he not return to morning's gates, the law
Of heaven reversing? Grant that I be borne aloft
In my ancestral car! Give me the reins, O sire,
Thy fiery team grant me to guide with lines of flame.
Then Corinth, though with double shore delaying fate,
Herself consumed with fire, shall light two seas with
    flame.
But no, this course alone remains, that I myself
Should bear the wedding torch, with acquiescent
    prayers,
And slay the victims on the altars consecrate.
Thyself inspect the entrails, and seek there the way
By prayer, if still, O soul, thou livest, if there still
Remaineth aught of old-time strength in thee! Away
With women's fears! Put on thy heart a breast-plate
    hard
And chill as Caucasus! Then all the wizard arts
That Phasis knew, or Pontus, shall be seen again
In Corinth. Now with mad, unheard-of, dreadful deeds,
Whereat high heaven and earth below shall pale and
    quake,
My pregnant soul is teeming; and my heart is full
Of pictured wounds and death and slaughter.—Ah,
    too long
On trifling ills I dwell. These were my virgin deeds.
Now that a mother's pains I've felt, my larger heart
Must larger crimes conceive. Then passion, gird thyself,
Put on thy strength, and for the issue now prepare!
Let my rejection pay as dread a fee as when,
Of old, through impious deeds of blood, I came to him.

Come, break through slow delay, and let the home once
    won
By crime, by equal deeds of crime be done away!

CHORUS (*chanting the epithalamium for the nuptials of
    Jason and Creüsa*):
Now on our royal nuptials graciously smiling,
Here may the lords of heaven and the deeps of the ocean
Come while the people feast in pious rejoicing!

First to the gods who sway the sceptre of heaven,
Pealing forth their will in the voice of thunder,
Let the white bull his proud head bow in tribute.

Then to the fair Lucina, her gift we offer,
White as the driven snow, this beautiful heifer,
Still with her neck untouched by the yoke of bondage.
Thou who alone canst rule the heart of the war-god,
Thou who linkest in peace the opposing nations,
Out of thy generous hand abundance pouring—
Thee we offer a daintier gift, O Concord!

Thou who, on the marriage torches attending,
Night's dark gloom with favouring hand dispellest,
Hither come with languishing footstep drunken,
Binding thy temples fair with garlands of roses!

Star of the evening, thou who to twilight leadest
The day, and hailest again the dawn of the morning,
All too slowly thou com'st for lovers impatient,
Eager to see thy sign in the glow of the sunset.

    The fairest of girls is she,
    The Athenian maids outshining,

Or the Spartan maiden with armour laden,
  No burden of war declining.

  Not by Alpheus' sacred stream,
  Nor Bœotia's musical water,
Is there any fair who can compare
  With our lovely Corinthian daughter.

  Our Thessalian prince excels,
  In beauty of form and face,
Even Bacchus, the son of the fierce-flaming one,
  Who yokes the wild tigers in place.

  The murmuring tripod's lord,
  Though the fairest in heavenly story,
The twins with their star bright gleaming afar—
  All yield to our Jason in glory.

When in her train of courtly maidens she mingles—
Like the bright sunshine paling the starry splendour,
Or the full moonlight quenching the Pleiads' brilliance,
So does she shine, all peerless, of fair ones the fairest.

Now, O Jason, freed from the hateful wedlock
That held thee bound to the barbarous Colchian woman,
Joyfully wed the fair Corinthian maiden,
While at last her parents' blessings attend thee.

  Ho then, youths, with licensed jest and rejoicing,
  Loud let the songs of gladness ring through the city;
  Rarely against our lords such freedom is given.

Fair and noble band of Bacchus, the thyrsus-bearer,
Now is the time to light the glittering torches of pine-
    wood.

Shake on high the festal fire with languishing fingers;

Now let the bold and merry Fescennine laughter and
    jesting
Sound through our ranks. Let Medea fare in silence and
    darkness,
If perchance another lord she shall wed in her exile.

Act II

MEDEA: We are undone! How harsh upon mine ears
    doth grate
The song! and even now I cannot comprehend
The vast extent of woe that hath befallen me.
Could Jason prove so false? Bereft of native land,
And home, and kingdom, could he leave me here
    alone
On foreign shores? Oh, cruel, could he quite reject
My sum of service, he who saw the fire and sea
With crime o'ercome for his dear sake? And does he
    think
That thus the fatal chapter can be ended? Wild,
Devoid of reason, sick of soul, my swift mind darts
In all directions seeking whence revenge may come!
I would he had a brother! But his wife—'gainst her
Be aimed the blow! Can thus my wrongs be satisfied?
Nay, nay—to meet my sum of woe must be heaped high
The crimes of Greece, of strange barbaric lands, and
    those
Which even thy hands have not known. Now lash thy
    soul
With memory's scourge, and call thy dark deeds in
    review:
The glory of thy father's kingdom reft away;
Thy brother, guiltless comrade of thy guilty flight,

All hewn in pieces and his corpse strewn on the deep,
To break his royal father's heart; and, last of crimes,
Old Pelias by his daughters slain at thy command.
O impious one, what streams of blood have flowed to
      work
Thy ends! And yet, not one of all my crimes by wrath
Was prompted. Love, ill-omened love, suggested all.
Yet, what could Jason else have done, compelled to
      serve
Another's will, another's law? He should have died
Before he yielded to the tyrant's will. Nay, nay,
Thou raging passion, speak not so! For, if he may,
I would that Jason still may live and still be mine,
As once he was; if not, yet may he still live on,
And, mindful of my merits, live without my aid.
The guilt is Creon's all, who with unbridled power
Dissolves the marriage bond, my children separates
From me who bore them, yea, and makes the strongest
      pledge,
Though ratified with straitest oath, of none effect.
Let him alone sustain my wrath; let Creon pay
The debt of guilt he owes! His palace will I bring
To utter desolation; and the whirling fire
To far-off Malea's crags shall send its lurid glare.
NURSE: Be silent now, I pray thee, and thy plaints con-
      fine
To secret woe! The man who heavy blows can bear
In silence, biding still his time with patient soul,
Full oft his vengeance gains. 'Tis hidden wrath that
      harms;
But hate proclaimed oft loses half its power to harm.
MEDEA: But small the grief is that can counsel take and
      hide
Its head; great ills lie not in hiding, but must rush
Abroad and work their will.

NURSE: Oh, cease this mad complaint,
My mistress; scarce can friendly silence help thee now.

MEDEA: But fortune fears the brave, the faint of heart o'erwhelms.

NURSE: Then valour be approved, if for it still there's room.

MEDEA: But it must always be that valour finds its place.

NURSE: No star of hope points out the way from these our woes.

MEDEA: The man who hopes for naught at least has naught to fear.

NURSE: The Colchians are thy foes; thy husband's vows have failed;
Of all thy vast possessions not a jot is left.

MEDEA: Yet I am left. There's left both sea and land and fire
And sword and gods and hurtling thunderbolts.

NURSE: The king must be revered.

MEDEA: My father was a king.

NURSE: Dost thou not fear?

MEDEA: Not though the earth produced the foe.

NURSE: Thou'lt perish.

MEDEA: So I wish it.

NURSE: Flee!

MEDEA: I'm done with flight.
Why should Medea flee?

NURSE: Thy children!

MEDEA: Whose, thou know'st.

NURSE: And dost thou still delay?

MEDEA: I go, but vengeance first.

NURSE: Th' avenger will pursue.

MEDEA: Perchance I'll stop his course.

NURSE: Nay, hold thy words, and cease thy threats, O foolish one.

Thy temper curb; 'tis well to yield to fate's decrees.

MEDEA: Though fate may strip me of my all, myself am
    left.

But who flings wide the royal palace doors? Behold,

'Tis Creon's self, exalted high in Grecian sway.

(*Medea retires to back of stage; exit Nurse; enter Creon*)

CREON: Medea, baleful daughter of the Colchian king,

Has not yet taken her hateful presence from our realm.

On mischief is she bent. Well known her treach'rous
    power.

For who escapes her? Who may pass his days in peace?

This cursèd pestilence at once would I have stayed

By force of arms; but Jason's prayers prevailed. She still

May live, but let her free my borders from the fear

Her presence genders, and her safety gain by flight.

                        (*He sees Medea approaching*)

But lo, she comes, with fierce and threatening mien, to
    seek

An audience with us. (*To attendants*) Slaves, defend
    us from her touch

And pestilential presence! Bid her silence keep,

And learn to yield obedience to the king's commands.

(*To Medea*) Go, speed thy flight, thou thing of evil,
    fell, and monstrous!

MEDEA: But tell me what the crime, my lord, or what
    the guilt

That merits exile?

CREON: Let the guiltless question thus.

MEDEA: If now thou judgest, hear me; if thou reign'st,
    command.

CREON: The king's command thou must abide, nor ques-
    tion aught.

MEDEA: Unrighteous sovereignty has never long endured.

CREON: Go hence, and to the Colchians complain.

MEDEA: I go,

But let him take me hence who brought me to thy
   shores.

CREON: Thy prayer has come too late, for fixed is my
   decree.

MEDEA: Who judges, and denies his ear to either side,
Though right his judgment, still is he himself unjust.

CREON: Didst lend thine ear to Pelias, ere thou judgedst
   him?

But come, I'll give thee grace to plead thy goodly cause.

MEDEA: How hard the task to turn the soul from wrath,
   when once

To wrath inclined; how 'tis the creed of sceptred kings
To swerve not from the purposed course they once have
   taken,

Full well I know, for I have tasted royalty.
For, though by present storms of ill I'm overwhelmed,
An exile, suppliant, lone, forsaken, all forlorn,
I once in happier times a royal princess shone,
And traced my proud descent from heavenly Phœbus'
   self.

My father's realm extended wide o'er all the land
Where Phasis' gentle waters flow, o'er Scythia's plains
Whose rivers sweeten Pontus' briny waves; where, too,
Thermodon's banks inclose the race of warlike maids,
Whose gleaming shields strike terror to their foes. All
   this

My father held in sway. And I, of noble birth,
And blessed of heaven, in royal state was high upraised.
Then princes humbly sought my hand in wedlock, mine,
Who now must sue. O changeful fortune, thou my throne
Hast reft away, and given me exile in its stead.
Trust not in kindly realms, since fickle chance may strew
Their treasures to the winds. Lo, this is regal, this
The work of kings, which time nor change cannot undo:
To succor the afflicted, to provide at need

A trusty refuge for the suppliant. This alone
I brought of all my Colchian treasure, this renown,
This very flower of fame, that by my arts I saved
The bulwark of the Greeks, the offspring of the gods.
My princely gift to Greece is Orpheus, that sweet bard
Who can the trees in willing bondage draw, and melt
The crag's hard heart. Mine too are Boreas' wingèd sons,
And Leda's heaven-born progeny, and Lynceus, he
Whose glance can pierce the distant view—yea, all the
    Greeks,
Save Jason; for I mention not the king of kings,
The leader of the leaders; he is mine alone,
My labour's recompense; the rest I give to you.
Nay, come, O king, arraign me, and rehearse my crimes.
But stay! for I'll confess them all. The only crime
Of which I stand accused is this—the Argo saved.
Suppose my maiden scruples had opposed the deed;
Suppose my filial piety had stayed my hand:
Then had the mighty chieftains fall'n, and in their fate
All Greece had been o'erwhelmed; then this, thy son-in-
    law,
Had felt the bull's consuming breath, and perished there.
Nay, nay, let fortune, when she will, my doom decree;
I glory still that kings have owed their lives to me.
But what reward I reap for all my glorious deeds
Is in thy hands. Convict me, if thou wilt, of sin,
But give him back for whom I sinned. O Creon, see,
I own that I am guilty. This much thou didst know,
When first I clasped thy knees, a humble suppliant,
And sought the shelter of thy royal clemency.
Some little corner of thy kingdom now I ask,
In which to hide my grief. If I must flee again,
Oh, let some nook remote within thy broad domain
Be found for me!

CREON: That I my power in mercy wield,

And spurn not those who seek my aid let Jason's self
My witness be, who, exiled, overwhelmed by fate,
And smitten sore with fear, a refuge found with me.
For lo, Thessalia's monarch, bent on vengeance dire,
Seeks Jason at my hand. The cause, indeed, is just:
For that his sire, o'erburdened with the weight of years,
Was foully taken off, while by the wicked guile
His guileless sisters' hands were nerved to do the deed.
If now our Jason can unlink his cause from thine,
'Tis easy his defense to make, for on his hands
No stain of blood is found. His arm no sword upraised,
And he has had no part nor lot in this thy crime.
No, thou and thou alone the arch contriver art,
Uniting in thy person woman's fertile wit
And man's effective strength; while in thy reckless heart
No thought of reputation dwells to check thy hand.
Then go thou hence and purge our kingdom of its stain;
Bear hence thy deadly poisons; free the citizens
From fear; abiding in some other land than this,
Outwear the patience of the gods.

MEDEA: Thou bid'st me flee?
Then give me back my bark wherein to flee. Restore
The partner of my flight! Why should I flee alone?
I came not thus. Or if avenging war thou fear'st,
Then banish both the culprits; why distinguish me
From Jason? 'Twas for him old Pelias was o'ercome;
For him the flight, the plunder of my father's realm,
My sire forsaken and my infant brother slain,
And all the guilt that love suggests; 'twas all for him.
Deep dyed in sin am I, but on my guilty soul
The sin of profit lieth not.

CREON: Why seek delay
By speech? Too long thou tarriest.

MEDEA: I go, but grant
This last request: let not the mother's fall o'erwhelm

Her hapless babes.

CREON: Then go in peace. For I to them
A father's place will fill, and take them to my heart.

MEDEA: Now by the fair hopes born upon this wedding
day,
And by thy hopes of lasting sovereignty secure
From changeful fate's assault, I pray thee grant from
flight
A respite brief, while I upon my children's lips
A mother's kiss imprint, perchance the last.

CREON: A time
Thou seek'st for treachery.

MEDEA: What fraud can be devised
In one short hour?

CREON: To those on mischief bent, be sure,
The briefest time is fraught with mischief's fatal power.

MEDEA: Dost thou refuse me, then, one little space for
tears?

CREON: Though deep-ingrafted fear would fain resist
thy plea,
A single day I'll give thee ere my sentence holds.

MEDEA: Too gracious thou. But let my respite further
shrink,
And I'll depart content.

CREON: Thy life shall surely pay
The forfeit if tomorrow's sun beholds thee still
In Corinth. But the voice of Hymen calls away
To solemnize the rites of this his festal day. (*Exeunt.*)

CHORUS: Too bold the man who first upon the seas,
The treacherous seas, his fragile bark confided;
Who, as the well-known shore behind him glided,
His life intrusted to the fickle breeze;

And, as his unknown seaward course he sped
Within his slender craft with foolish daring,

Midway 'twixt life and death went onward faring,
　　Along the perilous narrow margin led.

Not yet were sparkling constellations known,
Or sky, all spangled with the starry glory;
Not yet could sailors read the warning story
　　By stormy Hyades upon the heavens thrown.

Not yet was Zeus's foster-mother famed,
Nor slow Boötes round the north star wheeling;
Nor Boreas nor Zephyr gently stealing,
　　Each feared or welcomed, though as yet unnamed.

First Tiphys dared to spread his venturous sail,
The hidden lesson of the breezes learning,
Now all his canvas to the Zephyrs turning,
　　Now shifting all to catch the changing gale.

Now midway on the mast the yard remains,
Now at the head with all its canvas drawing,
While eager sailors lure the breezes blowing,
　　And over all the gleaming topsail strains.

The guiltless golden age our fathers saw,
When youth and age the same horizon bounded;
No greed of gain their simple hearts confounded;
　　Their native wealth enough, 'twas all they knew.

But lo, the severed worlds have been brought near
And linked in one by Argo's hand uniting;
While seas endure the oar's unwonted smiting,
　　And add their fury to the primal fear.

This impious bark its guilt in dread atoned
When clashing mountains were together driven,

And sea, from sea in mighty conflict riven,
   The stars besprinkled with the leaping foam.

Amid these perils sturdy Tiphys paled,
And from his nerveless hand the vessel bounded;
While stricken Orpheus' lyre no more resounded,
   And tuneful Argo's warning message failed.

What sinking terror filled each quaking breast,
When near the borders of sea-girt Pelorus,
There smote upon their ears the horrid chorus
   Of Scylla's baying wolves around them pressed.

What terror when they neared the Sirens' lair,
Who soothe the troubled waves with witching measures!
But Orpheus filled their souls with nobler pleasures,
   And left the foe in impotent despair.

And of this wild adventure what the prize,
That lured the daring bark with heroes laden?
The fleece of gold, and this mad Colchian maiden,
   Well fit to be the first ship's merchandise.

The sea, subdued, the victor's law obeys;
No vessel needs a goddess' art in framing,
Nor oars in heroes' hands, the ocean taming:
   The frailest craft now dares the roughest waves.

Now, every bound removed, new cities rise
In lands remote, their ancient walls removing;
While men of Ind by Caspian shores are roving,
   And Persia's face now greets the western skies.

The time will come, as lapsing ages flee,
When every land shall yield its hidden treasure;

When men no more shall unknown courses measure,
    For round the world no "farthest land" shall be.

ACT III

(*Medea is rushing out to seek vengeance, while the
    Nurse tries in vain to restrain her*)

NURSE: My foster-daughter, whither speedest thou
    abroad?

Oh, stay, I pray thee, and restrain thy passion's force.
(*Medea hastens by without answering. The Nurse
    soliloquizes*)

As some wild Bacchanal, whose fury's raging fire
The god inflames, now roams distraught on Pindus'
    snows,
And now on lofty Nysa's rugged slopes; so she,
Now here, now there, with frenzied step is hurried on,
Her face revealing every mark of stricken woe,
With flushing cheek and sighs deep drawn, wild cries,
    and tears,
And laughter worse than tears. In her a medley strange
Of every passion may be seen: o'ertopping wrath,
Bewailings, bitter groans of anguish. Whither tends
This overburdened soul? What mean her frenzied
    threats?
When will the foaming wave of fury spend itself?
No common crime, I fear, no easy deed of ill
She meditates. Herself she will outvie. For well
I recognize the wonted marks of rage. Some deed
Is threatening, wild, profane, and hideous.
(*Re-enter Medea*)

                                                    Behold
Her face betrays her madness. O ye gods, may these
Our fears prove vain forebodings!

MEDEA (*not noticing the Nurse's presence*): For thy
    hate, poor soul,

Dost thou a measure seek? Let it be deep as love.
And shall I tamely view the wedding torches' glare?
And shall this day go uneventful by, this day,
So hardly won, so grudgingly bestowed? Nay, nay,
While, poised upon her heights, the central earth shall
    bear
The heavens up; while seasons run their endless round,
And sands unnumbered lie; while days, and nights, and
    sun,
And stars in due procession pass; while round the pole
The ocean-fearing bears revolve, and tumbling streams
Flow downward to the sea; my grief shall never cease
To seek revenge, and shall forever grow. What rage
Of savage beast can equal mine? What Scylla famed?
What sea-engulfing pool? What burning Ætna placed
On impious Titan's heaving breast? No torrent stream,
Nor storm-tossed sea, nor breath of flame fanned by the
    gale,
Can check or equal my wild storm of rage. My will
Is set on limitless revenge!
                Will Jason say
He feared the power of Creon and Acastus' threats?
True love is proof against the fear of man. But grant
He was compelled to yield, and pledged his hand in
    fear:
He might at least have sought his wife with one last
    word
Of comfort and farewell. But this, though brave in heart,
He feared to do. The cruel terms of banishment
Could Creon's son-in-law not soften? No. One day
Alone was giv'n for last farewell to both my babes.
But time's short space I'll not bewail; though brief in
    hours,
In consequence it stretches out eternally.
This day shall see a deed that ne'er shall be forgot.

But now I'll go and pray the gods, and move high
    heaven
But I shall work my will!

NURSE: Thy heart all passion-tossed,
I pray thee, mistress, soothe, and calm thy troubled
    soul.

MEDEA: My troubled soul can never know a time of rest
Until it sees all things o'erwhelmed in common doom.
All must go down with me! 'Tis sweet such death to die.
                             (*Exit Medea*)

NURSE (*calling after her*): Oh, think what perils thou
    must meet if thou persist!
No one with safety may defy a sceptered king.

(*Enter Jason*)

JASON: O heartless fate, if frowns or smiles bedeck thy
    brow,
How often are thy cures far worse than the disease
They seek to cure! If, now, I wish to keep the troth
I plighted to my lawful bride, my life must pay
The forfeit; if I shrink from death, my guilty soul
Must perjured be. I fear no power that man can wield;
But in my heart paternal love unmans me quite;
For well I know that in my death my children's fate
Is sealed. O sacred Justice, if in heaven thou dwell'st,
Be witness now, that for my children's sake I act.
Nay, sure am I that even she, Medea's self,
Though fierce she is of soul and brooking no restraint,
Will see her children's good outweighing all her wrongs.
With this good argument my purpose now is fixed,
In humble wise to brave her wrath.

(*Enter Medea*)

                        At sight of me
Her raging fury flames anew! Hate, like a shield,
She bears, and in her face is pictured all her woe.

MEDEA: Thou see'st, Jason, that we flee. 'Tis no new
    thing
To suffer exile, but the cause of flight is strange;
For with thee I was wont to flee, not from thee. Yes,
I go. But whither dost thou send me whom thou driv'st
From out thy home? Shall I the Colchians seek again,
My royal father's realm, whose soil is steeped in blood
My brother shed? What country dost thou bid me seek?
What way by sea is open? Shall I fare again
Where once I saved the noble kings of Greece, and
    thee,
Thou wanton, through the threatening jaws of Pontus'
    strait,
The blue Symplegades? Or shall I hie me back
To fair Thessalia's realms? Lo, all the doors which I,
For thee, have opened wide, I've closed upon myself.
But whither dost thou send me now? Thou bid'st me
    flee,
But show'st no way or means of flight.

                           But 'tis enough:
The king's own son-in-law commands and I obey.
Come, heap thy torments on me; I deserve them all.
Let royal wrath oppress me, wanton that I am,
With cruel hand, and load my guilty limbs with chains;
And let me be immured in dungeons black as night:
Still will my punishment be less than my offense.
O ingrate! hast thou then forgot the brazen bull,
And his consuming breath? the fear that smote thee,
    when,
Upon the field of Mars, the earth-born brood stood forth
To meet thy single sword? 'Twas by my arts that they,
The monsters, fell by mutual blows. Remember, too,
The long-sought fleece of gold I won for thee, whose
    guard,

The dragon huge, was lulled to rest at my command;
My brother slain for thee. For thee old Pelias fell,
When, taken by my guile, his daughters slew their sire,
Whose life could not return. All this I did for thee.
In quest of thine advantage have I quite forgot
Mine own.

And now, by all thy fond paternal hopes,
By thine established house, by all the monsters slain
For thee, by these my hands which I have ever held
To work thy will, by all the perils past, by heaven
And sea that witnessed at my wedlock, pity me!
Since thou art blessed, restore me what I lost for thee:
That countless treasure plundered from the swarthy
    tribes
Of India, which filled our goodly vaults with wealth,
And decked our very trees with gold. This costly store
I left for thee, my native land, my brother, sire,
My reputation—all; and with this dower I came.
If now to homeless exile thou dost send me forth,
Give back the countless treasures which I left for thee.

JASON: Though Creon in a vengeful mood would have
    thy life,
I moved him by my tears to grant thee flight instead.

MEDEA: I thought my exile punishment; 'tis now, I see,
A gracious boon!

JASON: Oh, flee while still the respite holds;
Provoke him not, for deadly is the wrath of kings.

MEDEA: Not so. 'Tis for Creüsa's love thou sayest this;
Thou wouldst remove the hated wanton once thy wife.

JASON: Dost thou reproach me with a guilty love?

MEDEA: Yea, that,
And murder too, and treachery.

JASON: But name me now,
If so thou canst, the crimes that I have done.

MEDEA: Thy crimes—

Whatever I have done.

JASON: Why then, in truth, thy guilt
Must all be mine, if all thy crimes are mine.

MEDEA: They are,
They are all thine; for who by sin advantage gains,
Commits the sin. All men proclaim thy wife defiled.
Do thou thyself protect her, and condone her sin.
Let her be guiltless in thine eyes who for thy gain
Has sinned.

JASON: But gifts which sin has bought 'twere shame to
      take.

MEDEA: Why keep'st thou then the gifts which it were
      shame to take?

JASON: Nay, curb thy fiery soul! Thy children—for their
      sake
Be calm.

MEDEA: My children! Them I do refuse, reject,
Renounce! Shall then Creüsa brothers bear to these
My children?

JASON: But the queen can aid thy wretched sons.

MEDEA: May that day never dawn, that day of shame
      and woe,
When in one house are joined the low born and the high,
The sons of that foul robber Sisyphus, and these,
The sons of Phœbus.

JASON: Wretched one, and wilt thou then
Involve me also in thy fall? Begone, I pray.

MEDEA: Creon hath heard my prayer.

JASON: What wouldst thou have me do?

MEDEA: For me? I'd have thee dare the law.

JASON: The royal power
Doth compass me.

MEDEA: A greater than the king is here:
Medea. Set us front to front and let us strive;
And of this royal strife let Jason be the prize.

JASON: O'erwearied by my woes I yield. But be thou
ware,
Medea, lest too often thou shouldst tempt thy fate.
MEDEA: Yet fortune's mistress have I ever been.
JASON: But see,
With hostile front Acastus comes, on vengeance bent,
While Creon threatens instant death.
MEDEA: Then flee them both.
I ask thee not to draw thy sword against the king
Nor yet to stain thy pious hands with kindred blood.
Come, flee with me.
JASON: But what resistance can we make,
If war with double visage rear his horrid front,
If Creon and Acastus join in common cause?
MEDEA: Add, too, the Colchian armies with my father's
self
To lead them; join the Scythian and Pelasgian hordes:
In one deep gulf of ruin will I whelm them all.
JASON: Yet on the sceptre do I look with fear.
MEDEA: Beware,
Lest not the fear, but lust of power prevail with thee.
JASON: Too long we strive: have done, lest we suspicion
breed.
MEDEA: Now Jove, throughout thy heavens let the
thunders roll!
Thy mighty arm in wrath make bare! Thy darting flames
Of vengeance loose, and shake the lofty firmament
With rending storms! At random hurl thy vengeful bolts,
Selecting neither me nor Jason with thy aim;
That thus whoever falls may perish with the brand
Of guilt upon him; for thy hurtling darts can take
No erring flight.
JASON: Recall thee and in calmness speak
With words of peace and reason. Then if any gift
From Creon's royal house can compensate thy woes,

Take that as solace of thy flight.

MEDEA: My soul doth scorn
The wealth of kings. But let me have my little ones
As comrades of my flight, that in their childish breasts
Their mother's tears may flow. New sons await thy
    home.

JASON: My heart inclines to yield to thee, but love for-
    bids.
For these my sons shall never from my arms be reft,
Though Creon's self demand. My very spring of life,
My sore heart's comfort, and my joy are these my sons;
And sooner could I part with limbs or vital breath,
Or light of life.

MEDEA (*aside*): Doth he thus love his sons? 'Tis well;
Then is he bound, and in his armoured strength this flaw
Reveals the place to strike.

(*To Jason*) At least, ere I depart,
Grant me this last request: let me once more embrace
My sons. E'en that small boon will comfort my sad
    heart.
And this my latest prayer to thee: if, in my grief,
My tongue was over bold, let not my words remain
To rankle in thy heart. Remember happier things
Of me, and let my bitter words be straight forgot.

JASON: Not one shall linger in my soul; and curb, I
    pray,
Thy too impetuous heart, and gently yield to fate.
For resignation ever soothes the woeful soul.

(*Exit Jason*)

MEDEA: He's gone! And can it be? And shall he thus
    depart,
Forgetting me and all my service? Must I drop,
Like some discarded toy, out of his faithless heart?
It shall not be. Up then, and summon all thy strength
And all thy skill! And, this the fruit of former crime,

Count nothing criminal that works thy will. But lo,
We're hedged about; scant room is left for our designs.
Now must the attack be made where least suspicion
    wakes
The least resistance. Now Medea, on! and do
And dare thine utmost, yea, beyond thine utmost power!
(*To the Nurse*) Do thou, my faithful nurse, the comrade
    of my grief,
And all the devious wanderings of my checkered course,
Assist me now in these my plans. There is a robe,
The glory of our Colchian realm, the precious gift
Of Phœbus' self to king Æetes as a proof
Of fatherhood; a gleaming circlet, too, all wrought
With threads of gold, the yellow gold bespangled o'er
With gems, a fitting crown to deck a princess' head.
These treasures let Medea's children bear as gifts
To Jason's bride. But first infuse them with the power
Of magic, and invoke the aid of Hecate;
The woe-producing sacrifices then prepare,
And let the sacred flames through all our courts resound.
CHORUS: No force of flame or raging gale,
Or whizzing bolt so fearful is,
As when a wife, by her lord betrayed,
    Burns hot with hate.

Not such a force is Auster's blast,
When he marshals forth the wintry storms;
Nor Hister's headlong rushing stream,
Which, wrecking bridges in its course,
    Pours reckless on;

Nor yet the Rhone, whose current strong
Beats back the sea; nor when the snows,
Beneath the lengthening days of spring

And the sun's warm rays, melt down in streams
    From Hæmus' top.

Blind is the rage of passion's fire,
Will not be governed, brooks no reins,
And scoffs at death; nay, hostile swords
    It gladly courts.

Spare, O ye gods, be merciful,
That he who tamed the sea may live.
But much we fear, for the lord of the deep
Is wroth that his realm of the second lot
    Should be subdued.

The thoughtless youth who dared to drive
His father's sacred chariot,
Was by those fires, which o'er the heavens
He scattered in his mad career,
    Himself consumed.

The beaten path has never proved
The way of danger. Walk ye then
Where your forefathers safely trod,
And keep great nature's holy laws
    Inviolate.

Whoever dipped the famous oars
Of that bold bark in the rushing sea;
Whoe'er despoiled old Pelion
Of the thick, dark shade of his sacred groves;
Whoever dared the clashing rocks,
And, after countless perils passed,
His vessel moored on a barbarous shore,
Hoping to fare on his homeward way

The master of the golden fleece,
All by a fearful end appeased
    The offended sea.

First Tiphys, tamer of the deep,
Abandoned to an untrained hand
His vessel's helm. On a foreign shore,
Far from his native land he died;
And now within a common tomb,
'Midst unknown ghosts, he lies at rest.
In wrathful memory of her king
Lost on the sea, did Aulis then
Within her sluggish harbor hold
    The impatient ships.

Then he, the tuneful Muse's son,
At whose sweet strains the streams stood still,
The winds were silent, and the birds,
Their songs forgotten, flocked to him,
The whole wood following after—he,
Over the Thracian fields was hurled
In scattered fragments; but his head
Down Hebrus' grieving stream was borne.
The well-remembered Styx he reached,
And Tartarus, whence ne'er again
    Would he return.

The wingèd sons of Boreas
Alcides slew, and Neptune's son
Who in a thousand changing forms
Could clothe himself. But after peace
On land and sea had been proclaimed,
And after savage Pluto's realm
Had been revealed to mortal eyes,
Then did Alcides' self, alive,

On burning Œta's top lie down,
And give his body to the flames;
For sore distressed was he, consumed
By Deianira's deadly gift,
       The double blood.

A savage boar Ancæus slew;
Thou, Meleager, impiously
Thy mother's brother in wrath didst slay,
And by that angry mother's hand
Didst die. All these deserved their death.
But for what crime did Hylas die,
A tender lad whom Hercules
Long time but vainly sought? For he,
'Mid waters safe was done to death.
Go then, and fearlessly the deep
Plough with your daring ships; but fear
       The peaceful pools.

Idmon, though well he knew the fates,
A serpent slew on Afric sands;
And Mopsus, to all others true,
False to himself, died far from Thebes.
If he with truth the future sang,
Then Nauplius, who strove to wreck
The Argive ships by lying fires,
Shall headlong fall into the sea.
And for his father's daring crime
Shall Ajax, that Oïleus' son,
Make full atonement, perishing
       'Midst flame and flood.

And thou, Admetus' faithful mate,
Shalt for thy husband pay thy life,
Redeeming his from death. But he,

Who bade the first ship sail in quest
Of the golden spoil, King Pelias,
Seethed in a boiling cauldron, swam
'Mid those restricted waves. Enough,
O gods, have ye avenged the sea:
Spare him, we pray, who did but go
  On ordered ways.

Act IV

NURSE (*alone*): My spirit trembles, for I feel the near
  approach
Of some unseen disaster. Swiftly grows her grief,
Its own fires kindling; and again her passion's force
Hath leaped to life. I oft have seen her, with the fit
Of inspiration in her soul, confront the gods
And force the very heavens to her will. But now,
A monstrous deed, of greater moment far than these,
Medea is preparing. For, but now, did she
With step of frenzy hurry off until she reached
Her stricken home. There, in her chamber, all her stores
Of magic wonders are revealed; once more she views
The things herself hath held in fear these many years,
Unloosing one by one her ministers of ill,
Occult, unspeakable, and wrapt in mystery;
And, grasping with her hand the sacred altar-horn,
With prayers, she straightly summons all destructive
  powers,
The creatures bred in Libya's sands, and on the peaks
Of frigid Taurus, clad in everlasting snows.
Obedient to her potent charms, the scaly brood
Of serpents leave their darksome lairs and swarm to her;
One savage creature rolls his monstrous length along,
And darts his forkèd tongue with its envenomed sting,
Death-dealing; at the charming sound he stops amazed,

And fold on fold his body writhes in nerveless coils.
"But these are petty ills; unworthy of my hand,"
She cries, "are such weak, earth-born weapons. Potent charms
Are bred in heaven. Now, now 'tis time to summon powers
Transcending common magic. Down I'll draw from heaven
That serpent huge whose body lies athwart the sky
Like some great ocean stream, in whose constricting folds
The greater and the lesser Bears are held enthralled,
The greater set as guide for Grecian ships, the less
For Sidon's mariners! Let Ophiuchus loose
His hand and pour forth venom from his captive thrall!
And let the Python huge, that dared to rear its head
Against the heavenly twins, be present at my prayer!
Let Hydra's writhing heads, which by Alcides' hand
Were severed, all return to life and give me aid!
Thou too be near and leave thy ancient Colchian home,
Thou watchful dragon, to whose eyes the first sleep came
In answer to my incantations."

                       When she thus
Had summoned all the serpent brood, she cast her store
Of baleful herbs together; all the poisons brewed
Amid the rocky caves of trackless Eryx; plants
That flourish on the snowy peaks of Caucasus,
Whose crags were spattered with Prometheus' gore; the herbs
Within whose deadly juice the Arab dips his darts,
And the quiver-bearing Mede and fleeing Parthian;
Those potent juices, too, which, near the shivering pole,
The Suabian chieftains gather in Hyrcanian groves.
The seasons, too, have paid their tribute to her stores:

Whatever earth produces in the nesting time,
And when the stiff'ning hand of winter's frost has
    stripped
The glory from the trees and fettered all the land
With icy bonds; whatever flow'ring plant conceals
Destruction in its bloom, or in its twisted roots
Distils the juice of death, she gathers to her use.
These pestilential herbs Hæmonian Athos gave;
And these on lofty Pindus grew; a bloody knife
Clipped off these slender leaves on Macedonia's heights;
Still others grew beside the Tigris, whirling on
His flood to meet the sea; the Danube nourished some;
These grew on bright gem-starred Hydaspes' tepid
    stream;
And these the Bætis bore, which gave the land its name,
Displacing with its languorous tide, the western sea.
These felt the knife when early dawn begins to break;
The fruit of these was cut in midnight's gloomy hour;
This fatal crop was reaped with sickle magic-edged.
These deadly, potent herbs she takes and sprinkles o'er
With serpent venom, mixing all; and in the broth
She mingles unclean birds: a wailing screech-owl's
    heart,
A ghastly vampire's vitals torn from living flesh.
Her magic poisons all she ranges for her use.
The ravening power of hidden fire is held in these,
While deep in others lurks the numbing chill of frost.
Now magic runes she adds more potent far. But lo!
Her voice resounds! and, as with maddened step she
    comes,
She chants her charms, while heaven and earth convul-
    sive rock.
(*Enter Medea, chanting her incantations*)
MEDEA: I supplicate the silent throng, and you, the gods
Of death's sad rites, and groping chaos, and the home

Of gloomy Pluto, and the black abyss of death
Girt by the banks of Tartarus! Ye storied shades,
Your torments leave and haste to grace the festival
At Hymen's call! Let stop the whirling wheel that holds
Ixion's limbs and let him tread Corinthian ground;
Let Tantalus unfrighted drink Pirene's stream.
On Creon's stock alone let heavier torments fall,
And backward o'er the rocks let Sisyphus be hurled.
You too, the seed of Danaüs, whose fruitless toil
The ever-empty urns deride, I summon you;
This day requires your helping hands. Thou radiant
      moon,
Night's glorious orb, my supplications hear and come
To aid; put on thy sternest guise, thou goddess dread
Of triple form! Full oft have I with flowing locks,
And feet unsandaled, wandered through thy darkling
      groves
And by thy inspiration summoned forth the rain
From cloudless skies; the heaving seas have I subdued,
And sent the vanquished waves to ocean's lowest depths.
At my command the sun and stars together shine,
The heavenly law reversed; while in the Arctic sea
The Bears have plunged. The seasons, too, obey my will:
I've made the burning summer blossom as the spring,
And hoary winter autumn's golden harvests bear.
The Phasis sends his swirling waves to seek their source,
And Ister, flowing to the sea with many mouths,
His eager water checks and sluggish rolls along.
The billows roar, the mad sea rages, though the winds
All silent lie. At my command primeval groves
Have lost their shade; the sun, abandoning the day,
Has stood in middle heaven; while falling Hyades
Attest my charms.
                    But now thy sacred hour is come,
O Phœbe. Thine these bonds with bloody hand entwined

With ninefold serpent coils; these cords I offer thee,
Which on his hybrid limbs Typhœus bore, who shook
The throne of Jove. This vessel holds the dying blood
Of Nessus, faithless porter of Alcides' bride.
Here are the ashes of the pyre on Œta's top
Which drank the poisoned blood of dying Hercules;
And here the fatal billet that Althæa burned
In vengeance on her son. These plumes the Harpies left
Within their caverned lair when Zetes drove them forth;
And these the feathers of that vile Stymphalian bird
Which arrows, dipped in Lerna's deadly poison, pierced.

  But lo! mine altar fires resound!
  While in the tripod's answering voice
  Behold the present deity!
  I see the car of Trivia,
  Not full and clear as when she drives
  The livelong night to meet the dawn;
  But with a baleful, lurid glare,
  As, harried by Thessalian cries,
  She holds a more restricted course.
  Send such uncanny light abroad!
  Fill mortals with a dread unknown;
  And let our Corinth's priceless bronze
  Resound, Dictynna, for thy aid!
  To thee a solemn sacrifice
  On bloody altar do we pay!
  To thee, snatched from the mournful tomb,
  The blazing torch nocturnal burns;
  On thee I call with tossing head,
  And many a frantic gesture make;
  Corpselike upon the bier I lie,
  My hair with priestly fillet bound;
  Before thy awful shrine is waved
  The branch in Stygian waters dipped.

And, calling on thy name, with gleaming shoulders
    bared,
Like Bacchus' mad adorers, will I lash my arms
With sacrificial knife. Now let my life-blood flow!
And let my hands be used to draw the deadly sword,
And learn to shed belovèd blood!
(*She cuts her arm and lets the blood flow upon the
    altar.*)
Behold, self-stricken have I poured the sacrifice!
    But if too oft upon thy name I call,
    I pray forgive this importunity!
    The cause, O Hecate, of all my prayers
    Is ever Jason; this my constant care.
(*To attendants*) Take now Creüsa's bridal robe, and
    steep in these,
My potent drugs; and when she dons the clinging folds,
Let subtle flames go stealing through her inmost heart.
The fire that in this tawny golden circlet lurks
Prometheus gave, who, for his daring heavenly theft
In human aid, endured an ever-living death.
'Twas Vulcan showed the fires concealed in sulphur's
    veins;
While from my brother Phaëthon I gained a flame
That never dies; I have preserved Chimera's breath,
And that fierce heat that parched the fiery, brazen bull
Of Colchis. These dread fires commingled with the gall
Of dire Medusa have I bidden keep the power
    Of lurking evil. Now, O Hecate,
    Give added force to these my deadly gifts.
    And strictly guard the hidden seeds of flame.
    Let them deceive the sight, endure the touch;
    But through her veins let burning fever run;
    In fervent heat consume her very bones,
    And let her fiercely blazing locks outshine

Her marriage torches! Lo, my prayer is heard:
Thrice have replied the hounds of Hecate,
And she has shown her baleful, gleaming fires.
Now all is ready: hither call my sons,
And let them bear these presents to the bride.

(*Enter sons*)

Go, go, my sons, of hapless mother born,
And win with costly gifts and many prayers
The favor of the queen, your father's wife.
Begone, but quick your homeward way retrace,
That I may fold you in a last embrace.

(*Exeunt sons toward the palace, Medea in opposite
direction*)

CHORUS: Where hastes this Bacchic fury now,
All passion-swept? what evil deed
Does her unbridled rage prepare?
Her features are congealed with rage,
And with a queenly bearing, grand
But terrible, she sets herself
Against e'en Creon's royal power.
An exile who would deem her now?
Her cheeks anon with anger flush,
And now a deadly pallor show;
Each feeling quick succeeds to each,
While all the passions of her heart
Her changing aspect testifies.
She wanders restless here and there,
As a tigress, of her young bereft,
In frantic grief the jungle scours.
Medea knows not how in check
To hold her wrath nor yet her love;
If love and wrath make common cause,
What dire results will come?
When will this scourge of Corinth leave
Our Grecian shores for Colchis' strand,

And free our kingdom from its fear?
Now, Phœbus, hasten on thy course
With no retarding rein.
Let friendly darkness quickly veil the light,
And this dread day be buried deep in night.

Act V

MESSENGER (*comes running in from the direction of the palace*): Lo, all is lost! the kingdom totters from its base!
The daughter and the father lie in common dust!
CHORUS: By what snare taken?
MESSENGER: By gifts, the common snare of kings.
CHORUS: What harm could lurk in them?
MESSENGER: In equal doubt I stand;
And, though my eyes proclaim the dreadful deed is done,
I scarce can trust their witness.
CHORUS: What the mode of death?
MESSENGER: Devouring flames consume the palace at the will
Of her who sent them; there complete destruction reigns,
While men do tremble for the very city's doom.
CHORUS: Let water quench the fire.
MESSENGER: Nay here is added wonder:
The copious streams of water feed the deadly flames;
And opposition only fans their fiery rage
To whiter heat. The very bulwarks feel their power.
(*Medea enters in time to hear that her magic has been successful*)
NURSE (*to Medea*): Oh, haste thee, leave this land of Greece, in headlong flight!
MEDEA: Thou bid'st me speed my flight? Nay rather, had I fled,
I should return for this. Strange bridal rites I see!

(*Absorbed in her own reflections*) Why dost thou falter,
　　　O my soul? 'Tis well begun;
But still how small a portion of thy just revenge
Is that which gives thee present joy? Not yet has love
Been banished from thy maddened heart if 'tis enough
That Jason widowed be. Pursue thy vengeful quest
To acts as yet unknown, and steel thyself for these.
Away with every thought and fear of God and man;
Too lightly falls the rod that pious hands upbear.
Give passion fullest sway; exhaust thy ancient powers;
And let the worst thou yet hast done be innocent
Besides thy present deeds. Come, let them know how
　　　slight
Were those thy crimes already done; mere training they
For greater deeds. For what could hands untrained in
　　　crime
Accomplish? Or what mattered maiden rage? But now,
I am Medea; in the bitter school of woe
My powers have ripened.
　　　　　　　　　　　　(*In an ecstasy of madness*)
　　　Oh, the bliss of memory!
My infant brother slain, his limbs asunder rent,
My royal father spoiled of his ancestral realm,
And Pelias' guiltless daughters lured to slay their sire!
But here I must not rest; no untrained hand I bring
To execute my deeds. But now, by what approach
Or by what weapon wilt thou threat the treacherous foe?
Deep hidden in my secret heart have I conceived
A purpose which I dare not utter. Oh, I fear
That in my foolish madness I have gone too far—
I would that children had been born to him of this
My hated rival. Still, since she hath gained his heart,
His children too are hers—
That punishment would be most fitting and deserved.
Yes, now I see the final deed of crime, and thou,

My soul, must face it. You, who once were called my
    sons,
Must pay the penalty of these your father's crimes—
My heart with horror melts, a numbing chill pervades
My limbs, and all my soul is filled with sinking fear.
Now wrath gives place, and, heedless of my husband's
    sins,
The tender mother-instinct quite possesses me.
And could I shed my helpless children's blood? Not so,
Oh, say not so, my maddened heart! Far from my hand
And thought be that unnameable and hideous deed!
What sin have they that shedding of their wretched
    blood
Would wash away?
                Their sin—that Jason is their sire,
And, deeper guilt, that I have borne them. Let them
    die;
They are not mine. Nay, nay! they are my own, my sons,
And with no spot of guilt. Full innocent they are,
'Tis true—my brother, too, was innocent. O soul,
Why dost thou hesitate? Why flow these streaming tears,
While with contending thoughts my wavering heart is
    torn?
As when conflicting winds contend in stubborn strife,
And waves, to stormy waves opposed, the sea invade,
And to their lowest sands the briny waters boil;
With such a storm my heart is tossed. Hate conquers
    love,
And love puts impious hate to flight. Oh, yield thee,
    grief,
To love! Then come, my sons, sole comfort of my heart,
Come, cling within your mother's close embrace. Un-
    harmed
Your sire may keep you, while your mother holds you
    too.   (*Embraces her sons*)

But flight and exile drive me forth! And even now
My children must be torn away with tears and cries.
Then let them die to Jason since they're lost to me.
Once more has hate resumed her sway, and passion's fire
Is hot within my soul. Now fury, as of yore,
Reseeks her own. Lead on, I follow to the end!
I would that I had borne twice seven sons, the boast
Of Niobe! But all too barren have I been.
Still will my two sufficient be to satisfy
My brother and my sire.

   (*Sees a vision of the furies and her brother's ghost*)
         But whither hastes that throng
Of furies? What their quest? What mean their brand-
 ished fires?
Whom threats this hellish host with horrid, bloody
 brands?
I hear the writhing lash resound of serpents huge.
Whom seeks Megæra with her deadly torch? Whose
 shade
Comes gibbering there with scattered limbs? It is my
 brother!
Revenge he seeks, and we will grant his quest. Then
 come,
Within my heart plunge all your torches, rend me, burn;
For lo, my bosom open to your fury's stroke.
O brother, bid these vengeful goddesses depart
And go in peace down to the lowest shades of hell.
And do thou leave me to myself, and let this hand
That slew thee with the sword now offer sacrifice
Unto thy shade.   (*Slays her first son*)
     What sudden uproar meets my ear?
'Tis Corinth's citizens on my destruction bent.
Unto the palace roof I'll mount and there complete
This bloody sacrifice.
(*To her remaining son*) Do thou come hence with me.

But thee, poor senseless corse, within mine arms I'll bear.
Now gird thyself, my heart, with strength. Nor must this
    deed
Lose all its just renown because in secret done;
But to the public eye my hand must be approved.
JASON (*in the street below shouting to citizens*): Ho,
    all ye loyal sons, who mourn the death of kings!
Come, let us seize the worker of this hideous crime.
Now ply your arms and raze her palace to the ground.
MEDEA (*appearing on the housetop with her two
    sons*): Now, now have I regained my regal state,
    my sire,
My brother! Once again the Colchians hold the spoil
Of precious gold! And by the magic of this hour
I am a maid once more. O heavenly powers, appeased
At length! O festal hour! O nuptial day! On, on!
Accomplished is the guilt, but not the recompense.
Complete the task while yet thy hands are strong to act!
Why dost thou linger still? why dost thou hesitate
Upon the threshold of the deed? Thou canst perform it.
Now wrath has died within me, and my soul is filled
With shame and deep remorse. Ah me, what have I
    done,
Wretch that I am? Wretch that thou art, well mayst thou
    mourn,
For thou hast done it!
                        At that thought delirious joy
O'ermasters me and fills my heart which fain would
    grieve.
And yet, methinks, the act was almost meaningless,
Since Jason saw it not; for naught has been performed
If to his grief be added not the woe of sight.
JASON (*discovering her*): Lo, there she stands upon the
    lofty battlements!
Bring torches! fire the house, that she may fall ensnared

By those devices she herself hath planned.

MEDEA (*derisively*):   Not so,
But rather build a lofty pyre for these thy sons;
Their funeral rites prepare. Already for thy bride
And father have I done the service due the dead;
For in their ruined palace have I buried them.
One son of thine has met his doom; and this shall die
Before his father's face.

JASON: By all the gods, and by the perils of our flight,
And by our marriage bond which I have ne'er betrayed,
I pray thee spare the boy, for he is innocent.
If aught of sin there be, 'tis mine. Myself I give
To be the victim. Take my guilty soul for his.

MEDEA: 'Tis for thy prayers and tears I draw, not sheathe
    the sword.
Go now, and take thee maids for wives, thou faithless
    one;
Abandon and betray the mother of thy sons.

JASON: And yet, I pray thee, let one sacrifice atone.

MEDEA: If in the blood of one my passion could be
    quenched,
No vengeance had it sought. Though both my sons I
    slay,
The number still is all too small to satisfy
My boundless grief.

JASON: Then finish what thou hast begun—
I ask no more—and grant at least that no delay
Prolong my helpless agony.

MEDEA: Now hasten not,
Relentless passion, but enjoy a slow revenge.
This day is in thy hands; its fertile hours employ.

JASON: Oh, take my life, thou heartless one.

MEDEA: Thou bid'st me pity—
Well! (*Slays the second child*)—'Tis done!
No more atonement, passion, can I offer thee.

Now hither lift thy tearful eyes, ungrateful one.
Dost recognize thy wife? 'Twas thus of old I fled.
The heavens themselves provide me with a safe retreat.
(*A chariot drawn by dragons appears in the air*)
Twin serpents bow their necks submissive to the yoke.
Now, father, take thy sons; while I, upon my car,
With wingèd speed am borne aloft through realms of air.
                    (*Mounts her car and is borne away*)
JASON (*calling after her*): Speed on through realms of
    air that mortals never see:
But, witness heaven, where thou art gone no gods can be!

LUCAN

(Marcus Annæus Lucanus, 39 A.D.–65 A.D.)

*

From the Pharsalia

Translated by Sir Edward Ridley

The Crossing of the Rubicon

Lest newer glories triumphs past obscure,
Late conquered Gaul the bays from pirates won,
This, Magnus, was thy fear; thy roll of fame,
Of glorious deeds accomplished for the state
Allows no equal; nor will Cæsar's pride
A prior rival in his triumphs brook;
Which had the right 'twere impious to enquire;
Each for his cause can vouch a judge supreme;
The victor, heaven: the vanquished, Cato, thee.
Nor were they like to like: the one in years
Now verging towards decay, in times of peace
Had unlearned war; but thirsting for applause
Had given the people much, and proud of fame
His former glory cared not to renew,
But joyed in plaudits of the theatre,
His gift to Rome: his triumphs in the past,
Himself the shadow of a mighty name.
As when some oak, in fruitful field sublime,
Adorned with venerable spoils, and gifts

528

Of bygone leaders, by its weight to earth
With feeble roots still clings; its naked arms
And hollow trunk, though leafless, give a shade;
And though condemned beneath the tempest's shock
To speedy fall, amid the sturdier trees
In sacred grandeur rules the forest still.
No such repute had Cæsar won, nor fame;
But energy was his that could not rest—
The only shame he knew was not to win.
Keen and unvanquished, where revenge or hope
Might call, resistless would he strike the blow
With sword unpitying: every victory won
Reaped to the full; the favour of the gods
Pressed to the utmost; all that stayed his course
Aimed at the summit of power, was thrust aside:
Triumph his joy, though ruin marked his track.
As parts the clouds a bolt by winds compelled,
With crack of riven air and crash of worlds,
And veils the light of day, and on mankind,
Blasting their vision with its flames oblique,
Sheds deadly fright; then turning to its home,
Nought but the air opposing, through its path
Spreads havoc, and collects its scattered fires.

Such were the hidden motives of the chiefs;
But in the public life the seeds of war
Their hold had taken, such as are the doom
Of potent nations: and when fortune poured
Through Roman gates the booty of a world,
The curse of luxury, chief bane of states,
Fell on her sons. Farewell the ancient ways!
Behold the pomp profuse, the houses decked
With ornament; their hunger loathed the food
Of former days; men wore attire for dames
Scarce fitly fashioned; poverty was scorned,
Fruitful of warriors; and from all the world

Came that which ruins nations; while the fields
Furrowed of yore by great Camillus' plough,
Or by the mattock which a Curius held,
Lost their once narrow bounds, and widening tracts
By hinds unknown were tilled. No nation this
To sheathe the sword, with tranquil peace content
And with her liberties; but prone to ire;
Crime holding light as though by want compelled:
And great the glory in the minds of men,
Ambition lawful even at point of sword,
To rise above their country: might their law:
Decrees are forced from Senate and from Plebs:
Consul and Tribune break the laws alike:
Bought are the fasces, and the people sell
For gain their favour: bribery's fatal curse
Corrupts the annual contests of the Field.
Then covetous usury rose, and interest
Was greedier ever as the seasons came;
Faith tottered; thousands saw their gain in war.

    Cæsar has crossed the Alps, his mighty soul
Great tumults pondering and the coming shock.
Now on the marge of Rubicon, he saw,
In face most sorrowful and ghostly guise,
His trembling country's image; huge it seemed
Through mists of night obscure; and hoary hair
Streamed from the lofty front with turrets crowned:
Torn were her locks and naked were her arms.
Then thus, with broken sighs the Vision spake:
"What seek ye, men of Rome? and whither hence
Bear ye my standards? If by right ye come,
My citizens, stay here; these are the bounds;
No further dare." But Cæsar's hair was stiff
With horror as he gazed, and ghastly dread
Restrained his footsteps on the further bank.
Then spake he, "Thunderer, who from the rock

Tarpeian seest the wall of mighty Rome;
Gods of my race who watched o'er Troy of old;
Thou Jove of Alba's height, and Vestal fires,
And rites of Romulus erst rapt to heaven,
And God-like Rome; be friendly to my quest.
Not with offence or hostile arms I come,
Thy Cæsar, conqueror by land and sea,
Thy soldier here and wheresoe'er thou wilt:
No other's; his, his only be the guilt
Whose acts make me thy foe." He gives the word
And bids his standards cross the swollen stream.
So in the wastes of Afric's burning clime
The lion crouches as his foes draw near,
Feeding his wrath the while, his lashing tail
Provokes his fury; stiff upon his neck
Bristles his mane: deep from his gaping jaws
Resounds a muttered growl, and should a lance
Or javelin reach him from the hunter's ring,
Scorning the puny scratch he bounds afield.

  From modest fountain blood-red Rubicon
In summer's heat flows on; his pigmy tide
Creeps through the valleys and with slender marge
Divides the Italian peasant from the Gaul.
Then winter gave him strength, and fraught with rain
The third day's crescent moon; while Eastern winds
Thawed from the Alpine slopes the yielding snow.
The cavalry first form across the stream
To break the torrent's force; the rest with ease
Beneath their shelter gain the further bank.
When Cæsar crossed and trod beneath his feet
The soil of Italy's forbidden fields,
"Here," spake he, "peace, here broken laws be left;
Farewell to treaties. Fortune, lead me on;
War is our judge, and in the fates our trust."
Then in the shades of night he leads the troops

Swifter than Balearic sling or shaft
Winged by retreating Parthian, to the walls
Of threatened Rimini, while fled the stars,
Save Lucifer, before the coming sun,
Whose fires were veiled in clouds, by south wind driven,
Or else at heaven's command: and thus drew on
The first dark morning of the civil war.

Book I, Lines 136-266

‐≫※≪‐

PETRONIUS

(Gaius Petronius Arbiter, died 66 A.D.)

※

From the Satyricon

※

From Trimalchio's Dinner

Translated by Harry Thurston Peck

AFTER dressing, we took a preliminary stroll, and
presently espied a bald-headed old man, in red-
dish clothes, playing tennis in the midst of a number
of long-haired slaves. It was not the slaves, however,
that attracted us so much as the old gentleman himself
who, with slippers on his feet, was serving a green ball.
As soon as a ball fell to the ground he refused to touch
it again, but took a fresh one from a bag which a slave
by his side held out to the players. While I was watching
his luxurious manner of playing, up comes Menelaus and
says he:

"This is the gentleman at whose house you are going
to dine; and, in fact, this game is really a preliminary to
the dinner."

Before long, we entered the public bath and, after
remaining a while in the hot water, we changed to cold.
Trimalchio, after being carefully perfumed, was rubbed
down, though not with towels, but with mantles made of
the very softest wool; while three attendants who stood

there drank Falernian wine, of which they spilled a good deal in their wrangling; whereupon Trimalchio remarked that this was all his treat. Afterwards, wrapped up in a scarlet dressing-gown, he took his seat on a litter preceded by four gorgeously decorated footmen, and by a wheeled chair in which was his favourite slave, a blear-eyed old fellow, homelier even than his master. Then Trimalchio was carried off home, a musician marching beside him with a pair of shrill pipes and playing all the way as though he were saying something privately in his master's ear. We followed along, filled with admiration, and in Agamemnon's company we reached Trimalchio's front door, on one of whose posts was fastened a notice with this inscription:

IF ANY SLAVE SHALL LEAVE THE HOUSE WITHOUT HIS MASTER'S PERMISSION HE SHALL RECEIVE A HUNDRED LASHES.

At the entrance to the house was the doorkeeper, dressed in green with a cherry-coloured belt around his waist, and engaged in shelling peas into a silver dish. Above the threshold hung a golden cage in which a magpie kept saying, "How do you do?" to us as we entered. I fell to staring at all these things until I bent over backwards so far that I nearly broke my legs; for on the left as we entered, and not far from the janitor's room, was a great dog fastened by a chain and painted on the wall, while overhead in capital letters was the inscription:

BEWARE OF THE DOG!

My friends laughed at me; but I soon recovered my presence of mind and let my eyes rove over the entire wall; for on it was painted, first a slave auction, and then Trimalchio himself, with long hair and holding a wand in his hand, entering Rome guided by Minerva. Another painting represented him learning arithmetic, and another showed him as promoted to a stewardship. The meaning of all these things the thoughtful artist had carefully explained by legends painted under each. At the other end of the entrance, Mercury was represented as raising Trimalchio aloft by the chin, and there was also Fortune with her horn of plenty, and the three Fates twisting their golden threads. I observed in the portico a number of running footmen who were practising with their trainer, and in one corner I saw a large closet in a recess of which were household gods made of silver, a marble statuette of Venus, and a large gold box in which they said the master of the house kept his beard after it had been shaved off.

I fell to questioning the janitor as to what were the pictures in the middle, and he told me that they represented scenes from the *Iliad* and the *Odyssey*, and also the gladiatorial contests of a certain Lænas. I had very little time to gaze on them, however, for presently we entered the dining-room, near the door of which a bailiff was making up the accounts. What I most wondered at was that on the door-posts was a bundle of rods with axes, one end of which tapered off into the semblance of the beak of a ship with the legend:

TO GAIUS POMPEIUS TRIMALCHIO, AUGUSTAN COM-
MISSIONER, CINNAMUS, HIS STEWARD, HAS
CONSECRATED THIS.

Beneath the inscription a double lamp was suspended, and tablets were affixed to each door-post, one, if I remember rightly, bearing this announcement:

ON THE 30TH AND THE 31ST OF DECEMBER, OUR MASTER
DINES OUT.

On the other were painted the moon and the seven stars, and on a calendar a little knob served to indicate which days were lucky and which were unlucky.

Imbued with all these delightful facts, just as we were entering the dining-room a slave who had been assigned to this office called out, "Right foot first!" It quite upset us for a moment for fear lest any one of us should cross the threshold in an ill-omened way contrary to orders; but we managed to get our right feet in first, and just at this moment a slave, stripped of his outer clothing, threw himself at our feet and begged us to save him from punishment. He explained that the offence for which he was in peril was no great one; that he had simply allowed the steward's clothes to be stolen from the bath-house; and that these were worth only ten thousand sesterces. So we went back, right foot first, and begged the steward, who was counting his money in the outer hall, to let the slave off from punishment. The steward looked up disdainfully and replied:

"It isn't the loss that I'm vexed about, so much as the carelessness of this confounded slave! The clothes that he lost were my dinner-clothes which a dependent of mine gave me on my birthday. To be sure, they were of Tyrian purple, but they'd already been washed once. Well, well, I'll let him off for your sake."

Greatly impressed by this mark of favour, we had no sooner entered the dining-room than the slave whose punishment we had begged off rushed up to us, and to our surprise showered kisses upon us and thanked us for our kindness, saying finally:

"You'll find out pretty soon what sort of a man he is to whom you have done a favour. You know the master's wine is always the butler's gift."

Presently we took our places, and Alexandrian slaves poured water cooled with snow over our hands, while

others approached our feet and with great skill began
paring our corns; nor were they silent even over this
rather disagreeable task, but kept singing all the time. I
wanted to find out whether the whole household sang;
and so I asked for something to drink; whereupon a
slave served me, singing the while, like the others, a
shrill ditty; and in fact, every slave who was asked for
anything did exactly the same, so that you would have
imagined yourself in the green-room of a comic-opera
troupe rather than in the dining-room of a private
gentleman.

A very choice lot of *hors d'œuvres* was then brought
in; for we had already taken our places, all except Tri-
malchio himself for whom the seat of honour was
reserved. Among the objects placed before us was a
young ass made of Corinthian bronze and fitted with a
sort of pack-saddle which contained on one side pale
green olives and on the other side dark ones. Two dishes
flanked this; and on the margin of them Trimalchio's
name was engraved and the weight of the silver. Then
there were little bridge-like structures of iron which held
dormice seasoned with honey and poppyseed; and smok-
ing sausages were arranged on a silver grill which had
underneath it dark Syrian plums to represent black
coals, and scarlet pomegranate seeds to represent red-
hot ones.

In the midst of all this magnificence Trimalchio was
brought in to the sound of music and propped up on a
pile of well-stuffed cushions. The very sight of him
almost made us laugh in spite of ourselves; for his
shaven pate was thrust out of a scarlet robe, and around
his neck he had tucked a long fringed napkin with a
broad purple stripe running down the middle of it. On
the little finger of his left hand he wore a huge gilt
ring, and on the last joint of the next finger a ring that

appeared to be of solid gold, but having little iron stars upon it. Moreover, lest we should fail to take in all his magnificence, he had bared his right arm, which was adorned with a golden bracelet and an ivory circle fastened by a glittering clasp.

As he sat there picking his teeth with a silver tooth-pick, he remarked:

"Well, friends, it was just a bit inconvenient for me to dine now; but, so as not to delay you by my absence, I have denied myself a considerable amount of pleasure. You will allow me, however, to finish my game."

A slave came in carrying a backgammon-board of polished wood and also crystal dice; and I noted, as a very dainty detail, that instead of white and black pieces, he used, in playing, gold and silver coins. While he went on with his game, uttering as he played all sorts of Billingsgate, and while we were still eating the *hors d'œuvres*, a tray was brought in with a basket on which a wooden fowl was placed with its wings spread out in a circle after the fashion of setting hens. Immediately two slaves approached and amid a burst of music began to poke around in the straw, and having presently discovered there some pea-hens' eggs, they distributed them among the guests.

Trimalchio looked up during this operation and said, "Gentlemen, I had the hens' eggs placed under this fowl; but I'm rather afraid they have young chickens in them. Let's see whether they're still fit to suck."

So we took our spoons, which weighed not less than half a pound each, and broke the egg-shells, which were made of flour paste. As I did so, I was almost tempted to throw my egg on the floor, for it looked as though a chicken had just been formed inside; but when I heard an old diner-out by my side saying: "There's bound to be something good here," I thrust my finger through the shell and drew out a plump reed-bird, surrounded by yolk of egg well seasoned with pepper.

Trimalchio had now given up his game and called for the same dainties that we had had, inviting us with a loud voice to take a drink of honeyed wine also. Just then, however, at a signal given by music, all the dishes were swept off at once by a troop of slaves who sang over their work. Amid the bustle, a silver dish happened to fall on the floor, and when one of the servants started to pick it up, Trimalchio ordered him to be soundly cuffed, and told him to throw it down again; and presently there came in a servant, broom in hand, who swept up the silver dish along with the rest of the rubbish that lay upon the floor. After this, there entered two long-haired Æthiopian slaves carrying little bags such as are used for sprinkling the sand in the amphitheatre, and from these they poured wine over our hands; for water was not good enough to wash in at that house.

We complimented Trimalchio on all these elegant little details, and he observed complacently:

"Mars loves a fair field; so I had a separate table given to each guest. Incidentally, too, these wretched slaves will not overheat us by their crowding."

Immediately glass wine-jars were brought in, carefully sealed with plaster, and on their necks there were little tags with this legend: *"Falernian Opimian, one hundred years old."* While we were reading the tags, Trimalchio clapped his hands, and presently began to hold forth:

"Oh, dear, see how much longer-lived wine is than any poor mortal! Let's drink, then, and make merry, for wine is really life. Just look; here's genuine old Opimian. I didn't put nearly such good liquor as this on the table yesterday, and yet the people who dined with me then were socially very much superior to you."

As we were drinking the wine, and noting very carefully all his evidences of good taste, a slave brought him a silver skeleton ingeniously put together so that its limbs could be thrown out of joint and made to turn in any direction. This Trimalchio kept throwing again and again upon the table and making it assume all sorts of shapes, until at last he observed:

> "Alas and alack! what a nothing is man!
> We all shall be bones at the end of life's span:
> So let us be jolly as long as we can."

We were still complimenting him on his philosophy, when a course was served whose peculiarity attracted every one's attention; for a double tray in which it was set had the twelve signs of the Zodiac arranged in a circle and over each sign the chief butler had arranged some kind of food that was appropriate to it—over the Ram, some chick-peas with tendrils that curled like a ram's horns; over the Bull, a bit of beef; over the Twins, a pair of lamb's fries and kidneys; over the Crab, a garland; over the Lion, an African fig; over the Virgin, a sow's paunch; over the Balance, a pair of scales on one of which was placed a tart and on the other a cake; over the Scorpion, a crab; over Aquarius, a goose; over the Fish, two mullets. In the middle was a piece of fresh turf supporting a honeycomb. An Egyptian slave passed us some bread in a silver bread-plate, while Trimalchio croaked out a popular song from the musical farce called *The Garlic Eater*.

We were making ready to attack these absurd viands, though with no great eagerness, when Trimalchio remarked:

"Come, let's dine. This is really the very sauce of the dinner."

As he said this, four slaves came forward with a

solemn dance-step to the sound of music and took off the cover from the upper part of the tray. As soon as they had done this we saw, underneath the cover, capons and sows' breasts, and a hare with feathers stuck in its back so as to represent Pegasus. We observed also in the corner of the tray a figure of Marsyas, holding a wine-skin from which highly peppered fish-sauce flowed out over the fish, which swam in it as though they were in a brook. The slaves began to applaud, and we all joined in vigorously, laughing as we fell to, over these choice dainties. Trimalcho, equally delighted at this culinary surprise, called out, "Carver!" and at once a man provided with a knife and making elaborate gestures in time to the music, hacked up the meat in such a fashion that you would have imagined him to be a chariot-fighter slashing about to the sound of a water-organ. Trimalchio in a drawling tone kept up his exclamation, "Carver! Carver!" so that suspecting the repetition of this word to have some humorous intention, I did not hesitate to question the guest who sat beside me. He was quite familiar with the whole thing, and explained it by saying:

"Do you see the man who has carved the meat? His name is Carver. And so, as often as Trimalchio says, 'Carve her!' he calls the slave by name and at the same time tells him what to do."

* * *

The servants came and hung pieces of tapestry along the front of our couches, with hunting nets embroidered on them and huntsmen armed with spears, and all the paraphernalia of the hunt. We hardly knew what these preparations foreboded, when outside the dining-room a great hubbub began, and, lo and behold, Spartan dogs began dashing around the table. A tray followed them in which was set a boar of great size with a liberty-cap above him, while there hung from his tusks two little palm-leaf baskets, one full of nut-shaped dates, and the other full of Theban dates. All around were little pigs made of pastry and intent on the breasts, this signifying that the boar was supposed to represent a sow. These were intended for keepsakes to carry away.

The slave called Carver, who had mangled the capons, did not come in to cut up the boar; but instead, a big fellow with a beard, wearing leggings and with a light cloak on his shoulders, slashed the side of the boar vigorously with a drawn hunting-knife, till out of the gash live thrushes flew forth. Bird-catchers were at hand with long rods, and they caught the birds very quickly as they were fluttering around the dining-room. After Trimalchio had ordered a bird to be given to each guest, he added:

"Just see what a fine big acorn this wild boar had eaten!"

Directly after, the slaves went to the little baskets which hung from the boar's tusks, and distributed the dates among the guests to the accompaniment of music.

Meanwhile I in my remote corner was much distracted in mind as to why the boar had come in with a liberty-cap set upon him; so after I had eaten up all my sweetmeats, I resolved to question my informant.

"Oh," said he, "the slave here waiting on you can easily tell you that, for it isn't a puzzle but a perfectly obvious thing. This boar was brought on in the last course of yesterday's dinner, and was allowed by the guests to go untouched. So, you see, he comes back today to dinner like a freedman."

I fell to cursing my own stupidity, and asked no more questions lest I should appear never to have dined among gentlemen before.

While we were having this talk, a handsome young slave crowned with ivies and taking the part of Bacchus, the Free Father, passed grapes about in a basket and rendered his master's poems in a very shrill voice. Trimalchio turning in his direction said:

"Dionysus, I give you your freedom."

The slave at once took the liberty-cap off the boar and set it on his own head, upon which Trimalchio inquired of us all:

"Why am I of honourable birth? Because I have a Free Father."

We all commended this witty saying, and as the slave went around the table we kissed him warmly by way of congratulation.

After this course, Trimalchio got up to go to the lavatory; so that, feeling a certain freedom in the absence of our master, we began to draw each other into conversation. Dama, first of all, calling for a goblet, remarked:

"A day is nothing. Night comes before you can turn around. That's why I think there's nothing better than to go from your bed straight to the dining-room. It's a cold climate we have here. Even a bath scarcely warms me up. In fact, a hot drink is my wardrobe. I've had several stiff drinks already, so that I'm loaded for bear; for the wine has gone to my head."

*   *   *

The talk was passing back and forth in this way when Trimalchio returned, and, after wiping his forehead, washed his hands in perfumed water. Then, after a moment or two of delay, he said:

"You will excuse me, my friends, but my stomach for a good many days has been out of sorts, and the doctors don't know where they are at. However, I have been helped by pomegranate rind and a mixture of pitch and vinegar. I trust that my internal economy will soon feel ashamed of itself. Moreover there is a rumbling in my stomach so that you would imagine it to be a bull. And so if any of you wish to go out don't be bashful. You'll find all the conveniences. Flatulence goes to the head and kicks up a disturbance all through the body. I know of a good many persons who have died because they were too modest to speak the truth."

We thanked him for his kind generosity and concealed our laughter by taking numerous drinks. We had no idea, after all the rich things already eaten, that we hadn't yet, as they say, reached the top of the hill; but now, as soon as the table had been cleared off to the sound of music, three white swine were brought into the dining-room, decorated with muzzles and little bells. The slave who announced the guests said that one of the pigs was two years old, another three years old, and a third already six years old. I thought that rope dancers were coming in and that the pigs, as is often the case in the side-shows, were going to perform some remarkable tricks. But Trimalchio, putting an end to our suspense, said:

"Which of these pigs would you like to have served up at once on the table? Country cooks can prepare a fowl or a piece of beef and other trifles of that sort, but *my* cooks are accustomed to serve up whole calves boiled!"

Immediately he had the cook summoned; and not waiting for us to make a choice, he ordered the oldest pig to be slaughtered. Then he asked the slave in a loud voice:

"Which of my slave-gangs do you belong to?"

"The fortieth," said the cook.

"Were you purchased for me," said Trimalchio, "or born on my estate?"

"Neither," replied the cook. "I was left to you in Pansa's will."

"See then," said Trimalchio, "that you set the pig before us in good style. If you don't, I shall have you transferred to the gang of running footmen."

So the cook, after receiving this hint of his master's power, led the pig away to the kitchen. Trimalchio, looking at us with a genial countenance, then remarked:

"If the wine doesn't suit you, I'll have it changed; but you really must relish it. Thank God, I don't have to buy it; but everything that can make your mouth water is now produced on that estate of mine just outside the city, which I myself have not yet seen. It is said to be near Tarracina and Tarentum. I have a notion to add Sicily to my estates, so that when I take it into my head to go to Africa, I can sail between my own possessions. But tell me, Agamemnon, what rhetorical debate did you take part in today? For even though I don't plead cases myself, I have, nevertheless, some learning for home use. You are not to suppose that I think little of study. I have two libraries, one in Greek and one in Latin. So tell me, please, the subject of your debate."

"The subject," said Agamemnon, "is this: 'A poor man and a rich man were enemies—'"

"What on earth is a poor man?" interrupted Trimalchio.

"Oh, how witty!" cried out Agamemnon; and he went on to explain the subject of his argument. But Trimalchio at once interrupted him again and said:

"If all this really happened, there is no question to debate. If it didn't really happen, then there is nothing in it at all."

We received these and other sallies of his with the most effusive compliments.

"Tell me," said he, "my dear Agamemnon, do you remember the Twelve Labours of Hercules, or the story of Ulysses, and how the Cyclops twisted his thumb after he had been turned into a pig? When I was a boy I used to read these things in Homer; and with my own eyes I once saw the Sibyl at Cumæ hanging in a great jar, and when the young men asked her, 'Sibyl, what do you want?' she said, 'I want to die.'"

He had not yet finished blowing, when a tray was placed upon the table containing an immense pig. We fell to wondering at the rapidity with which it had been cooked; for we vowed that not even a barnyard fowl could have been thoroughly done in so short a time; and we wondered all the more because the pig seemed to us to be considerably larger than the live pig had appeared to be a little while before. Then Trimalchio, looking more and more intently at it, said:

"What? What? Hasn't this pig been drawn? No, by Jove, it hasn't! Just call the cook in."

Then when the cook, looking very much disconcerted, came to the table and admitted that he had forgotten to draw the pig, Trimalchio called out:

"What? Forgotten? One would imagine that this fellow had never handled pepper and salt. Strip him!"

Immediately the cook was stripped of his outer garments, and took his place in a dejected way between two slaves whose duty it was to administer a flogging. All the guests began to beg him off and said:

"This sort of thing often happens. We beg you, let him off, and if he should ever do it again, none of us will plead for him."

I, however, being a man of unflinching sternness,

could not restrain myself, but putting my mouth to Aga-memnon's ear, said:

"Really, this must be a most worthless slave. Could any one really forget to draw a pig? By Jove, I wouldn't forgive him if he had forgotten to clean even a fish."

But not so Trimalchio, whose countenance relaxed into a genial expression as he said:

"Well, since your memory is so bad, just draw him here in our presence."

So the cook put on his tunic and, seizing his knife, cut into the pig's stomach this way and that way with a careful hand. Instantly, after the cuts had been made and by reason of the pressure from within, sausages of various kinds came tumbling out. The whole company broke out into spontaneous applause and called out:

"Good for Gaius!"

The cook was rewarded with a drink, a silver crown, and a cup on a salver of Corinthian bronze. As Aga-memnon began to examine this salver very closely, Trimalchio remarked:

"I'm the only person who has genuine Corinthian bronze."

I imagined that, in accordance with the rest of his conceit, he was going to say that his bronze had been brought to him from Corinth; but he gave the thing a better turn than that by saying:

"Perhaps you would like to know why I'm the only man who has true Corinthian bronze. Well, it's because the bronze-dealer from whom I buy it is called Corin-thus; for how can anything be Corinthian unless one has a Corinthus to make it? And lest you imagine that I'm an ignorant person, I'll let you know that I under-stand how Corinthian bronze first came to be made. When Troy was taken, Hannibal, a clever fellow, and a sly dog, had all the bronze and gold and silver statues heaped up into one pile and built a fire under them. The various metals all melted down into a single one, and then from the blended mass the artisans took metal and made dishes, and plates, and statuettes. That's the way that Corinthian bronze was first produced—a single metal made out of all the others and itself neither one nor the other. You will excuse me for what I' am going to say, but for my part I prefer vessels of glass, for they have no smell to them. Indeed, if they couldn't be broken, I should prefer them even to gold. But now, of course, they're cheap. Nevertheless, there once lived an artisan who made a glass bottle that couldn't possibly be broken. He gained admission to the emperor's presence with his invention; and making as if to hand it over to Cæsar, he let it fall on the stone floor. Cæsar naturally supposed that it had been broken, but the artisan picked up the bottle from the floor, and, lo and behold, it was simply dented like a vessel of bronze. Then, taking a little hammer from his pocket, he straightened the bottle out with perfect ease. He naturally thought that he had made a great hit, especially after Cæsar asked him:

" 'Does any one else understand this manner of making glass?'

"Listen now: when the workman had said no, Cæsar ordered him to be beheaded, because if the secret of this manufacture should leak out, gold would become as cheap as dirt. I'm a good deal of a connoisseur in silver. I have a hundred large goblets, more or less, made of that metal, on which Cassandra is represented as killing her sons, and the dead boys are depicted so vividly that you would think they were alive. I have also a thousand sacrificial bowls which Mummius left

to my former owner, and on which is shown Dædalus
shutting up Niobe in the Trojan Horse. I have, too, the
battles of Hermeros and of Petrais depicted on drink-
ing-cups, all of them very heavy. In fact, I wouldn't
sell my special knowledge for any money."

While he was saying this, a boy let a cup fall on the
floor. Looking at him, Trimalchio said:

"Be off quickly and commit suicide, for you're a fool!"

Immediately the boy, with quivering lip, began to
beg. Trimalchio asked:

"Why do you beg of me as though I had done any-
thing to you? I advise you to beg yourself not to be
such a fool."

At length, however, persuaded by us, he let off the
boy, who at once ran about the table, while Trimalchio
exclaimed:

"Out with the water and in with the wine!"

We applauded his witty geniality, and especially
did Agamemnon applaud it, for he knew by what sort
of services he would get another invitation to dinner.
Trimalchio, after having been duly flattered, fell to
drinking merrily, and now being nearly drunk, he said:

"Aren't any of you going to ask my Fortunata to
dance for you? Believe me, no one can do the coochee-
coochee better than she."

And spreading his hands above his head, he gave us
an imitation of Syrus, the actor, while all his slaves
droned out together:

"Well done, by Jove! Well done!"

* * *

A troupe immediately came in, clattering their shields
and spears. Trimalchio sat up on his couch, and while
the Homeric actors in a pompous fashion began a dia-

logue in Greek verse, he read a book aloud in Latin
with a singsong tone of voice. Presently, when the rest
had become silent, he said:

"Do you know what play they're acting? Diomede
and Ganymede were two brothers. Their sister was
Helen. Agamemnon carried her off and put a deer in
her place for Diana, and so now Homer explains how
the Trojans and the Parentines are waging war. Aga-
memnon, you must know, came off victor and gave
his daughter Iphigenia to be the wife of Achilles. There-
upon Ajax went mad, and presently now will show us
the denouement."

As Trimalchio said this, the Homeric actors set up a
shout, and while the slaves bustled about, a boiled calf
was brought on in an enormous dish and with a helmet
placed upon it. The actor who took the part of Ajax
followed with a drawn sword, fell upon it as though
he were mad, and hacking this way and that he cut
up the calf and offered the bits to us on the point of
his sword, to our great surprise.

We had no time to admire these elegant proceedings,
for all of a sudden the ceiling of the room began to
rumble and the whole dining-room shook. In consterna-
tion I jumped up, fearing lest some acrobat should
come down through the roof; and all the other guests
in surprise looked upward as though they expected
some miracle from heaven. But lo and behold! the panels
of the ceiling slid apart, and suddenly a great hoop
as though shaken off from a hogshead was let down,
having gold crowns with jars of perfume hanging about
its entire circumference. These things we were invited
to accept as keepsakes, and presently a tray was set
before us full of cakes with an image of Priapus as a
centre-piece made of confectionery and holding in its
generous bosom apples of every sort and grapes, in the

usual fashion, as being the god of gardens. We eagerly
snatched at this magnificent display, and suddenly re-
newed our mirth at discovering a novel trick; for all
the cakes and all the apples, when pressed the least bit,
squirted forth saffron-water into our faces. Thinking
that there was something of a religious turn to a course
that was so suggestive of divine worship, we all rose
up together and pronounced the formula, "Success to
Augustus, Father of his Country!" But some of us, even
after this solemn act, snatched up the apples and filled
our napkins with them to carry away—a thing which
I did myself, for I thought that I could not heap up
enough presents in Giton's lap.

While this was going on, three slaves dressed in
white tunics entered, two of whom placed images of
the household gods upon the table, and the other one
carrying around a bowl of wine called out: "God bless
us all!" Trimalchio told us that one image was the
image of the God of Business, the second the image of
the God of Luck, and the third the image of the God of
Gain. There was a very striking bust of Trimalchio also,
and as everybody else kissed it, I was ashamed not to
do the same.

Presently, after all of us had invoked health and
happiness for ourselves, Trimalchio, looking in the direc-
tion of Niceros, said:

"You used to be better dinner-company. Somehow
or other now, though, you're absolutely mum and don't
open your head. I beg you, if you wish to oblige me,
tell me some of your experiences."

Niceros, flattered by the notice of his friend, said:

"May I never make another farthing if I am not
bursting with joy to see you in such good form; so let's
be as happy as we can, though I am awfully afraid of
these learned persons present for fear they should laugh

at me. However, that's their affair. I'll spin my yarn all the same; for what harm does any one do me who laughs at me? It's a great deal better to be laughed at, than to be laughed down."

And then he began the following story:

"When I was still a slave I used to live in a little street where Gavilla lives now. At that time, as the gods would have it, I fell in love with the wife of Terence, the innkeeper. You must have known her—her name was Melissa, a native of Tarentum, and a very kissable girl, too. Yet there wasn't anything wrong in my love for her, but I just liked her because she had such nice ways. Whatever I asked of her she gave me. If she made a penny she gave me half of it, and whatever I had I turned over to her to keep for me, and never was cheated. As it happened, her husband died at his place in the country and so I tried by hook and by crook to get to her, for you know a friend in need is a friend indeed. As chance would have it, my master had gone to Capua to look after some wares; and so, seizing the opportunity, I asked a man who was staying with us to go with me as far as the fifth milestone. He was a soldier, as bold as hell. We set off about cock-crow, while the moon was still shining as bright as midday. At last we came to a cemetery and my companion went off among the tombstones, while I took a rest, humming a tune and counting the monuments. Presently, when I looked at my companion, he had undressed and had put all his clothes by the roadside. My heart was in my mouth, and I sat there like a dead man; but he walked around his clothes and all of a sudden was turned into a wolf. Now don't imagine that I'm fooling you, for I wouldn't tell any lies for the world. But, as I was going on to say just now, he was turned into a wolf, and began to howl, and then ran off into the woods. At first

I didn't know where I was at, but when I went up to
his clothes to pick them up—lo and behold, they had
all been turned into stone! Well, I was about ready
to die of fright, but I drew my sword and all along
the road I cut and thrust at every shadow until I reached
my friend's house. When I entered as pale as a ghost
I almost fainted. The sweat was running down my
crotch, my eyes were fixed, and it was with the greatest
difficulty that I was brought to. Melissa wondered at
me to think that I was out so late and she said, 'If you'd
only come sooner you might have been of some help to
us; for a wolf has just entered the grounds and attacked
our flocks and made them bleed like a butcher. He
didn't get off unhurt, however, for one of my slaves
stuck him in the neck with a spear.' After I had heard
this I couldn't close my eyes; but as soon as it was
bright daylight, I hurried home like a plundered pedlar;
and when I came to the place where the clothes had
been turned into stone I found nothing there but a
pool of blood. But when I reached home, there lay my
friend the soldier, in his bed like a stuck pig with
the doctor putting a plaster on his neck. Then I knew
that he was a werewolf, and from that day on I couldn't
have eaten a mouthful of bread with him even if you
had killed me. I leave it to others to say what they think
of this; but if I've lied to you I hope your honours will
have nothing more whatever to do with me."

After we had all expressed our wonder, Trimalchio
remarked:

"If you'll believe me, my hair stood on end, because
I know that Niceros never tells any idle yarns, but he's
a straightforward fellow, and by no means fond of
hearing himself talk. Now I'm going to tell you a
frightful thing myself, as strange as an ass on the house-
tops. When I was still a long-haired boy—for even from

early youth I led a pretty gay life—my master's favourite died, a regular jewel, a rare fellow, and one that could turn his hand to anything. His poor mother was mourning over him and we were all of us in a very sad state of mind, when suddenly we heard witches shrieking so that you would imagine that it was a pack of hounds chasing a hare. We had with us at that time a Cappadocian, a tall fellow, very bold and so strong that he could have picked up a mad bull. He drew his sword valiantly, rushed out of the house, and, wrapping his left arm carefully in his cloak, he thrust a hag right through the middle. We heard a groan, yet (really, I'm not lying) we couldn't see the witches themselves. Presently, however, our man came in again and threw himself down on the bed, and—lo and behold, his body was all black and blue as though it had been scourged because, no doubt, an evil hand had touched him! Closing the door, we went on about our business, but when the mother went to embrace her son's body, she touched it and found nothing but a dummy made of litter, with no heart, no vitals, nothing at all. So you see that the witches had swooped down on the boy and put a puppet in his place. Believe me, there *are* witches, real night hags, and they turn everything upside down. But as for this stout fellow of ours, after what had happened he never came to himself again, and after a few days he died raving crazy."

We all expressed alike our wonder and our entire belief, and we touched the table with our lips, begging the night hags to stay in their own haunts when the time came for us to go home from dinner.

❀   ❀   ❀

A little later, after Trimalchio had ordered the second part of the dinner to be brought in, his slaves took

away all the tables and brought in new ones, sprinkling
the floor with red and yellow sawdust, and also with
mica ground to powder, a thing which I had never
before seen done. Straightway Trimalchio observed:

"I could be perfectly satisfied myself with this course
alone, for you now have really a second dinner. Still,
if there's anything else especially choice, bring it on."

Meanwhile an Alexandrian slave who was serving
the hot drinks, began to imitate the song of the night-
ingale, Trimalchio calling out from time to time:

"Change your tune!" and then, lo and behold, came
another diversion; for the slave who sat at Habinnas's
feet, having got the hint, I imagine, from his master,
sung out all of a sudden in a droning voice these lines
from the *Æneid*:

> "Meanwhile Æneas, with majestic sweep,
> Skimmed with his fleet the waters of the deep."

A more excruciating sound never struck my ears;
for, apart from the crescendo and diminuendo of his
barbarous rendering, he interpolated other lines, so that
for the first time I found even Virgil tiresome. When
he had finished, however, Habinnas applauded him,
remarking:

"He never had to learn these things, but I educated
him up to it by sending him out to listen to the per-
formances in the street, with the result that he hasn't
his match at imitating the mule-drivers and the mounte-
banks. He's awfully clever, for he can take the part
of a cobbler, or a cook, or a baker; in fact, he is a per-
fect Jack-of-all-trades. To be sure, he has two faults,
apart from which he is really out of sight—he has been
circumcised and he snores, for as to the fact that he's
squint-eyed, I don't mind that, for they say that Venus
herself has a cast in her eyes. These two faults, how-

ever, have this result: he is never silent and he keeps an eye on everything. I paid three hundred denarii for him."

Scintilla interrupted him in the midst of his talk, observing:

"Yes, but you don't tell all the accomplishments of this wretched slave. He is a pimp, and I shall see that he gets branded for it."

Trimalchio laughed at this.

"I recognize in him," said he, "a real Cappadocian. He's very good to himself, and, by Jove! I praise him for it, for this is the only way for a man to do. But don't be jealous, Scintilla. Depend upon it, I understand you both. As sure as I'm alive, I used in my time to be *aux petits soins* with my master's wife, so that even my master had a sort of inkling of it, and that's why he had me transferred to the stewardship of his country place. But least said, soonest mended."

On this the miserable slave, precisely as though he had received high praise, pulled a clay lamp out of his pocket, and for half an hour or more gave us an imitation of trumpeters, Habinnas chiming in, flipping his lower lip with his finger. At last the slave sat up in the midst of us and gave us an imitation of flute-players with their instruments, and later, putting on his cloak and taking a whip, he took the part of mule-drivers, until Habinnas called him and kissed him and offered him a drink, saying:

"Bully for you, Massa! I'm going to give you a pair of brogans!"

These tiresome proceedings would never have come to an end had not a dessert been brought in, consisting of thrushes made of pastry and stuffed with nuts and raisins. Following these came quinces stuck full of thorns so as to represent hedgehogs. One could have stood these things, had not the disgusting abundance of the course made us prefer to die of hunger; for after there had been set before us, as we supposed, a fat goose surrounded by fish and every kind of birds, Trimalchio remarked:

"My friends, whatever you see set before you here has been made out of one single kind of material."

Thereupon, I, being a man of great insight, immediately understood what it was, as I thought, and looking at Agamemnon I said:

"I shouldn't be surprised if all these things were made of filth, or at any rate, out of mud, for I have seen at Rome at the time of the Saturnalia the very same thing in the way of a dinner."

But before I had finished speaking, Trimalchio observed:

"As I hope to grow in wealth and lose in flesh, this cook of mine made all these things out of pork. There cannot be a more valuable fellow to have around than he. Should he take a fancy to do so, he could make you fish out of a sow's paunch, and pigeon out of bacon, a turtle-dove out of ham, and a chicken out of a knuckle of beef. And that's why, by a happy thought of mine, I have given him a first rate name, for he is called Dædalus; and because he has his wits about him I brought him from Rome a present of some knives made of Noric steel."

These he at once ordered to be brought out, and after we had looked at them he expressed his admiration. He even made us test the edges of the knives on our cheeks.

All of a sudden there came in two slaves, who had been quarrelling apparently at the town-pump; for they still carried their water-jars on their necks. While Trimalchio was hearing the case between these two brawlers, neither one of them accepted his decision, but each

broke the other's water-jar with a club. In our surprise
at the rudeness of the drunken pair, we fixed our eyes
on them as they quarrelled, and I noted that out of
the broken vessels came tumbling oysters and scallops
which a slave collected in a dish and carried around.
The clever cook matched these dainties, for he had
served up snails on a silver gridiron, singing all the
time himself with a quavering and disagreeable voice.

*　　*　　*

After some trifling dainties had been consumed, Tri-
malchio, looking around at the servants, said:
"Well, haven't you had your dinner yet? Go and get
it, and let other servants come here and wait upon us."
Directly, then, another set came in, those who went
out exclaiming, "Farewell, Gaius!" and those who came
in saluting him with, "Hail, Gaius!" Soon after, for the
first time, our mirth was checked; for when a young
slave who was by no means bad looking had come in
among the new servants, Trimalchio pounced upon him
and began to kiss him for a long time. Whereupon
Fortunata, in order to prove her equal right in the
household, began to abuse Trimalchio, styling him the
scum of the earth and a disgraceful person. At last she
called him a dog. Taking offence at this vituperation,
Trimalchio threw a cup in her face, and she, as though
she had lost an eye, shrieked and placed her trembling
hands before her face. Scintilla also was very much
disturbed and hid the cowering woman in her robe.
A slave at once in an officious maner placed a cold jug
against her cheek leaning upon which Fortunata began
to moan and cry.
On his side Trimalchio exclaimed:
"How now? The jade doesn't remember that I took
her off the stage and made an honest woman of her;

she puffs herself up like a frog and fouls her own nest
—a faggot and not a lady. But, as the saying goes, one
who was born in a garret doesn't fit a palace. So
help me gracious, I'll see that this clodhopping tragedy
queen is brought up with a round turn. I, when I was
only a poor devil, had a chance to marry a fortune of
ten million sesterces, and you know I'm not lying about
it. Agatho, who sold perfume to a lady who lived next
door, took me aside and said: 'I beg you not to let your
race perish from the earth'; but just because I was a
good fellow and didn't want to seem fickle, I fastened
this ball-and-chain to my leg. Very well, now, I'll teach
you to claw me, and just to show you on the spot what
you've brought upon yourself, I order you, Habinnas,
not to put her statue on my tomb, lest even after my
death I should be having scraps with her. In fact, to
teach her how severe I can be, I forbid her to kiss me
when I am dead."

After this thunderous blast, Habinnas fell to begging
him not to be angry, saying:

"None of us is perfect. We are men, you know, not
gods."

And Scintilla also, weeping, addressed him in the
same way and exhorted him by his better nature to be
mollified, calling him, "Gaius." On this Trimalchio could
not keep back his tears and remarked:

"I beg you, Habinnas, as you hope to be lucky, if I
have done anything wrong, just spit in my face. I kissed
this excellent young slave, not because of his good looks
but because of his intelligence. He can say his table of
'ten times,' he can read a book at sight, and he's saved
up some money for himself out of his daily food allow-
ance, and bought a little stool and two ladles with his
own money. So doesn't he deserve to have me keep my
eye on him? But of course Fortunata won't have it. Isn't

that so, you bandy-legged creature? You'd better be thankful for your blessings, you bird of prey, and not make me show my teeth, you dainty darling, or else you shall find out what my anger is like. You know *me!* What I've once decided on is as sure as fate. But come, let's think of something more cheerful. I hope you're all comfortable, my friends. I used to be myself the same sort of person that you all are, but, by my own merits, I became what I am. It's brain that makes men, and everything else is all rot. One man'll tell you one rule of life, and another'll tell you another. But *I* say, 'Buy cheap and sell dear,' and so you see I'm just bursting with wealth. (Well, grunter, are you still crying? Pretty soon I'll give you something to cry for!) Well, as I was going on to say, my clever management brought me to my present good fortune. When I came from Asia, I was about the height of this candle-stick here, and, in fact, I used to measure myself against it every day. And so as to get a beard on my mug, I used to smear my lips with lamp-oil. I was a great favourite with my master for fourteen years, and I was on pretty good terms with my master's wife. You understand what I mean. I'm not saying anything about it, because I'm not one of the boastful kind; but, as the gods would have it, I was really master in the house myself and I took his fancy greatly. Well, there's no need of a long story. He made me his residuary legatee, and I came into a fortune fit for a senator. But nobody never gets enough. I became crazy to go into business; and, not to bore you, I had five ships built, loaded them with wine (and wine at that time was worth its weight in gold), and sent them to Rome. You'd imagine that it had been actually planned that way, for every blessed ship was wrecked, and that's fact and not fable. On one single day the sea swallowed down thirty million sesterces. Do you think I gave up?

Not much! This loss just whetted my appetite as though
it had been a mere nothing. I had other ships built,
bigger and better, and they were luckier too, so that
everybody said I was a plucky fellow. You know the
proverb, that it takes great courage to build a great ship.
I loaded them with wine once more, with bacon, beans,
ointment, and slaves, and at that crisis Fortunata did a
very nice thing, for she sold all her jewelry and even all
her clothes, and put a hundred gold pieces in my hand.
And this was really the germ of my good fortune. What
the gods wish happens quickly. In a single round trip I
piled up ten million sesterces, and immediately bought
in all the lands that had belonged to my former owner.
I built me a house and bought all the cattle that were
offered for sale, and whatever I touched grew as rich as
a honeycomb. After I began to have more money than
my whole native land contains, then, says I, enough. I
retired from business and began to lend money to freed-
men. A fortune-teller, a young Greek named Serapa, a
man who was on very good terms with the gods, gave
me some points when I was making up my mind to go
out of business. He told me of things that even I had for-
gotten. He set them forth down to the finest possible
point. He knew my very insides, and the only thing he
didn't tell me was what I had had for dinner the day
before. You would imagine that he had lived in the same
house with me. I say, Habinnas, you were there, I think.
Didn't he say this? *'You have married a wife from such-
and-such a position. You are unlucky in your friends.
No one is ever as grateful to you as he ought to be.
You have great estates. You are cherishing a viper in
your bosom.'* And he also told me something that I
haven't mentioned—that there remains to me now of life
just thirty years, four months, and two days. Moreover,
I'm going to come into a legacy pretty soon. That's what

my horoscope tells me. But if I shall be so lucky as to unite my Apulian estates, I shall not have lived in vain. In the mean time, while my luck held, I built this house which, as you know, was once a mere shanty, but is now a palace. It has four regular dining-rooms, twenty bed-rooms, two marble porticoes, an upstairs dining-room, a bedroom in which I sleep myself, a sitting-room for this viper here, and an excellent janitor's office. It holds as many strangers as a hotel. Indeed, when Scaurus came here, he wouldn't put up anywhere else, even though he has his father's house to go to, on the sea-shore. There are a good many other things that I'm going to show you presently; but, believe me, a man is worth just as much as he has in his pocket; and according to what you hold in your hand so will you be held in es-teem by others. This is what your friend has to say to you, a man who once, as they say, was a cat, but now is a king. Meanwhile, Stichus, bring out my grave-clothes in which I want to be buried, and bring out also some ointment, and a snack from that wine-jar there from which I wish to have my bones washed."

Stichus immediately complied and brought a white coverlet and a purple tunic into the dining-room; where-upon Trimalchio asked us to feel whether they were all wool or not, and then, smiling, he said:

"See to it, Stichus, that neither the mice nor the moths get hold of these; for if they do I'll have you burnt alive. I want to be buried in a glorious fashion, so that all the people will bless me."

Then he opened a jar of ointment and anointed us all, saying as he did it:

"I hope that everything will please me as much when I'm dead as it does while I'm alive."

Then he ordered wine to be poured into a wine-cooler and observed:

"Consider that you have received an invitation to my funeral."

The thing had gone to a disgusting extreme, when Trimalchio, sodden with drink, hit upon a new sort of exhibition, and had hornblowers brought into the dining-room. Then, having been propped up on a number of pillows, he sprawled himself out upon the lowest couch and said:

"Imagine that I am dead. Say something nice about me."

The hornblowers blew a funeral march; and one of them, the slave of the undertaker, who was really the most respectable man in the crowd, blew such a tremendous blast that he roused up the whole neighbourhood. The police who were on duty in the vicinity, thinking that Trimalchio's house was on fire, suddenly broke down the door, and rushed in with axes and water, as was their right. Seizing this very favourable opportunity, we gave Agamemnon the slip, and made our escape as hastily as though we were really fleeing from a conflagration.

There was no light in front of the house to show us the way as we wandered about, nor did the intense stillness of the night give us any hope of meeting wayfarers with torches. The effects of the wine, moreover, and our ignorance of the locality would have confused us even had it been in the daytime; and so, after we had dragged our bleeding feet for almost an hour over the sharp stones and bits of broken pottery that lay in the street, we were at last saved by the ingenuity of Giton; for he, fearing to lose his way even in daylight, had cleverly marked all the pillars and columns of the houses with chalk, and these marks were visible even in the thick darkness, and by their whiteness showed us the way as we wandered about. Nevertheless, we had considerable trouble even after we reached our inn; for the old woman who kept it, having passed a good deal of time in drinking with her various guests, would not have known it even though the place had been on fire. We might very well, therefore, have spent the entire night on the doorsteps had not Trimalchio's courier with ten wagons come upon us, and after clamouring for a little while, at last smashed the door of the inn and thus enabled us to enter.

MARTIAL

(Marcus Valerius Martialis, 40? A.D.–?104 A.D.)

❋

From the Epigrams

❋

I:32 To Sabidius
Translated by Thomas Brown

I do not love thee, Dr. Fell;
The reason why I cannot tell.
But this I know, and know full well,
I do not love thee, Dr. Fell.

❋

II:4 To Ammianus
Translated by F. A. Wright

You fondle your mother and she fondles you:
    You're her "brother" and she is your "sister."
Why those mischievous names, I should much like to
    know?
    Why are you not her son when you've kissed her?
If you think that such conduct is merely a jest,
    You're mistaken, my innocent brother;
When a mother as "Sister" would fain be addressed,
    She's neither the one nor the other.

565

II:35 Your legs so like the moon
Translated by W. T. Webb

Your legs, so like the moon at crescent,
    A bathing-tub will scarce look neat in;
So here I send you, for a present,
    A drinking-horn to wash your feet in.

II:84 Thou art a cuckold
Translated by Sir Charles Sedley

Thou art a cuckold; so great Cæsar was:
    Eat'st till thou spew'st; Antonius did the same:
Thou lovest whores; Jove loves a bucksome lass:
    But that thou'rt whipped is thy peculiar shame.

IV:12 At night no man do you refuse
Translated by F. A. Wright

At night no man do you refuse,
    And what is worse, dear Nancy,
There's nothing you refuse to do,
    Whatever be his fancy.

IV:69 Setine and Massic at your board abound
Translated by J. A. Pott

Setine and Massic at your board abound,
Yet some aver your wine is hardly sound;
'Twas this relieved you of four wives, they say;
A libel—but I will not dine today.

V:34 Thou Mother dead
Translated by J. A. Pott

Thou Mother dead, and thou my Father's shade,
To you I now commit the gentle maid,
    Erotion, my little love, my sweet;
    Let not her shuddering spirit fear to meet
The ghosts, but soothe her lest she be afraid.
How should a baby heart be undismayed
    To pass the lair where Cerberus is laid?
    The little six-year maiden gently greet.
Dear reverend spirits, give her kindly aid
And let her play in some Elysian glade,
    Lisping my name sometimes—and I entreat,
    Lie softly on her, kindly earth; her feet,
Such tiny feet, on thee were lightly laid.

V:43 Thaïs for black
Translated by W. T. Webb

Thaïs for black, Lycænia
  For milk-white teeth is known.
For why? Lycænia's teeth were bought,
  While Thaïs wears her own.

VI:66 In Fabius' will
Translated by J. A. Pott

In Fabius' will sole legatee,
  Why is Labienus glad?
In courting the testator, he
  Had spent far more than Fabius had.

X:47 The Meanes to Attaine Happy Life
Translated by Henry Howard, Earl of Surrey

Martiall, the thinges that doe attain
The happy life, be these I finde,
The riches left, not got with pain;
The fruitfull ground, the quiet minde,
The egall frend; no grudge, no strife;
No charge of rule, nor governaunce;
Without disease, the healthful life;
The houshold of continuance:

The meane dyet, no delicate fare;
Trew wisedome joynde with simplenesse;
The night discharged of all care;
Where wine the witte may not oppresse.
The faithfull wife, without debate;
Such slepes as may begile the night;
Contented with thine owne estate,
Ne wish for death, ne feare his might.

X: 47 The things that make a life to please

Translated by Sir Richard Fanshawe

The things that make a life to please
(Sweetest Martial), they are these:
Estate inherited, not got:
A thankful field, hearth always hot:
City seldom, law-suits never:
Equal friends agreeing ever:
Health of body, peace of mind:
Sleeps that till the morning bind:
Wise simplicity, plain fare:
Not drunken nights, yet loos'd from care:
A sober, not a sullen spouse:
Clean strength, not such as his that ploughs;
Wish only what thou art, to be;
Death neither wish, nor fear to see.

✳

X:61 Epitaph on Erotion
Translated by Leigh Hunt

Underneath this greedy stone,
Lies little sweet Erotion;
Whom the Fates, with hearts as cold,
Nipp'd away at six years old.
Thou, whoever thou mayst be,
That hast this small field after me,
Let the yearly rites be paid
To her little slender shade;
So shall no disease or jar
Hurt thy house, or chill thy Lar;
But this tomb be here alone
The only melancholy stone.

TACITUS

(Publius Cornelius Tacitus, 55? A.D.-?117 A.D.)

From the Annals

Translated by John Jackson

*

The Government of Rome

KINGS held dominion in the city of Rome from its
foundation: Lucius Brutus instituted liberty and
the consulate. Dictatorships were resorted to in tempo-
rary emergencies: neither the power of the decemvirs
continued in force beyond two years, nor the consular au-
thority of the military tribunes for any length of time.
The domination of Cinna did not continue long, nor that
of Sulla: the influence of Pompey and Crassus quickly
merged in Cæsar: the arms of Lepidus and Antony in
Augustus, who, with the title of prince, took under his
command the commonwealth, exhausted with civil dis-
sensions. But the affairs of the ancient Roman people,
whether prosperous or adverse, have been recorded by
writers of renown. Nor were there wanting authors of
distinguished genius to have composed the history of
the times of Augustus, till by the spirit of flattery, which
became prevalent, they were deterred. As to Tiberius,
Caligula, Claudius, and Nero, whilst they yet reigned the
histories of their times were falsified through fear; and

after they had fallen, they were written under the influence of recent detestation. Thence my own design of recounting a few incidents respecting Augustus, and those towards the latter part of his life; and, after that, of giving a history of the reign of Tiberius and the rest; uninfluenced by resentment and partiality, as I stand aloof from the causes of them.

When, after the fall of Brutus and Cassius, there remained none to fight for the commonwealth; when Sextus Pompeius was utterly defeated at Sicily; and Lepidus being deprived of his command, and Mark Antony slain, there remained no leader even to the Julian party but Octavius; having put off the name of triumvir, styling himself consul, and pretending that all he aimed at was the jurisdiction attached to the tribuneship for the protection of the commons; when he had cajoled the soldiery by donations, the people by distribution of corn, and men in general by the charms of peace, he (Octavius) began by gradations to exalt himself over them; to draw to himself the functions of the senate and of the magistrate, and the framing of the laws; in which he was thwarted by no man: the boldest spirits having fallen in some or other of the regular battles, or by proscription; and the surviving nobility being distinguished by wealth and public honours, according to the measure of their promptness to bondage; and as these innovations had been the cause of aggrandisement to them, preferring the present state of things with safety, to the revival of ancient liberty with personal peril. Neither were the provinces averse to that condition of affairs; since they mistrusted the government of the senate and people, on account of the contentions among the great and the avarice of the magistrates: while the protection of the laws was enfeebled and borne down by violence, intrigue, and bribery.

Moreover, Augustus, as supports to his domination, raised his sister's son, Claudius Marcellus, a mere youth, to the dignity of pontiff and curule ædile; aggrandised by two successive consulships Marcus Agrippa, a man meanly born, but an accomplished soldier, and the companion of his victories; and soon, on the death of Marcellus, chose him for his son-in-law. The sons of his wife, Tiberius Nero and Claudius Drusus, he dignified with the title of Imperator, though there had been no diminution in the members of his house. For into the family of the Cæsars he had already adopted Lucius and Caius, the sons of Agrippa; and though they had not yet laid aside the puerile garment, vehement had been his ambition to see them declared princes of the Roman youth, and even designed to the consulship; while he affected to decline the honours for them. Upon the decrease of Agrippa, they were cut off, either by a death premature but natural, or by the arts of their stepmother Livia; Lucius on his journey to the armies in Spain, Caius on his return from Armenia, ill of a wound: and as Drusus had been long since dead, Tiberius Nero was the only survivor of his stepsons. On him every honour was accumulated (to that quarter all things inclined); he was by Augustus adopted for his son, assumed colleague in the empire, partner in the tribunitian authority, and presented to the several armies; not from the secret machinations of his mother, as heretofore, but at her open suit. For over Augustus, now very aged, she had obtained such absolute sway, that he banished into the isle of Planasia his only surviving grandson, Agrippa Posthumus; a person destitute indeed of liberal accomplishments, and a man of clownish brutality with great bodily strength, but convicted of no heinous offence. The emperor, strange to say, set Germanicus, the son of Drusus, over eight legions quartered upon the Rhine, and or-

dered that he should be engrafted into his family by
Tiberius by adoption, though Tiberius had then a son
of his own on the verge of manhood; but the object was
that he might stand firm by having many to support and
protect him. War at that time there remained none, ex-
cept that in Germany, kept on foot rather to blot out
the disgrace sustained by the loss of Quintilius Varus,
with his army, than from any ambition to enlarge the
empire, or for any advantage worth contending for. In
profound tranquillity were affairs at Rome. The magis-
trates retained their wonted names; of the Romans, the
younger sort had been born since the battle of Actium,
and even most of the old during the civil wars: how
few were then living who had seen the ancient free state!

The character of the government thus totally changed;
no traces were to be found of the spirit of ancient in-
stitutions. The system by which every citizen shared in
the government being thrown aside, all men regarded
the orders of the prince as the only rule of conduct and
obedience; nor felt they any anxiety for the present,
while Augustus, yet in the vigour of life, maintained
the credit of himself and house, and the peace of the
state. But when old age had crept over him, and he was
sinking under bodily infirmities—when his end was at
hand, and thence a new source of hopes and views was
presented—some few there were who began to talk idly
about the blessings of liberty: many dreaded a civil war
—others longed for one; while far the greatest part
were occupied in circulating various surmises reflecting
upon those who seemed likely to be their masters: "That
Agrippa was naturally stern and savage, and exasperated
by contumely; and neither in age nor experience equal
to a task of such magnitude. Tiberius, indeed, had ar-
rived at fulness of years, and was a distinguished cap-
tain, but possessed the inveterate and inherent pride

of the Claudian family; and many indications of cruel
nature escaped him, in spite of all his arts to disguise
it; that even from his early infancy he had been trained
up in an imperial house; that consulships and triumphs
had been accumulated upon him while but a youth. Not
even during the years of his abode at Rhodes, where
under the plausible name of retirement, he was in fact
an exile, did he employ himself otherwise than in medi-
tating future vengeance, studying the arts of simulation,
and practising secret and abominable sensualities. That
to these considerations was added that of his mother, a
woman with the ungovernable spirit peculiar to her sex;
that the Romans must be under bondage to a woman,
and moreover to two youths, who would meanwhile op-
press the state, and, at one time or other, rend it piece-
meal."

While the public mind was agitated by these and
similar discussions, the illness of Augustus grew daily
more serious, and some suspected nefarious practices
on the part of his wife. For some months before, a
rumour had gone abroad that Augustus, having singled
out a few to whom he communicated his purpose, had
taken Fabius Maximus for his only companion, had
sailed over to the island of Planasia, to visit Agrippa;
that many tears were shed on both sides, many tokens
of mutual tenderness shown, and hopes from thence
conceived that the youth would be restored to the
household gods of his grandfather. That Maximus had
disclosed this to Martia, his wife—she to Livia; and that
the emperor was informed of it: and that Maximus, not
long after, dying (it is doubtful whether naturally, or
by means sought for the purpose), Martia was observed,
in her lamentations at his funeral, to upbraid herself
as the cause of her husband's destruction. Howsoever
that matter might have been, Tiberius was scarce

entered Illyrium when he was summoned by a letter from his mother, forwarded with speed; nor is it fully known whether, at his return to Nola, he found Augustus yet breathing, or already lifeless. For Livia had carefully beset the palace, and all the avenues to it, with vigilant guards; and favourable bulletins were from time to time given out, until, the provisions which the conjuncture required being completed, in one and the same moment were published the departure of Augustus, and the accession of Tiberius.

The first atrocity of this new reign was the murder of Posthumus Agrippa: the assassin, a bold and determined centurion, found him destitute of arms, and little apprehending such a destiny, yet was scarce able to dispatch him. Of this transaction Tiberius avoided any mention in the senate; he pretended that orders had been given by his father, in which he enjoined the tribune appointed to the custody of his person, "not to delay to slay Agrippa whensoever he himself had completed his last day." It is very true, that Augustus, having made many and vehement complaints of the young man's demeanour, had obtained that his exile should be sanctioned by a decree of the senate; but he never hardened himself to the extent of inflicting death upon any of his kindred; neither is it credible that he murdered his grandson for the security and establishment of his stepson. More probable it is, that Tiberius and Livia, the former from motives of fear, the latter impelled by a stepmother's aversion, expedited the destruction of this young man, the object of their jealousy and hatred. When the centurion, according to the custom of the army, acquainted Tiberius "that his commands were executed," he answered, "he had commanded no such execution, and that he must appear before the senate, and be answerable to them for it." When this came to the knowledge of Sallustius Crispus, who shared in his secret counsels, and had sent the centurion the warrant, he dreaded that he should be arraigned on a false charge of the assassination; and perceiving it to be equally perilous to confess the truth or invent a falsehood, he warned Livia "that the secrets of the palace, the counsels of friends, and the ministerial acts of soldiers, should not be divulged; that Tiberius should not enfeeble the force of princely authority by referring all things to the senate; that such were the conditions of sovereign authority, that an account should not stand good otherwise than if it were rendered to one alone."

Now at Rome, consuls, senators, and knights were rapidly degenerating into a state of abject servitude; and the higher the quality of any, so much the more false and forward; all carefully framing their countenances so as not to appear overjoyed at the departure of the prince, nor over sorrowful in the commencement of a new reign, they intermingled tears with gladness, and wailings with adulation. Sextus Pompeius and Sextus Apuleius, at that time consuls, took first an oath of fidelity to Tiberius; then administered it to Seius Strabo and Caius Turranius; the former, captain of the prætorian guards, the other, intendant of the public stores; next, to the senate, to the people, and to the soldiery: for Tiberius began all things by the consuls, as if the ancient republic still subsisted, and he were yet unresolved about assuming the sovereign rule; even his edict for summoning the senate, he issued not but under the title of the tribunitian power, received by him under Augustus. The words of the edict, too, were few, and extremely modest. It imported that "he should consult them on the funeral honours proper to be paid his father: for himself, he would not depart from the corpse; and that this alone of the public functions he took upon himself." Yet when Augustus was dead, he had given the word to the prætorian cohorts, as Imperator; sentinels were stationed about the palace; had soldiers under arms, and all the other appendages of a court; went guarded into the forum, guarded to the senate; wrote letters to the armies in the style of one who had obtained princedom; nor did he ever hesitate, but when he spoke to the senate. The chief cause proceeded from fear lest Germanicus, who was master of so many legions, numberless auxiliaries, of the allies, who was wonderfully in favour with the people, might wish rather to possess the empire than to wait for it: he likewise sacrificed somewhat to fame, that he might seem chosen and called to the empire by the voice of the people, rather than to have crept darkly into it by the intrigues of a wife, and by adoption from a superannuated prince. It was afterwards found, that this irresolution was counterfeited, that he might also penetrate into the designs and inclinations of the great men: for, warping their words and their looks into crimes, he stored them up in his heart.

On the first day the senate met, he would suffer no other business to be transacted but that about the funeral of Augustus, whose last will, brought in by the vestal virgins, appointed Tiberius and Livia his heirs. Livia was adopted into the Julian family, and dignified with the name of Augusta: in the second degree of succession he appointed his grandchildren and their children; and in the third degree he had named the great men of Rome, most of them hated by him: but out of vainglory, and for future renown. His legacies were not beyond the measure of a Roman citizen; except that he left to the Roman people 435,000 great sesterces, part to them as a body, and part to be distributed individually: to every soldier of the prætorian guards a thousand small sesterces; to every soldier of the Roman legions, and to every man in the cohorts of Roman citizens, three hundred. The funeral honours were next considered. Of these, the most signal appeared the following: Asinius Gallus moved, that "the funeral should pass through the triumphal gate": Lucius Arruntius, "that the titles of the laws which he had made, and the names of all the nations which he had conquered, should be carried before the corpse": Valerius Messala added that "the oath of allegiance to Tiberius should be renewed every year"; and being asked by Tiberius, "whether at his instigation he had made that motion?" Messala said "he spoke it of his own accord; nor would he ever be determined by any but his own counsel, in things which concerned the commonweal; even though with the hazard of giving offence." This was the only form of flattery which was left to the age. The senators then concurred in a loud cry, "that upon their own shoulders they must bear the body to the pile." Tiberius granted the request with modest insolence, and cautioned the people by an edict, "that they would not insist that the corpse of Augustus should be burnt rather in the forum, than in the field of Mars, which was the place appointed, and act as they did on a former occasion, when from an excess of zeal they had disturbed the funeral solemnities of the sainted Julius." On the funeral day the soldiers were stationed as for a guard, a circumstance which excited deep derision in those who had either seen, or had received from their fathers, a description of that day of slavery yet crude and immature, and of liberty unsuccessfully reclaimed, when the assassination of the dictator Cæsar was regarded by some as a deed of unexampled atrocity, by others an achievement of superlative glory; "that now an aged prince, who had been long in possession of power, after having provided resources for his heirs, to be employed against the commonwealth—that such an one, forsooth, must be protected by a guard of soldiers in order that his interment might be undisturbed!"

Much discourse concerning Augustus himself followed: the multitude expressing their wonderment at things of no importance; "that the last day of his life, and the first of his reign, was the same; that he died at Nola, in the same house, and in the same chamber, where his father Octavius died. Even the number of his consulships, equal to those of Valerius Corvinus and of Caius Marius together, was much talked of: that he had exercised the power of the tribuneship seven-and-thirty continued years: that he was one-and-twenty times proclaimed Imperator; with other honours repeated to him, or created for him." On the other hand, by men of deeper discernment, his life was variously lauded or censured. His admirers said "that by his filial piety to his father Cæsar, and the necessities of the republic, where the laws no longer governed, he had been driven into civil war; which can never be begun or carried on by just and gentle means. Indeed, provided he might be revenged on the murderers of his father, he had made many sacrifices to Antony; many to Lepidus: but when Lepidus became torpid with sloth, and Antony was lost in sensuality, there was then no other remedy for his distracted country than the sovereignty of one: that the republic, however, had not been settled by him in the form of a kingdom or a dictatorship, but placed under the government of one with the title of prince; that by him the empire was fenced in by the ocean and rivers far remote; the legions, the provinces, the navy, and all things were systematically connected; justice was dispensed to the citizens, moderation observed towards the allies, and Rome herself was adorned with magnificent structures: in a very few instances had force been employed, and in those only to secure the peace of the whole."

In answer to this it was urged that "his filial piety, and the exigencies of the republic, were laid hold of as a pretence; but that from an ardent lust of reigning, the veteran soldiers were worked upon by means of his largesses: and though a private youth, he had levied an army; had corrupted the legions of the consul; that his interest with the party of Pompey was simulated: that soon after, when, in virtue of a decree of the senate, he possessed himself of the fasces and the authority of the prætorship, when Hirtius and Pansa, the two consuls, were slain, he had seized both their armies (whether it was that the consuls fell by the enemy, or whether Pansa was killed by pouring poison into his wounds; and Hirtius cut off by his own soldiers, and Cæsar the contriver of this treason): that by terror he had extorted the consulship in spite of the senate; and turned against the commonwealth the very arms with which the commonwealth had entrusted him for her defence against Antony. To these were added his proscription of citizens; the divisions of lands; which were not commended even by the very persons who carried out the measure. But admitting that the deaths of Cassius and the Bruti were sacrifices offered to his father's hate of them (though eternal justice demanded that he should have made personal animosities yield to public good), yet he betrayed Pompey by the phantom of a peace, Lepidus by a specious show of friendship. And afterwards, that Antony, having been ensnared by treaties, those of Tarentum and Brundusium, and by the marriage of his sister, paid with his life the penalty of that insidious alliance. After these things no doubt there was peace, but it was a bloody peace. There were, too, the disasters of Lollius, and of

Varus; and at Rome, the Varrones, the Egnatii, the Juli, put to death." Nor was his domestic life spared upon this occasion. "The abduction of Nero's wife—the pontiffs consulted in mockery as to whether she might marry him consistently with religion, having conceived but not yet brought forth—the excesses of Quintus Tedius and Vedius Pollio; lastly, his wife Livia had proved a cruel mother to the commonwealth, and to the Julian house a more cruel stepmother: nothing was left by him for the honours of the gods, since it was his pleasure to have temples dedicated to himself, to be represented under the similitude of the powers above, and be ministered unto by flamens and priests: nor had he adopted Tiberius for his successor, either out of affection for him, or from concern for the public welfare; but having discovered in him a spirit proud and cruel, he sought glory for himself by the contrast of a character consummately base." For, Augustus, when, a few years before, he solicited the senate to grant to Tiberius another term of the authority of the tribuneship, though in a laudatory speech, had thrown out some observations upon his personal peculiarities, his tastes and course of life, in order that under colour of apologising for them he might brand him with infamy.

However, as soon as the funeral of Augustus was over a temple and divine worship were decreed him. The prayers of the senate were then turned to Tiberius; but he replied evasively, descanting on the magnitude of the task of governing, and his own unaspiring disposition; he said that "the genius of the sainted Augustus was alone capable of the mighty charge: that for himself, having been called by him to a participation of his cares, he had learnt by experience how difficult to bear was the burthen of government, and how subject to the caprices of fortune: that a number of persons would more easily discharge the functions of the public administration by sharing its toils amongst them: he therefore implored them that in a state supported by so many illustrious patriots, they would not cast the whole administration upon one." Such was his speech; but there was more dignity of sentiment in it than sincerity; and the words of Tiberius, which, even upon subjects on which he sought not disguises, were dark and cautious, whether from nature, or from habit, at this juncture, indeed, as he laboured wholly to hide his heart, were more than ever involved in ambiguity and uncertainty: but the senators, whose sole fear was to seem to understand him, burst into tears, plaints, and vows: with extended arms they supplicated the gods, invoked the image of Augustus, and embraced the knees of Tiberius. He then commanded the imperial register to be produced and recited. It contained a summary of the resources of the state, the number of Romans and auxiliaries in the armies, the amount of the navy, kingdoms, provinces, tributes, customs, the public expenditure, and largesses. This register was all written by the hand of Augustus; and he had added a recommendation to keep the empire within fixed limits; but whether from apprehension for its safety, or jealousy of future rivals, is uncertain.

Meanwhile, the senate stooping to the most humiliating importunity, Tiberius happened to say, that, "as he was unequal to the weight of the whole government; so if they entrusted him with any particular part, whatever it were, he would undertake it." Hereupon Asinius Gallus says, "I beg to know, Cæsar, what part of the government you desire to be committed to you?" He was confounded at the unlooked-for question. For a short space he continued mute; but recovering himself, answered, that "it ill became his modesty to choose or reject any particular branch of the administration, when he desired rather to be excused from the whole." Gallus rejoined (for he concluded from his countenance that he had given offence), "by this question he did not mean that he should divide things which were inseparable; but that he might be convinced out of his own mouth, that the commonwealth is but one body, and can be governed only by the mind of one." He added an encomium upon Augustus, and reminded Tiberius himself of his many victories, of the many civil employments which he had long and admirably sustained: nor even thus could he mollify his wrath, who had long hated him, from a suspicion that having married Vipsania, daughter of Marcus Agrippa, and formerly wife of Tiberius, he meant to soar above the rank of a subject, and inherited the haughty spirit of Asinius Pollio, his father.

Lucius Arruntius incurred his displeasure next, by a speech not much unlike that of Gallus; though towards him Tiberius bore no inveterate rancour; but he regarded with jealousy Arruntius, as being rich, energetic, accomplished, and, accordingly, in repute with the people. Indeed Augustus, shortly before his decease, mentioning those who would be capable of obtaining the supreme power, but would not accept it; or unequal to it, yet wished for it; or who had both ambition and sufficiency, had said that "Marcus Lepidus was qualified, but would reject it; Asinius would be aspiring, but had inferior talents; and that Lucius Arruntius was not unworthy of it, and upon a proper occasion would attempt it." That he spoke thus of Lepidus and Asinius, is agreed; but, instead of Arruntius, some writers have transmitted the name of Cneius Piso: and every one of these great men, except Lepidus, were afterwards cut off, under imputations of various crimes, all concocted by Tiberius. Quintus Haterius also, and Mamercus

Scaurus excited his jealous spirit; the first by asking him, "How long, Cæsar, wilt thou suffer the commonwealth to remain destitute of a head?" Scaurus, because he had said, "There was room to hope that the prayers of the senate would not prove abortive, since he had not put his veto on the motion of the consuls, as he might have done, according to the privilege of the tribunitian authority." He inveighed against Haterius on the instant. Scaurus, towards whom his resentment was more implacable, he passed over in profound silence. Wearied at last with the general importunity, and the expostulations of individuals, he relaxed by little and little; not so far as to declare openly that he would undertake the empire, but only to avoid the uneasiness of rejecting solicitation. It is well known that Haterius, when he went next day to the palace to implore pardon, and embraced the knees of Tiberius who was walking, narrowly escaped being slain by the soldiers, because Tiberius had fallen down, whether by chance or entangled in the arms of Haterius; his anger, however, was not appeased by the danger which threatened so great a man, until Haterius supplicated Augusta, whose most earnest entreaties obtained protection for him.

Towards Livia, too, extravagant was the adulation of the senate. Some were for decreeing her the appellation of Parent, others of Mother of her Country; and almost all were of opinion, that to the name of Tiberius should be added, The son of Julia. Tiberius urged impatiently that "public honours to women ought to be cautiously adjudged; and that with the same moderation he would receive such as were presented to himself." But, torn with jealousy, and regarding the elevation of a woman as the depression of himself, he suffered not so much as a lictor to be decreed her, and even forbade the raising an altar upon her late adoption, and other similar honours. But for Germanicus he asked the proconsular power; and deputies were sent to present it to him, and at the same time to condole with him on the death of Augustus. The same honour was not solicited for Drusus, because he was present, and already consul-elect. He then named twelve candidates for the prætorship, the number settled by Augustus; and though the senate requested him to increase it, he bound himself by an oath never to exceed it.

The assemblies for electing magistrates were now first transferred from the Campus Martius to the senate; for though the emperor had conducted all affairs of moment at his pleasure; yet, till that day, some were still transacted according to the inclination of the tribes. Neither did the regret of the people for the seizure of these their ancient rights rise higher than some impotent grumbling: the senate, too, released from the charge of buying votes, and from the shame of begging them, willingly acquiesced in the regulation, by which Tiberius contented himself with the recommendation of four candidates only, to be accepted without opposition or canvassing. At the same time, the tribunes of the people asked leave to celebrate, at their own expense, certain games in honour of Augustus, which were called after his name, and which were now inserted in the calendar. But it was decreed that the charge should be defrayed out of the exchequer, and that the tribunes should in the circus wear the triumphal robe; but to be carried in chariots was denied them. The annual celebration of these plays was, for the future, transferred to the prætors, to whom should fall the jurisdiction of deciding suits between citizens and strangers.

Book I, Chapters 1-15

✳

From Germany

Translated by *William Peterson*

✳

The German Character

No people are more addicted to divination by omens
and lots. The latter is performed in the following simple
manner. They cut a twig from a fruit-tree, and divide it
into small pieces, which, distinguished by certain marks,
are thrown promiscuously upon a white garment. Then,
the priest of the canton, if the occasion be public;
if private, the master of the family; after an invocation
of the gods, with his eyes lifted up to heaven, thrice
takes out each piece, and, as they come up, interprets
their signification according to the marks fixed upon
them. If the result prove unfavourable, there is no more
consultation on the same affair that day; if propitious,
a confirmation by omens is still required. In common
with other nations, the Germans are acquainted with the
practice of auguring from the notes and flight of birds;
but it is peculiar to them to derive admonitions and pres-
ages from horses also. Certain of these animals, milk-
white, and untouched by earthly labour, are pastured
at the public expense in the sacred woods and groves.
These, yoked to a consecrated chariot, are accompanied
by the priest, and king, or chief person of the com-
munity, who attentively observe their manner of neigh-
ing and snorting; and no kind of augury is more credited,
not only among the populace, but among the nobles and

priests. For the latter consider themselves as the ministers of the gods, and the horses, as privy to the divine will. Another kind of divination, by which they explore the event of momentous wars, is to oblige a prisoner, taken by any means whatsoever from the nation with whom they are at variance, to fight with a picked man of their own, each with his own country's arms; and, according as the victory falls, they presage success to the one or to the other party.

On affairs of smaller moment, the chiefs consult; on those of greater importance, the whole community; yet with this circumstance, that what is referred to the decision of the people, is first maturely discussed by the chiefs. They assemble, unless upon some sudden emergency, on stated days, either at the new or full moon, which they account the most auspicious season for beginning any enterprise. Nor do they, in their computation of time, reckon, like us, by the number of days, but of nights. In this way they arrange their business; in this way they fix their appointments; so that, with them, the night seems to lead the day. An inconvenience produced by their liberty is, that they do not all assemble at a stated time, as if it were in obedience to a command; but two or three days are lost in the delays of convening. When they all think fit, they sit down armed. Silence is proclaimed by the priests, who have on this occasion a coercive power. Then the king, or chief, and such others as are conspicuous for age, birth, military renown, or eloquence, are heard; and gain attention rather from their ability to persuade, than their authority to command. If a proposal displease, the assembly reject it by an inarticulate murmur; if it prove agreeable, they clash their javelins; for the most honourable expression of assent among them is the sound of arms.

Before this council, it is likewise allowed to exhibit

accusations, and to prosecute capital offences. Punishments are varied according to the nature of the crime. Traitors and deserters are hung upon trees: cowards, dastards, and those guilty of unnatural practices are suffocated in mud under a hurdle. This difference of punishment has in view the principle, that villainy should be exposed while it is punished, but turpitude concealed. The penalties annexed to slighter offences are also proportioned to the delinquency. The convicts are fined in horses and cattle: part of the mulct goes to the king or state; part to the injured person, or his relations. In the same assemblies chiefs are also elected, to administer justice through the cantons and districts. A hundred companions, chosen from the people, attend upon each of them, to assist them as well with their advice as their authority.

The Germans transact no business, public or private, without being armed: but it is not customary for any person to assume arms till the state has approved his ability to use them. Then, in the midst of the assembly, either one of the chiefs, or the father, or a relation, equips the youth with a shield and javelin. These are to them the manly gown; this is the first honour conferred on youth: before this they are considered as part of a household; afterwards, of the state. The dignity of chieftain is bestowed even on mere lads, whose descent is eminently illustrious, or whose fathers have performed signal services to the public; they are associated, however, with those of mature strength, who have already been declared capable of service; nor do they blush to be seen in the rank of companions. For the state of companionship itself has its several degrees, determined by the judgment of him whom they follow; and there is a great emulation among the companions, which shall possess the highest place in the favour of their chief; and among the chiefs, which shall excel in the number and valour of his companions. It is their dignity, their strength, to be always surrounded with a large body of select youth, an ornament in peace, a bulwark in war. And not in his own country alone, but among the neighbouring states, the fame and glory of each chief consists in being distinguished for the number and bravery of his companions. Such chiefs are courted by embassies; distinguished by presents; and often by their reputation alone decide a war.

In the field of battle, it is disgraceful for the chief to be surpassed in valour; it is disgraceful for the companions not to equal their chief; but it is reproach and infamy during a whole succeeding life to retreat from the field surviving him. To aid, to protect him; to place their own gallant actions to the account of his glory, is their first and most sacred engagement. The chiefs fight for victory; the companions for their chief. If their native country be long sunk in peace and inaction, many of the young nobles repair to some other state then engaged in war. For, besides that repose is unwelcome to their race, and toils and perils afford them a better opportunity of distinguishing themselves; they are unable, without war and violence, to maintain a large train of followers. The companion requires from the liberality of his chief, the warlike steed, the bloody and conquering spear: and in place of pay, he expects to be supplied with a table, homely indeed, but plentiful. The funds for this munificence must be found in war and rapine: nor are they so easily persuaded to cultivate the earth, and await the produce of the seasons, as to challenge the foe, and expose themselves to wounds; nay, they even think it base and spiritless to earn by sweat what they might purchase with blood.

During the intervals of war, they pass their time less in hunting than in a sluggish repose, divided between sleep and the table. All the bravest of the warriors, committing the care of the house, the family affairs, and the lands, to the women, old men, and weaker part of the domestics, stupefy themselves in inaction: so wonderful is the contrast presented by nature, that the same persons love indolence, and hate tranquillity! It is customary for the several states to present, by voluntary and individual contributions, cattle or grain to their chiefs; which are accepted as honorary gifts, while they serve as necessary supplies. They are peculiarly pleased with presents from neighbouring nations, offered not only by individuals, but by the community at large; such as fine horses, heavy armour, rich housings, and gold chains. We have now taught them also to accept of money.

It is well known that none of the German nations inhabit cities; or even admit of contiguous settlements. They dwell scattered and separate, as a spring, a meadow, or a grove may chance to invite them. Their villages are laid out, not like ours in rows of adjoining buildings; but every one surrounds his house with a vacant space, either by way of security against fire, or through ignorance of the art of building. For, indeed, they are unacquainted with the use of mortar and tiles; and for every purpose employ rude unshapen timber, fashioned with no regard to pleasing the eye. They bestow more than ordinary pains in coating certain parts of their buildings with a kind of earth, so pure and shining that it gives the appearance of painting. They also dig subterraneous caves, and cover them over with a great quantity of dung. These they use as winter-retreats, and granaries; for they preserve a moderate temperature; and upon an invasion, when the open country is plundered, these recesses remain unviolated, either because the enemy is ignorant of them, or because he will not trouble himself with the search.

The clothing common to all is a sagum fastened by a clasp, or, in want of that, a thorn. With no other covering, they pass whole days on the hearth, before the fire. The more wealthy are distinguished by a vest, not flowing loose, like those of the Sarmatians and Parthians, but girt close, and exhibiting the shape of every limb. They also wear the skins of beasts, which the people near the borders are less curious in selecting or preparing than the more remote inhabitants, who cannot by commerce procure other clothing. These make choice of particular skins, which they variegate with spots, and strips of the furs of marine animals, the produce of the exterior ocean, and seas to us unknown. The dress of the women does not differ from that of the men: except that they more frequently wear linen, which they stain with purple; and do not lengthen their upper garment into sleeves, but leave exposed the whole arm, and part of the breast.

The matrimonial bond is, nevertheless, strict and severe among them; nor is there anything in their manners more commendable than this. Almost singly among the barbarians, they content themselves with one wife; a very few of them excepted, who, not through incontinence, but because their alliance is solicited on account of their rank, practice polygamy. The wife does not bring a dowry to her husband, but receives one from him. The parents and relations assemble, and pass their approbation on the presents—presents not adapted to please a female taste, or decorate the bride; but oxen, a caparisoned steed, a shield, spear, and sword. By virtue of these, the wife is espoused; and she in her turn makes a present of some arms to her husband. This they consider as the firmest bond of union; these, the sacred mysteries, the conjugal deities. That the woman may not think herself excused from exertions of fortitude, or exempt from the casualties of war, she is admonished by the very ceremonial of her marriage, that she comes to her husband as a partner in toils and dangers; to suffer and to dare equally with him, in peace and in war: this is indicated by the yoked oxen, the harnessed steed, the offered arms. Thus she is to live; thus to die. She receives what she is to return inviolate and honoured to her children; what her daughters-in-law are to receive, and again transmit to her grandchildren.

They live, therefore, fenced around with chastity; corrupted by no seductive spectacles, no convivial incitements. Men and women are alike unacquainted with clandestine correspondence. Adultery is extremely rare among so numerous a people. Its punishment is instant, and at the pleasure of the husband. He cuts off the hair of the offender, strips her, and in presence of her relations expels her from his house, and pursues her with stripes through the whole village. Nor is any indulgence shown to a prostitute. Neither beauty, youth, nor riches can procure her a husband: for none there looks on vice with a smile, or calls mutual seduction the way of the world. Still more exemplary is the practice of those states in which none but virgins marry, and the expectations and wishes of a wife are at once brought to a period. Thus, they take one husband as one body and one life; that no thought, no desire, may extend beyond him; and he may be loved not only as their husband, but as their marriage. To limit the increase of children, or put to death any of the later progeny, is accounted infamous: and good habits have there more influence than good laws elsewhere.

In every house the children grow up, thinly and meanly clad, to that bulk of body and limb which we

594 THE SILVER AGE

behold with wonder. Every mother suckles her own children, and does not deliver them into the hands of servants and nurses. No indulgence distinguishes the young master from the slave. They lie together amidst the same cattle, upon the same ground, till age separates, and valour marks out, the freeborn. The youths partake late of the pleasures of love, and hence pass the age of puberty unexhausted: nor are the virgins hurried into marriage; the same maturity, the same full growth, is required: the sexes unite equally matched, and robust; and the children inherit the vigour of their parents. Children are regarded with equal affection by their maternal uncles as by their fathers: some even consider this as the more sacred bond of consanguinity, and prefer it in the requisition of hostages, as if it held the mind by a firmer tie, and the family by a more extensive obligation. A person's own children, however, are his heirs and successors; and no wills are made. If there be no children, the next in order of inheritance are brothers, paternal and maternal uncles. The more numerous are a man's relations and kinsmen, the more comfortable is his old age; nor is it here any advantage to be childless.

It is an indispensable duty to adopt the enmities of a father or relation, as well as their friendships: these, however, are not irreconcilable or perpetual. Even homicide is atoned by a certain fine in cattle and sheep; and the whole family accepts the satisfaction, to the advantage of the public weal, since quarrels are most dangerous in a free state. No people are more addicted to social entertainments, or more liberal in the exercise of hospitality. To refuse any person whatever admittance under their roof, is accounted flagitious. Every one according to his ability feasts his guests: when his provisions are exhausted, he who was late the host, is now the guide and companion to another hospitable board. They enter the next house uninvited, and are received with equal cordiality. No one makes a distinction with respect to the rights of hospitality, between a stranger and an acquaintance. The departing guest is presented with whatever he may ask for; and with the same freedom a boon is desired in return. They are pleased with presents; but think no obligation incurred either when they give or receive.

Their manner of living with their guests is easy and affable. As soon as they arise from sleep, which they generally protract till late in the day, they bathe, usually in warm water, as cold weather chiefly prevails there. After bathing they take their meal, each on a distinct seat, and at a separate table. Then they proceed, armed, to business; and not less frequently to convivial parties, in which it is no disgrace to pass days and nights, without intermission, in drinking. The frequent quarrels that arise amongst them, when intoxicated, seldom terminate in abusive language, but more frequently in blood. In their feasts, they generally deliberate on the reconcilement of enemies, on family alliances, on the appointment of chiefs, and finally on peace and war; conceiving that at no time the soul is more opened to sincerity, or warmed to heroism. These people, naturally void of artifice or disguise, disclose the most secret emotions of their hearts in the freedom of festivity. The minds of all being thus displayed without reserve, the subjects of their deliberation are again canvassed the next day; and each time has its advantages. They consult when unable to dissemble; they determine when not liable to mistake.

Their drink is a liquor prepared from barley or wheat brought by fermentation to a certain resemblance of wine. Those who border on the Rhine also purchase wine. Their food is simple; wild fruits, fresh venison, or coagulated milk. They satisfy hunger without seeking the elegances and delicacies of the table. Their thirst for liquor is not quenched with equal moderation. If their propensity to drunkenness be gratified to the extent of their wishes, intemperance proves as effectual in subduing them as the force of arms.

They have only one kind of public spectacle, which is exhibited in every company. Young men, who make it their diversion, dance naked amidst drawn swords and presented spears. Practice has conferred skill at this exercise, and skill has given grace; but they do not exhibit for hire or gain: the only reward of this pastime, though a hazardous one, is the pleasure of the spectators. What is extraordinary, they play at dice, when sober, as a serious business: and that with such a desperate venture of gain or loss, that, when everything else is gone, they set their liberties and persons on the last throw. The loser goes into voluntary servitude; and, though the youngest and strongest, patiently suffers himself to be bound and sold. Such is their obstinacy in a bad practice—they themselves call it honour. The slaves thus acquired are exchanged away in commerce, that the winner may get rid of the scandal of his victory.

The rest of their slaves have not, like ours, particular employments in the family allotted them. Each is the master of a habitation and household of his own. The lord requires from him a certain quantity of grain, cattle, or cloth, as from a tenant; and so far only the subjection of the slave extends. His domestic offices are performed by his own wife and children. It is usual to scourge a slave, or punish him with chains or hard labour. They are sometimes killed by their masters: not through severity of chastisement, but in the heat of passion, like an enemy; with this difference, that it is done with impunity. Freedmen are little superior to slaves; seldom filling any important office in the family; never in the state, except in those tribes which are under regal government. There, they rise above the free-born, and even the nobles: in the rest, the subordinate condition of the freedmen is a proof of freedom.

Lending money upon interest, and increasing it by usury, is unknown amongst them: and this ignorance more effectually prevents the practice than a prohibition would do. The lands are occupied by townships, in allotments proportional to the number of cultivators; and are afterwards parcelled out among the individuals of the district, in shares according to the rank and condition of each person. The wide extent of plain facilitates this partition. The arable lands are annually changed, and a part left fallow; nor do they attempt to make the most of the fertility and plenty of the soil, by their own industry in planting orchards, inclosing meadows, and watering gardens. Corn is the only product required from the earth: hence their year is not divided into so many seasons as ours; for, while they know and distinguish by name Winter, Spring, and Summer, they are unacquainted equally with the appellation and bounty of Autumn.

Their funerals are without parade. The only circumstance to which they attend, is to burn the bodies of eminent persons with some particular kinds of wood. Neither vestments nor perfumes are heaped upon the pile: the arms of the deceased, and sometimes his horse, are given to the flames. The tomb is a mound of turf. They contemn the elaborate and costly honours of monumental structures, as mere burthens to the dead. They soon dismiss tears and lamentations; slowly, sorrow and regret. They think it the women's part to bewail their friends, the men's to remember them.

Chapters 10-27

JUVENAL

(Decimus Junius Juvenal, 60? A.D.–?140 A.D.)

From the Satires

Translated by John Dryden

*

The Third Satyr

Griev'd tho I am, an Ancient Friend to lose,
I like the Solitary Seat he chose:
In quiet *Cumæ* fixing his Repose:
Where, far from Noisy *Rome* secure he Lives,
And one more Citizen to *Sybil* gives;
The road to *Bajæ*, and that soft Recess
Which all the Gods with all their Bounty bless.
Tho I in *Prochyta* with greater ease
Cou'd live, than in a Street of Palaces.
What Scene so Desart, or so full of Fright,
As tow'ring Houses tumbling in the Night,
And *Rome* on Fire beheld by its own Blazing Light?
But worse than all, the clatt'ring Tiles; and worse
Than thousand Padders, is the Poet's Curse.
Rogues that in Dog-days cannot Rhime forbear:
But without Mercy read, and make you hear.

   Now while my Friend, just ready to depart,
Was packing all his Goods in one poor Cart;
He stopp'd a little at the Conduit-Gate,

Where *Numa* modell'd once the *Roman* State,
In Mighty Councels with his Nymph retir'd:
Though now the Sacred Shades and Founts are hir'd
By Banish'd Jews, who their whole Wealth can lay
In a small Basket, on a Wisp of Hay;
Yet such our Avarice is, that every Tree
Pays for his Head; not Sleep it self is free:
Nor Place, nor Persons now are Sacred held,
From their own Grove the Muses are expell'd.
Into this lonely Vale our Steps we bend,
I and my sullen discontented Friend:
The Marble Caves, and Aquæducts we view;
But how Adult'rate now, and different from the true!
How much more Beauteous had the Fountain been
Embellish't with her first Created Green,
Where Crystal Streams through living Turf had run,
Contented with an Urn of Native Stone!
   Then thus *Umbricius* (with an Angry Frown,
And looking back on this degen'rate Town,)
Since Noble Arts in *Rome* have no support,
And ragged Virtue not a Friend at Court,
No Profit rises from th' ungrateful Stage,
My Poverty encreasing with my Age,
'Tis time to give my just Disdain a vent,
And, Cursing, leave so base a Government.
Where *Dedalus* his borrow'd Wings laid by,
To that obscure Retreat I chuse to fly:
While yet few furrows on my Face are seen,
While I walk upright, and Old Age is green,
And *Lachesis* has somewhat left to spin.
Now, now 'tis time to quit this cursed place,
And hide from Villains my too honest Face:
Here let *Arturius* live, and such as he;
Such Manners will with such a Town agree.
Knaves who in full Assemblies have the knack

Of turning Truth to Lies, and White to Black;
Can hire large Houses, and oppress the Poor
By farm'd Excise; can cleanse the Common-shoare;
And rent the Fishery; can bear the dead;
And teach their Eyes dissembled Tears to shed,
All this for Gain; for Gain they sell their very Head.
These Fellows (see what Fortune's pow'r can do)
Were once the Minstrels of a Country Show:
Follow'd the Prizes through each paltry Town,
By Trumpet-Cheeks and Bloated Faces known.
But now, grown rich, on drunken Holy-days,
At their own Costs exhibit Publick Plays;
Where influenc'd by the Rabble's bloody will,
With Thumbs bent back, they popularly kill.
From thence return'd, their sordid Avarice rakes
In Excrements again, and hires the Jakes.
Why hire they not the Town, not ev'ry thing,
Since such as they have Fortune in a String?
Who, for her pleasure, can her Fools advance;
And toss 'em topmost on the Wheel of Chance.
What's *Rome* to me, what bus'ness have I there,
I who can neither Lye, nor falsely Swear?
Nor Praise my Patron's undeserving Rhimes,
Nor yet comply with him, nor with his Times;
Unskill'd in Schemes by Planets to foreshow,
Like Canting Rascals, how the Wars will go:
I neither will, nor can Prognosticate
To the young gaping Heir, his Father's Fate:
Nor in the Entrails of a Toad have pry'd,
Nor carry'd Bawdy Presents to a Bride:
For want of these Town Virtues, thus, alone,
I go conducted on my way by none:
Like a dead Member from the Body rent;
Maim'd, and unuseful to the Government.
    Who now is lov'd, but he who loves the Times,

Conscious of close Intrigues, and dipt in Crimes;
Lab'ring with Secrets which his Bosom burn,
Yet never must to publick light return?
They get Reward alone who can Betray:
For keeping honest Counsels none will pay.
He who can *Verres,* when he will, accuse,
The Purse of *Verres* may at Pleasure use:
But let not all the Gold which *Tagus* hides,
And pays the Sea in Tributary Tides,
Be Bribe sufficient to corrupt thy Breast;
Or violate with Dreams thy peaceful rest.
Great Men with jealous Eyes the Friend behold,
Whose secrecy they purchase with their Gold.

    I haste to tell thee, nor shall Shame oppose,
What Confidents our Wealthy *Romans* chose:
And whom I most abhor: To speak my Mind,
I hate, in *Rome,* a *Grecian* Town to find:
To see the Scum of *Greece* transplanted here,
Receiv'd like Gods, is what I cannot bear.
Nor *Greeks* alone, but *Syrians* here abound,
Obscene *Orontes,* diving under Ground,
Conveys his Wealth to *Tyber's* hungry Shoars,
And fattens *Italy* with Foreign Whores:
Hither their crooked Harps and Customs come;
All find Receipt in Hospitable *Rome.*
The Barbarous Harlots crowd the Publick Place:
Go Fools, and purchase an unclean Embrace;
The painted Mitre court, and the more painted Face.
Old *Romulus,* and Father *Mars* look down,
Your Herdsman Primitive, your homely Clown
Is turn'd a *Beau* in a loose tawdry Gown.
His once unkem'd, and horrid Locks, behold
Stilling sweet Oyl; his Neck inchain'd with Gold:
Aping the Foreigners, in ev'ry Dress;
Which, bought at greater cost, becomes him less.

Mean time they wisely leave their Native Land,
From *Sicyon, Samos,* and from *Alaband,*
And *Amydon,* to *Rome* they Swarm in Shoals:
So Sweet and Easie is the Gain from Fools.
Poor Refugies at first, they purchase here:
And, soon as Denizen'd, they domineer:
Grow to the Great, a flatt'ring Servile Rout:
Work themselves inward, and their Patrons out.
Quick Witted, Brazen-fac'd, with fluent Tongues,
Patient of Labours, and dissembling Wrongs
Riddle me this, and guess him if you can,
Who bears a Nation in a single Man?
A Cook, a Conjuror, a Rhetorician,
A Painter, Pedant, a Geometrician,
A Dancer on the Ropes, and a Physician.
All things the hungry *Greek* exactly knows:
And bid him go to Heav'n, to Heav'n he goes.
In short, no *Scythian, Moor,* or *Thracian* born,
But in that Town which Arms and Arts adorn.
Shall he be plac'd above me at the Board,
In Purple Cloath'd, and lolling like a Lord?
Shall he before me sign, whom t' other Day
A small-craft Vessel hither did convey;
Where, stow'd with Prunes, and rotten Figs, he lay?
How little is the Priviledge become
Of being born a Citizen of *Rome!*
The *Greeks* get all by fulsom Flatteries;
A most peculiar Stroke they have at Lies.
They make a Wit of their Insipid Friend;
His blobber-Lips, and beetle-Brows commend;
His long Crane Neck, and narrow Shoulders Praise;
You'd think they were describing Hercules.
A creaking Voice for a clear Trebble goes;
Tho harsher than a Cock that Treads and Crows.
We can as grosly praise; but, to our Grief,

No Flatt'ry but from *Grecians* gains belief.
Besides these Qualities, we must agree
They Mimick better on the Stage than we
The Wife, the Whore, the Shepherdess they play,
In such a Free, and such a Graceful way,
That we believe a very Woman shown,
And fancy something underneath the Gown.
But not *Antiochus*, nor *Stratocles*,
Our Ears and Ravish'd Eyes can only please:
The Nation is compos'd of such as these.
All *Greece* is one Commedian: Laugh, and they
Return it louder than an Ass can bray:
Grieve, and they Grieve; if you Weep silently,
There seems a silent Eccho in their Eye:
They cannot *Mourn* like you; but they can Cry.
Call for a Fire, their Winter Cloaths they take:
Begin but you to shiver, and they shake:
In Frost and Snow, if you complain of Heat,
They rub th' unsweating Brow, and Swear they Sweat.
We live not on the Square with such as these:
Such are our Betters who can better please:
Who Day and Night are like a Looking-Glass;
Still ready to reflect their Patron's Face.
The Panegyrick Hand, and lifted Eye,
Prepar'd for some new Piece of Flattery.
Ev'n Nastiness, Occasions will afford;
They praise a belching, or well-pissing Lord.
Besides, there's nothing Sacred, nothing free
From bold Attempts of their rank Leachery
Through the whole Family their labours run;
The Daughter is debauch'd, the Wife is won:
Nor scapes the Bridegroom, or the blooming Son.
If none they find for their lewd purpose fit,
They with the Walls and very Floors commit.
They search the Secrets of the House, and so

Are worshipp'd there, and fear'd for what they know.
  And, now we talk of *Grecians,* cast a view
On what, in Schools, their Men of Morals do;
A rigid Stoick his own Pupil slew.
A Friend, against a Friend, of his own Cloath,
Turn'd Evidence, and murther'd on his Oath.
What room is left for *Romans,* in a Town
Where *Grecians* rule, and Cloaks control the Gown?
Some *Diphilus,* or some *Protogenes,*
Look sharply out, our Senators to seize:
Engross 'em wholly, by their Native Art,
And fear no Rivals in their Bubbles heart:
One drop of Poison in my Patron's Ear,
One slight suggestion of a senseless fear,
Infus'd with cunning, serves to ruine me;
Disgrac'd, and banish'd from the Family.
In vain forgotten Services I boast;
My long dependance in an hour is lost:
Look round the World, what Country will appear,
Where Friends are left with greater ease than here?
At *Rome* (nor think me partial to the Poor)
All Offices of ours are out of Door:
In vain we rise, and to their Levees run;
My Lord himself is up, before, and gone:
The Prætor bids his Lictors mend their pace,
Lest his Collegue outstrip him in the Race:
The childless Matrons are, long since, awake;
And for Affronts the tardy Visits take.
  'Tis frequent, here, to see a free-born Son
On the left-hand of a Rich Hireling run:
Because the wealthy Rogue can throw away,
For half a Brace of Bouts, a Tribune's pay
But you, poor Sinner, tho you love the Vice,
And like the Whore, demurr upon the Price:
And, frighted with the wicked Sum, forbear

To lend a hand, and help her from the Chair.
    Produce a Witness of unblemish'd life,
Holy as *Numa*, or as *Numa's* Wife,
Or him who bid th' unhallow'd Flames retire;
And snatch'd the trembling Goddess from the Fire.
The Question is not put how far extends
His Piety, but what he yearly spends:
Quick, to the Bus'ness; how he Lives and Eats;
How largely Gives; how splendidly he Treats:
How many thousand Acres feed his Sheep,
What are his Rents, what Servants does he keep?
Th' Account is soon cast up; the Judges rate
Our Credit in the Court, by our Estate.
Swear by our Gods, or those the *Greeks* adore,
Thou art as sure Forsworn, as thou art Poor:
The Poor must gain their Bread by Perjury;
And even the Gods, that other Means deny,
In Conscience must absolve 'em, when they lye.
    Add, that the Rich have still a Gibe in store;
And will be monstrous witty on the Poor:
For the torn Surtout and the tatter'd Vest,
The Wretch and all his Wardrobe are a Jest;
The greasie Gown, sully'd with often turning,
Gives a good hint, to say The Man's in Mourning:
Or if the Shoo be ript, or patches put,
He's wounded! see the Plaister on his Foot.
Want is the Scorn of ev'ry Wealthy Fool;
And Wit in Rags is turn'd to Ridicule.
    Pack hence, and from the Cover'd Benches rise
(The Master of the Ceremonies cries),
This is no place for you, whose small Estate
Is not the Value of the settled Rate:
The Sons of happy Punks, the Pandars Heir,
Are priviledg'd to sit in triumph there,
To clap the first, and rule the Theatre.

Up to the Galleries, for shame, retreat:
For, by the *Roscian* Law, the Poor can claim no Seat.
Who ever brought to his rich Daughter's Bed
The Man that poll'd but Twelve-pence for his Head?
Who ever nam'd a poor Man for his Heir,
Or call'd him to assist the Judging Chair?
The Poor were wise, who by the Rich oppress'd,
Withdrew, and sought a Sacred Place of Rest.
Once they did well, to free themselves from Scorn;
But had done better never to return.
Rarely they rise by Virtues aid, who lie
Plung'd in the depth of helpless Poverty.

  At *Rome* 'tis worse; where House-rent by the Year,
And Servants Bellies cost so Dev'llish dear;
And Tavern Bills run high for hungry Chear.
To drink or eat in Earthen Ware we scorn,
Which cheaply Country Cupboards does adorn:
And coarse blue Hoods on Holydays are worn.
Some distant parts of *Italy* are known,
Where none, but only dead Men, wear a Gown:
On Theatres of Turf, in homely State,
Old Plays they act, old Feasts they Celebrate:
The same rude Song returns upon the Crowd,
And, by Tradition, is for Wit allow'd.
The Mimick Yearly gives the same Delights;
And in the Mother's Arms the Clownish Infant frights.
Their Habits (undistinguish'd by degree)
Are plain, alike; the same Simplicity,
Both on the Stage, and in the Pit, you see.
In his white Cloak the Magistrate appears;
The Country Bumpkin the same Liv'ry wears.
But here, Attir'd beyond our Purse we go,
For useless Ornament and flaunting Show:
We take on trust, in Purple Robes to shine;
And Poor, are yet Ambitious to be fine.

This is a common Vice, tho all things here
Are sold, and sold unconscionably dear.
What will you give that *Cossus* may but view
Your Face, and in the Crowd distinguish you;
May take your Incense like a gracious God;
And answer only with a Civil Nod?
To please our Patrons, in this vicious Age,
We make our Entrance by the Fav'rite Page:
Shave his first down, and when he Polls his Hair,
The Consecrated Locks to Temples bear:
Pay Tributary Cracknels, which he sells;
And, with our Offerings, help to raise his Vails.

   Who fears, in Country Towns, a House's fall,
Or to be caught betwixt a riven Wall?
But we Inhabit a weak City here;
Which Buttresses and Props but scarcely bear:
And 'tis the Village Masons daily Calling,
To keep the World's Metropolis from falling,
To cleanse the Gutters, and the Chinks to close;
And, for one Night, secure his Lord's Repose.
At *Cumæ* we can sleep, quite round the Year,
Nor Falls, nor Fires, nor Nightly Dangers fear;
While rolling Flames from *Roman* Turrets fly,
And the pale Citizens for Buckets cry.
Thy Neighbour has remov'd his Wretched Store,
(Few Hands will rid the Lumber of the Poor)
Thy own third Story smoaks; while thou, supine,
Art drench'd in Fumes of undigested Wine.
For if the lowest Floors already burn,
Cock-lofts and Garrets soon will take the Turn.
Where thy tame Pidgeons next the Tiles were bred,
Which in their Nests unsafe, are timely fled.

   Codrus had but one Bed, so short to boot,
That his short Wife's short Legs hung dangling out;
His Cup-board's Head six Earthen Pitchers grac'd,

Beneath 'em was his Trusty Tankard plac'd:
And, to support this Noble Plate, there lay
A bending Chiron cast from honest Clay:
His few Greek Books a rotten Chest contain'd,
Whose Covers much of mouldiness complain'd:
Where Mice and Rats devour'd Poetick Bread,
And with Heroick Verse luxuriously were fed.
'Tis true, poor *Codrus* nothing had to boast,
And yet poor *Codrus* all that Nothing lost;
Beg'd naked through the Streets of wealthy *Rome;*
And found not one to feed, or take him home.
  But if the Palace of *Arturius* burn,
The Nobles change their Cloaths, the Matrons mourn;
The City Prætor will no Pleadings hear;
The very Name of Fire we hate and fear:
And look agast, as if the *Gauls* were here.
While yet it burns, th' officious Nation flies,
Some to condole, and some to bring supplies:
One sends him Marble to rebuild, and one
White naked Statues of the *Parian* Stone,
The Work of *Polyclete*, that seem to live;
While others, Images for Altars give;
One Books and Skreens, and *Pallas* to the Brest;
Another Bags of Gold, and he gives best.
Childless *Arturius*, vastly rich before,
Thus by his Losses multiplies his Store:
Suspected for Accomplice to the Fire,
That burnt his Palace but to build it higher.
  But, cou'd you be content to bid adieu
To the dear Play-house, and the Players too,
Sweet Country Seats are purchas'd ev'ry where,
With Lands and Gardens, at less price, than here
You hire a darksom Doghole by the year.
A small Convenience, decently prepar'd,
A shallow Well, that rises in your yard,

That spreads his easie Crystal Streams around,
And waters all the pretty spot of Ground.
There, love the Fork; thy Garden cultivate,
And give thy frugal Friends a *Pythagorean* Treat.
'Tis somewhat to be Lord of some small Ground;
In which a Lizard may, at least, turn round.

   'Tis frequent, here, for want of sleep to dye;
Which Fumes of undigested Feasts deny;
And, with imperfect heat, in languid Stomachs fry.
What House secure from noise the poor can keep,
When ev'n the Rich can scarce afford to sleep?
So dear it costs to purchase Rest in *Rome;*
And hence the sources of Diseases come.
The Drover who his Fellow-drover meets,
In narrow passages of winding Streets:
The Waggoners, that curse their standing Teams,
Would wake ev'n drowsie *Drusus* from his Dreams.
And yet the Wealthy will not brook delay;
But sweep above our Heads, and make their way;
In lofty Litters born, and read and write,
Or sleep at ease: The Shutters make it Night.
Yet still he reaches, first, the Publick Place:
The prease before him stops the Client's pace.
The Crowd that follows, crush his panting sides,
And trip his heels; he walks not, but he rides.
One elbows him, one justles in the Shole:
A Rafter breaks his Head, or Chairman's Pole:
Stockin'd with loads of fat Town-dirt he goes;
And some Rogue-Souldier, with his Hobnail'd Shoos,
Indents his Legs behind in bloody rows.
See with what Smoke our Doles we celebrate:
A hundred Ghests, invited, walk in state:
A hundred hungry Slaves, with their *Dutch* Kitchins
    wait.
Huge Pans the Wretches on their heads must bear;

Which scarce Gygantick *Corbulo* cou'd rear:
Yet they must walk upright beneath the load;
Nay run, and running blow the sparkling flames abroad.
Their Coats, from botching newly brought, are torn:
Unwieldy Timber-trees, in Waggons born,
Stretch'd at their length, beyond their Carriage lye;
That nod, and threaten ruin from on high.
For, should their Axel break, its overthrow
Wou'd crush, and pound to dust, the Crowd below;
Nor Friends their Friends, nor Sires their Sons cou'd
    know:
Nor Limbs, nor Bones, nor Carcass wou'd remain:
But a mash'd heap, a Hotchpotch of the Slain.
One vast destruction; not the Soul alone,
But Bodies, like the Soul, invisible are flown.
Mean time, unknowing of their Fellows Fate,
The Servants wash the Platter, scour the Plate,
Then blow the Fire, with puffing Cheeks, and lay
The Rubbers, and the Bathing-sheets display;
And oyl them first; and each is handy in his way.
But he, for whom this busie care they take,
Poor Ghost, is wandring by the Stygian Lake:
Affrighted with the Ferryman's grim Face;
New to the Horrours of that uncouth place;
His passage begs with unregarded Pray'r:
And wants two Farthings to discharge his Fare.
    Return we to the Dangers of the Night;
And, first, behold our Houses dreadful height:
From whence come broken Potsherds tumbling down;
And leaky Ware, from Garret Windows thrown:
Well may they break our Heads, that mark the flinty
    Stone.
'Tis want of Sence to sup abroad too late;
Unless thou first hast settled thy Estate.
As many Fates attend, thy Steps to meet,

As there are waking Windows in the Street.
Bless the good Gods, and think thy chance is rare
To have a Piss-pot only for thy share.

The scouring Drunkard, if he does not fight
Before his Bed-time, takes no rest that Night,
Passing the tedious Hours in greater pain
Than stern *Achilles*, when his Friend was slain:
'Tis so ridiculous, but so true withall,
A Bully cannot sleep without a Braul:
Yet tho his youthful Blood be fir'd with Wine,
He wants not Wit, the Danger to decline:
Is cautious to avoid the Coach and Six,
And on the Lacquies will no Quarrel fix.
His Train of Flambeaus, and Embroider'd Coat
May Priviledge my Lord to walk secure on Foot.
But me, who must by Moon-light homeward bend,
Or lighted only with a Candle's end,
Poor me he fights, if that be fighting, where
He only Cudgels, and I only bear.
He stands, and bids me stand: I must abide;
For he's the stronger, and is Drunk beside.

Where did you whet your Knife to Night, he cries,
And shred the Leeks that in your Stomach rise?
Whose windy Beans have stuff't your Guts, and where
Have your black Thumbs been dipt in Vinegar?
With what Companion Cobler have you fed,
On old Ox-cheeks, or He-Goats tougher Head?
What, are you Dumb? Quick with your Answer, quick,
Before my Foot Salutes you with a Kick.
Say, in what nasty Cellar, under Ground,
Or what Church-Porch, your Rogueship may be found?
Answer, or Answer not, 'tis all the same:
He lays me on, and makes me bear the blame.
Before the Bar, for beating him, you come;
This is a Poor Man's Liberty in *Rome*.

You beg his Pardon; happy to retreat
With some remaining Teeth, to chew your Meat.

Nor is this all; for, when Retir'd, you think
To sleep securely; when the Candles wink,
When every Door with Iron Chains is barr'd,
And roaring Taverns are no longer heard;
The Ruffian Robbers by no Justice aw'd,
And unpaid cut-Throat Soldiers, are abroad;
Those Venal Souls, who, harden'd in each ill
To save Complaints and Prosecution, kill.
Chas'd from their Woods and Bogs, the Padders come
To this vast City, as their Native Home:
To live at ease, and safely sculk in *Rome*.

The Forge in Fetters only is employ'd;
Our Iron Mines exhausted and destroy'd
In Shackles; for these Villains scarce allow
Goads for the Teams, and Plough-shares for the Plough.
Oh happy Ages of our Ancestours,
Beneath the Kings and Tribunitial Pow'rs!
One Jayl did all their Criminals restrain;
Which, now, the Walls of *Rome* can scarce contain.

More I cou'd say, more Causes I cou'd show
For my departure; but the Sun is low:
The Waggoner grows weary of my stay;
And whips his Horses forwards on their way.

Farewell; and when, like me, o'erwhelm'd with care.
You to your own *Aquinum* shall repair,
To take a mouthful of sweet Country air,
Be mindful of your Friend; and send me word,
What Joys your Fountains and cool Shades afford:
Then, to assist your Satyrs, I will come;
And add new Venom, when you write of *Rome*.

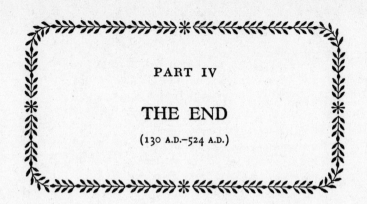

PART IV

THE END

(130 A.D.–524 A.D.)

THE causes of the slow decline of the Roman Empire are beyond the province of the purely literary historian; but its effects are plain in a kind of listlessness. In an attempt to stop the economic rot, imperial edicts bound the subjects of the Empire to follow in their fathers' callings; the Empire became one great, stratified serfdom. Under the early Empire, Tacitus had put into the mouth of a barbarian the great challenge to the boast of the *Pax Romana*: "*Solitudinem faciunt, pacem appellant*"—"They make a desert and call it peace." Now it might be said that Rome made a prison and called it peace. Slavery is fatal to inventiveness, because it is so easy to let the slaves do the work; for instance, the Romans never learned to tack a ship, and they never made much use even of the water mill, which had been invented by the Alexandrine Greeks. The only expedient that Rome was able to invent was more servitude. The desperate expedient worked, for a time; bureaucracy and serfdom kept the wheels turning slowly. As one watches the Empire creak downhill, one is reminded of E. M. Forster's fantasy, "The Machine Stops," a beehive society where all wants were supplied by one vast machine; when the machine began to break down here and there, nobody knew what to do about it.

A few works of the declining Empire suggest a kind of too early spring, a budding of the romanticism which was to flower in the Middle Ages. *The Golden Ass* of Apuleius, with its witches and enchantments, has the real romantic feeling. The episode of Cupid and Psyche —which means Love and the Soul—is a foreshadowing of allegory, especially the allegory of Love, which was one of the dominant forms of the Middle Ages; while the underlying idea, that the Soul betrays Love and regains him through suffering, is one which (though Apuleius would have rejected this indignantly) could hardly have occurred to a pagan before the coming of Christianity.

Then there is that haunting poem, the "Pervigilium Veneris," or "The Vigil of Venus." In form it marks the beginning of the re-emergence of the old native accentual rhythm. It is written in a long trochaic line, in which the normal stress accent coincides with the verse beat much oftener than in the hexameter and other meters employed by the classic poets; some lines, like "*Ipsa gemmis purpurantem pingit annum floridis,*" might be scanned by accent alone. The next step in this direction was taken by Venantius Fortunatus, who used the same measure for the earliest hymns of the Church but scanned it entirely by accent: "*Pange, lingua, gloriosi prœlium certaminis*"—"Speak, my tongue, and tell the battle, tell the glory of the strife." The next step would be rhyme, but that does not appear until the Middle Ages. In spirit, the "Pervigilium Veneris" is altogether romantic. One translator has boldly rendered the title "The Eve of Saint Venus"; perhaps too boldly, for the Venus of the poem is certainly still the pagan goddess of earthly love. And yet her paganness, bound up as it is with the wildwood in springtime, is less like the Mother of Rome in Lucretius or Virgil than like the enchantress of the Tannhäuser legend. At the end the poet suddenly abandons his theme, in a manner that no classical poet would have allowed himself, to cry out in his own person and lament the loss of his gift of song. Coming where they do, those lines are one of those historic accidents that seem too perfectly symbolic to be accidental. They are like the story of the ship, at the time of the crucifixion of Christ in Jerusalem, that approached an unfamiliar shore and heard the people wailing, "Great Pan is dead!" We can guess with certainty that it was the local festival for one of the innumerable gods who died and were reborn; and yet to us, as to the sailors, it seems a lamentation for the death of God, who is All. So, in the last lines of her last great poem, we hear the voice of Rome herself crying out because the god of song has forsaken her. The romantic spirit was putting out its first buds; but there was soon to come the long, hard frost of the Dark Ages.

Christianity added little to literature, as distinct from theology. Its preoccupation with the state of the soul led to a kind of introspectiveness exemplified in the *Confessions* of Saint Augustine, which may be called the beginning of the modern novel and indeed of modern psychology; but it cannot be said that either the Church Fathers or the early writers of unrhymed hymns have much to offer apart from edification.

As was fitting, the last work of the ancient world was written by a Christian, and might have been written by a pagan, if the pagan was a Neoplatonist. Rome had fallen at last. Theodoric the Ostrogoth ruled in the city. Anicius Boëthius, who has been called the last of the Romans and the first of the Scholastics, had been a consul under King Theodoric—the names of the Republican offices persisted even yet. He was accused of conspiring with Justin, the still ruling emperor in the East, "to maintain the integrity of the Senate and restore Rome to liberty"—how familiar it sounds! He was imprisoned and ultimately put to death. While in prison he wrote his *De Consolatione Philosophiæ*, an eloquent and deeply thought consideration of good and evil in the form of a dialogue between the prisoner Boëthius and Philosophy, who comes to instruct and console him. One passage in it, concerned with the problem of man's free will and God's foreknowledge, contains speculations about the nature of time which are an anticipation of some of the most modern theories. Boëthius was a Christian, but he limited himself to "natural theology," to the ideas which reason alone put within the reach of any man, Christian or pagan; the God of whom he writes might have been conceived by any of the followers of Plato who had learned to look for the One behind the many. So, as the lights go out all over the Western world, the last of the Romans tells us that among the ancients there is still to be found the consolation of philosophy.

LUCIUS APULEIUS

(born 125? A.D.)

✱

From The Golden Ass

✱

Cupid and Psyche

Translated by *Walter Pater*

IN A CERTAIN city lived a king and queen who had three daughters exceeding fair. But the beauty of the elder sisters, though pleasant to behold, yet passed not the measure of human praise, while such was the loveliness of the youngest that men's speech was too poor to commend it worthily and could express it not at all. Many of the citizens and of strangers, whom the fame of this excellent vision had gathered thither, confounded by that matchless beauty, could but kiss the finger-tips of their right hands at sight of her, as in adoration to the goddess Venus herself. And soon a rumor passed through the country that she whom the blue deep had borne, forbearing her divine dignity, was even then moving among men, or that by some fresh germination from the stars, not the sea now, but the earth, had put forth a new Venus, endued with the flower of virginity.

This belief, with the fame of the maiden's loveliness, went daily further into distant lands, so that many people were drawn together to behold that glorious

619

model of the age. Men sailed no longer to Paphos, to Cnidus or Cythera, to the presence of the goddess Venus: her sacred rites were neglected, her images stood uncrowned, the cold ashes were left to disfigure her forsaken altars. It was to a maiden that men's prayers were offered, to a human countenance they looked, in propitiating so great a godhead: when the girl went forth in the morning they strewed flowers on her way, and the victims proper to that unseen goddess were presented as she passed along. This conveyance of divine worship to a mortal kindled meantime the anger of the true Venus. "Lo! now the ancient parent of nature," she cried, "the fountain of all elements! Behold me, Venus, benign mother of the world, sharing my honours with a mortal maiden, while my name, built up in heaven, is profaned by the mean things of earth! Shall a perishable woman bear my image about with her? In vain did the shepherd of Ida prefer me! Yet shall she have little joy, whosoever she be, of her usurped and unlawful loveliness!" Thereupon she called to her that winged, bold boy, of evil ways, who wanders armed by night through men's houses, spoiling their marriages; and stirring yet more by her speech his inborn wantonness, she led him to the city, and showed him Psyche as she walked.

"I pray thee," she said, "give thy mother a full revenge. Let this maid become the slave of an unworthy love." Then, embracing him closely, she departed to the shore and took her throne upon the crest of the wave. And lo! at her unuttered will, her ocean-servants are in waiting: the daughters of Nereus are there singing their song, and Portunus, and Salacia, and the tiny charioteer of the dolphin, with a host of Tritons leaping through the billows. And one blows softly his sounding sea-shell, another spreads a silken web against the sun, a third

presents the mirror to the eyes of his mistress, while
the others swim side by side below, drawing her chariot.
Such was the escort of Venus as she went upon the sea.

Psyche meantime, aware of her loveliness, had no fruit
thereof. All people regarded and admired, but none
sought her in marriage. It was but as upon the finished
work of the craftsman that they gazed upon that divine
likeness. Her sisters, less fair than she, were happily
wedded. She, even as a widow, sitting at home, wept
over her desolation, hating in her heart the beauty in
which all men were pleased.

And the king, supposing that the gods were angry,
inquired of the oracle of Apollo, and Apollo answered
him thus: "Let the damsel be placed on the top of a
certain mountain, adorned as for the bed of marriage
and of death. Look not for a son-in-law of mortal birth;
but for that evil serpent-thing, by reason of whom even
the gods tremble and the shadows of Styx are afraid."

So the king returned home and made known the
oracle to his wife. For many days she lamented, but at
last the fulfilment of the divine precept is urgent upon
her, and the company was made ready to conduct the
maiden to her deadly bridal. And now the nuptial torch
gathers dark smoke and ashes: the pleasant sound of
the pipe is changed into a cry: the marriage hymn con-
cludes in a sorrowful wailing: below her yellow wed-
ding-veil the bride shook away her tears; insomuch that
the whole city was afflicted together at the ill-luck of
the stricken house.

But the mandate of the god impelled the hapless
Psyche to her fate, and, these solemnities being ended,
the funeral of the living soul goes forth, all the people
following. Psyche, bitterly weeping, assists not at her
marriage but at her own obsequies, and while the
parents hesitate to accomplish a thing so unholy the

daughter cries to them: "Wherefore torment your luck-
less age by long weeping? This was the prize of my
extraordinary beauty! When all people celebrated us
with divine honours, and with one voice named the New
Venus, it was then ye should have wept for me as one
dead. Now at last I understand that that one name of
Venus has been my ruin. Lead me and set me upon the
appointed place. I am in haste to submit to that well-
omened marriage, to behold that goodly spouse. Why
delay the coming of him who was born for the destruc-
tion of the whole world?"

She was silent, and with firm step went on the way.
And they proceeded to the appointed place on a steep
mountain, and left there the maiden alone, and took
their way homeward dejectedly. The wretched parents,
in their close-shut house, yielded themselves to per-
petual night; while to Psyche, fearful and trembling
and weeping sore upon the mountain-top, comes the
gentle Zephyrus. He lifts her mildly, and, with vesture
floating on either side, bears her by his own soft breath-
ing over the windings of the hills, and sets her lightly
among the flowers in the bosom of a valley below.

Psyche, in those delicate grassy places, lying sweetly
on her dewy bed, rested from the agitation of her soul
and arose in peace. And lo! a grove of mighty trees, with
a fount of water, clear as glass, in the midst; and hard
by the water, a dwelling-place, built not by human
hands but by some divine cunning. One recognized,
even at the entering, the delightful hostelry of a god.
Golden pillars sustained the roof, arched most curiously
in cedar-wood and ivory. The walls were hidden under
wrought silver, all tame and woodland creatures leaping
forward to the visitor's gaze. Wonderful indeed was the
craftsman, divine or half divine, who by the subtlety

of his art had breathed so wild a soul into the silver!
The very pavement was distinct with pictures in goodly
stones. In the glow of its precious metal the house is its
own daylight, having no need of the sun. Well might it
seem a place fashioned for the conversation of gods
with men!

Psyche, drawn forward by the delight of it, came near,
and, her courage growing, stood within the doorway.
One by one, she admired the beautiful things she saw;
and, most wonderful of all! no lock, no chain, nor living
guardian protected that great treasure-house. But as she
gazed there came a voice—a voice, as it were, unclothed
of its bodily vesture. "Mistress!" it said, "all these things
are thine. Lie down, and relieve thy weariness, and rise
again for the bath when thou wilt. We thy servants,
whose voice thou hearest, will be beforehand with our
service, and a royal feast shall be ready."

And Psyche understood that some divine care was
providing, and, refreshed with sleep and the bath, sat
down to the feast. Still she saw no one: only she heard
words falling here and there, and had voices alone to
serve her. And the feast being ended, one entered the
chamber and sang to her unseen, while another struck
the chords of a harp, invisible with him who played on
it. Afterwards the sound of a company singing together
came to her, but still so that none was present to sight;
yet it appeared that a great multitude of singers was
there.

And the hour of evening inviting her, she climbed into
the bed; and as the night was far advanced, behold, a
sound of a certain clemency approaches her. Then,
fearing for her maidenhood, in so great solitude, she
trembled, and more than any evil she knew dreaded that
she knew not. And now the husband, that unknown hus-

band, drew near, and ascended the couch, and made her his wife; and lo! before the rise of dawn he had departed hastily. . . .

One night the bridegroom spoke thus to his beloved, "O Psyche, most pleasant bride! Fortune is grown stern with us, and threatens thee with mortal peril. Thy sisters, troubled at the report of thy death and seeking some trace of thee, will come to the mountain's top. But if by chance their cries reach thee, answer not, neither look forth at all, lest thou bring sorrow upon me and destruction upon thyself." Then Psyche promised that she would do according to his will. But the bridegroom was fled away again with the night. And all that day she spent in tears, repeating that she was now dead indeed, shut up in that golden prison, powerless to console her sisters sorrowing after her, or to see their faces; and so went to rest weeping.

And after a while came the bridegroom again, and embracing her as she wept, complained, "Was this thy promise, my Psyche? What have I to hope from thee? Even in the arms of thy husband thou ceasest not from pain. Do now as thou wilt. Indulge thine own desire, though it seeks what will ruin thee. Yet wilt thou remember my warning, repentant too late." Then, protesting that she is like to die, she obtains from him that he suffer her to see her sisters, and present to them moreover what gifts she would of golden ornaments; but therewith he ofttimes advised her never at any time, yielding to pernicious counsel, to inquire concerning his bodily form, lest she fall, through unholy curiosity, from so great a height of fortune, nor feel ever his embrace again. "I would die a hundred times," she said, cheerful at last, "rather than be deprived of thy most sweet usage. I love thee as my own soul, beyond comparison even with Love himself. Only bid thy servant Zephyrus bring hither my sisters, as he brought me. My honey-comb! My husband! Thy Psyche's breath of life!" So he promised; and after the embraces of the night, ere the light appeared, vanished from the hands of his bride.

And the sisters, coming to the place where Psyche was abandoned, wept loudly among the rocks, and called upon her by name, so that the sound came down to her, and running out of the palace distraught, she cried, "Wherefore afflict your souls with lamentation? I whom you mourn am here." Then, summoning Zephy-rus, she reminded him of her husband's bidding; and he bare them down with a gentle blast. "Enter now," she said, "into my house, and relieve your sorrow in the company of Psyche your sister."

And Psyche displayed to them all the treasures of the golden house, and its great family of ministering voices, nursing in them the malice which was already at their hearts. And at last one of them asks curiously who the lord of that celestial array may be, and what manner of man her husband? And Psyche answered dissem-blingly, "A young man, handsome and mannerly, with a goodly beard. For the most part he hunts upon the mountains." And lest the secret should slip from her in the way of further speech, loading her sisters with gold and gems, she commanded Zephyrus to bear them away.

And they returned home, on fire with envy. "See now the injustice of fortune!" cried one. "We, the elder chil-dren, are given like servants to be the wives of strangers, while the youngest is possessed of so great riches, who scarcely knows how to use them. You saw, Sister! what a hoard of wealth lies in the house; what glittering gowns; what splendor of precious gems, besides all that gold trodden under foot. If she indeed hath, as she said, a bridegroom so goodly, then no one in all the world is happier. And it may be that this husband, being of divine nature, will make her too a goddess. Nay! so in truth it is. It was even thus she bore herself. Already she looks aloft and breathes divinity; who, though but a woman, has voices for her handmaidens, and can command the winds." "Think," answered the other, "how arrogantly she dealt with us, grudging us these trifling gifts out of all that store, and when our company a burden, causing us to be hissed and driven away from her through the air!" . . .

And the bridegroom, whom still she knows not, warns her thus a second time, as he talks with her by night: "Seest thou what peril besets thee? Those cunning wolves have made ready for thee their snares, of which the sum is that they persuade thee to search into the fashion of my countenance, the seeing of which, as I have told thee often, will be the seeing of it no more for ever. But do thou neither listen nor make answer to aught regarding thy husband. Besides, we have sown also the seed of our race. Even now this bosom grows with a child to be born to us, a child, if thou but keep our secret, of divine quality; if thou profane it, subject to death." And Psyche was glad at the tidings, rejoicing in that solace of a divine seed, and in the glory of that pledge of love to be, and the dignity of the name of mother. Anxiously she notes the increase of the days, the waning months. And again, as he tarries briefly beside her, the bridegroom repeats his warning: "Even now the sword is drawn with which thy sisters seek thy life. Have pity on thyself, sweet wife, and upon our child, and see not those evil women again." But the sisters make their way into the palace once more, crying to her in wily tones, "O Psyche! and thou too wilt be a mother! How great will be the joy at home! Happy indeed shall we be to have the nursing of the golden child. Truly if he be answerable to the beauty of his parents, it will be a birth of Cupid himself."

So, little by little they stole upon the heart of their sister. She, meanwhile, bids the lyre to sound for their delight, and the playing is heard: she bids the pipes to move, the quire to sing, and the music and the singing come invisibly, soothing the mind of the listener with sweetest modulation. Yet not even thereby was their malice put to sleep: once more they seek to know what manner of husband she has, and whence that seed. And Psyche, simple over-much, forgetful of her first story, answers, "My husband comes from a far country, trading for great sums. He is already of middle age, with whitening locks." And therewith she dismisses them again.

And returning home upon the soft breath of Zephyrus one cried to the other, "What shall be said of so ugly a lie? He who was a young man with goodly beard is now in middle life. It must be that she told a false tale: else is she in very truth ignorant of what manner of man he is. Howsoever it be, let us destroy her quickly. For if she indeed knows not, be sure that her bridegroom is one of the gods: it is a god she bears in her womb. And let that be far from us! If she be called mother of a god, then will life be more than I can bear."

So, full of rage against her, they returned to Psyche, and said to her craftily, "Thou livest in an ignorant bliss, all incurious of thy real danger. It is a deadly serpent, as we certainly know, that comes to sleep by thy side. Remember the words of the oracle, which declared thee destined to a cruel beast. There are those who have seen it at nightfall, coming back from its feeding. In no long time, they say, it will end its blandishments. It but waits for the babe to be formed in thee, that it may devour thee by so much the richer. If indeed the solitude of this musical place, or it may be the loathsome commerce of a hidden love, delight thee, we at least in sisterly piety have done our part." And at last the unhappy Psyche, simple and frail of soul, carried away by the terror of their words, losing memory of her husband's precepts and her own promise, brought upon herself a great calamity. Trembling and turning pale, she answers them, "And they who tell those things, it may be, speak the truth. For in very deed never have I seen the face of my husband, nor know I at all what manner of man he is. Always he frights me diligently from the sight of him, threatening some great evil should I too curiously look upon his face. Do ye, if ye can help your sister in her great peril, stand by her now."

Her sisters answered her, "The way of safety we have well considered, and will teach thee. Take a sharp knife, and hide it in that part of the couch where thou art wont to lie: take also a lamp filled with oil, and set it privily behind the curtain. And when he shall have drawn up his coils into the accustomed place, and thou hearest him breathe in sleep, slip then from his side and discover the lamp, and, knife in hand, put forth thy strength, and strike off the serpent's head." And so they departed in haste.

And Psyche left alone (alone but for the furies which beset her) is tossed up and down in her distress, like a wave of the sea; and though her will is firm, yet, in the moment of putting hand to the deed, she falters, and is torn asunder by various apprehensions of the great calamity upon her. She hastens and anon delays, now full of distrust, and now of angry courage: under one bodily form she loathes the monster and loves the bridegroom. But twilight ushers in the night; and at length in haste she makes ready for the terrible deed. Darkness

came, and the bridegroom; and he first, after some faint
essay of love, falls into a deep sleep.

And she, erewhile of no strength, the hard purpose
of destiny assisting her, is confirmed in force. With lamp
plucked forth, knife in hand, she put by her sex; and
lo! as the secrets of the bed become manifest, the
sweetest and most gentle of all creatures, Love himself,
reclined there, in his own proper loveliness! At sight
of him the very flame of the lamp kindled more gladly!
But Psyche was afraid at the vision, and, faint of soul,
trembled back upon her knees, and would have hidden
the steel in her own bosom. But the knife slipped from
her hand; and now, undone, yet ofttimes looking upon
the beauty of that divine countenance, she lives again.
She sees the locks of that golden head, pleasant with
the unction of the gods, shed down in graceful entangle-
ment behind and before, about the ruddy cheeks and
white throat. The pinions of the winged god, yet fresh
with the dew, are spotless upon his shoulders, the deli-
cate plumage wavering over them as they lie at rest.
Smooth he was, and, touched with light, worthy of
Venus his mother. At the foot of the couch lay his bows
and arrows, the instruments of his power, propitious to
men.

And Psyche, gazing hungrily thereon, draws an arrow
from the quiver, and trying the point upon her thumb,
tremulous still, drave in the barb, so that a drop of blood
came forth. Thus fell she, by her own act, and unaware,
into the love of Love. Falling upon the bridegroom, with
indrawn breath and a hurry of kisses from her eager and
open lips, she shuddered as she thought how brief that
sleep might be. And it chanced that a drop of burning
oil fell from the lamp upon the god's shoulder. Ah! mala-
droit minister of love, thus to wound him from whom all
fire comes; though 't was a lover, I trow, first devised

thee, to have the fruit of his desire even in the darkness!
At the touch of the fire the god started up, and behold-
ing the overflow of her faith, quietly took flight from
her embraces.

And Psyche, as he rose upon the wing, laid hold on
him with her two hands, hanging upon him in his pas-
sage through the air, till she sinks to the earth through
weariness. And as she lay there, the divine lover, tarry-
ing still, lighted upon a cypress tree which grew near,
and, from the top of it, spake thus to her, in great emo-
tion. "Foolish one! unmindful of the command of Venus,
my mother, who had devoted thee to one of base de-
gree, I fled to thee in his stead. Now know I that that
was vainly done. Into mine own flesh pierced mine
arrow, and I made thee my wife, only that I might seem
a monster beside thee—that thou shouldst seek to
wound the head wherein lay the eyes so full of love to
thee! Again and again, I thought to put thee on thy
guard concerning these things, and warned thee in lov-
ing kindness. Now I would but punish thee by my flight
hence." And therewith he winged his way into the deep
sky.

Psyche, prostrate upon the earth, and following far
as sight might reach the flight of the bridegroom, wept
and lamented; and when the breadth of space had
parted him wholly from her, cast herself down from the
bank of a river which was nigh. But the stream, turning
gentle in honour of the god, put her forth again unhurt
upon its margin. And as it happened, Pan, the rustic
god, was sitting just then by the waterside, embracing,
in the body of a reed, the goddess Canna; teaching her
to respond to him in all varieties of slender sound. Hard
by, his flock of goats browsed at will. And the shaggy
god called her, wounded and outworn, kindly to him
and said, "I am but a rustic herdsman, pretty maiden,

yet wise, by favour of my great age and long experience; and, if I guess truly by those faltering steps, by thy sorrowful eyes and continual sighing, thou labourest with excess of love. Listen then to me, and seek not death again, in the stream or otherwise. Put aside thy woe and turn thy prayers to Cupid. He is in truth a delicate youth: win him by the delicacy of thy service."

So the shepherd-god spoke, and Psyche, answering nothing, but with a reverence to his serviceable deity, went on her way. And while she, in her search after Cupid, wandered through many lands, he was lying in the chamber of his mother, heart-sick. And the white bird which floats over the waves plunged in haste into the sea, and approaching Venus as she bathed, made known to her that her son lies afflicted with some grievous hurt, doubtful of life. And Venus cried, angrily, "My son, then, has a mistress! And it is Psyche, who witched away my beauty and was the rival of my godhead, whom he loves!"

Therewith she issued from the sea, and returning to her golden chamber, found there the lad, sick, as she had heard, and cried from the doorway, "Well done, truly! to trample thy mother's precepts under foot, to spare my enemy that cross of an unworthy love; nay, unite her to thyself, child as thou art, that I might have a daughter-in-law who hates me! I will make thee repent of thy sport, and the savour of thy marriage bitter. There is one who shall chasten this body of thine, put out thy torch and unstring thy bow. Not till she has plucked forth that hair, into which so oft these hands have smoothed the golden light, and sheared away thy wings, shall I feel the injury done me avenged." And with this she hastened in anger from the doors.

And Ceres and Juno met her, and sought to know the meaning of her troubled countenance. "Ye come in season," she cried; "I pray you, find for me Psyche. It must needs be that ye have heard the disgrace of my house." And they, ignorant of what was done, would have soothed her anger, saying, "What fault, Mistress, hath thy son committed, that thou wouldst destroy the girl he loves? Knowest thou not that he is now of age? Because he wears his years so lightly must he seem to thee ever but a child? Wilt thou for ever thus pry into the pastimes of thy son, always accusing his wantonness, and blaming in him those delicate wiles which are all thine own?" Thus, in secret fear of the boy's bow, did they seek to please him with their gracious patronage. But Venus, angry at their light taking of her wrongs, turned her back upon them, and with hasty steps made her way once more to the sea.

Meanwhile Psyche, tost in soul, wandering hither and thither, rested not night or day in the pursuit of her husband, desiring, if she might not soothe his anger by the endearments of a wife, at the least to propitiate him with the prayers of a handmaid. And seeing a certain temple on the top of a high mountain, she said, "Who knows whether yonder place be not the abode of my lord?" Thither, therefore, she turned her steps, hastening now the more because desire and hope pressed her on, weary as she was with the labours of the way, and so, painfully measuring out the highest ridges of the mountain, drew near to the sacred couches. She sees ears of wheat, in heaps or twisted into chaplets; ears of barley also, with sickles and all the instruments of harvest, lying there in disorder, thrown at random from the hands of the labourers in the great heat. These she curiously sets apart, one by one, duly ordering them; for she said within herself, "I may not neglect the shrines, nor the holy service, of any god there be, but must rather win by supplication the kindly mercy of them all."

And Ceres found her bending sadly upon her task, and cried aloud, "Alas, Psyche! Venus, in the furiousness of her anger, tracks thy footsteps through the world, seeking for thee to pay her the utmost penalty; and thou, thinking of anything rather than thine own safety, hast taken on thee the care of what belongs to me!" Then Psyche fell down at her feet, and sweeping the floor with her hair, washing the footsteps of the goddess in her tears, besought her mercy, with many prayers: "By the gladdening rites of harvest, by the lighted lamps and mystic marches of the Marriage and mysterious Invention, by thy daughter Proserpine, and by all beside that the holy place of Attica veils in silence, minister, I pray thee, to the sorrowful heart of Psyche! Suffer me to hide myself but for a few days among the heaps of corn, till time have softened the anger of the goddess, and my strength, out-worn in my long travail, be recovered by a little rest."

But Ceres answered her, "Truly thy tears move me, and I would fain help thee; only I dare not incur the ill-will of my kinswoman. Depart hence as quickly as may be." And Psyche, repelled against hope, afflicted now with twofold sorrow, making her way back again, beheld among the half-lighted woods of the valley below a sanctuary builded with cunning art. And that she might lose no way of hope, howsoever doubtful, she drew near to the sacred doors. She sees there gifts of price, and garments fixed upon the door-posts and to the branches of the trees, wrought with letters of gold which told the name of the goddess to whom they were dedicated, with thanksgiving for that she had done. So, with bent knee and hands laid about the glowing altar, she prayed saying, "Sister and spouse of Jupiter' be thou to these my desperate fortunes, Juno the Auspicious! I know that thou dost willingly help those in travail with child; deliver me from the peril that is upon me." And as she prayed thus, Juno in the majesty of her godhead was straightway present, and answered: "Would that I might incline favorably to thee; but against the will of Venus, whom I have ever loved as a daughter, I may not, for very shame, grant thy prayer."

And Psyche, dismayed by this new shipwreck of her hope, communed thus with herself, "Whither, from the midst of the snares that beset me, shall I take my way once more? In what dark solitude shall I hide me from the all-seeing eye of Venus? What if I put on at length a man's courage, and yielding myself unto her as my mistress, soften by a humility not yet too late the fierceness of her purpose? Who knows but that I may find him also whom my soul seeketh after, in the abode of his mother?"

And Venus, renouncing all earthly aid in her search, prepared to return to heaven. She ordered the chariot to be made ready, which Vulcan had wrought for her as a marriage-gift, with a cunning of hand which had left his work so much the richer by the weight of gold it lost under his tool. From the multitude which housed about the bed-chamber of their mistress, white doves came forth, and with joyful motions bent their painted necks beneath the yoke. Behind it, with playful riot, the sparrows sped onward, with other birds sweet of song, making known by their soft notes the approach of the goddess. Eagle and cruel hawk alarmed not the quireful family of Venus. And the clouds broke away, as the uttermost ether opened to receive her, daughter and goddess, with great joy.

And Venus passed straightway to the house of Jupiter to beg from him the service of Mercury, the god of speech. And Jupiter refused not her prayer. And Venus and Mercury descended from heaven together; and as they went, the former said to the latter, "Thou knowest, my brother of Arcady, that never at any time have I done anything without thy help; for how long time, moreover, I have sought a certain maiden in vain. And now nought remains but that, by thy heraldry, I proclaim a reward for whomsoever shall find her. Do thou my bidding quickly." And therewith she conveyed to him a little scrip, in the which was written the name of Psyche, with other things; and so returned home.

And Mercury failed not in his office; but departing into all lands, proclaimed that whosoever delivered up to Venus the fugitive girl, should receive from herself seven kisses—one thereof full of the inmost honey of her throat. With that the doubt of Psyche was ended. And now, as she came near to the doors of Venus, one of the household, whose name was Use-and-Wont, ran out to her, crying: "Hast thou learned, Wicked Maid! now at last! that thou hast a mistress?" and seizing her roughly by the hair, drew her into the presence of Venus. And when Venus saw her, she cried out, saying, "Thou hast deigned then to make thy salutations to thy mother-in-law. Now will I in turn treat thee as becometh a dutiful daughter-in-law!"

And she took barley and millet and poppy-seed, every kind of grain and seed, and mixed them together, and laughed, and said to her: "Methinks so plain a maiden can earn lovers only by industrious ministry: now will I also make trial of thy service. Sort me this heap of seed, the one kind from the others, grain by grain; and get thy task done before the evening." And Psyche, stunned by the cruelty of her bidding, was silent, and moved not her hand to the inextricable heap. And there came forth a little ant, which had understanding of the difficulty of her task, and took pity upon the consort of the god of Love; and he ran deftly hither and thither, and called together the whole army of his fellows. "Have pity," he cried, "nimble scholars of the Earth, Mother of all things! have pity upon the wife of Love, and hasten to help her in her perilous effort." Then, one upon the other, the hosts of the insect people hurried together; and they sorted asunder the whole heap of seed, separating every grain after its kind, and so departed quickly out of sight.

And at nightfall Venus returned, and seeing that task finished with so wonderful diligence, she cried, "The work is not thine, thou naughty maid, but his in whose eyes thou hast found favour." And calling her again in the morning, "See now the grove," she said, "beyond yonder torrent. Certain sheep feed there, whose fleeces shine with gold. Fetch me straightway a lock of that precious stuff, having gotten it as thou mayst."

And Psyche went forth willingly, not to obey the command of Venus, but even to seek a rest from her labour in the depths of the river. But from the river, the green reed, lowly mother of music, spake to her: "O Psyche! pollute not these waters by self-destruction, nor approach that terrible flock; for, as the heat groweth, they wax fierce. Lie down under yon plane-tree, till the quiet of the river's breath have soothed them. Thereafter thou mayst shake down the fleecy gold from the trees of the grove, for it holdeth by the leaves."

And Psyche, instructed thus by the simple reed, in the humanity of its heart, filled her bosom with the soft golden stuff, and returned to Venus. But the goddess smiled bitterly, and said to her, "Well know I who was the author of this thing also. I will make further trial of thy discretion, and the boldness of thy heart. Seest thou the utmost peak of yonder steep mountain? The dark stream which flows down thence waters the Stygian fields, and swells the flood of Cocytus. Bring me now, in this little urn, a draught from its innermost source." And therewith she puts into her hands a vessel of wrought crystal.

And Psyche set forth in haste on her way to the mountain, looking there at last to find the end of her hapless life. But when she came to the region which borders on the cliff that was showed to her, she understood the deadly nature of her task. From a great rock, steep and slippery, a horrible river of water poured forth, falling straightway by a channel exceeding narrow into the unseen gulf below. And lo! creeping from the rocks on either hand, angry serpents, with their long necks and sleepless eyes. The very waters found a voice and bade her depart, in smothered cries of, *Depart hence!* and *What doest thou here? Look around thee!* and *Destruction is upon thee!* And then sense left her, in the immensity of her peril, as one changed to stone.

Yet not even then did the distress of this innocent soul escape the steady eye of a gentle providence. For the bird of Jupiter spread his wings and took flight to her, and asked her, "Didst thou think, simple one, even thou! that thou couldst steal one drop of that relentless stream, the holy river of Styx, terrible even to the gods? But give me thine urn." And the bird took the urn, and filled it at the source, and returned to her quickly from among the teeth of the serpents, bringing with him of the waters, all unwilling—nay! warning him to depart away and not molest them.

And she, receiving the urn with great joy, ran back quickly that she might deliver it to Venus, and yet again satisfied not the angry goddess. "My child!" she said, "in this one thing further must thou serve me. Take now this tiny casket, and get thee down even unto hell, and deliver it to Proserpine. Tell her that Venus would have of her beauty so much at least as may suffice for but one day's use, that beauty she possessed erewhile being forworn and spoiled, through her tendance upon the sick-bed of her son; and be not slow in returning."

And Psyche perceived there the last ebbing of her fortune—that she was now thrust openly upon death, who must go down, of her own motion, to Hades and the Shades. And straightway she climbed to the top of an exceeding high tower, thinking within herself, "I will cast myself down thence: so shall I descend most quickly into the kingdom of the dead." And the tower again broke forth into speech: "Wretched Maid! Wretched Maid! Wilt thou destroy thyself? If the breath quit thy body, then wilt thou indeed go down into Hades, but by no means return hither. Listen to me. Among the pathless wilds not far from this place lies a certain mountain, and therein one of hell's vent-holes. Through the breach a rough way lies open, following which thou wilt come, by straight course, to the castle of Orcus. And thou must not go empty-handed. Take in each hand a morsel of barley-bread, soaked in hydromel; and in thy mouth two pieces of money. And when thou shalt be now well onward in the way of death, then wilt thou overtake a lame ass laden with wood, and a lame driver, who will pray thee reach him certain cords to fasten the burden which is falling from the ass; but be thou cautious to pass on in silence. And soon as thou comest to the river of the dead, Charon, in that crazy bark he hath, will put thee over upon the further side. There is greed even among the dead; and thou shalt deliver to him, for the ferrying, one of those two pieces of money, in such wise that he take it with his hand from between thy lips. And as thou passest over the stream, a dead old man, rising on the water, will put up to thee his mouldering hands, and pray thee to draw him into the ferry-boat. But beware that thou yield not to unlawful pity.

"When thou shalt be come over, and art upon the causeway, certain aged women, spinning, will cry to thee to lend thy hand to their work; and beware again that thou take no part therein; for this also is the snare of Venus, whereby she would cause thee to cast away one at least of those cakes thou bearest in thy hands. And think not that a slight matter; for the loss of either one of them will be to thee the losing of the light of day. For a watch-dog exceeding fierce lies ever before the threshold of that lonely house of Proserpine. Close his mouth with one of thy cakes; so shalt thou pass by him, and enter straightway into the presence of Proserpine herself. Then, do thou deliver thy message, and taking what she shall give thee, return back again; offering to the watch-dog the other cake, and to the ferryman that other piece of money thou hast in thy mouth. After this manner mayst thou return again beneath the stars. But withal, I charge thee, think not to look into, nor open, the casket thou bearest, with that treasure of the beauty of the divine countenance hidden therein."

So spake the stones of the tower; and Psyche delayed not, but proceeding diligently after the manner enjoined, entered into the house of Proserpine, at whose feet she sat down humbly, and would neither the delicate couch nor that divine food which the goddess offered her, but did straightway the business of Venus. And Proserpine filled the casket secretly, and shut the lid, and delivered it to Psyche, who fled therewith from Hades with new strength. But coming back into the light of day, even as she hasted now to the ending of her service, she was seized by a rash curiosity. "Lo! now," she said within herself, "my simpleness! who bearing in my hands the

divine loveliness, heed not to touch myself with a par-
ticle at least therefrom, that I may please the more by
the fervor of it, my fair one, my beloved!" Even as she
spoke, she lifted the lid; and behold! within, neither
beauty, nor anything beside, save sleep only, the sleep
of the dead, which took hold upon her, filling all her
members with its drowsy vapour, so that she lay down
in the way and moved not, as in the slumber of death.

And Cupid, being healed of his wound, because he
would endure no longer the absence of her he loved,
gliding through the narrow window of the chamber
wherein he was holden, his pinions being now repaired
by a little rest, fled forth swiftly upon them, and com-
ing to the place where Psyche was, shook that sleep
away from her, and set him in his prison again, awaken-
ing her with the innocent point of his arrow. "Lo! thine
old error again," he said, "which had like once more to
have destroyed thee! But do thou now what is lacking
of the command of my mother: the rest shall be my
care." With these words, the lover rose upon the air; and
being consumed inwardly with the greatness of his love,
penetrated with vehement wing into the highest place of
heaven, to lay his cause before the father of the gods.
And the father of gods took his hand in his, and kissed
his face, and said to him, "At no time, my son, hast thou
regarded me with due honour. Often hast thou vexed my
bosom, wherein lies the disposition of the stars, with
those busy darts of thine. Nevertheless, because thou
hast grown up between these mine hands, I will accom-
plish thy desire." And straightway he bade Mercury to
call the gods together; and, the council-chamber being
filled, sitting upon a high throne, "Ye gods," he said, "all
ye whose names are in the white book of the Muses, ye
know yonder lad. It seems good to me that his youthful
heats should by some means be restrained. And that

all occasion may be taken from him, I would even confine him in the bonds of marriage. He has chosen and embraced a mortal maiden. Let him have fruit of her love, and possess her for ever."

And thereupon he bade Mercury produce Psyche in heaven; and holding out to her his ambrosial cup, "Take it," he said, "and live for ever; nor shall Cupid ever depart from thee." And the gods sat down together to the marriage-feast. On the first couch lay the bridegroom, and Psyche in his bosom. His rustic serving-boy bare the wine to Jupiter; and Bacchus to the rest. The Seasons crimsoned all things with their roses. Apollo sang to the lyre, while a little Pan prattled on his reeds, and Venus danced very sweetly to the soft music. Thus, with due rites, did Psyche pass into the power of Cupid; and from them was born the daughter whom men call Voluptas.

Book IV, Chapter 28, through Book VI, Chapter 24

❧❧❧✳❧❧❧

ANONYMOUS

✳

The Vigil of Venus

Translated by F. L. Lucas

Loveless hearts shall love tomorrow, hearts that have
loved shall love anew.
Spring is young now, spring is singing, in the spring
the world first grew;
In the spring the birds are wedded, in the spring-
time true hearts pair,
Under the rain of her lover's kisses loose the forest
flings her hair.
Now in shadows of the woodland She that binds all
true loves' vows,
She shall build them bowers tomorrow of Her own
green myrtle-boughs.
There Dione high enthronéd on her lovers lays her
law—
Loveless hearts shall love tomorrow, hearts that have
loved shall love once more.

She it is that paints the springtide, flower-be-
jewelled, purple-drest,
She that swells the young bud's bosom with low
whispers from the west,
Till it breaks in balmy blossom; She that in the
wake of night,
O'er the fields where darkness flung them, spreads
the dewdrops' liquid light.

642

See how, trembling, all but falling, each one glit-
ters like a tear!

Yet they fall not—in its station clings so fast each
tiny sphere.

See, the Rose comes forth in crimson, shows her
blush of maiden shame!

Dew that through the windless midnight from the
starry Heavens came,

Bathes tomorrow morn her bosom, strips its mantle
dank and green;

Venus bids at morn tomorrow wed shall every Rose
be seen.

Child of kisses Love hath given, born of blood the
Cyprian shed,

Bred of gem's and flame's refulgence, of the sun's
own crimson bred,

Then the Rose shall rend the splendour of the
bridal veil she wore

And her life's one wedlock show her flushed with
the beauty no man saw.

Loveless hearts shall love tomorrow, hearts that have
loved shall love once more.

Now Her nymphs Love's Lady biddeth muster
where Her myrtles sway;

There's a boy shall be their playmate—"Yet can
Love keep holiday?

Can Love play among Her maidens, if his hand
still holds the bow?"

"Maidens, fear not. Love comes maying. Weapon-
less he comes, your foe.

He is bidden to disarm him, bidden come with
limbs laid bare,

Lest his firebrand, or his arrows, or his bow make
mischief there.

And yet, maidens, watch and ward ye! Cupid hath
a comely hue.
And when Love comes bare and naked, Love wears
all his armour too.
Loveless hearts shall love tomorrow, hearts that have
loved shall love anew."

But to thee, O Maid of Delos, Venus sends maids
chaste as thou,
For this single boon to beg thee—grant through
all thy woodlands now
That no wild thing's blood tomorrow stain the
grasses of the glade,
That in peace o'er its young blossoms green may
glide the westering shade.
She Herself would come to pray thee, might She
move thy maiden heart;
She Herself would bid thee join us, were it but a
maiden's part—
Bid thee gaze while we go dancing through our
three nights' revelry,
Dance with multitudes about us down the glens
that honour thee,
Dance amid a rain of garlands down the lanes of
myrtle-bowers,
With us Ceres, with us Bacchus—yea, the Lord of
Song is ours.
Up now, wake the dark with revel, sing aloud the
long night through!
Bow, ye forests, to Dione! Thou, Diana, shun our
view!
Loveless hearts shall love tomorrow, hearts that have
loved shall love anew.

Lo, Love's Lady comes to judgment. At Her side
 the Graces meet.

Fair with all the flowers of Hybla deck today Her
 judgment-seat.

Hybla, broadcast fling thy blossoms, all that Spring
 bears in her hands;

Of thy flowers make thee a mantle, wide as Ætna's
 meadowlands.

Nymphs of meadow, nymphs of mountain, hither
 all are gathering,

Nymphs of coppice and of forest, nymphs that
 haunt the hidden spring.

She hath bid them all draw hither, She whose
 womb the wing'd Love bore:

"Maids," She laughs, "though Love come naked, no
 more trust him than before."

Loveless hearts shall love tomorrow, hearts that have
 loved shall love once more.

For tomorrow is the morning when high Heaven
 first was wed

And the cycle of the seasons from the clouds of
 spring was bred.

Soft in showers His love descended on the gentle
 lap of Earth,

Quickened all Her mighty body, brought all living
 things to birth.

But the Sea's far-circling surges, quickened by far
 other rain,

Red with blood that streamed from heaven, where
 sea-horses shook their mane

And the blue sea-monsters gambolled, tossed Dione
 from the foam—

Her the Mother, Her the Mighty, Her whose spirit
 hath its home

In the inmost mind of all things, in the blood Her
     power sways
While through earth, through sea, through heaven
     onward wind Her hidden ways.
That day first the paths She fashioned for life's seed
     the wide world o'er,
All the roads of birth revealing, procreation's mystic
     lore.
Loveless hearts shall love tomorrow, hearts that have
     loved shall love once more.

She it was that brought Her Trojans hither to the
     Latin land,
She that gave Her son Æneas the Laurentine
     maiden's hand,
Gave to Mars that other maiden, virgin guard of
     Vesta's fire,
Gave the daughters of the Sabine to the Roman
     youths' desire.
So sprang Ramnes and Quirites; so at last She
     raised to reign
Both our Cæsars, sire and nephew, lest the race of
     Rome should wane.
Loveless hearts shall love tomorrow, hearts that have
     loved shall love again.

Love bids all our fields grow fruitful; well the fields
     Love's Lady know;
Love Himself was born, 'tis whispered, in the
     meadows, long ago.
Him, when all was spring and blossom, Venus
     to Her bosom drew,
On soft kisses of the flowers there She nursed him,
     till he grew.

Loveless hearts shall love tomorrow, hearts that have
loved shall love anew.

Look, beneath the broomy shadows now the great
bulls lie apart,
Each at ease beside his chosen, who hath won and
bound his heart;
In the shadows, look, are lying, mated now, the
bleating sheep;
Yea, today Dione biddeth all the birds their carols
keep.
Hark, the chattering swans are calling hoarse across
the mirrored mere,
While the tragic bride of Tereus through the pop-
lars answers clear—
Sings as clear as happy lover, sings as if forgot at
last
Savage lord and ravished sister, all the anguish of
the past.

Ah, she sings. But we are silent. When shall *my*
spring come to me?
When shall *I* grow as a swallow, and my lips at last
be free?
For my silence Phœbus scorns me and the Muse
her face withdrew:
So it was that its own silence old Amyclæ over-
threw—
Yet loveless hearts shall love tomorrow, hearts that have
loved shall love anew.

SAINT AUGUSTINE

(Aurelius Augustinus, 354 A.D.–430 A.D.)

✳

From the Confessions

Translated by William Watts

✳

How He Robbed a Pear-Tree

SURELY thy law, O Lord, punishes thievery; yea, and this law is so written in our hearts, that iniquity itself cannot blot it out. For what thief does willingly abide another man to steal from him? No, not a rich thief, him that is driven to steal upon necessity. Yet had I a desire to commit thievery; and did it, compelled neither by hunger nor poverty; but even through a cloyedness of well doing, and a pamperedness of iniquity. For I stole that, of which I had enough of mine own, and much better. Nor when I had done, cared I to enjoy the thing which I had stolen, but joying in the theft and sin itself. A pear-tree there was in the orchard next our vineyard, well laden with fruit, not much tempting either for colour or taste. To the shaking and robbing of this, a company of lewd young fellows of us went late one night (having, according to our pestilent custom in the game-places, continued our sports even till that season): thence carried we huge loadings, not for our own lickerishness, but even to fling to the hogs, though perhaps we ate some of it. And all this we did, because we would go whither we should not. Behold my heart, O Lord, which thou hadst pity on in the very bottom of the bottomless pit. Now, behold, let my heart tell thee, what it sought for there, that I should be thus evil for nothing, having no other provocation to ill, but ill itself. It was foul, yet I loved it, I loved to undo myself, I loved mine own fault, not that for which I committed the fault, but even the very fault itself; a base soul, shrinking back thus from my holdfast upon thee, even to utter destruction; not affecting anything from the shame, but the shame itself.

Book II, Chapter 4

BOËTHIUS

(Anicius Manlius Severinus Boëthius, 480 A.D.–524 A.D.)

*

From The Consolation of Philosophy

Translated by H. R. James

"GOD is eternal; in this judgment all rational be-
ings agree. Let us then consider what eternity
is. For this word carries with it a revelation alike of
the Divine nature and of the Divine knowledge. Now
eternity is the possession of endless life whole and per-
fect at a single moment. What this is becomes more
clear and manifest from a comparison with things tem-
poral. For whatever lives in time is a present proceed-
ing from the past to the future, and there is nothing set
in time which can embrace the whole space of its life
together. Tomorrow's state it grasps not yet, while it
has already lost yesterday's; nay, even in the life of today
ye live no longer than one brief transitory moment.
Whatever therefore is subject to the condition of time,
although, as Aristotle deemed of the world, it never
have either beginning or end, and its life be stretched
to the whole extent of time's infinity, it yet is not such
as rightly to be thought eternal. For it does not include
and embrace the whole space of infinite life at once, but
has no present hold on things to come, not yet accom-
plished. Accordingly, that which includes and possesses

the whole fulness of unending life at once, from which
nothing future is absent, from which nothing past has
escaped, this is rightly called eternal; this must of
necessity be ever present to itself in full self-possession,
and hold the infinity of movable time in an abiding
present. Wherefore they deem not rightly who imagine
that on Plato's principles the created world is made co-
eternal with the Creator, because they are told that he
believed the world to have had no beginning in time,
and to be destined never to come to an end. For it is
one thing for existence to be endlessly prolonged, which
was what Plato ascribed to the world, another for the
whole of an endless life to be embraced in the present,
which is manifestly a property peculiar to the Divine
mind. Nor need God appear earlier in mere duration of
time to created things, but only prior in the unique
simplicity of His nature. For the infinite progression
of things in time copies this immediate existence in the
present of the changeless life, and when it cannot suc-
ceed in equalling it, declines from movelessness into
motion, and falls away from the simplicity of a perpetual
present to the infinite duration of the future and the
past; and since it cannot possess the whole fulness of
its life together, for the very reason that in a manner it
never ceases to be, it seems, up to a certain point, to
rival that which it cannot complete and express by at-
taching itself indifferently to any present moment of
time, however swift and brief; and since this bears some
resemblance to that ever-abiding present, it bestows
on everything to which it is assigned the semblance of
existence. But since it cannot abide, it hurries along
the infinite path of time, and the result has been that
it continues by ceaseless movement the life the com-
pleteness of which it could not embrace while it stood

still. So, if we are minded to give things their right
names, we shall follow Plato in saying that God indeed
is eternal, but the world everlasting.

"Since, then, every mode of judgment comprehends
its objects conformably to its own nature, and since
God abides forever in an eternal present, His knowledge,
also transcending all movement of time, dwells in the
simplicity of its own changeless present, and, embrac-
ing the whole infinite sweep of the past and of the
future, contemplates all that falls within its simple
cognition as if it were now taking place. And therefore,
if thou wilt carefully consider that immediate present-
ment whereby it discriminates all things, thou wilt more
rightly deem it not foreknowledge as of something
future, but knowledge of a moment that never passes.
For this cause the name chosen to describe it is not pre-
vision, but providence, because, since utterly removed
in nature from things mean and trivial, its outlook em-
braces all things as from some lofty height. Why then
dost thou insist that the things which are surveyed by
the Divine eye are involved in necessity, whereas clearly
men impose no necessity on things which they see? Does
the act of vision add any necessity to the things which
thou seest before thy eyes?"

"Assuredly not."

"And yet, if we may without unfitness compare God's
present and man's, just as ye see certain things in this
your temporary present, so does He see all things in His
eternal present. Wherefore this Divine anticipation
changes not the natures and properties of things, and
it beholds things present before it, just as they will here-
after come to pass in time. Nor does it confound things
in its judgment, but in the one mental view distinguishes
alike what will come necessarily and what without
necessity. For even as ye, when at one and the same

time ye see a man walking on the earth and the sun
rising in the sky, distinguish between the two, though
one glance embraces both, and judge the former volun-
tary, the latter necessary action: so also the Divine
vision in its universal range of view does in no wise con-
fuse the characters of the things which are present to its
regard, though future in respect of time. Whence it
follows that when it perceives that something will come
into existence, and yet is perfectly aware that this is
unbound by any necessity, its apprehension is not
opinion, but rather knowledge based on truth. And if to
this thou sayest that what God sees to be about to come
to pass cannot fail to come to pass, and that what can-
not fail to come to pass happens of necessity, and wilt
tie me down to this word necessity, I will acknowledge
that thou affirmest a most solid truth, but one which
scarcely anyone can approach to who has not made the
Divine his special study. For my answer would be that
the same future event is necessary from the standpoint
of Divine knowledge, but when considered in its own
nature it seems absolutely free and unfettered. So, then,
there are two necessities—one simple, as that men are
necessarily mortal; the other, conditioned, as that, if
you know that some one is walking, he must necessarily
be walking. For that which is known cannot indeed be
otherwise than as it is known to be, and yet this fact
by no means carries with it that other simple necessity.
For the former necessity is not imposed by the thing's
own proper nature, but by the addition of a condition.
No necessity compels one who is voluntarily walking to
go forward, although it is necessary for him to go for-
ward at the moment of walking. In the same way, then,
if Providence sees anything as present, that must neces-
sarily be, though it is bound by no necessity of nature.
Now, God views as present those coming events which

happen of free will. These, accordingly, from the standpoint of the Divine vision are made necessary conditionally on the Divine cognizance; viewed, however, in themselves, they desist not from the absolute freedom naturally theirs. Accordingly, without doubt, all things will come to pass which God foreknows as about to happen, but of these certain proceed of free will; and though these happen, yet by the fact of their existence they do not lose their proper nature, in virtue of which before they happened it was really possible that they might not have come to pass.

"What difference, then, does the denial of necessity make, since, through their being conditioned by Divine knowledge, they come to pass as if they were in all respects under the compulsion of necessity? This difference, surely, which we saw in the case of the instances I formerly took, the sun's rising and the man's walking; which at the moment of their occurrence could not but be taking place, and yet one of them before it took place was necessarily obliged to be, while the other was not so at all. So likewise the things which to God are present without doubt exist, but some of them come from the necessity of things, others from the power of the agent. Quite rightly, then, have we said that these things are necessary if viewed from the standpoint of the Divine knowledge; but if they are considered in themselves, they are free from the bonds of necessity, even as everything which is accessible to sense, regarded from the standpoint of Thought, is universal, but viewed in its own nature particular. 'But,' thou wilt say, 'if it is in my power to change my purpose, I shall make void providence, since I shall perchance change something which comes within its foreknowledge.' My answer is: Thou canst indeed turn aside thy purpose;

but since the truth of providence is ever at hand to see that thou canst, and whether thou dost, and whither thou turnest thyself, thou canst not avoid the Divine foreknowledge, even as thou canst not escape the sight of a present spectator, although of thy free will thou turn thyself to various actions. Wilt thou, then, say: 'Shall the Divine knowledge be changed at my discretion, so that, when I will this or that, providence changes its knowledge correspondingly?'"

"Surely not."

"True, for the Divine vision anticipates all that is coming, and transforms and reduces it to the form of its own present knowledge, and varies not, as thou deemest, in its foreknowledge, alternating to this or that, but in a single flash it forestalls and includes thy mutations without altering. And this ever-present comprehension and survey of all things God has received, not from the issue of future events, but from the simplicity of His own nature. Hereby also is resolved the objection which a little while ago gave thee offence—that our doings in the future were spoken of as if supplying the cause of God's knowledge. For this faculty of knowledge, embracing all things in its immediate cognizance, has itself fixed the bounds of all things, yet itself owes nothing to what comes after.

"And all this being so, the freedom of men's will stands unshaken, and laws are not unrighteous, since their rewards and punishments are held forth to wills unbound by any necessity. God, who foreknoweth all things, still looks down from above, and the ever-present eternity of His vision concurs with the future character of all our acts, and dispenseth to the good rewards, to the bad punishments. Our hopes and prayers also are not fixed on God in vain, and when they are rightly directed

cannot fail of effect. Therefore, withstand vice, practise
virtue, lift up your souls to right hopes, offer humble
prayers to Heaven. Great is the necessity of righteous-
ness laid upon you if ye will not hide it from yourselves,
seeing that all your actions are done before the eyes of
a Judge who seeth all things."

THE VIKING PORTABLE LIBRARY

The Portable Beat Reader
Edited by Ann Charters

The Portable Blake
Edited by Alfred Kazin

The Portable Chekhov
Edited by Avrahm Yarmolinsky

The Portable Emerson
*Edited by Carl Bode and
Malcolm Cowley*

The Portable Faulkner
Edited by Malcolm Cowley

The Portable Greek Historians
Edited by M. I. Finley

The Portable Thomas Jefferson
Edited by Merrill D. Peterson

The Portable James Joyce
Edited by Harry Levin

The Portable Jung
Edited by Joseph Campbell

The Portable Abraham Lincoln
Edited by Andrew Delbanco

The Portable Machiavelli
*Edited by Peter Bondanella and
Mark Musa*

The Portable Karl Marx
Edited by Eugene Kamenka

The Portable Medieval Reader
*Edited by James Bruce Ross and
Mary Martin McLaughlin*

The Portable Nietzsche
Edited by Walter Kaufmann

The Portable North American
Indian Reader
Edited by Frederick Turner

The Portable Dorothy Parker
Edited by Brendan Gill

The Portable Plato
Edited by Scott Buchanan

The Portable Poe
Edited by Philip Van Doren Stern

The Portable Romantic Poets
*Edited by W. H. Auden and
Norman Holmes Pearson*

The Portable Shakespeare
Edited by Marshall Best

The Portable Thoreau
Edited by Carl Bode

The Portable Mark Twain
Edited by Bernard De Voto

The Portable Walt Whitman
Edited by Mark Van Doren

The Portable Oscar Wilde
Revised Edition
*Edited by Richard Aldington and
Stanley Weintraub*

The Portable World Bible
Edited by Robert O. Ballou

FOR THE BEST IN PAPERBACKS, LOOK FOR THE

In every corner of the world, on every subject under the sun, Penguin represents quality and variety—the very best in publishing today.

For complete information about books available from Penguin—including Penguin Classics, Penguin Compass, and Puffins—and how to order them, write to us at the appropriate address below. Please note that for copyright reasons the selection of books varies from country to country.

In the United States: Please write to *Penguin Group (USA), P.O. Box 12289 Dept. B, Newark, New Jersey 07101-5289* or call 1–800–788–6262.

In the United Kingdom: Please write to *Dept. EP, Penguin Books Ltd, Bath Road, Harmondsworth, West Drayton, Middlesex UB7 0DA.*

In Canada: Please write to *Penguin Books Canada Ltd, 10 Alcorn Avenue, Suite 300, Toronto, Ontario M4V 3B2.*

In Australia: Please write to *Penguin Books Australia Ltd, P.O. Box 257, Ringwood, Victoria 3134.*

In New Zealand: Please write to *Penguin Books (NZ) Ltd, Private Bag 102902, North Shore Mail Centre, Auckland 10.*

In India: Please write to *Penguin Books India Pvt Ltd, 11 Panchsheel Shopping Centre, Panchsheel Park, New Delhi 110 017.*

In the Netherlands: Please write to *Penguin Books Netherlands bv, Postbus 3507, NL-1001 AH Amsterdam.*

In Germany: Please write to *Penguin Books Deutschland GmbH, Metzlerstrasse 26, 60594 Frankfurt am Main.*

In Spain: Please write to *Penguin Books S. A., Bravo Murillo 19, 1° B, 28015 Madrid.*

In Italy: Please write to *Penguin Italia s.r.l., Via Benedetto Croce 2, 20094 Corsico, Milano.*

In France: Please write to *Penguin France, Le Carré Wilson, 62 rue Benjamin Baillaud, 31500 Toulouse.*

In Japan: Please write to *Penguin Books Japan Ltd, Kaneko Building, 2-3-25 Koraku, Bunkyo-Ku, Tokyo 112.*

In South Africa: Please write to *Penguin Books South Africa (Pty) Ltd, Private Bag X14, Parkview, 2122 Johannesburg.*